Tomorrow Perhaps the Future

Also by Sarah Watling

The Olivier Sisters

Tomorrow Perhaps the Future

Writers, Outsiders,
and the Spanish Civil War

SARAH WATLING

ALFRED A. KNOPF
NEW YORK, 2023

Grateful acknowledgment is made to the following for permission to reprint previously published material:

Carcanet Press Limited: Excerpts from "Madrid 1936" and "Yes, It Is Spain" from *Selected Poems* by Nancy Cunard, edited by Sandeep Parmar. Originally published by Carcanet Press Limited, London, in 2016. Reprinted by permission of Carcanet Press Limited.

Granta Publications: Excerpt from *The Diary of Virginia Woolf, Volume 5* by Virginia Woolf. Reprinted by permission of Granta Publications.

Grove Atlantic: Excerpts from *The Face of War* by Martha Gellhorn. Copyright © 1937, 1938, 1940, 1941, 1942, 1943, 1944, 1945, 1959, 1966, 1967, 1983, 1985, 1986, 1987, 1988 by Martha Gellhorn. Reprinted by permission of Grove Atlantic, Inc. Any third-party use of this material, outside of this publication, is prohibited.

HarperCollins Publishers: Excerpt from *The Diary of Virginia Woolf, Volume 3.* Diary and Appendix II copyright © 1980 by Quentin Bell and Angelica Garnett. Excerpt from *The Starched Blue Sky of Spain and Other Memoirs* by Josephine Herbst. Copyright © 1991 by the Estate of Josephine Herbst. Excerpt from *Three Guineas* by Virginia Woolf. Copyright © 1938 by Harcourt, Inc., copyright renewed 1966 by Leonard Woolf. Reprinted by permission of HarperCollins Publishers.

Library of Congress Cataloging-in-Publication Data
Names: Watling, Sarah, author.
Title: Tomorrow perhaps the future : writers, outsiders, and the Spanish Civil War / Sarah Watling.
Description: New York : Alfred A. Knopf, 2023. | Includes bibliographical references and index.
Identifiers: LCCN 2022049910 (print) | LCCN 2022049911 (ebook) | ISBN 9780593319666 (hardcover) | ISBN 9780593313732 (trade paperback) | ISBN 9780593319673 (ebook)
Subjects: LCSH: Spain—History—Civil War, 1936–1939—Literature and the war. | Spain—History—Civil War, 1936–1939—Participation, Foreign. | Literature—Women authors—History and criticism. | LCGFT: Literary criticism.
Classification: LCC DP269.8.L5 W38 2023 (print) | LCC DP269.8.L5 (ebook) | DDC 946.081/—dc23/eng/20230118
LC record available at https://lccn.loc.gov/2022049910
LC ebook record available at https://lccn.loc.gov/2022049911

Jacket photo by Gerda Taro
Jacket design by Maddie Partner

Manufactured in the United States of America

First American Edition

For Cat

'To-morrow, perhaps the future.
[. . .] But to-day the struggle.'

W. H. Auden, 'Spain'

'Today it is Spain. Tomorrow it will be some other country . . .'

Julio Álvarez del Vayo at the League of Nations, September 1937

'But in Spain no. Perhaps and Tomorrow – in Spain it is HERE.'

Nancy Cunard, 'To Eat Today'

Contents

Bay of Biscay

Atlantic Ocean

FRANCE

Santander
Bilbao
ANDORRA
Perpignan
La Junquera
Portbou
Gerona
R. Ebro
Barcelona

PORTUGAL

El Escorial
Madrid
Guadalajara
Brunete
Morata de Tajuña
Teruel
Huete
Castellón
Valencia
Palma de Mallorca

Badajoz

Alicante

Almería

Mediterranean Sea

Cádiz
Málaga

Tangier

Spain, 31 July 1936

Republican zone

Nationalist zone

Santa Cruz de Tenerife
Las Palmas de Gran Canaria

0   50   100   150   200 kilometres
0   25   50   75   100 miles

No Perhaps, No Tomorrow

Put it this way: an old woman sits alone in a darkened movie theatre and cries uncontrollably. That there is no one seated nearby she considers a mercy, because the room's night-like privacy is necessary to her. The film has triggered her memory so intensely that she feels both as if she is dying and that she is already dead. On the screen she watches the most important experiences of her life flicker by inexorably, and admits to herself that that is what they were. There is no sign of Josephine Herbst in the footage and yet it shows her most alive, it shows the time when everything mattered. After the screening she will sit in the lobby and smoke for a long while, mulling over the ways in which history has disappointed her, which is another way of thinking about what her own life has failed to deliver.

While she sits there, gathering herself, she is also sobbing over lunch again in Toulouse in 1937. Just sitting there, ridiculous, weeping over an omelette her starved stomach is hankering for.

What is the street outside to Josephine Herbst? It contains not a single person who could understand the movie she's just seen. It contains nobody who would understand flying out of Barcelona with relief and landing in another country in despair.

In Toulouse, it is like being in a nightmare where you are separated from the world in some fundamental but gossamer way that only you perceive. The world goes about its business and you are cut off by knowing, now, how little any of it matters, how short a time this peace will last. And by flying out of Barcelona and landing in Toulouse, you have left everything that counts behind.

Finally, smoking in the lobby in 1966, she works her way to the truth. She is seventy-four (or, in harsher terms, three years from death) and the fact is, she writes afterwards, that those thirty years ago, *in the most real sense my most vital life did indeed end with Spain. Nothing so vital, either in my personal life or in the life of the world, has ever come again. And in a deep sense, it has all been a shadow picture for years and years.*

A different place and time, a more composed woman: Martha Gellhorn is seventy-four years old and Josephine Herbst is dead so cannot hate her any longer. Provoked by the young man interviewing her, she stubs out her cigarette and says, 'I don't even know what you *mean* exactly by objective.'

Or take Sylvia Townsend Warner, one year younger and exchanging bright, literary letters with her editor at the *New Yorker*. In passing he mentions his donations to the Spanish Republic thirty years before. Enough, he thinks, to be suspected of 'premature anti-fascism' (FBI code for dangerous communist). 'Prematurely anti-Fascist'? she exclaims, reaching out through time and distance to seize a new-found comrade. 'It soars above all other mortal distinctions.'

Or picture a grieving woman, fifty-eight years old and ten months from her death; Virginia Woolf putting down in her own defence: 'Thinking is my fighting.'

One final scene. Consider a woman, sixty-four years old and five years from the end, reeling out of Spain under expulsion, not-so-fresh from several days in jail and devastated in more ways than one. Raging, she makes her way to England through a series of scuffles and shouts and confrontations. The French police arrest her, then the English ones do. On the King's Road in London they pick her up for soliciting, and then add on drunk and disorderly. She scraps. She throws her shoes at the magistrate. She ends up in a mental hospital. From there, she does what she has done countless times before in the service of any number of causes: with aristocratic presumption, she emits a stream of letters to her dearest friends and to eminent people, between whom there is some degree of overlap, protesting her incarceration. It all goes back, she says, to the Spanish Civil War. In some ways, she's right. Her friends are worried, upset, outraged. Some accept that she has lost her mind, others don't. Nancy Cunard, one will write, was 'not mad, but maddened'.

★

I could go on. There is Dorothy Parker, that famous wit, declaring at the end of Spain's war that 'there is nothing funny in the world anymore'. There is Jessica Mitford on the radio in 1977, choosing as the one record that meant the most to her an old German anthem, composed in concentration camps, that her long-dead husband learned in the International Brigades. There is President Roosevelt admitting in 1939, as Europe accelerated into the Second World War, that not offering support to the Spanish Republic had been a 'grave mistake'.

Clearly Spain mattered. But what's unusual about the Spanish Civil War, which ravaged the country between 1936 and 1939 and brought its young democracy to an end, is how much it mattered to people who had nothing to do with Spain. This is not a book about Spaniards. It's not even, really, a book about war. This is a book about individuals – outsiders – and how they understood their role in the history of humanity.

It's a book about a cluster of people I was drawn to some time ago now: individuals, most of them writers, for whom the Spanish war and its challenges never lost their force. The writers produced literature during those years that stayed with me, that stays with me still: poems, memoirs, stories and essays that warranted attention and opened windows onto the late 1930s that had been left boarded up by the male canon I'd inherited.

I had been thinking about activism and retreat, responsibility, freedom and solidarity, and about how one might respond to fearful calamities on the horizon. There they were with their own generations' calamities, their own responses. I might as well admit to a weakness for people with an instinct for rebellion, for women who do not go out of their way to please when more important matters are at stake. Nancy Cunard, Martha Gellhorn, Josephine Herbst, Sylvia Townsend Warner and Virginia Woolf all resisted in some way the lives they had been offered. The poet, activist, journalist Nancy Cunard fought hard to overwrite the heiress-muse script drafted by others, emerging unapologetic and determined, heartfelt and erring. Helplessly I admired Martha Gellhorn's uncompromising, outspoken approach to life and to war reporting; her hard-cased empathy and endless capacity for outrage. I could not resist the radical novelist Josephine Herbst's bad temper, her willingness to scrap, complain and question, to take male grandstanding down with a single swipe at the knees. Sylvia Townsend Warner's self-deprecating drollery (in fiction, journalism and manner) seduced me not least because it came from the pen of a woman so sure, in fact, of her position and its rightness. She knew how her detractors could dismiss her and she had a disarming ability to take the words right out of their mouths. And who has ever made better use of words than Virginia Woolf, a woman whose curiosity about humanity was endless and yet bounded by a fear of trespass – of others into her own intellectual sanctuaries, certainly, but also of the imagination into other lives, when so many voices are silenced?

The Spanish war began in July 1936 when a group of disaffected generals – including Francisco Franco, who would emerge as their leader – attempted to launch a coup against their country's elected government. The reaction of foreign powers was significant from the start. Fascist Italy and Nazi Germany offered decisive material support to Franco's side (the nationalists) while the Republican government received from its fellow democracies in France, the United States and Great Britain only a queasy refusal to intervene. As the Republic battled to survive this well-resourced attack, relying on a tenacious popular resistance to the military takeover and on arms from Soviet Russia and Mexico, many observers understood the war as an opportunity to halt the global advance of fascism: one that their own governments seemed loath to take up.

Some months in, Nancy Cunard challenged her fellow writers to make public statements on the war in an urgent call that framed things like this:

It is clear to many of us throughout the whole world that now, as certainly never before, we are determined or compelled, to take sides.

The equivocal attitude, the Ivory Tower, the paradoxical, the ironic detachment, will no longer do.

This was where the Spanish Civil War began to matter to me. It happened that, when I first found this eye-catching statement, I was living through an era of national and international upheaval that made Nancy's eighty-year-old challenge snatch up my attention.

It was possible, in her day, to see democracy as a teetering edifice, a system that had outlived, even failed, its potential. Alternatives vied for dominance. The Great Depression in America, that 'citadel of capitalism', had not only destabilised economies around the world but shaken faith in the capitalist system itself – proving, to some minds, the validity of the Marxist theory that had predicted its collapse. The twenties and early thirties had seen military dictators or non-democratic forms of government gain the upper hand in a raft of countries: Hungary, Poland, Yugoslavia, Romania, Japan, Portugal, Austria, Bulgaria, Greece and, of course, even earlier, Russia. By 1936, Germany and Italy had been governed by fascists for years. Their regimes found plenty of sympathisers in countries shaken by the First World War and ensuing Depression. The British Union of Fascists, for instance, was already almost four years old. Nor was fascist aggression on the international stage something new. Italy had invaded Ethiopia in 1935; Germany was openly remilitarising – something forbidden by the terms of the peace imposed at the end of the First World War. For some, the great dichotomy of the 1930s was provided by fascism and communism. For many others (including those who weren't convinced of a meaningful difference between the two), Spain was perhaps simpler still: fascism or opposition to fascism.

By my day it had become fairly common to hear people drawing dark parallels with the 1930s: that decade in which Mussolini and Hitler crushed opposition and raised their armies, and Franco took over Spain, and 'Blackshirts' marched in the streets of London. We thought we knew these facts, but it seemed they were losing their power to terrify or forewarn; that acknowledging them belonged to an old tyranny of decency and truth that others were ready to throw off.

It's an absurd kind of grandiosity, in a way, to relate the darkest past
to your own moment and its preoccupations. Yet I felt many of the
things I had taken for granted dropping away around the time I first
started reading about Nancy Cunard. Democratic processes, mechanisms of justice, truth itself: all were under renewed threat. My country seemed a less moderate, less peaceful place than I was used to, and
newly emboldened extremists were taking eagerly to the public stage.
Inequalities of wealth and opportunity were widening. The urgency
of the climate crisis felt increasingly clamorous. It was difficult not to
simply feel hopeless; pinioned into a narrow space of outraged despair.

And yet, it was quite convenient to have so much out in the open.
It was something to respond to. It gave Nancy's uncompromising
position a certain appeal – even offered, perhaps, a kind of permission. I kept remembering a feminist demonstration I had taken part
in years before, when I was twenty-one. Meeting friends in a park
afterwards, one of them had punctured our exultant mood: the turn-
out I'd bragged of was more or less meaningless, he opined, an act of
preaching to the choir. What was the point when everyone on the
march was already persuaded? By 2019 – a year in which, though abortion rights had just been extended in Ireland, the UN Deputy High
Commissioner for Human Rights could describe US policy on abortion as 'gender-based violence against women, no question' and the
anti-feminist, far-right Vox party made unprecedented gains in Spain,
raising the uncomfortable spectre of Franco – the response I should
have made was becoming clearer to me. My twenty-one-year-old self
had marched to give notice of her resistance. There was nothing to be
gained by trying to understand the point of view we were protesting
(that the way women dressed could provoke rape), but much to be
risked from letting that idea exist in the world unchallenged.

Nancy's 'taking sides' has an air of immaturity about it, perhaps
precisely because of the playground training most of us receive in it.
So much prudence and fairness is signified by resisting these easy allegiances, by seeing 'two sides to every story' – a terminology that tends
to imply that truth or moral superiority can only ever exist in not
choosing either one. And it was becoming clear that polarisation serves
the extremes best of all. But something about Nancy's construction

spoke to me. It suggested that there is power in the act of taking a side; that there are moments on which history rests, when nuance or hesitation (perhaps or tomorrow) will prove fatal, when it is vital to know – and to acknowledge – which side you are on.

The worst times can take on an appearance of simplicity and war is exactly the kind of aberration that removes options, leaving the single choice of one side or another in its place. Yet when Nancy and thousands of other foreigners to Spain acted *voluntarily* in support of the Spanish Republic, they made their beliefs public. Their actions proposed the worst times as periods of opportunity, too: invitations to reclaim principles from the privacy of our thoughts and conversations and ballot boxes, and make them decisive factors in the way we live and act. This is why this book is not about the Spanish experience of the war, but rather about the people who had the option not to involve themselves and decided otherwise.

Writers are good for thinking through. I was interested in the question of critical distance – whether it is always possible or even, as I'd instinctively assumed, always desirable – and I could think of no better individual to shed light on this than a writer (or intellectual) in wartime. But people from all walks of life understood the Spanish war as a question, a provocation that demanded an answer. Thousands from across the world volunteered on behalf of the Republic, going so far as to travel to the country as combatants and auxiliaries. Others declared themselves through campaigning and fundraising. Martha Gellhorn defined herself as 'an onlooker': I wanted to explore, too, the experience of people whose commitment drew them closer to the action.

Alongside her in this book are the British Communist Nan Green and her husband, George, who wrenched themselves from their children to volunteer with medical and military units in Republican Spain. There is a young African American nurse named Salaria Kea who saw her service there as a calling. There is one of the boldest photographers to contribute to the memory of the war: Gerda Taro, a refugee from Germany for whom the fight against fascism was personal. They left their own accounts of the conflict, whether through images or text, and following their stories taught me much about how historical narratives are formed in the first place; why leaving a record can be one of the most instinctive, and contested, human impulses. When I went looking for Salaria Kea, the negotiations and challenges her story had undergone became as interesting to me as the missing pieces. A woman of colour deemed a political radical, a nurse and not a writer: hers was a voice that rarely received a welcome hearing. This book voices many of my questions, but with Salaria so much was unclear that I realised I could only tell her story by narrating the pursuit and leaving the questions open.

'Rebels', like Franco, turn military might against the government they're meant to serve. But I found that all the people I chose to follow fulfilled the word's other definition, of those who 'resist authority, control, or convention'. I wanted to know why they believed that the moment had come, with Spain, for taking sides. Or, rather, I wanted to know how they recognised the Spanish war as the moment for doing something about the way their present was heading, and what 'taking sides' had meant in practice. I wanted to know whether Nancy really thought the mere act of declaring a side could make a difference, as she suggested when she put out that urgent call. I wanted to know why she had addressed it specifically to 'Writers and Poets'.

The Spanish war is often remembered for, and through, its writers – and notably writers from outside the country. Of all the defeats in history, perhaps only Troy has been as well served by literature as Republican Spain was during and after the ascension of Franco, who would eventually rule in Spain for almost forty years. Countless novels and memoirs, a handful of them the greatest books by the greatest writers of their generation; reams of poetry, both brilliant and pedestrian, have preserved the memory of its cause.

As I read, I began to think that their authors' position had something to say about the nature of writing itself. It seemed significant that each of the writers in this book saw themselves, whether at home or abroad, as an outsider. If not belonging was a fundamental part of that identity, taking sides on Spain only crystallised a series of pressing questions about the purpose and privileges of writers. The 1930s was a decade of art colliding with politics, of artists determining to marry the two. Presented with the trauma of the Great Depression, the unavoidable phenomenon of Soviet Russia and the spread of fascism, there were journalists and poets alike who sought new modes and new material. Writers questioned their obligations to society, asked what art could achieve; they interrogated the intellectual life to expose its value and its limitations.

The list of foreigners who spent time in Spain during the war reads like a roll call of the most celebrated voices of the era: think of the Spanish war and I imagine you think of Ernest Hemingway and George Orwell, perhaps Stephen Spender, John Dos Passos, W. H. Auden. Delve a little further and you will find a far greater array of authors, including writers who were female, writers of colour, writers who did not write in English (though the wealth of Spanish-language literature falls beyond the scope of a book interested in the outsiderness of writers). They went because, as Martha Gellhorn put it, 'We knew, we just *knew* that Spain was the place to stop Fascism', or because they believed in the liberal project of the Republic and wanted to raise awareness of its plight, or because they wanted to observe, or even participate in, the cause célèbre of the moment. They saw history coming and went out to meet it.

Nancy made three long trips to Spain over the three-year war; Martha went twice in 1937 and again in 1938. Sylvia and Josephine went less – twice with her partner, the poet Valentine Ackland, for Sylvia; Josephine only once – and Virginia not at all. (Gerda Taro came and went as the reporters did; Salaria Kea and the Greens stayed for long, unbroken periods.) Writing this book, I claimed the freedom to pick up each life story that seemed relevant and put it down when it went beyond where I needed to go. The book turns to these women not merely because they are women but because they posed and addressed, in work and in life, the very questions that seemed worth pursuing. It transpires that the famous men aren't all there is to know about the Spanish Civil War.

Martha arrived in Madrid as a restless twenty-eight-year-old, and there began a career of covering humanity at its best and worst that would sustain her for the rest of her life. If it was the start of something for her, for Josephine Herbst, a seasoned political radical whose short time in Spain was inversely proportional to how much it meant

to her, the war instead represented a kind of ending: a dwindling
of her own political allegiances and, as she saw it, of a decade that
reverberated with faith in the individual's ability to make a difference. In anarchist Barcelona in 1936, Sylvia and Valentine would
discover the promise of a liberatory future unthinkable at home,
where their seizure of personal and political fulfilment as Communists and queer women had proved 'an exile'. And then, with-
holding where Nancy dived in, was Nancy's old acquaintance but
never friend, Virginia Woolf, struggling, and failing, to keep the
war out of her life.

When Nancy took aim at the refuge of the 'Ivory Tower', she was
articulating a live debate around the writing life – one that continued
as responses to her challenge flooded in from interested writers. As
a sanctuary for thinking and creating, the ivory tower was essential
to some and a moral failing to others. Yet this supposed distinction
between creation (or scholarship) and involvement in the 'real' world
could not explain why Spain meant so much to the writers in this
book, nor how it proved the seeding ground for some of Martha's best
reportage, not to mention her anguished 1940 novel *A Stricken Field*;
or for some of the finest writing among Josephine's memoirs – the
genre for which she had the greatest talent; or for Sylvia's 1938 novel
After the Death of Don Juan and the hauntingly poignant poetry she and
Valentine wrote of this time; or the modernist chronicle that Nancy
would work on for the rest of her life, trying to express the extrane-
ous matter of history – the grief and questioning and protest – in her
many, many poems about 'Spain-my-Spain'. Instead, for me, it set up
another question that these writers had lived, and worked, through.

As so often happens, the further I explored, the more certain people
announced themselves, collecting like burrs to the challenges posed
by Nancy Cunard. There were other writers I chanced across in the
Spanish war, far from the landscapes I had mentally assigned them, and
though we didn't accompany each other for the duration, they summoned distinct experiences of that era that I couldn't do without. The
journalist Virginia Cowles, as glamorous and well connected as her
friend Martha Gellhorn – though perhaps more level-headed – offered

a different approach from Martha's frustration with objectivity. A year after Nancy, Sylvia and Valentine first came to Spain, the American poet and playwright Langston Hughes arrived in Madrid, already a veteran of the tussles involved in harnessing politics to art. The teenage rebels Esmond Romilly and Jessica Mitford (whose writing career began much, much later) lived out the deep incursions that politics can make when they excised themselves from their families to go to Spain – theirs a less harrowing rupture than civil war inescapably imposes on some families. Jessica and her (in)famous sisters raised humour as another of the questions I was asking of literature as resistance or refuge.

'We [writers],' Martha imperiously informed her colleagues in 1937, 'have the obligation of seeing and understanding what happens, of telling the truth, of fighting constantly for a clarification of the issues. We have, in short, the vital job of shaping history as it happens.' History was part of the reason the Spanish Civil War inspired writers, why it made them think they had something to offer. Reporters laid down a first draft, often preserving memories that were suppressed later. But all those writing in response to what they saw in Spain had the opportunity to address the future. By chronicling the struggle, they posted flags for posterity, marking out opposition to fascism even where that opposition failed.

In a certain way, the Republican cause became something capacious and unwieldy – it became whatever each individual chose to make it. Solidarity meant identifying the ways in which a phenomenon like fascism was not confined by national boundaries; it meant finding common cause with people not like you – and that sometimes meant bringing your own experiences and causes to the table. This was interesting, and troubling, to me. It suggested preliminaries for meaningful change, but it also suggested that attempts to enact solidarity carry within them the risk of drowning out your chosen allies.

None of the individuals in this book went untouched by the terrible assault to hope of the 1930s and early 1940s but they each found ways to engage. In them I found activism with a human face. A way of living their ideals that was indeed a struggle – a struggle that did not always succeed and was not, even, always well done – but one that sought to draw what they believed they could offer the world into coherence with what they believed was right. That, I thought, was the way to live. With them, there could be beauty and love and personal rewards within a movement for political change – it was part of how they knew the change would bring in a better world. There could be solidarity based on common interests – that is what made it seem viable. There could be failure without despair. 'Grim as my view has come to be,' Josephine wrote long after the Republic's defeat, 'I still think it absolutely necessary, to continue on any line available, the harassment and the protest.' It is not always easy to discern the questions your time is asking you – or perhaps it is too easy to silence them. These outsiders of mine could see how high the stakes had grown by the late 1930s. Their varied and various contributions throw up thorny questions about solidarity and allyship that have not left us today, but they also remind us that it can be done.

There I was with certain questions occupying me and these encounters on the horizon. I wanted to know what it had meant to take a side, and how it had been done, and I wanted to know what writing had to do with it. Josephine's reason for going to Spain echoed down the generations: 'I was probably trying to find some answers to the confusions in my own mind.' Sometimes you're seeking a way through the questions, and you find yourself writing a book.

Preludes
1935–36

Where do you start?

Josephine Herbst arrived in Cuba under false pretences, girded with accreditation from moderate magazines she wouldn't be writing for, intending to reach the resistance. But the whole point of an underground resistance is that it isn't easy to find.

The pose was lady journalist researching the Cuban sugar industry. The reality was something like: short story writer and fearless novelist of growing reputation, a woman who compulsively fictionalised the traumas and grievances of her life and background so unflinchingly that she had made some of it unpublishable, who had only lately hit upon the real meaning of that material – the real method for giving it a purpose – but who had been temporarily rerouted by her emergence as an intrepid, politically committed, as-far-left-as-you-can-go journalist. The reality was a commission from the Marxist-aligned *New Masses* to write about revolutionaries in a volatile dictatorship where a military officer named Fulgencio Batista was crushing dissent. If only the world weren't so clamorous, Josephine Herbst could have got back to the novels she was meant to be writing. But she also believed that, without the clamour of the world, there would be no novels.

It took her weeks to gain the trust of the Cuban underground in 1935 – weeks she spent interviewing local politicians and American businessmen, building up a picture of a country at the mercy of US business interests. She even managed to speak with Batista himself, a man she presciently judged was 'ready to make a military dictatorship'. All the while she was seeking a way up into the mountains, where peasants in a region called Realengo 18 were said to be holding out against sugar companies' attempts to seize their land. At first her contacts would take her only as far as Santiago, where the scarred bodies of the activists she met were explanation enough of the reasons for their caution. Then, finally, there was a five-day journey on horseback, along 'trails that go steeply up a mountain side through thick virgin forest and jungle, sprouting ferns and vines as tangled as hair' to 'the secret mountainsides of "Realengo 18"'.

It was so remote that she was the first foreign journalist ever to meet them, yet the people there, armed and friendly, expressed no sense of their isolation. 'The district of Realengo is small in comparison to Cuba and Cuba is only a tiny island,' she wrote, 'but no one in Realengo feels alone in the fight for freedom. They talk too much of what is going on in the world. They know too much to be alone.'

This knowledge and these connections were important. Over the past few years, covering the Depression-era radicalisation of American farmers, Josephine had remarked on surprising cooperations. What made a white man from an old farming family find common cause with 'the impoverished Negro share cropper from Alabama'? 'Nothing except the conviction that their struggle against mass ruin is the same.' Within the right kinds of alliances, she believed, and with the willingness to struggle, was a solution not just to economic inequality but to imperialism and racial prejudice too.

Those overarching connections would be driven home to her again on May Day, weeks after her return from Cuba, when she heard her Pennsylvania neighbours sing exactly the same leftist anthem she had sung into the dark night with her hosts in the mountains. Which is to say, maybe you start in Cuba. But the story can't be told without the USA and '*el imperialismo yanqui*', or the isolated rebels who identify as citizens of the world, or the memory of them surfacing the next time you're reporting on a farmers' conference and the crowd sings 'The Internationale'. You try to tell the story of one people, and all the others come crowding in.

By the time Josephine got back to Havana from the mountains, everything had escalated. A general strike called in opposition to Batista's repression triggered a violent clampdown. She was in a theatre when a bomb went off outside. Most people stayed where they were; Josephine dashed out to find pools of blood on the pavement. She wrote up her articles while gunfire spat in the streets, then had them smuggled out of the country when the authorities restricted the mail. She soon followed, unable to do anything more while her contacts were being hunted down and disappearing.

Fortunately, it was not far from Cuba to an old friend's bolthole in Key West in Florida. She spent a few days recuperating with Ernest Hemingway, then it was onwards to New York, where she was due to speak at a writers' conference.

Onstage at the Mecca Temple, she knew why she'd been asked. Last-minute panic: a great gathering of progressive American writers and they'd forgotten to arrange a female speaker for the opening night. This was typical of the various Communist productions she'd appeared at; they wanted her for her profile more than for her opinions. In 1935, she was, in the words of her biographer many years later, 'a leading lady' of the country's radical Left. That was partly due to her own work and reputation, and partly because her husband, John Herrmann, had shifted his focus from literature to Communist organising.

As the fascist threat in Europe, and Stalin's wary eye on it, prompted a new mood of broad leftist cooperation – often heralded as a 'Popular Front' – Josephine's political connections were bringing her to larger audiences. Yet she hated the 'smuggies' of the Left's 'New York political elite', who went around giving stirring speeches to strikers on lives they knew nothing about. Nor had she ever responded well to being told how or what to write: at the Writers' Congress she sniped with friends that they should call the proposed League of American Writers the 'League Against American Writing', since literary quality was apparently not the priority. 'Don't get me wrong', she would write years later, when such things were dangerous to admit, 'I went as far left as you can go', but she never counted herself among 'the Faithful' (and there's no evidence that she ever actually joined the Communist Party). Perhaps her scepticism showed: a sketch of the Congress speakers has the forty-three-year-old grim-faced beneath a wide, unlovely hat.

Onstage she spoke about her own ancestors, farming people from Pennsylvania, and she spoke of Cuba. She spoke of what really mattered: resistance, revolution. Then she went home, where her husband had passed through briefly with his mistress, making things awkward with the neighbours. There were other reasons not to linger: there was, for instance, the pressing problem of Adolf Hitler.

Since he had come to power in Germany in 1933, voices of opposition had been falling ominously silent. The National Socialist German Workers' Party (NSDAP) was now the only party allowed by law; Dachau, their first concentration camp for political prisoners, was already two years old. The Nuremberg Laws, stripping German Jews of basic rights, would be instituted that September. It was said that the Nazis had wiped out their opponents entirely, and if there was no one standing up to Hitler at home, there seemed to be little appetite for confronting him internationally either. Josephine negotiated an assignment from the *New York Post* and headed for Berlin.

Berlin was a risk. It could be dangerous to go there, and there was no guarantee she'd find anything to report. Exiles had furnished her with contacts, but these came with warnings attached: people might have disappeared, or her drawing attention could cause them to.

In Germany, it was summertime and everything was as neat and orderly as the world had been led to believe. 'To the eye,' she admitted, 'streets are clean, window boxes are choked with flowers, children hike to the country in droves, singing songs. The slogans of the opposition groups have been white-washed from the walls.' It was a contrast to the hungry, unsettled Berlin she had known during her two years there in the 1920s, when she had been ashamed of the affluence her American dollars brought her in the inflation-stricken city. In 1935, the contrast had its own message. She sensed 'a changed and sick country', a smothered one. Describing attributes which supposedly give dictatorships their appeal, she also confronted the costs at which they are achieved: 'On the surface things appear cheerful. Boys bicycle on country roads. Who sees a concentration camp? Yet silence is over the very countryside . . . Talk does not bubble up anymore.'

Later she would write of 'that cautious, wary, dead quality that numbs masses of Germans in their daily living', pinpointing a shared characteristic of totalitarian regimes wherever and whenever they descend: the effect of the loss of all safe spaces for the mind or voice.

(What she didn't yet realise is that this is what Stalinism would look like, though her own 1930 visit to the USSR had signally failed to swell her enthusiasm.)

Fear stalked her in Berlin, just as it had done in Cuba and would, for a time, in Spain. The courage it took to find these stories came not from the absence of fear but the unceasing struggle with it. Look into her hotel room in Havana and you would see a middle-aged woman, puffy beneath the eyes and half-mad, writing a frantic stream of vitriol and appeal to the husband preparing to leave her. With the collapse of her own life so insistently significant, she asked herself whether she was up to the challenge of these assignments, whether she could do justice to other emergencies when so hard-pressed by her own. Her mind was as frightening to her as the very real dangers of investigating the abuses of dictatorships. They were all terrifying places to be.

In Berlin she sent a letter to her old friend Katherine Anne Porter, knowing it was risky to write too freely, trying to psych herself into courage: 'Everything very quiet, muzzled in fact but no more of that until I see you again. I felt dreadfully depressed at first, did even this morning with a kind of horror of being alone that goes to the very bone. I'm not sure I can pull off the business here & am not going to be frightened if I don't. I am not going to be terrified of failing for the moment.'

Josephine had gone to Germany intending to lay her ear to the ground and listen for the sound of resistance; eventually, at a whisper, she heard it. She set up secret meetings, was told about suppressed strikes and workers who defiantly attended the funerals of murdered comrades; she began to pick up jokes that expressed discontent with the regime, and learned of opposition leaflets cascading from waterspouts into the street with the rain. She managed to uncover a hidden reality of opposition − not, as her biographer notes, from the conservative aristocrats who would be commemorated for their belated intervention against Hitler, but from housewives on buses, industrial workers, brave leaflet circulators and slogan painters. She wrote a report that ran over five consecutive days on the *New York Post* front page. They called it 'Behind the Swastika'.

★

Brave leaflet circulators are not born, but made. When she was just into her twenties, Gerta Pohorylle – Gerda Taro, as she became – promised to send her best friend details of all the admirers she was accumulating in Leipzig. Then she added a quick caveat, droll and dangerous: 'if the Nazis don't kill me [first]'. Within two years, those same Nazis had won the Reichstag elections. That was in March 1933. By April, there was a boycott of Jewish businesses in Leipzig. In May they burned books. Gerda had already been arrested.

In a well-known photograph, taken in either 1934 or 1935, she sits at a Parisian café table with her tongue out, winking roguishly. It's a self-possessed look, and she dares you not to take things so seriously. Perhaps she's at one of the Left Bank establishments crowded in those years with émigrés, eking out coffees, arguing over politics yet basking in the broad solidarity of anti-fascism. Given a common enemy, those on the left had gained a whole host of new allies, too.

Gerda was small – barely over five feet tall – and slender, with a boyish crop of blonde-red hair. When people didn't like her they said she was pushy. It's true she retained the poise and ambition of her earlier years. She didn't leave her gaiety and promise behind her when she left Germany, but in Paris there were so many ways in which they were thwarted.

Gerda's family originally came from Galicia, a part of the Austro-Hungarian Empire that was once home to the largest Jewish population in the world. In the empire's post-war dismemberment Galicia became part of Poland, making German-speaking families like Gerda's into Poles. But the Pohorylles settled in Stuttgart in Germany, in the bosom of a prosperous extended family that kept Gerda well dressed and well educated. She was a good student at a prestigious school, spent a year at a Swiss finishing school, excelled at languages; was a ravishing and assimilated member of the bourgeoisie.

With the volatile crumbling of the Weimar Republic, when German politics reached for extremes, that life had begun to feel insufficient. Her friends weren't interested in politics. They also weren't Jewish. When she was nineteen, her family moved to Leipzig after the failure of her father's business, and there Gerda fell in with a left-leaning Jewish milieu – people who understood, as her old friends apparently didn't, what growing antisemitism in the country meant to her.

'When you met her,' one of the Leipzig crowd remembered, 'the immediate impression was of someone who was cheerful, happy, full of the joys of life. And bright. Not a fighter or in sackcloth and ashes.' Her boyfriend could list many enthusiasms: 'going to parties, dancing late into the night, sitting in fine restaurants, meeting new people'. She wasn't so much inclined to politics as someone whose life was over-taken by it. In Leipzig she began distributing anti-Nazi leaflets. Her brothers were more audacious: they tipped the flyers into the street from the rooftop of a department store, sparking a scandal in which at least sixty people, including Gerda, were arrested (her brothers went underground just in time).

In the crowded cell where she spent two weeks, Gerda distinguished herself by her supply of cigarettes, her ability to sing hit American jazz songs with the correct pronunciation, and her idea for what they should do with the bell they'd discovered in their cell. When the women were kept awake at night by the screaming from the men's sections, they rang it, incessantly, until the beatings stopped.

Meanwhile, Gerda's parents were making use of their ill-fitting Polish passports to appeal to the Polish consul, who demanded an explanation for her arrest. Gerda was released but remained under surveillance. Late in 1933, she left alone for Paris.

In France, they let refugees in but they were hardly universally wel-comed, especially as the numbers only kept on growing. The country offered women like her a safe haven – but who was to say it was a permanent one?

★

Where Josephine Herbst had written of window boxes choked by their flowers, Virginia Woolf, driving through Germany only a few weeks before her, described 'docile hysteria': a similarly sinister sense of unreality, of threat lingering beneath an immaculate upper-air pic-ture. She'd had an inkling about what things might be like there: she and her husband, who was Jewish, had been warned that the trip could be risky, and when Leonard disappeared into a German customs building for longer than she expected, Virginia quickly took fright. But Leonard had wanted to see for himself what fascism looked like in operation. The 'savage silliness' of this Germany confounded him. How were people like him and Virginia – intelligent, thoughtful people – supposed to take it seriously?

They spent three days motoring across the country, from Holland to Austria, in glorious weather, stately in their convertible, and the whole thing had something of the air of a Mad Hatter's tea party. For a start, they had their pet monkey, Mitz, in the car with them. While she provoked raptures of delight wherever they went, Virginia and Leonard found themselves susceptible to the atmosphere. The relief when officials smiled on their pet. Virginia felt it: 'the first stoop in our back'. It was a feeling that stiffened into anger.

On the Rhine in the May sunshine they were caught up in a rally for Hermann Goering, though at the time they feared they were about to come face to face with Hitler. Presented with children waving flags beneath banners that read 'The Jew is our enemy', they pressed on, grim and chastened, until their car passed beyond the reach of what Virginia called 'the docile hysterical crowd'. Docility does not quite imply toothlessness. If she didn't believe in its spontaneity, for Virginia the obedience of those people (made docile perhaps because they've ceased thinking for themselves) was dangerous in itself. Clearly the coercion of the moment reached her too: in her notes from the trip, she recorded lifting her hand in response to the crowd's delight in Mitz. That will raise a lot of questions. Did she wave? Give a fascist salute? Did she, in that moment, connect her own occasional jokes about Leonard's nose with the hatred on the banners? Fascism offends her, but so too, it had always seemed, did her husband's Jewishness.

It's probably no coincidence that in 1935 Virginia rekindled her practice, started earlier in the decade, of keeping scrapbooks of newspaper clippings. Already the author of *Mrs Dalloway*, *To the Lighthouse*, *Orlando* and *The Waves*, Virginia was, at fifty-three, a woman cresting intellectual and literary eminence, celebrated as a modernist sphinx. She had begun to think of reaching a wider audience. 'Can there be grand Old Women of literature?' she ruminated. Because if there could, she wanted to be one.

In the 1930s, as the prospect of war encroached further and further into everyday life, she was formulating a message she wanted heard. In the scrapbooks, stories of prejudice and oppression accumulated to fuel the two books occupying her mind that year. One, *The Years*, was a novel that would become her greatest commercial success to date; the other was a strange, slender volume called *Three Guineas* that she privately conceived of as her anti-fascist pamphlet but which would rarely be accepted as such. By now several years into the novel, Virginia was approaching dangerous psychological waters. In order to buy herself the time to write the second book, she would have to survive the experience of writing the first.

1935 was also the year in which Sylvia Townsend Warner and her partner began keeping their own compilations of newspaper clippings. Theirs was an almost daily record that ranged from the desperate effects of poverty and unemployment in Britain to fascist outrages abroad, maintained so thoroughly that they even added an index. Such was the scope of their interest in the world – and the scope of their activities, too. Coursing through their shared life was a passion for social justice that animated their work both literary and political.

It was almost a decade since Sylvia's bestselling debut novel about a spinster drawn to witchcraft, *Lolly Willowes; or The Loving Huntsman*, had gained her rave reviews on both sides of the Atlantic. Sylvia had been in her early thirties then. Since the death of her beloved father, a schoolmaster who had fostered her precocious intelligence, she had worked as a music editor in London. She was quick, dark and lean; bespectacled and frizzy of hair; a talented conversationalist. While her contemporaries like Nancy Cunard were revelling in modernism (they both published poetry collections in 1925, the year before *Lolly Willowes*'s release), Sylvia's work was steeped in the English pastoral and not preoccupied with experimentation. She was drawn to forms that her biographer would describe as 'not simply traditional but almost quaint'. The subversiveness of *Lolly Willowes*, then, much like the subversiveness of its author, ran below the radar. Sylvia wasn't above playing up to the dotty eccentric. When Virginia Woolf asked, at a lunch arranged so the two writers could meet, how Sylvia knew so much about witches, Sylvia told her it was because she was one. Yet whimsical though the magic in Lolly's picturesque Chilterns village may be, there is something worldly wise and dangerous to society about a female character who would rather sell herself to the Devil than be owned by the bourgeois middle-class family.

If there was no actual pact with the Devil to avoid this fate, in conservative Britain the lesbian, communist household Sylvia established in rural Dorset ran pretty close. In 1930, radicalism had entered her life in the form of a striking twenty-four-year-old called, rather appropriately, Valentine (she had changed her name from Molly).

Valentine was, and would remain, little known or published as a poet. In contrast to Sylvia's bookish childhood, she had been raised an affluent socialite – albeit one who could occasionally compensate for her father's lack of sons. She could shoot and preferred to dress in trousers; had also modelled for Augustus John and Eric Gill. Sent, at fifteen, to Paris to be finished, she had returned in love with another girl, an 'unnaturalness' for which her father never forgave her. At nineteen she married a gay friend in Westminster Cathedral while in the midst of an affair with another woman. The union was annulled within a year. When she met Sylvia, Valentine was unhappy and shy and already prone to self-medicating with booze. But it was the outrageous, androgynous good looks that people noticed first.

It was Valentine who prompted Sylvia into political commitment. Sylvia once listed to her the things that had long provoked her ire – 'priests in their gowns, anti-semitism, the white man who is the black man's burden, warmongers' – but knowing them was simply to acknowledge 'convictions' that had 'remained unacted desires. Perhaps this was not enough.' In 1935, they took the step of joining the British Communist Party together, adding to its modest but growing membership.

In a small world, Sylvia had become one of the party's key intellectuals, quickly trusted to join delegations abroad when writers gathered to discuss peace and fascism. She had all the domineering tendencies and bulldozing abilities of the Women's Institute ladies she satirised so winningly in stories for the *New Yorker*, though she tended to get her own way on behalf of rather different causes. The couple busied themselves organising their local community (a qualified success), writing to papers, selling the *Daily Worker* and pasting up posters attacking the British Union of Fascists. Valentine acquired a duplicating machine on which she produced leaflets and bulletins; there was also the cherished asset of a green MG Midget in which she ferried villagers to polling stations and demonstrations – a time-consuming business since the car had only two seats. Sylvia discovered a flair for heckling. Their house – though damp, unluxurious and marooned in a field – became a hub of community and activism; before long Sylvia was threatening to 'have a notice painted saying, "This way to the Olde Communiste's Reste" '. (Much later, Nancy Cunard was one of the radicals to take her rest there.) It was hardly necessary. They were swiftly – but, it must be said, fairly ineffectually – placed under police surveillance. 'Their chief occupation,' the bewildered local police report observed, 'appears to be the writing of stories.'

Both of them were contributors to the *Left Review*, a magazine established in 1934 in response to the spread of the extreme Right, and founding members of the local Left Book Club's writers' and readers' group. (The Left Book Club, which was exactly what it sounds like, boasted almost 60,000 members by the end of the 1930s: evidence of an audience hungry for politically inflected intellectual debate.) Home was also a lending library geared towards recruitment, because literature was how they knew to reach people. Sylvia was developing firm ideas about the kind of writing that mattered, commending authors who rejected 'the slough of Art for Art's sake' for 'the better foundation of Art for Man's sake'. Her own novels now bore a purpose that was inextricable from her beliefs. 'However bewitched her pen,' a friend and fellow writer would note, 'however bewitching, she lived wholly in an unambiguous world where the only duty lies in taking sides. The books as well as the author are always partisan.'

The Communist Party had attracted them, Sylvia later said, by being the only party that appeared to be doing anything. Given what was accumulating in the scrapbooks, doing something seemed pressing. It also simplified the options. 'The choice for all who think and feel is already between Fascism and socialism', Sylvia wrote. Hitler's contempt for individual rights could 'mean nothing but destruction'.

★

Nan Green agreed. That was why, if you were passing Russell Square station of an evening, you might see her selling the *Daily Worker* outside: a neat, energetic figure with short dark hair, plying her trade beside an ageing prostitute and a man selling chestnuts from a barrow.

Nan's husband, George, was a cellist. When they married, he was making a living accompanying silent films in the cinema, but the work in Manchester dried up overnight when the talkies arrived. Nan's first baby was born in 1931, in the midst of the Depression; her second arrived the following year, while George was away in London looking for work. When she joined him in the flat he'd found in Hampstead, Nan was ill and both children had developed whooping cough. She had desperate days: exhausted, hard-pressed to keep the babies fed and clean and alive; diminished by poverty and a hostile landlady.

Nan was only twenty-seven when they moved to London, but she had already worked so many dreary jobs. In 1928, the year that the vote was extended to women over twenty-one, she'd had a manager who instructed her to make sure none of her colleagues voted Labour. Intrigued, she had visited the local offices and ended up joining the party. But in Hampstead she found the local branch full of patronising intellectuals, adding a new strand to her new loneliness. Then George picked up a copy of John Strachey's *The Coming Struggle for Power*: the book all the political types were reading. They shared it excitedly, George reading it during the day and Nan in the evenings. For them, as for many others, it prompted a turn towards communism.

Years earlier, Nan had worked for an insurance company, calculating payouts for those hurt or killed in industrial accidents, and she could not forget the derisive values placed on some people's lives. Experience had taught her all she needed to know about the absence of safeguards for most people, the way certain bodies and minds were dispensable: there to be drained by employers and cast aside. George and Nan joined the Communist Party and began the same stream of activities that kept Sylvia and Valentine so busy: leaflets, slogans, posters, meetings.

To the Greens, liberal democracy was showing its age and failing its people. High unemployment had sent swathes of the British population into destitution, yet no government seemed equal to the challenge of rescuing them. Change was an urgent necessity, but some of the solutions proposed were just as alarming. When Nan took to the streets, it was often in direct opposition to the British fascist party established by the aristocratic politician Oswald Mosley in 1932, which had reached a membership height of about 50,000 members in only two years. Though a reputation for hooliganism was costing it mainstream appeal, the BUF had boasted the noisy support of the *Daily Mail*, as well as subsidies from Mussolini and Hitler's governments.

If the coming revolution crystallised the future into two sides of a struggle – those who were for the revolution and those against it – by 1935 Nan's side could sometimes make temporary expansions for the greater goal. That year – the year in which the British Communist Party won its first parliamentary seat in years – Nan, like Sylvia and Valentine, was campaigning on behalf of the local Labour candidate in the general election (though it was hard to tell whether Communist support cost him more votes than it gained him).

Nan sold the *Daily Worker* even when people spat at her and old men propositioned her; at other times she got up early to distribute it outside factory gates. When George was employed to play in Lyons tea houses, he managed to persuade every colleague in each new branch he worked at to join the musicians' union. The couple produced its newsletter, *Crescendo*, at home in the flat. Their young children, Frances and Martin, learned to turn the handle of the duplicating machine while Nan printed, reciting as they went:

> I am driving
> A nail
> Into the coffin
> Of capitalism.

That she had the energy to do any of it – what with work and kids and money troubles – seems extraordinary when you think about it. But that was how she was: somehow undefeatable. Plus, 'it was a matter of extreme urgency', she later wrote, this reality of stark positions forming: 'democracy and peace, or fascism and war'. It wasn't only developments at home that concerned her. Abroad, fascist countries were growing confidently aggressive. In the months after the Woolfs' driving holiday, Hermann Goering, whom they'd so narrowly avoided, took on responsibility for rearming Germany. That same year, in October 1935, Mussolini launched his invasion of Ethiopia (then usually referred to in Europe as Abyssinia). Nan was paying attention to all of it. The urgency only galvanised her: 'there was so much to be done'.

In New York, Salaria Kea followed the news about Ethiopia closely. The African American press was deeply interested in that invasion. Ethiopia was a bastion of independence in an Africa dominated by Europe's colonial powers. It was also a member of the League of Nations, that post-war vote of confidence in international diplomacy, and it appealed to the League for support against Italian aggression. The appeals continued over the following months as Ethiopian resistance was defeated by Italian armies wielding mustard gas, securing Mussolini the beginnings of the empire he so desperately desired. If any warning were needed of what fascism meant for people of colour the world over, there it was, and the twenty-two-year-old Salaria heard it loud and clear. With her fellow nurses at Harlem Hospital, she raised money to send medical supplies to the beleaguered country; she even hoped to volunteer her medical skills there, though this soon proved impossible.

Salaria, who had once dreamed of becoming a nun, knew how much she had to offer. The problem was getting other people to appreciate it. When floods devastated parts of the American Midwest the following year, the Red Cross would tell her that a black nurse would be 'more trouble than [she] was worth' there. Nor was her home town interested in her services at all; she had trained in New York because in Ohio she would not have been able to practise. Even nursing was something she had turned to only because segregation made her hopes of teaching impossible. It was difficult to become a PE teacher when you weren't allowed into the local swimming pool.

When Salaria qualified, there were twenty-six hospitals in New York but only four in which a black nurse could find employment. At the beginning of her career, she had found herself caring for a ward of terminal cases at Seaview, a tuberculosis sanatorium on Staten Island. Salaria was young, clever and energetic. She was also small and slight, standing at five foot five and weighing only ninety-six pounds, and working in a place considered too dangerous for white nurses, where staff frequently succumbed to the disease being treated. The National Association for the Advancement of Colored People (NAACP) called a meeting to protest conditions there, an event Salaria always remembered because it gave her a chance to speak up.

Action was a lesson she had kept on learning. Seated in the dining room at Harlem Hospital, where she was training and would later return to work, she had once been told she was sitting in a white nurse's place. She and four others stood up. They weren't going anywhere: the table was. Five pairs of hands tipped the whole thing over. Older black nurses had warned Salaria and her fellow students not to draw attention to themselves, but it was the noisy clatter of cutlery – followed by noisy student organising – that got the dining room desegregated.

Salaria found her people among her more politicised colleagues. There were doctors on the staff in Harlem who had come from Germany. They told her things – news that astonished her. Until she heard what was happening to Jews under Hitler, she'd assumed that white people inflicted terror only on people who looked like her.

★

Nancy Cunard picked a side in the Ethiopian war too, and no one was going to be spared her opinions. She went to Geneva, to the heart of the League's deliberations. Determined to do more than follow the crisis from a distance, she had found work as a correspondent for the Associated Negro Press (ANP), an agency in Chicago that provided copy predominantly for black papers – not an obvious match for a white aristocrat, but in this case there was an unusual alignment of interests. It may well have been her articles that Salaria was reading in Harlem.

'Everything but reporting was out of the question for me during those strenuous days,' Nancy wrote afterwards. League meetings were long, and reporting on them sometimes meant writing through the night. This was the kind of thing that could hold her attention – the kind of worthwhile absorption it had taken her a long time to find.

In her early twenties, Nancy had admitted to finding life 'quite impossible': 'I cannot enjoy a thing without carrying it to all the extremes and then nearly dying of the reaction.' At forty, she was still the kind of person who needed to approach everything at full tilt. She always would be. She seemed unable to tolerate steadiness or equilibrium – the kind of states that make life weatherable. To keep pace with herself, she had tried all sorts of substances, some of which, like sex and alcohol and jazz, gave her a certain exciting charm. Young Nancy had judged this tendency of hers 'weak-minded'. Yet weak-minded doesn't seem quite the term for Nancy Cunard.

Her start in life held few clues to the grind she'd follow in Geneva. She was born at Nevill Holt, a 13,000-acre estate in the Leicestershire countryside, in 1896. Her mother was an American heiress called Maud, who conquered English high society and renamed herself Emerald. Her father, Sir Bache, was a grandson of the founder of the iconic Cunard line of steamships, a man who preferred 'country pursuits' to dinner parties and who found himself unable to contain his much younger wife for long. Aristocrats, politicians, painters and writers clustered around Lady Cunard and her munificence. During her childhood in the vast, imposing house, Nancy was usually ignored but, depending on the season, had opportunities to observe the glamorous people her mother collected. She also liked to watch homeless men tramp across the grounds, and dreamed of joining them.

The ANP was hardly her debut with the press. Ever since Lady

Cunard had abandoned Leicestershire – and her husband – and Nancy had spent her London adolescence among the 'Corrupt Coterie' (socialites with famous surnames), Nancy had been a person strangers might recognise from the magazines. In pictures taken by Man Ray and Cecil Beaton she is thin-lipped and challenging of gaze; a small neat head, with strong make-up and cropped hair. She dressed in out-landish clothes and had exploits like getting arrested for swimming in Hyde Park's Serpentine lake at night.

During the First World War she had married, and fallen in love with someone else. Her lover was killed. Divorce eventually followed Armistice, and Paris became her home – a rowdy, eye-catching life beyond the reach of her mother. The atmosphere suited her: the 'per-manent state of *avant-gardisme* whose activities and creativeness were for ever stimulating'. Between Paris and London, she knew and col-laborated with Imagists, Vorticists, Surrealists, Dadaists, you name it. She began a long affair with the Surrealist Louis Aragon. Her body bore the brunt of her lifestyle: smoker's cough, aches, extreme thin-ness. Yet she carried it all off with an alluring physical grace. To some-one who met her in the 1920s she was 'incomparably bewitching'. To others she appeared to be at the centre of everything. The novelist Kay Boyle spent nights tracking Nancy through the cafés and bars and clubs of Paris, convinced she '*had* to find her, or else . . . it seemed the night would die'.

They weren't the only ones bewitched. Nancy had an untamed quality and the liberty that wealth brings. She hated food, but her appetites for everything else were voracious. A novelist could have invented her, and they did, inscribing a creature that was irresistible, insatiable, sometimes threatening and sometimes plain ridiculous; not quite or not entirely human. Aldous Huxley was inspired to create 'a perfumed imitation of a savage or an animal', a woman unhindered by ideals or economics and yet utterly intoxicating; a danger to men. Characters drawn by Richard Aldington, Wyndham Lewis and the bestselling Michael Arlen gave similar impressions. It's worth men-tioning that they were all her former lovers.

Already one of 'the most photographed young women', in those years Nancy became an icon associated with many of the groups and movements that were setting the post-war direction for the arts. By 1925, she had produced three volumes of poetry. The last was *Parallax*, which bore the influence of T. S. Eliot's *The Waste Land* and was published by Virginia and Leonard Woolf at the Hogarth Press. In 1928, unperturbed by their warning that she'd spend the rest of her life with her hands covered in ink, she had turned her attention to publishing. She moved an ancient hand press to her newly acquired home in Normandy – a cottage known as Le Puits Carré 'in lush, smiling country' near the village of La Chapelle-Réanville – and set up the Hours Press. It had closed by the time she dropped everything for Ethiopia, but for almost four years the venture had showcased her connections and her instinct for the modern; she printed, among other works, Ezra Pound's first thirty *Cantos*, and Laura Riding and Robert Graves and the then-unknown Irish writer Samuel Beckett. She was a successful publisher and a talented translator – work she approached with sincere diligence. Nancy took the arts seriously. 'Her concern with poetry,' Sylvia Townsend Warner confirmed, 'was carnal and passionate: she pursued the word, the phrase, with the patience of a weasel, the concentration of a falcon.'

Yet the gossip columns that had come into their own in her youth specialised in making people famous for being famous. They were more willing to embrace her style than any hints of substance. 'She writes poetry that we can't for the life of us understand,' the *London Mail* remarked cheerfully beside her photo in 1921, 'even when we try ever so hard.'

So, enough of the twenties. 'Why this apocryphal smarming over times that seemed, *then*, in no wise extraordinary?' she would demand, revealing something about how extraordinary the next part of her life was. The 1930s? Those 'were worth while'. By the thirties, and not unconnectedly, she had a vast collection of ivory bracelets, which she wore in abundant stacks that extended above both elbows; it was said she used them as weapons. She had burned all her bridges with her mother, or perhaps it was the other way round. Her focus was on activism – anti-imperialism, anti-racism and anti-fascism – which she often expressed through journalism, poetry and publishing.

Not everyone was on board with the new Nancy, the one who would storm off to Geneva because something important was happening. That frantic energy was still carrying her beyond where most people would go, yet to some – perhaps pining for the parties – it seemed as though the times had changed her. According to Solita Solano, a writer and editor who met Nancy in Paris, she had been fun and charming in the twenties but in the thirties she was working 'for the rights of man' and for this 'Nancy functioned best in a state of fury'. The habits of that rail-thin figure – dashing, with her 'water wagtail's' gait, from League to typewriter at night – were already characteristic. 'Sleep? Warmth? Food?' Solano would recall. 'No! Somewhere someone was suffering . . .'

There is no question about the pillars of Nancy's life by 1936, as she listened to Haile Selassie make his last unsuccessful call on the League of Nations to awake from its inertia. They were her work, her friends, her politics. For which we could also say: poetry, love, causes.

There were plenty of views on Nancy Cunard; the more things went on this way, the more unfriendly voices joined the chorus. But the poet Langston Hughes appreciated his friend's attraction to grand ideals and historic-scale conflicts. He would one day imagine her in a Spanish air, with her 'piñata of a heart in the center of a mobile at fiesta time with bits of her soul swirling in the breeze in honor of life and love and Good Morning to you, *Bon Jour, Muy Buenos, Muy Buenos! Muy Buenos!*'

And it is this image that lingers: Nancy, thin as paper, wearing her convictions right on the surface of her life, arrestingly suspended in just such a way as to receive a beating.

★

Nancy didn't have to go to Geneva to report on conflict. Politics were adversarial enough in her adopted home that she was writing anxiously in 1936 about the possibility of civil war. That year, a Popular Front coalition won the spring election in France, bringing in the country's first-ever Jewish and Socialist premier (a consolation for refugees like Gerda). But France still had its own powerful right wing that looked admiringly towards the order and strength on display in

Germany, a neighbour that offered a stark contrast to French chaos. Not long before his election, prime minister Léon Blum was beaten almost to death by right-wing extremists. After it, he had to contend with a wave of strikes that threatened to paralyse the country (his government introduced a series of reforms, including higher wages and the forty-hour work week).

Across France's southern border, in Spain, elections had also returned a victory for a broad coalition of left-wing parties that year. Another Popular Front administration was born: a tenuous Republican-Socialist collaboration brought about by the bloody repressions of the previous conservative government.

The Second Spanish Republic was itself only five years old in 1936. It had come into being with the end of Miguel Primo de Rivera's military dictatorship and the departure of King Alfonso XIII. Since then, a political system that favoured coalitions had more or less wiped out the Spanish middle ground. Popular Front parties lined up against the Right. In a country long dominated by the Catholic church, with illiteracy rates as high as 50 per cent in most places on the eve of the Republic and an average life expectancy of only forty-nine years old (more than a decade lower than in the UK and US), principles like education and land reform, women's and workers' rights, had proved hugely contentious. Lawlessness mounted, and for everyone who welcomed the reforms implemented by the first left-wing government's 1931 constitution, there were plenty for whom they didn't go far enough.

For too long, the streets had been menaced by an assertive radical Left as well as the disruptive efforts of the Falange, Spain's homegrown fascist movement (more well financed than actually popular), whose members drove around in some places in cars fitted with machine guns. And if anything embodied that lost middle ground, it was perhaps the government brought in by the 1936 elections – a government not only abhorred by the old ruling elites for its leftist character, but one that failed to satisfy the Socialists and anarchists, the primary forces of the Spanish Left.

★

That summer, Martha Gellhorn was planning on writing a novel about pacifists. If she ever finished it, it would be her third book: not a bad innings for a twenty-seven-year-old university dropout. For research she went from France, where she was living, into Germany, to a library in Stuttgart that specialised in material about the 1914–18 war. It was there that she became an anti-fascist.

Martha had lived, on and off, in Europe since she was twenty-one, but she had only recently returned from a longish stint in her native US. There she had trained herself to look closely at terrible things. When she'd arrived, Roosevelt's government was still scrambling to get a handle on the scale of the devastation wrought by the Wall Street Crash. The administration was initially hampered by a lack of hard data, but Harry Hopkins, the man tasked with running the New Deal relief programme, was conscious that the thoughts, needs and grievances of those most affected by the crisis also remained a mystery. His solution to that particular lacuna was to assemble a team of writers to fan out across the country and send back reports on the American experience of the Depression. Martha had been assigned the textile regions of the Carolinas and New England.

She had spent gruelling weeks on the road feeling isolated and increasingly demoralised. She came from an engaged and active home, the daughter of a doctor and a woman who campaigned vigorously for social and political reform, but she had never seen anything like this. She visited families in their derelict homes, spoke to doctors, relief workers, factory owners; she encountered degradation of a kind she hardly knew, yet, how to articulate. In Massachusetts she confessed, with all the preoccupations of a female correspondent who has yet to prove herself, that everything was 'so grim that whatever words I use will seem hysterical and exaggerated'. 'I haven't been in one house', she wrote to Hopkins, 'that hasn't offered me the spectacle of a human being driven beyond his or her powers of endurance and sanity . . . It is hard to believe that these conditions exist in a civilised country.' The more she saw, the angrier she became; Hopkins, getting what he'd asked for, was not spared her outrage. She detailed incompetence, corruption and insensitivity in the distribution of state aid. 'Politics is bad enough in any shape,' she told him, 'but it shouldn't get around to manhandling the destitute.' When the job came to an end (she was fired for inciting exploited labourers to an act of civil disobedience), Martha channelled the experience into *The Trouble I've Seen*, a recounting in four novellas of what she had been trying to show her boss. The only excuse for allowing such outrages, she believed, was not knowing about them. And yet later she would realise how easy it can be to overlook evil; how in Germany she had seen 'only a bit of the surface scum'.

She had that uneasy, unfamiliar sense of oppression, that sense Josephine and Virginia picked up on: of the peace having something false about it. In the street, she caught sight of what looked like a group of louts harassing an elderly couple. It seemed as though the couple were on their hands and knees, scrubbing the pavement, but she couldn't quite believe her eyes. Then, in the library, she watched an encounter between the librarian and her new Nazi boss. You could say she saw what happened to scholarship under fascism. The librarian had already confided, in whispers, that the library seemed unlikely to survive much longer. The First World War, a conflict in which Germany had suffered a devastating defeat, was not a popular topic in the Third Reich. Martha was there when the new director arrived, making an eye-catching entrance on horseback. 'He was young, blond and handsome' – all things Martha was then – and dressed in a Brownshirt uniform. 'He made a lot of noise in that silent place.' Martha couldn't follow the exchange they had, nor would the librarian tell her anything about it afterwards. She drew her conclusions simply from watching the woman's face while they spoke, from an expression she didn't fully understand how to interpret: 'I was unused to the look of fear.'

It was during this trip that she read of an outbreak of violence in Spain. The German papers described nationalists heroically fighting a revolt by 'Red swine dogs', despite the fact that technically it was the nationalists who were trying to overthrow the newly elected government. (According to the Nazi way of seeing things, those loyal to the Republic were the 'dogs'.) Martha had no trouble deciding her sympathies lay with the loyalists. 'The Nazi papers had one solid value: Whatever they were against, you could be for.'

★

In Spain, the first hours of the rebellion unfolded in a series of betrayals and bloody confrontations, as local garrisons declared for or against the government. Disorganised and tentative, ministers discovered the progress of their enemies by phoning individual governors in the provinces and seeing who picked up.

That summer, mere geography decided millions of fates: people were caught in either a Nationalist zone or a Republican one. Yet, faced with the overthrow of their young democracy, thousands of Spaniards had suddenly to choose a side. The Republic found most of its supporters among the labouring classes and progressive middle class, while aristocracy and church largely rallied to Franco. As the government dithered, attempting negotiations and then reshuffling itself, the trade unions clamoured for arms. The nationalists were said to be slaughtering potential opponents as they advanced across the country, and workers did not want to meet them undefended. Dolores Ibárruri, a Communist parliamentary deputy soon to become famous as 'La Pasionaria', launched a wartime career of bloodthirsty speeches. 'It is better to die on your feet than to live on your knees!' she proclaimed. '¡*No pasarán!*' ('They shall not pass!') The government allowed precious hours to go by, and then threw open the armouries.

Nancy Cunard was following the news but stuck in Geneva, watching in disgust as the assembled powers broke 'their own clauses and covenants, with suprahuman cynicism' and withdrew the sanctions against Italy that had failed to impede its invasion of Ethiopia. Meanwhile, the Spanish government was proving unable to halt its well-armed and well-organised opponents, though the nationalists were finding the popular resistance to their takeover more intense than expected. Spanish democracy survived the first attack, but it had not defeated its enemies. What might have been a decisive coup was now a civil war.

Nancy had told Langston Hughes that she was putting together an anthology of black poetry, but in August she had to confess the project was on hold. 'Events in France have been too much for the quiet collecting of poems! The strikes – wonderful; then Geneva; now this. What a summer . . .' Now she was in Spain, in a war zone. 'I am alone. I am having a fine time.' Spain was 'wonderful', 'tremendous', 'terrible'. She wanted to know when he was coming.

PART ONE

Beginnings

Nancy Cunard, Sylvia Townsend Warner, Valentine Ackland

Barcelona: summer, autumn 1936

Nancy was on a train to Barcelona three weeks after the rebellion. By the time she got there, on 11 August, there were two Spains: the Republican and Nationalist (rebel) zones. The nationalists held much of the north-west of the country. Except for the surrounded coastal regions of Asturias, Santander and the Basque Country, their territory arched over Madrid and descended some way along the border with Portugal. They also controlled the islands of Mallorca, Ibiza and Formentera, and the southernmost tip of Spain, around Cádiz. On the mainland, they ruled over 11 million people, compared with 14 million remaining in the Republican zone.

One Spain was a military state where strikes were punishable by death, left-wing newspapers were closed, and membership of trade unions or Popular Front parties (and, in some places, merely having voted for them) was grounds for arrest and often execution. Working-class populations were systematically terrorised, while church leaders generally intervened only to insist on offering confession to the murdered before they were killed. 'There was', the historian Hugh Thomas later wrote, 'a silence in Nationalist cities which strongly contrasted with the babel-like conditions in the Republic.' There, a wavering government had been overtaken by people's revolutions that brought with them assassinations and vandalism – particularly directed at churches – as well as radical reforms and social and economic experimentation.

Nancy arrived in Barcelona on a press visa that gave her three months to come to grips with what was happening. The weeks that followed were 'so engrossing', she said, 'that I could think of nothing else . . . The things of Spain took hold of me entirely.'

~

To one traveller at the end of the 1920s, Barcelona appeared as 'a blur of smoke by the edge of the Mediterranean'. Beneath the haze, this industrial heartland had been embellished by the wealth of its bourgeoisie into a showcase of confidence and of art nouveau and modernist flourishing. The Hotel Majestic, which became the haunt of foreign correspondents in the city, stood on the grand boulevard of the Passeig de Gràcia, where wrought-iron streetlamps adorned with leafy arabesques accompanied the undulating stone façades and jewel-like fantasias of homes built by Antoni Gaudí. By 1930, Barcelona had become Spain's most populous city, a city of millionaires and of shanty housing, of working-class districts where families crammed into 'beehive' flats and disease raced through unsanitary spaces, and heat or rain could bring buildings down. Every year between 1900 and 1936, the Barcelona region saw the highest number of industrial accidents in the country – years in which boys typically began work between the ages of eight and ten, and their mothers protested food prices or simply requisitioned what they needed from shops with the protection of armed members of the CNT trade union.

Capital of the independently spirited (and, under the Republic, self-governing) region of Catalonia, Barcelona was also an anarchist stronghold. Anarchism was one of the great forces in Spanish political life: almost 2 million workers were affiliated with anarchist unions. Nowhere else in Europe was the movement so significant. Rejecting all forms of centralised power, its leaders had always refused to cooperate with the democratic parties. They represented a 'huge, self-absorbed and passionate movement, already throbbing with anonymous violence'.

The Barcelona of 1936 was no place for equivocal attitudes. When nationalist officers marched their men through the heart of the city on 19 July, the workers were ready for them. Factory sirens blared and people poured into the streets, bearing weapons that had circulated throughout the night. Those not involved in the fighting threw up barricades to block the soldiers' way into the centre.

There, the nationalists had been dealt a key defeat. Seizing the initiative with their resistance, the unions found themselves supported by their old enemies in the Civil Guard and the Assault Guard (local para-military forces); in the midst of street battles, some soldiers were even persuaded to switch sides to preserve the Republic. Having secured the city, for the first time in their history anarchists agreed to cooperate with the government to defeat a common enemy.

For a time, though, Catalonia's armed defenders had carte blanche. 'The government does not exist,' declared Andreu Nin of the Trot-skyist POUM (Partido Obrero de Unificación Marxista: Workers' Marxist Unification Party). 'We collaborate with them, but they can do no more than sanction whatever is done by the masses.' In the chaos unleashed by the nationalist uprising, law and order dis-integrated. To the horror of many leaders of the Left, long-festered scores were settled against police officials, churches and industrialists known for the suppression of unions.

When Nancy arrived in August, the worst of this was already con-tained; she was impressed by 'the discipline in this town, the order'. What she saw was a city in which the revolutionary potential of 1936 was made manifest. If war was itself disastrous, the confidence on display in Barcelona explains the paradox of her reaction: why even then – especially then – Spain could seem 'wonderful'.

With the old structures of authority blasted suddenly away, it seemed possible that a new form of society was being trialled in Bar-celona. It was on these streets that visitors like George Orwell – who arrived in December and swiftly volunteered for a POUM militia – were made, for however short a period, to believe: to chance hope in a cause that seemed viable in that very moment and that very place. Fac-tories, shops and banks had been requisitioned and were now run by their employees; the Ritz Hotel became 'Gastronomic Unit Number One', a public canteen for anyone who needed it; revolutionary com-mittees took over responsibilities once held by the authorities; and Catalonia was run by a coalition of anti-fascist militias. The people on the street seemed sure of themselves, assertive; unbowed by old oppressions and scornful of old hierarchies, like branches springing up as they shed a winter load.

Nancy, fluent in both Spanish and Catalan, would have noticed that formal forms of address – markers of deference – had been abandoned. Everywhere one was greeted with '¡*Salud!*' and the clenched-fist salute. Tips and taxi fares were declined. 'The people are lovely,' she reported enthusiastically; '[they] have been through hell'. She was already the type to stop and talk to strangers – and then to question them about their living conditions and view of local politics. She picked up people wherever she went and she had never restricted her curiosity to her own class: she was at home in Barcelona. At the Hotel Majestic she would form a lasting friendship with Angel Goded, a waiter whose children would one day be taught to bless her name.

Solidarity was expected in Barcelona and visitors welcomed. A revolution needs witnesses and heralds, and the city had a message for the international community. 'We are going to inherit the earth,' the anarchist leader Buenaventura Durruti announced to a Canadian journalist. 'The bourgeoisie may blast and ruin their world before

Boys in CNT caps on a barricade in Barcelona (Gerda Taro)

they leave the stage of history. But we carry a new world in our hearts.'

Nancy got to work spreading the word. She filed three or four articles a week, writing for the Associated Negro Press, for Sylvia Pankhurst's *New Times* and for various newsletters focused on Spain. Over the course of the war she would also write for the French press, for the London *News Chronicle*, the *Manchester Guardian*, the *New Statesman*, the *Nation*, the *Left Review* and others. In mid-September, one of her articles caught the attention of Valentine Ackland and Sylvia Townsend Warner.

Sylvia and Valentine had hoped that the Communist Party would arrange to send them to Spain. 'We are perpetually half-packed, and half-hoped,' Sylvia wrote to a friend that August, 'and each secretly convinced that the other will be chosen and the one left to pine.' They were sure there was work for them with one of the medical units assembling to volunteer in the Republican zone: Valentine could drive and Sylvia excelled at organising – she also felt she would be valuable as a journalist. But after a flurry of cryptic notes about meetings with party officials in Valentine's appointments diary, there was only 'Waiting'. (Meanwhile Sylvia made a three-day dash to Brussels to take part in a Communist-organised International Peace Congress.)

After Nancy's direct appeal for 'active material aid' for the Republic, Valentine tried announcing her own, more flamboyant, plan to chivvy the party organisers into action. She wrote a letter to the *Daily Worker* and the *News Chronicle*, proposing to lead a convoy of volunteers to Spain herself in the MG Midget. Later she admitted that her intentions had been largely symbolic: to make 'a gesture towards the United Front'. Given the international situation, signalling solidarity in person seemed as urgent as the cash donations she and Sylvia were mustering as they waited.

While individuals rallied to the Republican cause, the British government was responding with similar speed but markedly different sympathies. Determined to avoid – apparently at any cost – another European war like the one that had blighted Nancy and Sylvia's youths, the government was also peopled by upper-class conservatives who had no desire to support the European Left. The Foreign Secretary announced an embargo on arms sales to the Republic, despite the fact that, as a recognised government, the Spanish administration was legally entitled to buy arms on the international market. (It also became increasingly clear that not only fascist countries, but also British and American businesses, were aiding the nationalists.) At the time of Nancy's trip to Barcelona, the British government threw its considerable influence behind the Non-Intervention Agreement, by which twenty-seven nations – including, crucially, France, Great Britain, Germany, Italy and the USSR – committed to aiding neither side. (The Germans, Italians and Russians ignored it.) In vain, the Spanish foreign minister warned the League of Nations in September that 'the blood-stained soil of Spain is already, in fact, the battle field of a world war'. A Non-Intervention Committee was convened in London, and presided doggedly over what would be described as 'the supreme farce of our time'. In claiming neutrality, Britain's venerable democracy had loaded the dice against the survival of a far younger counterpart. It was an 'attitude', Nancy said, that 'never surprised' her.

Sylvia felt that 'respectables' in Britain worked to ensure that sympathetic accounts of the Republic did not reach the public; later she would have trouble getting her own 'propaganda' published. Whatever sympathy there undoubtedly was among ordinary people was tempered by an overwhelming opposition to the idea of another world war. Meanwhile, the conservative press indulged in lurid and exaggerated accounts of a 'Red Terror' tearing through places like Barcelona (sex-crazed anarchists and violated nuns). Less was said in those papers about the methodical 'cleansing' Franco had embarked upon as he began his campaign to destroy Spanish republicanism forever. The bias of such stories in the French press was partly what had sent Nancy to Spain to see for herself; it was the only way, she said, to 'find out what truly was happening'.

Finally, Sylvia and Valentine were both summoned to help a British volunteer medical unit that was being organised from Barcelona. They arrived at the French border with Spain towards the end of September but found themselves stalled again. With things shifting rapidly, papers that had been adequate when they left home were subjected to new scrutiny only days later, and their first welcome was at gunpoint. Valentine logged a series of aborted crossings in her diary as the couple skirted the frontier, seeking an opportunity. 'Sent back' twice at Portbou, a fishing village at the foot of the Pyrenees, it at last proved their gateway into Spain.

★

'At the border between France and Spain there is a tunnel,' Langston Hughes would later recall, 'a long stretch of darkness through which the night express from Paris passes in the early morning. When the train comes out into the sunlight, on the Spanish side of the mountain, with a shining blue bay where children swim in the Mediterranean, you see the village of Portbou.' To arrive in Spain via this uppermost point of the Costa Brava (literally its 'Wild Coast') was to find a country of tree-tufted mountains, of rocky coastline with dark sand beaches and dazzling ocean: a beautiful, inaccessible place, one welcoming but not laid out for your ease. To arrive in 1936 was to find both things true: visitors like Sylvia and Valentine proceeded from there by long, uncomfortable journeys, requiring a discombobulating array of passes – sometimes even passwords – provided by different authorities, and met people whose welcome they would never forget. Portbou was a village dominated by a large, elegant railway station, from which it was still possible to reach Barcelona.

Sylvia immediately took to the garrulousness of Barcelona, to its certainty and hope. The air reverberated with news and music issuing from loudspeakers in the trees; the organ grinders played 'The Internationale'. Trams were garlanded with flowers and there was not a car or bus unadorned with the initials of one of the political associations – which had organised themselves into militias. Browsing the little stalls on the plaza, she bought trinkets decorated with their names for the *Daily Worker* to auction off at home: 'the anarchist F.A.I. and C.N.T., the Trotskyist P.O.U.M., the Communist P.S.U.C. and U.G.T.' She felt they were seeing the very beginnings of a revolution, as if they had landed in 'the early days of the USSR'.

For Sylvia, this was an especially stirring prospect. In 1936 there were signs of unease among Western enthusiasts for the Russian revolution disconcerted by the first trials in what became Stalin's nightmarish purges, or by glimpses of famine and oppression on visits to the USSR itself. Sylvia was not one of them. She was among those (and they included many distinguished figures) who still believed in Soviet Russia as a thrilling experiment in a new, better, social order. If anything, the creep of doubt made the need for loyalty all the fiercer, because with these hotly contested criticisms emerging from former admirers it seemed that the enemies of progress were appearing in unexpected guises.

The militias in Barcelona were a highly visible sign of the war raging outside of the city. Since roughly half of the regular army had sided with the rebels in July, the Republic had been forced to scramble recruits for a People's Army. Soldiers looked suspiciously young. They wore mismatching, ad hoc uniforms. Some of them were even female. Trainees drilled on the beaches and in public squares; they marched proudly through the pouring rain to ecstatic crowds. 'If one wants to please a child,' Sylvia noticed, 'one allows him or her to play with fire-arms.'

In streets crammed with hundreds of thousands of refugees, Sylvia and Valentine spent much of the three weeks they had in Spain queuing patiently at various committee offices, where the many stamps and permits and passes necessary for getting anything done (or just getting anything) could be secured. With no central authority in charge, and revolutionary fervour at a pitch of hypervigilance, the more stamps that could be secured on passes the better. Sylvia was in her element.

Embarrassingly, she and Valentine had arrived wearing hats, trappings of bourgeois respectability that they quickly discarded to fit in with the women of Barcelona. They were first housed in a hotel, but were soon offered a room in one of the requisitioned 'palaces' in the city's wealthy suburbs. The threatened opulence was not ideal, since they fully intended to live, as one of the other guests put it, 'as much like proletarians as possible'. Fortunately, they were given the job of preparing the building for its new life as a hospital.

In the *New Yorker*, Sylvia described her work in Barcelona as 'excursions ranging from buying large iron frying pans for the hospital kitchen to combing Barcelona for a café where newly arrived [volunteers for British Medical Aid] could be restored with buttered toast'. By these efforts, 'in my humble, stammering way, I, too, helped to combat Fascism'. (If the intention was simply to offer her services, to do something, then sending positive accounts of the city to a magazine with the reach of the *New Yorker* was itself no small contribution.)

Marginal many times over – female, unmarried, countryside-dwelling, politically unconventional, lesbian and now almost middle-aged – Sylvia was used to going unnoticed. She played up to this nothing-to-see-here persona in much of her writing, letting what was radical infiltrate beneath a comforting sense of eccentricity. In cheerful *New Yorker* style, she allowed for the absurdities of their position in Barcelona, describing the naïve good intentions and faintly ridiculous sincerity of the foreign volunteers in a way that made everyone seem well intentioned and quite probably ineffectual; harmless, in other words, especially to the status quo. Her account is peppered with 'affable' and 'benevolent' visitors, 'children of angelic serenity' and even 'puppy dogs'. One of the volunteers is on a funny diet; Sylvia's favourite person, their housekeeper Asunción ('shaped so exactly like a bear'), passes wet Sundays tearing up and down in the basement pretending to be a bullfighter.

Yet there are clues to less cosy realities, like Asunción's other habit, when wishing to express disapproval, 'of turning herself into a machine gun and saying, "Poum, poum, poum, poum!"'

'You cannot imagine,' Sylvia reported to a friend, 'after this mealy-mouthed country [Britain], the pleasure of seeing an office with a large painted sign, Organisation for the Persecution of Fascists.' What exactly she understood by 'Persecution' she didn't say. Like Nancy, she and Valentine had missed the early bloodletting, and Sylvia was impressed by what she described as the 'sturdily tranquil' atmosphere in Barcelona. Where she found destruction, she approved of the targets. In the *Left Review*, she openly defended the ransacking of the city's churches, contrasting it with the preservation of the mansions whose owners had fled for the Nationalist zone. Sylvia toured many of these buildings looking for a suitable rest home for British nurses and found that, though items deemed to be of artistic value had been formally appropriated, the houses were otherwise intact: no signs of frenzied mobs having passed through with a free rein. This proved to her the ideological basis of the assaults on religious buildings. The churches, she explained, 'have been cleaned out exactly as sick-rooms are cleaned out after a pestilence. Everything that could preserve the contagion has been destroyed.'

It's a cool, even clinical, spin on the revolution in Barcelona, designed to defend the anarchists from the 'Red hordes' slurs broadcast by Franco and his supporters, and reflective of her approval. Nancy, who was shown armouries in churches and told of priests firing on the people in July, took a similar view. 'Here all the churches, the insides that is, have been burnt out,' she told Langston soon after arriving: 'the eradication of the pest of religion.'

Sylvia and Valentine admired the resolution of the Catalan people and their spirited determination against the odds. They knew that enemy planes could reach the city from Mallorca in less than twenty minutes and that there were nowhere near enough air-raid shelters. They could see that many of the soldiers marching off proudly to the front had not been issued guns. They felt themselves to be on the right side of a conflict that transcended borders. 'People like Asunción', Sylvia claimed, 'just belong to the good.'

Judging by a letter Valentine wrote almost a month before they left for Spain, there was a point that summer when it seemed Sylvia's fears would come true and that Valentine would be sent without her. 'If I go to Spain, and if I am killed there,' Valentine told her, Sylvia was to remember first and foremost 'that I love you most deeply, passionately and happily, and that I have loved you like this ever since we first lay together, without any break.'

Six years previously, Valentine and Sylvia had first been united in outrage. Believing that a girl in the Dorset village where they were both staying was being mistreated, they had stormed over together to confront her employer. 'Righteous indignation', Sylvia reflected afterwards, 'is a beautiful thing.' That night they began to speak quiet confidences through the partition wall that separated their bedrooms, and Sylvia discovered that her cool, self-contained housemate feared herself 'utterly unloved'. 'The forsaken grave wail of her voice smote me,' she wrote later, 'and had me up, and through the door, and at her bedside. There I stayed, till I got into her bed, and found love there.'

The first novel Sylvia finished after the revelations of Valentine was published while they were in Spain. In one of its most striking scenes, the protagonist, Sophia Willoughby, listens as the captivating storyteller Minna holds a room transfixed with her description of witnessing the thawing of a frozen river as a child. Drawn first by the noise, Minna remembers, her younger self was stirred and mesmerised as the revivified current wrenched chunks of ice into the wash of the river: 'It was like a battle. It was like a victory. The rigid winter could stand no longer, it was breaking up, its howls and vanquished threats swept past me, its strongholds fell and were broken one against another, it was roused at last.'

The novel is set during the Parisian revolutions of 1848, and the adult Minna links the unstoppable force of the waters to Liberty: the ice of the status quo giving way under the gathering momentum of change. But it could just as easily stand for the revolution of feeling that Sophia, on the brink of her first lesbian affair, experiences as the novel unfolds.

By this time in her life, Sylvia understood the great surge of fulfilment that living in defiance of conventional society – facing down its howls and threats – could bring. Having experienced the emotional revolution of finding love with Valentine, she longed to live the fulfilment of other 'unacted desires' she had discovered in the 1930s. In Barcelona she excitedly believed herself to be as close as it was possible to get to that touchstone of Russia in 1917. 'I've never seen people who I admired more,' Sylvia told an interviewer many years later. 'I never again saw a country I loved as much as I loved Spain.'

Secretly, love was the key. While inspecting gutted churches, meeting official persecutors ('The head persecutor was one of the nicest men I have ever met'), and preparing a trenchant criticism of her British comrades for their disorganised efforts in Spain, Sylvia was also writing poems for Valentine. In these poems it is love – something that was once theirs alone – that makes their involvement in humanity real to them and gains them entrance to Barcelona and all it signifies. In her private love-letter record of the visit, handwritten in an exuberant red-and-white booklet, the trip is like a honeymoon and they the happy couple emanating a goodwill that is reflected back at them by comrade after comrade.

To read this account is to understand how truly liberating the trip was – a period when a new frankness about their relationship was possible. In her *New Yorker* piece, Sylvia mentions a curious conversation with Asunción, who would come to mean a great deal to her. When two of the volunteers disappear together, Asunción mistakenly assumes an assignation (it is a meeting, she guesses knowingly, 'under the pine trees'). Hating to disappoint her, Sylvia reveals a 'real romance' instead:

> We told her of another couple from among our group – neither of them, I fear, from her point of view remarkable for youth or beauty – who were linked not only by the prevalent sense of duty but also by a real desire to retire together under the pine trees.
>
> Her jaw dropped; she looked incredulous, and even aghast. But in a moment she had recovered her philosophy, her geniality, her warmth of heart; and raising her fist in the Popular Front salute, she exclaimed, '*Viva la República!*'

Reading the article for details of their stay, it took me a moment to register the strange vagueness of this description. I wondered if it was Sylvia's cryptic way of saying that she and Valentine had confided their own relationship, a partnership they regarded as a marriage: an exchange that could not be divulged explicitly in print but was equally too precious to omit entirely. The revolutionary mood seems integral to Asunción's welcoming acceptance – saluting the Republic as if personal and political can't be put asunder, and new freedom in one realm can only mean freedom in the other.

The out-of-history sense of possibility in Barcelona is palpable in Sylvia's own intense and heady freedom to proclaim herself – to

Valentine, perhaps to Asunción, and, it seems, in the very streets of the city. It's there in her celebration of the noise and the voices – the liberty to say what was previously unsayable – that comparison with 'mealy-mouthed' Britain, which must have been particularly potent for a couple who could not ordinarily acknowledge the enormity of what they meant to each other. In England, living on the edge of a thatched-cottage hamlet, their marriage was denied by their neighbours' polite refusal to enquire; it was denied by the very language the state permitted them. Presented with the problem of a census, they had not been able to call themselves married but only 'companion' and 'spinster: annulled'.

Valentine had never been ashamed of her sexuality, but her father's discovery of her first girlfriend had revealed the potential for a punitive gulf between her joy in love and others' conception of it: 'I remember very vividly the expression of disgust on his face.' Yet in Barcelona, Sylvia and Valentine clearly felt themselves among friends, part of a great collective effort of emancipation. Marginalised at home by their politics as much as by their commitment to living the truth of their love – decisions which liberated them in fundamental ways – as Sylvia's poems attest, in Barcelona she and Valentine had ceased to be outsiders: 'No longer was our own / Freedom an exile [. . .]'.

Barcelona offered the extraordinary rush of walking hand in hand, 'like children allowed / Out by themselves' – finally trusted with an exhilarating autonomy. Untethered from the society that sought to exclude and deny them, new realms of solidarity revealed themselves. 'We could look people openly in the face,' Sylvia savours. Love wasn't new to them – 'We did not go there with hearts unexercised' – but in Barcelona's revolutionary openness its capacities seemed newly realised.

For love poems about war, those in the booklet are largely (some might say inappropriately) unmarked by loss. Everything is expansion, revelation. Sylvia and Valentine love the people they meet, they love the cause. They are so bound to it that they share its pulse, and hold so close to one another that its beating comforts Sylvia through her lover's body when she imagines fascist bombers speeding on their way:

> Embraced with all my power
> Of love, not only you
> I clasp, not only you I greet.

In a puckish account of their palatial accommodation in the fourth poem of the booklet's six, Sylvia revels in the idea that their presence has been directly enabled by the driving out of the old world, taking transgressive pleasure in imagining the pious enemies whose marital bed they have usurped. 'But in that bed with lean bodies and laughing minds we lay.'

This, perhaps, was their reward – or a promise of greater rewards to come with victory. For living as they did was already their gift for the future, their legacy to others who might yet live their freedom. 'I love you with the arrogance of first love, that knows no one in the world loved just so, or so completely, ever before,' Valentine told Sylvia when she thought she might have to go to Spain alone. 'But I hope very many people will after us, sweetheart – and we've done our best to make it possible.'

When I first saw the booklet Sylvia made for Valentine, their papers were being housed temporarily in a large brick building – one of several large brick buildings that seemed to have been built as an afterthought to the car park they sat in. I had read the poems long before, in an article that had singled them out as 'unprecedented' among English poetic responses to the war for their 'combination of radical politics and queer desire', but if discovering the poems had been a thrilling intellectual signpost, the booklet itself was a physical, confirmatory talisman of the meaning Barcelona held for the couple. Its existence in the nondescript reading room seemed deeply incongruous.

I had the same feeling later that day, exploring the picturesque Dorset villages where they had lived together and were buried together. Red telephone boxes and a thatched pub aren't what immediately spring to mind when you think of Communist activists. Then the parts coalesced to give me Sylvia and Valentine as resident outsiders: women with experience in making themselves at home, through hard work and imperviousness, wherever felt right. Barcelona had been one of those places.

In Sylvia's poems, love isn't just saccharine indulgence; it doesn't enbubble the couple but rather draws them into closer commitment to the cause. There is an odd parallel to the glowy goodwill of the booklet in Sylvia's party-functionary severity elsewhere, her unruffled eliding of the violence. What Sylvia likes about Asunción, who is also mentioned in the poems, is not only her kind hospitality but her revolutionary ruthlessness. 'Nor did I lose sight for a moment', she informed readers of the *New Masses* (an audience rather further to the left than that of the *New Yorker*), '[of] the fact that both the persecutor and [Asunción] would (and probably had) kill fascists as one kills cockroaches.' The 'ability to kill and the ability to remain kind' were nurtured, she believed, 'from the same root of conviction and experience'.

Sylvia had no intention of killing anyone in Barcelona (though Valentine, who was an excellent shot, considered joining a militia), but her lack of qualms about the deaths there is striking. Was this a determination not to be naïve, a resolution to acknowledge the stakes involved when resisting those on the right who didn't see the poor or the queer as human? Or just a recklessness with other people's lives that came at little cost to herself? It's clear that Asunción made her feel safe, as though purpose and principle were the true indicators of who belonged to the good.

Only one poem in the series of six written for Valentine – the only one that was published – restricts itself to a more sombre palette, to images of drought and a gathering storm, to politics and propaganda. It admits to the presence of death in a way reminiscent of another poem Sylvia published about the war: 'Portbou', in which she speaks of 'the resolved fury / of those who fight for Spain'. Both poems return from the honeymoon postcards to a hardened single-mindedness, the kind of ruthlessness that would prove famously controversial in W. H. Auden's better-known poem 'Spain' (which Nancy loved, published on her return to France and echoed in parts of her own poetry) with its reference to 'necessary murder'.

Love, rage. They're themes that ought to be jarring – are jarring – and yet they found a marriage in Sylvia's approach to the war. In Barcelona, it was clearly possible for her to find joy in a movement she had faith in whilst having few illusions about all it entailed. A life worth living may still be lived at a cost, after all, and it may need to be fought for. Those warning hints smuggled into the *New Yorker* article are there in the poems, too – in the hard edge to Sylvia's love, the rage that isn't assuaged but is instead intensified by seeing how good the world could be. She promises to weaponise her knowledge of utopia:

> [. . .] We should be vilely their debtor
>   If we do not love further henceforth, and hate better.

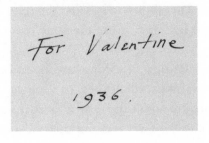

★

Valentine's idea of joining a militia wasn't unthinkable. Female militia members were one of the most publicised features of the early war. The partners Robert Capa and Gerda Taro, who were among the photographers arriving in Barcelona at around the same time as Nancy, captured numerous images of women training in these new identities. In one of the most iconic, Gerda held a *miliciana* in a close frame as she knelt on the sand, resting her arm on her bent knee in front of her, aiming a pistol into the distance. The woman looks young and picturesque; her hair, overalls and neat, heeled shoe all dark against the backdrop, with only the small gun in her hand shining bright as the sky behind.

Nor were the female combatants all Spanish. The first British casualty of the Republican side was Felicia Browne, an artist and

Communist who found herself in Barcelona on 19 July and enlisted in a militia. She was killed during a failed attempt to blow up an enemy munitions train in Aragon within weeks of Nancy's arrival. Browne had come to see her art pale in significance beside the inequalities that enabled her to live in relative leisure. 'I can only make out of what is valid and urgent to me,' she explained to a friend. 'If painting and sculpture were more valid and more urgent to me than the earthquake which is happening in the revolution, or if these two were reconciled so that the demands of one didn't conflict (in time, even, and concentration) with the demands of the other, I should paint and make sculpture.'

The brilliant French intellectual Simone Weil, only twenty-seven at the time, also arrived in Catalonia before Sylvia and Valentine, or even Nancy, to volunteer for an anarchist militia. 'When I realised that, try as I would, I could not prevent myself from participating morally in [the] war – in other words, from hoping all day and every day for the victory of one side and the defeat of the other', she told a friend, 'I took the train to Barcelona, with the intention of enlisting.'

Weil was a tenacious researcher, capable of an almost total disregard for her own well-being. At home in France she was technically a *lycée* teacher, though lately she had been preoccupied with infiltrating factories in order to study working conditions. What she had gained from that experience was a visceral understanding of the physical exhaustion, degradation and imprisonment entailed in industrial capitalism. What she had lost was 'a certain lightness of heart which, it seems to me, will never again be possible'.

Her revolutionary foray in Spain did not last long. Shortly after helping to sabotage a railway line, she strolled straight into a pot of boiling cooking oil that had been concealed in a ditch to hide the flames from enemy view. Horribly burned, she limped back to Barcelona and was eventually taken home by her long-suffering parents.

The mishap was probably not the worst outcome they had imagined. Their daughter was already in poor health and notoriously clumsy. For all her courage, it is hard to see what she thought she was contributing to the militia she insisted on joining; easier to ridicule the hard-headed efforts of this fragile intellectual. She could hardly have been oblivious to her own physical shortcomings, or the strain these placed on her comrades, and she gave no sign of thinking she had anything specific to contribute to the Republic. Seeing the situation for herself was certainly crucial for writing first-hand accounts for the press or persuasive fundraising material, but there was also clearly something significant to Simone Weil about experience.

Sylvia valued her period of working in a munitions factory during the First World War for the direct comprehension it gave her of conditions she'd later oppose. Weil, too, used her experiences, at the factory and now at the front, as material to think with. According to her biographer, the time after her return from Spain was 'a period rich in reflection which marked a turning-point in her political thought'. When it came to the causes that occupied her, she had a kind of dedication to integrity, to involving herself both physically and intellectually, which elevated authenticity of experience to an almost moral level. Her efforts at factory and militia life seem attempts at true solidarity that resulted in a sometimes-perverse determination to spare herself nothing. In this, she was a little like Nancy Cunard, who could, it was said, harden 'her will to overcome exhaustion, courting physical discomfort, indifferent to calumny, smiling at risks' when her cause demanded it – a self-abnegation that rarely endears you to others. (Weil's austerity was more deliberate, more wearing than energising. During the Second World War, alone in Britain and limiting herself to the rations her compatriots in France received, she would die of tuberculosis at thirty-four.)

'War is a malignant disease, an idiocy, a prison,' Martha Gellhorn, a woman who would become an expert, once wrote, 'and the pain it causes is beyond telling or imagining'. The intricacies of the Spanish war, its origins and evils, are unavoidably significant and yet did not matter. Not to those, like Nancy and Sylvia, who believed the situation to be dreadfully simple. To them, it was right and wrong, good and evil, hope and despair: resisting fascism or succumbing to it. Choosing a side in the war was a moral imperative and a straightforward one. The things they saw in the Republican zone confirmed a position already taken. To say that there were atrocities on both sides is both significant and true – which is to say, the truth would not be complete without acknowledging it – but also obscures the fact that the scale and targets of the destruction perpetrated by each side were very different, and that the two sides represented deeply opposed ideologies.

For these women, the decision to head for Spain was an obvious one. It was obvious because, as Nancy put it, 'of the ghastliness, the magnitude and the closeness of the civil war in Spain', and it was obvious because the prospect of another war, 'engineered by the alliances of the fascist leaders of diverse countries', was now looming. This meant that 'every single other matter, (things that were vital and immediate until the Spanish war began), [was] now secondary to this'.

But there were plenty of people – millions – who did not put every single other matter aside. For the vast majority, it was the individual, the day-to-day, that remained the paramount emergency, the motivating force: the only world real enough to be worth suffering for. Leaving for Spain may have been easier for Nancy, Sylvia and Valentine because they were childless; because, despite their unconventionality, they retained certain safety nets of their class. If they sometimes suffered for their freedom, they also put it to good use.

Valentine believed that part of the mainstream reticence about the plight of Republican Spain was because it wasn't pitiable enough. This confidence of the downtrodden – this 'free, cultured, intellectual people, fighting magnificently and with much reason to hope for victory' – was too threatening to the established order to be broadcast. It was not the suffering of the people in Barcelona that was the problem, but their liberation. Like Nancy and Sylvia, Valentine reacted to her time in Spain with a rush of writing: poems, letters and articles were all logged in her diary during the first days back at home. Non-intervention, the mealy-mouthed not-looking-too-closely that saved people from confrontation (that allowed her and Sylvia to live together in peace but imposed upon them a shame they did not feel) would, as Nancy put it the following year, 'no longer do'.

For people paying such close attention to the currents of the time, there was a terrible fear behind the decision to go to Spain. 'Don't die – Live,' Valentine had begged in what she believed – when it seemed she might be summoned alone – could be her final letter to Sylvia. 'And if you have to die (as I <u>dread</u> you may) in Fascism or war or persecution – remember me and love me. If I could shelter you I would – I would.' Neither inaction nor engagement could shelter them – the risk of either was annihilation, the stakes inordinately high. With the future darkening at pace, those looking towards it had to wrest some defiant response from the beckoning of despair.

The Battle for Madrid

Nancy Cunard

Madrid: autumn, winter 1936

At the end of the last day of August 1936, Nancy Cunard sat down in the desert in Aragon and gazed at immensity. 'It had been a day that got out of hand, somehow.' She had spent it with a young mother whose 'little dead daughter' Nancy had photographed in her coffin. In gratitude for that brisk gift – a record of her child's existence – the woman had insisted on offering food and drink. Afterwards, Nancy's instinct had been to take herself away on a 'thundering long walk', but the light was going, and getting lost in a war zone pure foolish selfishness. Instead, she struck away from her companions to sit alone on the sand in an empty landscape that set her 'utterly at peace': a condition so rare that she promised herself she would return one day. 'To me it was infinity. . . . It was total and complete.'

That day, in the desert, death was on her mind. When they'd carried the child's coffin out into the blazing sun (she'd had to explain that the gloom in the house was too dark for her Kodak), she'd wondered how many more bodies she would see before she left. Her conscience was troubling her. She'd come to Spain to cover the war and she hadn't yet found a way to the front.

A month later, she had spent 'days and days' with the militias in Aragon ('a marvellous experience'), having met two soldiers on a train who presumably agreed to take her with them. It was fortunate that she was resourceful, determined: her journeys were cobbled-together opportunisms of buses, lifts, chance encounters. Travelling with soldiers brought people running with the clenched-fist salute. The young mother in Aragon was far from the only bereaved woman to hail her. Told Nancy's reason for coming, they instructed her to 'continue, work, tell the truth'. From villages at the front, she made her way west to Madrid. From there she wrote a letter to the *Manchester Guardian*. Convinced that readers would be 'in sympathy with the legal Government of Spain and with its heroic defenders, the People's Militias (amongst whom are fighting many of the Spanish intellectuals), in their hard struggle against international Fascism', she urged donations 'without delay'. The Republic's forces were ill-equipped and the harsh Spanish winter already hung ominously over the capital. Later, Nancy would remember 'snow in the new craters there'. She'd had a feeling that Madrid would be 'hard', but what she discovered was 'little by little, progressively, terrible'.

In the week she wrote her letter, the nationalists began a rapid advance on the capital and Nancy got her transport to another front. There was every expectation that Madrid would be occupied within days. Nationalist generals could count on trained and disciplined men, many of whom, unlike the loyal members of the Spanish regular army, had previous combat experience. This was because the backbone of their strength was the Army of Africa, a colonial force of 40,000 men and a bloodthirsty reputation. Franco's initial plan to transfer these troops to Spain on warships had been scuppered when the crews mutinied against their nationalist officers. But then Hitler and Mussolini stepped in with planes that saved the day, carrying the first 12,000 men into Spain over two months and helping the nationalists continue their charge across the country.

'Every day', one Madrileño would write, 'news came which showed how the armies of the rebels were fanning out like locust swarms, advancing on Madrid from all sides'. They moved so fast that when the prime minister tried calling the Republican commander at Illescas, a town on the Toledo road out of Madrid, he found it had already fallen to the enemy. On 21 October, nationalist troops were just thirty kilometres from the city. Two days later, Junkers Ju 52 planes sent from Germany dropped bombs over the capital. Nancy heard reports of people killed in the suburbs. She kept moving, hitching lifts on trucks and walking long distances to get near the fighting, which kept drawing closer.

In the notes she made for her articles there was no question of impartiality. She wrote of how far 'we' had advanced; whether a demolished bridge was blown up 'by us or enemy'. She recorded rapid-fire impressions, jottings that would find their echoes in the poetry she composed obsessively about the war.

On 19, 21, 23 and 24 October she headed towards Illescas, returning in the evenings to the sight of refugees streaming into the city. For months people had been rushing north, bearing harrowing stories of the brutality and pillaging that arrived with the nationalists. The Army of Africa heralded systematic terror: mass slaughter, the abuse of women, bodies displayed for days in the streets to drive home the message. Over the radio, the nationalist general Queipo de Llano indulged in graphic descriptions of what Madrid's women could expect from his soldiers. Nancy estimated she'd seen 4,000 women and children arrive in the city in a single evening.

Republican militiamen were falling back too, and their tales were no more encouraging. Illescas had fallen on 19 October, but over the coming days the Republicans struggled unsuccessfully to recover it. Nancy had no experience as a war reporter but she did have a determination to get close to the action. She fell in with Scottish ambulance drivers as she followed the Republican counter-attack. Weapons shortages meant there was little protection from the enemy planes: 'The ambulance has much to do.' Exploring further west – in the direction of Móstoles and Navalcarnero, where the nationalists were also pressing in – she drove in a car camouflaged with thistles and leaves. As the net closed around Madrid, she issued regular and detailed accounts to the press. Diligently she picked up knowledge ('A little rise in the ground on the right; natural protection from enemy fire, increased by dug-out trench at its base; they shoot over top') and sketched out the felt experience of the conflict. 'We run across the road, ducking, then talking with those in the trenches . . . Bullets pass. NOISE. In the distance more and bigger noise, muted by distance.' She was so close to the action that it was sometimes impossible to tell what was happening. Pushing on towards Illescas, she recorded 'sounds of war, heavy; artillery, considerable; distant machine guns. Three planes pass over us, very high. Said to be enemy . . . it is not possible to know at this moment whether Illescas is ours or theirs. The fighting is going on.'

~

In the first days of November, General Franco announced that Madrid could soon expect to be 'liberated'. He had lorries of food for its inhabitants standing ready just behind his artillery, and long lists of arrests prepared.

Nancy wrote that the air raids were 'constant', yet she was struck by the stoicism on the streets. 'Population just looked at the sky,' she wrote, 'continued on its way.' But Franco's forces, backed by squadrons of German and Italian airmen, seemed unstoppable; others were less sanguine. On 6 November, the government judged the situation so hopeless that they abruptly evacuated to Valencia, leaving General José Miaja, Minister of War, with responsibility for the defence of the city. The Communist deputy Antonio Mije, who also remained, pledged that his forces would 'defend Madrid house by house'. Trade union leaders were summoned and given orders to mobilise 50,000 men overnight. Elsewhere, the execution of political prisoners began.

At dawn on 7 November, Radio Madrid called for the building of barricades as the nationalists began a heavy artillery bombardment that signalled their attempt on the city. La Pasionaria's voice echoed from loudspeakers in the streets, calling on housewives to prepare pots of boiling oil to hurl over the heads of Franco's men. Ill-equipped Spanish workers made for the front; those without arms planning to acquire them as their comrades fell. Children worked at the barricades, while a battalion of women assembled before the Segovia bridge and fighter planes sent from Russia appeared in the sky.

The Madrileños – many of whom had learned how to use a rifle only hours before – were still holding out the following day. Then, as orders for a total mobilisation issued from the radio at two-minute intervals, and foreign reporters confidently predicted the fall of the city, and telegrams congratulating Franco were delivered to Miaja, reinforcements appeared in a column along the Gran Vía. They were almost 2,000 soldiers from the International Brigade, in corduroy uniforms and steel helmets, heralded on their progress towards the city by peasants yelling, '¡No pasarán!'

★

It's estimated that over 30,000 people, from fifty-three different countries, volunteered for the International Brigades over the course of the war. Thousands of others arrived from abroad to serve in different Republican militias, and still more acted on their sympathies by coming as ambulance drivers and medics. Steel workers from Hungary clung to the undersides of trains to get to Spain; Poles, Romanians and Yugoslavs, coordinated by French and Italian Communists in Paris, joined them in evading right-wing governments at home. Two and a half thousand recruits joined the British Battalion. Over four and a half thousand volunteered from Canada and the US. Germans and Italians who had already lost the fight at home, Irish republicans, African Americans, Jews from Europe and North America: all offered their lives in an unprecedented wave of international solidarity, often inspired by communism but overwhelmingly as a stand against fascism. The Botwin Company, named for a Jewish communist killed in Poland, put the message on its flag in Yiddish, Polish and Spanish: 'For your freedom and ours.'

It was a momentous year for internationalism and for left-wing cooperation. Facing threatening developments on the far right, liberals and moderates sought to overcome the fragmentation that had benefited their opponents. In Spain, the parties of the Left and centre-Left had worked strenuously to create the electoral alliance that won the February elections. Even the Comintern had indicated a cautious policy change in Moscow in 1935, offering communist parties around the world the flexibility to cooperate with other (non-communist) anti-fascist groups. This was the 'United Front' Valentine had spoken of joining.

People like Nancy, who believed passionately in internationalism's potential to create change but had been disappointed by the toothlessness of bodies like the League of Nations, were primed to see Spain as the ultimate expression of global leftist solidarity. The apparent cohesion of the anti-democratic far Right, its crushing success in countries like Italy, Germany and Austria, made alliances across very different groups seem necessary, even desirable, and sent Europe hurtling into confrontations of ever-higher stakes. (It also explains why many of the writers heading to Spain apparently saw no contradiction in claiming the Spanish war as a fight for democracy whilst claiming as allies communists with proven records of hostility to democracy.) One American journalist remembered reporting from the Republican zone as an experience that 'gave courage and faith in humanity; it taught us what internationalism means'. As foreigners offered their lives to the Spanish Republic, they did so in a moment of possibility and imperatives.

'Madrid didn't look very exciting,' the seventeen-year-old volunteer Esmond Romilly wrote later of his arrival there, 'mostly tramlines and barricades.' But its significance was massive. Germany, Italy and Portugal had all recognised Franco's government 'on the pretext that it was in control of [the capital]'. Preserving Madrid from the rebels would show the international community that the Republic had a chance at survival.

Esmond was one of a handful of British volunteers to participate in the early defence of Madrid. He had cycled across France by himself before boarding a boat to Spain with other recruits, feeling bashful about his lack of military experience. At Valencia's port his instinctive sympathy was rewarded with an enormous welcome: a crowd ready with the favourite slogan, 'No Pas-ar-án!' 'The cheers and salutations went on for an hour.'

In mid-November, around the time Nancy's visa expired and she was forced to leave, the nationalists broke across the Manzanares river, reaching as far as the University City, a grand, unfinished campus on the city's western edge. After days of close combat, the Republican forces managed to halt the nationalist advance before the Hall of Philosophy and Letters. Gunfire flew between Philosophy and Law, and desperate skirmishes were fought in buildings where book-lined walls provided ineffective shelter. In the fierce fighting nearby, Esmond saw death and met mortal fear, witnessing scenes that would haunt him. Later he remembered sheltering in a National Guard building with 'dead lying in the room, in the passage, and heaped upon the stairs. . . . A machine-gun post was established behind a window on the first floor . . . Every ten minutes someone would be carried down wounded'.

In December, he took part in an infamously bloody attempt to repulse the nationalist pressure at Boadilla del Monte, a village twenty kilometres from Madrid. Parts of that experience stayed clear to him afterwards: Englishmen banded together on a grassy slope, caught in crossfire; his mind screaming at him that the friend slumped beside him was dead; the sense of dashing forward with no idea of why or where he was going. Much of it was blurred. Esmond started out as one of eighteen British volunteers in his battalion. By the end of that three-day battle there were two.

Madrid had been almost universally expected to fall, but the defence scrambled that winter managed to stave off the nationalists. Nancy knew that conditions in the city had only got worse after she left, become 'hellish'. Looking back in a poem called 'Madrid 1936', she immediately faltered: 'I cannot see the landscape for the tears'.

Interviewed in Paris on her return, though, she insisted on sounding a note of hope, one that for the moment proved justified. 'It is ghastly how the rebels are smashing up so much of that beautiful country,' she said, 'but I still think Madrid may be able to drive them off, unbelievable as that seemed at the time I left.'

The Paradoxical

Where Nancy Cunard Was Coming From

France: late 1936 – early 1937

Pablo Neruda first saw Nancy's home in the moonlight and in the snow. It was late, and flakes billowed whitely around the lonely house like curtains. He took a walk that soon disoriented him. Perhaps the lunar quiet was too stark a contrast with the clamours of Madrid. Transferred to France from his job in Spain for openly supporting the Republic, Neruda had followed Nancy to Normandy to help with her latest publication. Together they would put together proofs for a series of six poetry pamphlets she would call, with eye-catching grandeur, *The Poets of the World Defend the Spanish People*.

The affair with Pablo had been part of the intensity of Nancy's time in Madrid, part of how poetry, love, causes coalesced. At thirty-two, he was already an acclaimed poet. He had lived in Madrid since his appointment as Chilean consul in 1934, and during her stay he introduced her to a close-knit network of Spanish writers and publishers. When they met, Pablo was mourning his friend, the playwright Federico García Lorca, who had disappeared at the beginning of the war. (Lorca had been executed by nationalists and his body dumped in an unmarked grave.) A towering figure in Spanish arts, who had affairs with men and sought to 'rehumanise' poetry, who directed a government-sponsored travelling theatre group that took culture out into the provinces: Lorca represented much that the nationalists despised. At Pablo's apartment in the Casa de las Flores, where the windows looked out over the University City that would host such carnage, Nancy had been ushered into a convivial community that was coming to terms with the strength of its enemies and seeking to clarify its *raison d'être*.

Artists in the Republican zone were working feverishly to harness their talents for the war effort. The Alianza de Intelectuales Antifascistas, a forum that ran cultural programmes, marshalled artists to maintain various bulletins and magazines. When Langston Hughes stayed in its Madrid venue in 1937, he found a hub where artists came and went, composing songs and poems, posters and plays, and operating a press donated by French comrades. One of his hosts ran theatre groups that sometimes toured the trenches, director and cast mingling with the audience after performances to discuss the work. Others gave lessons and lectures to soldiers, helped edit brigade newspapers. 'In time of war, what can writers and artists do that is useful, entertaining, and beautiful in a living, vital way?' Langston would ask in a radio broadcast, before listing the activities he knew were happening, describing a kind of cultural outreach intended to help people take possession of the war that had overtaken their lives – making it theirs as they narrated it.

Nancy was proud to learn from the poet Manuel Altolaguirre that the Hours Press had inspired him to set up his own publishing house, which was now disseminating literature at the front, where literacy drives were underway in earnest. Neruda unleashed a series of twenty-one poems that were published as *España en el corazón* (*Spain in Our Hearts*), printed by every means available along Republican lines. Soldiers learned to set type; paper was produced from old flags and captured enemy uniforms. In this way, art was deployed on the front lines. It came to symbolise the deprivations of the past and the promise of victory; it became a rallying point that was used to distinguish the Republic from the enemy – a distilled expression of the cause.

Nancy had form with pamphlets. She was also still working out how to harness literature and politics, and had a history of charging at 'solidarity' in ways that could miss the mark. Neruda found her 'quixotic, unalterable, fearless, and pathetic . . . one of the strangest persons I have ever known': all of which could stand as a description of the development of her activism, which had taken form from a grab bag of political awakening, literary instinct and desire.

In 1931 Nancy had detonated her relationship with her wealthy mother by berating the confined, hypocritical and racist milieu she came from in a booklet of only eleven pages. That story had even older origins. You could place it in the 'hectic spin' of Venice in the summer of 1928, when she met a man named Henry Crowder. Nancy, in her early thirties, in a city she had loved for a long time: palazzos, 'balls, fancy-dress galas and festivities'.

Her cousin took her to hear the jazz violinist Eddie South and his Chicago band, the Alabamians, at the Hotel Luna. Henry Crowder was on piano. 'They played in that "out of this world" manner,' Nancy remembered. 'Such Jazz and such Swing and such improvisations! And all new to me in style! Well, so ravishing was it all that when they stepped from the band-stand at the end of their last number we rose to our feet with one accord and asked them to sit down and have a drink with us.'

As much as the music, it was the band members themselves who were apparently so 'new' to Nancy that the word she seems to be reaching for is 'exotic': they were 'people so different to all I had ever known that they seemed as strange to me as beings from another planet. They were Afro-Americans . . .' Entranced by the men – struck by their music, style and manners; physically attracted too – she went to hear them night after night. 'A new element had come into my life, suddenly.'

Except it wasn't quite so sudden. Jazz was already one of her passions. She was among the crowds in Paris besotted with black American stars like Josephine Baker. She was at one with the Surrealist interest in 'primitive' art, trawling port towns with Louis Aragon to seek out old ivories sold by sailors and building a collection of African and Oceanic work. All of them interests she regarded as connected.

By her own accounting, Nancy's attraction to Henry reads like straightforward fetishisation. Her desire for him, her admiration for a culture and community she would seek to reach through him ('a people', she wrote, 'so utterly rich in natural grace and beauty'), often reads like an exercise in reduction rather than seeing. Their relationship would never truly escape a fug of exploitation – though who was using whom wasn't always the clearest – and yet it did re-route Nancy's life, via her interests and attractions, towards some of her most meaningful fixations.

Henry Crowder was, by most accounts, a serious and reserved man. Nancy described him as 'a tall, imposing, handsome man of color'. Several years older, he was also temperamentally worlds away. Where Henry's favourite refrain was 'Opinion reserved!', to Nancy, 'nothing – nor opinion nor emotion nor love nor hate – could be "reserved" for one instant on the score of the things this Man-Continent-People gradually revealed to me about his race and the life of his race'. Their affair would last, on and off, for the next seven years. Much later she would say that Henry 'introduced an entire world' to her, that he 'made' her. He stripped parts of her ignorance from her. From him she learned facts about racial prejudice (and especially about life for a black man in America) that amazed and infuriated her.

Nancy's pamphlet of 1931 was a commemorative one. It marked a year, she explained by way of introduction, since 'the Colour Question first presented me personally with its CLASH or SHOCK aspect'. In other words, it marked a year since her mother had been introduced to the idea of Henry Crowder. In December 1930, Nancy and Henry had been living together for two years and had made several visits to London but, though he met most of Nancy's friends, Henry and Lady Cunard seem never to have been introduced. Emerald learned about Nancy's relationship when the famous Margot Asquith (widow of a prime minister), asked after her daughter with the words 'What is it now – drink, drugs or [n—s]?'

This at least is the story that made its way back to Nancy, who included it in her pamphlet as the trigger for the 'dreadful confusion' that ensued. Lady Cunard frantically rang round town asking Nancy's friends if it was true that her daughter knew a black man. Threats were issued that might have been less alarming had Emerald not been so well connected. Police arrived at Nancy and Henry's hotel when they came to London and the proprietor received sinister telephone calls. Nancy, harassed, went as far as consulting a lawyer about the possibility of

Emerald being able to get Henry deported, which she had apparently threatened to do. After her return to France, Nancy was told that new financial constraints had forced her mother to reduce her allowance. Friends continued to report interrogations from Lady Cunard about Henry and the extent of his blackness.

By the time Henry and Nancy went to stay with a friend in Austria in early 1931, Nancy was in a bad way. She turned up 'full of the London row and her Ladyship's detectives' and, drinking steadily, became more and more erratic: aggressive with Henry and verging on predatory with their host – undone, he felt, by alcohol 'plus never drawing the line'. Some of her behaviour – smashing every pane of glass in her window, banging her head against the wall – sounds a lot like a woman trapped inside the kind of incapacitated, incapacitating fury that quickly becomes self-destructive.

As Nancy explained to another friend, the past months of her relationship had been violently revelatory about 'the colour question, viz the inferiority of the African race in particular to the white races. Till now these convictions have not been challenged in me; they are now being so.' Her mother's similarly volcanic reaction to Henry had broken through the euphoria of interrogating her own previously unexamined prejudices to hammer home the inescapability of other people's. All around, Nancy was heard to mutter, were 'enemies, enemies' and no obvious way to fight back.

To Henry's alarm, she decided she wanted to travel to America. The trip was a nightmare for him. Despite all the research she'd done, grilling him (an interest he'd at first relished) and taking herself off to the British Library to discover more, Nancy had not entirely escaped her ignorance. In the US, she wanted to go everywhere and see everything; demanded to know why he failed to defend himself when they were insulted on the street. 'I could not make her understand that New York was not Paris. She proposed doing many, many things that I knew could not be done.' Spoiling for a fight, she put him in danger.

Staying in Harlem, she met with the editors of W. E. B. Du Bois's *Crisis* magazine and afterwards wrote an article for them, mocking her mother's attitudes. Then she expanded it into her pamphlet and

posted it out at Christmastime to hundreds of her friends, relations
and acquaintances – and her mother's.

It's part of the magic of books that they're such secretive, unimposing
objects: small of form and capacious of promise. But when I picked
up a copy of *Black Man and White Ladyship* – a thin and age-softened
thing – I couldn't help thinking that Nancy's text was somehow
showed up by its flimsiness. In places her essay is trenchant, sarcastic,
provocative and unflinching. (Impressed, Neruda would write that
he had 'never seen anything more vitriolic'.) It strips the protection
of privacy from those unused to being challenged, confronting them
with their own words and attitudes. Nancy used what she considered
a personal betrayal to protest a culture of prejudice in Britain and the
US. Yet in connecting the two, the balance went somehow awry.
From her mother's hypocrisy, the pamphlet hurtles unhesitatingly
into a summary of the history of slavery and American lynchings,
but never entirely gets away from Nancy's grievances, so that after a
while it reads like a list of childish complaints: Nancy's allowance cut!
Paintings by Manet promised to her perhaps withdrawn! We strain to
sympathise! She unleashes an outrage that is a little too general – she
hasn't done the work of sorting through its sources to judge the sa-
lient issues – so that her exposé of how British upper-class prejudice
operates also becomes a long account of her loss of income, something
that receives more space on the page than lynching does. The pamphlet becomes contained by a spat between a daughter and her mother,
which gave most of its recipients an excuse not to engage at all.

It was an early example of Nancy's ability to make things (seem)
simple, oppositional: one that resurfaced forcefully with the Spanish
war. There is a certain appeal in that. Striving to understand points
of view to which you are fundamentally opposed can seem like a
waste of time when lives are being lost. Yet Nancy is also an example
of how good intentions – the first galvanising flame of outrage – fall
very short of meaningful support for a cause. Ultimately, *Black Man
and White Ladyship* was a hand grenade lobbed by someone who surely

knew her target too well to think it would prompt any self-reflection. It drew attention, but more to Nancy and her rebellion than to the matters she now cared about.

When it came to activism, Nancy began to reveal a new capacity for devotion. Causes like the infamous Scottsboro case, in which a group of young black men were unjustly convicted of raping two white women and sentenced to death, became the focus of tireless efforts. She marched in demonstrations, circulated petitions, threw fundraisers; for many years she corresponded with at least one of the accused directly. In 1933, she established the Scottsboro Defence Committee and acted as treasurer for its fund. (Virginia Woolf was among those who supported the appeal.) And with *Black Man and White Ladyship* out of her system, she came to a far more ambitious and productive idea: the compilation and editing of an anthology of, and about, black life and culture, which was eventually published in 1934. The *Negro* anthology took over Nancy's life and finances for years (she closed the Hours Press during this time). It was born of the combative mood in which she had apparently taken up permanent residence: the 'indignation, the fury, the disgust, the contempt, the longing to fight'.

When she returned to New York to collect contributions for it, Henry refused to join her. Nancy checked into Harlem's Grampion Hotel, the first white woman to stay there, and was quickly discovered by the press. A Movietone segment showed her entering a 'Harlem Negro Hotel'; tabloid headings proliferated, smearing her with innuendo. It was reported (falsely) that she had broken up the marriage of the singer and actor Paul Robeson. British papers stooped to headlines like 'Auntie Nancy's Cabin – Down Among the Black Gentlemen of Harlem'. The predictable slurry of hate mail arrived.

Nancy saw these invented sex scandals as a concerted effort to undermine her intentions in New York, a hysterical scrambling of the issues which allowed the press to attack efforts towards understanding and equality without acknowledging them. 'No chance is ever missed by the American press,' she wrote soon afterwards, 'to stir up as much fury as possible against Negroes and their white friends. . . . As in the South it is always the lie of the "rape" of white women by black men, so in

the North it is always the so-called "scandal" of inter-racial relations.'
Instead of dodging the attention, she tried to harness it for her own ends.
She called a press conference and solicited donations to the Scottsboro
fund, inviting at the same time contributions to her *Negro* anthology.

For others, it was all an unwelcome kind of publicity. Many of the
black writers and intellectuals she approached in Harlem regarded her
with suspicion. Her personal and unmethodical approach was hardly
guaranteed to inspire confidence, and Henry wasn't the only one
annoyed that Nancy did not consider the possible implications for the
people around her of her excursions into their lives. The journalist Henry
Lee Moon summed up the obvious first impression when recalling his
own dismissal: 'Just another white woman sated with the decadence of
Anglo-Saxon society, rebelling against its restrictive code, seeking new
fields to explore, searching for color, she was not to be taken seriously.'

But if a pamphlet is, by its nature, an ephemeral thing – an urchin
sent out to spread a message through a crowd – the copy of the *Negro*
anthology I sought out at the British Library speaks of weightier intentions. It is a big book – the kind you lift with both hands and set down
with a sense of reverence. More than eight hundred pages. One hundred and fifty contributors, two hundred and fifty separate entries,
hundreds of illustrations. In girth and heft and no-expense-spared
production quality, the *Negro* anthology makes the kind of claims to
import that an *Encyclopaedia Britannica* does.

Open the cover, though, and the thirties font hints at an anarchic
younger cousin. The sheer work and determination it must have taken
to compile are daunting – and there is some great writing in it – but
the emphasis is noticeably uneven. It takes in contemporary news
and culture, poetry, history and ethnography and politics. Continu-
ing her tactic of dragging prejudice into full view, Nancy included
some of the hate mail she'd received. (The proceeds from libel cases she
launched over the Robeson story had gone some way to covering her
substantial printing costs.) In execution and content, Nancy's project
was more reminiscent of the scrapbooks she made: the attention span
is global, the contents list reveals the breadth of her connections and
research – contributions by Langston Hughes and Countee Cullen;

W. E. B. Du Bois and Zora Neale Hurston – but there is less sober intentionality and more grabbing at what's in front of her. It's a collection indelibly stamped with its creator's personality.

The ambition matters, though. Six years before Nancy arrived, Harlem had been described by the scholar Alain Locke as a 'race capital': home not only to a concentration of New York's black residents but to the cultural flourishing of the 1920s that bore its name. Other anthologies had emerged from the Harlem Renaissance (including Locke's 1925 volume *The New Negro*) but Nancy's has been acknowledged as 'one of the first works to attempt the production of knowledge about African cultures on a global scale'. Locke himself heralded it as 'the finest anthology in every sense of the word ever compiled on the Negro'. He shared her conviction that such a collection could challenge prejudice and oppression, and prove wrong those who denied the possibility of black civilisation.

The book I'd held was a far rarer thing than Nancy would have hoped. Hundreds of unsold copies were still languishing in the publishers' warehouse in the 1940s when it was destroyed in the Blitz. After the furore over her travel for the project, she was disappointed by the lack of serious attention the book received. For decades, the *Negro* anthology was almost impossible to get hold of. (A facsimile edition was only released in 2018.) Scholars looking for similar material simply began again, unaware of its existence: a dispiriting repetition of efforts since the anthology has more recently been recognised as a 'major, unique and original', though not unproblematic, achievement.

In his 1940 memoir, Langston Hughes (who was enthusiastic about the *Negro* anthology) mentioned an anecdote about Salvador Dalí being asked at a party if he 'knew anything about Negroes'. 'Everything!' Dalí replies. 'I've met Nancy Cunard!'

If that tells something about Nancy's proselytising, it also has something arch to say about the paradox of white enthusiasts being accepted as authorities on black culture. Nancy clearly began to appreciate how much oxygen her notoriety absorbed in the limited public space allowed to black writers and questions of racial justice. She gestured towards correcting the balance in the anthology, where she allowed room for author photos beside only 'the writings of Negroes or of those of Negro descent'. No photograph, then, of Josephine Herbst, to whom Nancy wrote personally to request permission for reprinting her article on one of the Scottsboro trials, 'Lynching in the Quiet Manner'. Visual space was reserved for young men of colour relaxing in a park, for an annual conference of the NAACP, for Henry Crowder, the Scottsboro accused and members of their families, for the movie stars Nina Mae McKinney and Daniel Haynes.

She did something similar in the poetry pamphlets compiled in Normandy in 1937. Though they were sold in London and Paris to raise money for Spanish relief, they included poems in Spanish as well as in French and English, giving voice to the Spaniards whose literary record of their country's tragedy was destined to be elided by death and exile, and by the more famous work of their Anglophone sympathisers.

Contributions were arriving from Rafael Alberti, Stephen Spender, Tristan Tzara and Louis Aragon, as well as Pablo Neruda and many others. Nancy included work by Lorca, and she would be the first person to publish Auden's 'Spain', probably the most acclaimed poem to come out of the war.

Seeking a contribution from Langston in the US, she asked explicitly for a poem 'from the heart and from the revolutionary angle'. Alain Locke had once put his immediate hope for change in 'the revaluation by white and black alike of the Negro in terms of his artistic endowments and cultural contributions'. But by the year of Nancy's first visit to Harlem, a more radical – more overtly political – direction had emerged. After the Scottsboro trial, and as the Depression worsened poverty in black America, the optimism of the Harlem Renaissance had waned. To Langston it had seemed that it had never reached the majority of black people anyway – it certainly 'hadn't raised their wages any'. Yet neither he nor Nancy had jettisoned their faith in the arts. Instead, in 1931, Langston had challenged 'beauty-makers' to face new directions in a poem called 'Call to Creation': 'Look at harshness, look at pain, / Look at life again.'

For Pablo Neruda five years later, the murder of Lorca was like the murder of poetry. It revolutionised the way he conceived of his own work and what it should do; it changed the way he wrote. Why was the romance gone from his poems, he imagined his readers asking in 'I Explain Some Things'; where was the 'metaphysics laced with poppies'? Look at Spain, came his response: 'Come and see the blood in the streets'.

The 'time-instinct', Valentine Ackland wrote, is 'the only true guide an artist has'. That the poet is not set apart from her environment but must rise to the challenges of the times was a point of view entirely in sympathy with Nancy's expectations of poets and poetry. As orchestrator of these collections, she could marshal artistic cross-currents into brief confluences of collective action. There was little ego in the ways she worked, which ranged through the chores of publishing. At Le Puits Carré, she patiently taught Pablo to set type. With him at her side, she had the conditions in which she could thrive: companionship and a period of intense work, camaraderie that did not aggravate a nature that had learned solitude early on. That balance was there in the pamphlets, in the collective efforts of activism borne by the private communion of the arts.

She too was writing poems of protest and exhortation. Her outrage over the nationalist and fascist abuses could not be contained in a single form, so that poetry was harnessed for activism and journalism resurfaces in modernist poems, tethering her literary response to the unavoidably literal. Her Spanish poetry (and she wrote it, both about Spain and in Spanish, for the rest of her life) was shot through with grief and challenge. 'Madrid 1936' contains a demand. 'They have died and died in Madrid', she writes early on. And then, later: 'PEOPLES, WHAT IS YOUR ANSWER?'

'[The United States will] scrupulously refrain from any interference whatsoever in the unfortunate Spanish situation.'

William Phillips, acting Secretary of State, 7 August 1936

'Spain, Germany, Russia – all are elbowed out. The marriage [between Edward VIII and Wallis Simpson] stretches from one end of the paper to another.'

Virginia Woolf, diary for Monday, 7 December 1936

'There will be weeping and wailing and gnashing of teeth in the boudoirs of such American-born London hostesses as Lady Emerald Cunard, favourite hostess of the former King and Mrs. Simpson.'

'Society Here Swings Swiftly to New King', New York *Daily News*, 11 December 1936

Facing Facts

Virginia Woolf and Nancy Cunard

London: November 1936

It was in November that Virginia Woolf really seemed to notice the Spanish Civil War. In the spring, before the Spanish war broke out but as the German army remilitarised areas it had been banned from since the First World War, she had assured her politically minded nephew, Julian, that 'we never stop facing facts. Every day almost I get rung up to be asked to sign this, subscribe to that . . . what good they do I don't know; but I sign & I protest & so on.' In the summer, she had even been moved to sign an open letter calling on the government to support the Republic.

But by then, the strain of finishing her latest novel, *The Years*, was such that her family feared she was headed for another breakdown. For parts of 1936 she was entirely incapacitated with headaches; then she couldn't sleep, lost weight, was frighteningly reminded of her previous plunges from reason and felt perilously close to suicide. The scope of her tolerance for impressions narrowed to the company of her sister – Julian's mother, Vanessa Bell – to Leonard, and to the novel. International crises aggravated her worries over *The Years*, so that Hitler and the book became part of the same strain, and the madness of the outside world can hardly have seemed more terrifying than the prospect of losing her grip on her own sanity.

In November she was recovering. Finally, she admitted to Julian that the Spanish war was 'the most flaming of all the problems'. Days later she described a drive back to her London house with Leonard in a dreamlike diary entry. Much is vague and only odd details strike out clearly from the gloom, as the drive becomes a literal (re)emergence through one of the city's infamous fogs.

Figures suddenly emerged. The kind man with a paper. I walked by his side leading the car. It crashed into a wall. The wing buckled. Walked by the kerb all through Wimbledon & Wandsworth. The kerb ended. Here I was lost in a trackless mist. & so on & on. A little boy emerged – a street ruffian. People lined the pavement watching the lost cars. Another man led us; offered me a rest. In the car I looked & found the paper was The Blackshirt. Out again. Just as we thought we must find a garage & come home by tube a bus driver told us that in 200 yards it would be clear. So, miraculously, it was. Glass clear – lit up, & so home.

There's no explanation of how the BUF newspaper got into the car in the first place (a gift from the kind man, presumably), yet among the impressions of people subsiding into and out of the murk, it's the fascist rag that is most distinct. It's as if the mist of her ordeal is lifting to reveal horrors drawn unexpectedly close in the dark.

That statement of Nancy's was hovering, her insistence that, in 1937, 'the equivocal attitude, the Ivory Tower, the paradoxical, the ironic detachment, will no longer do'.

The equivocal attitude, the ironic detachment, the ivory tower: she was pretty clear on some of the prime mechanisms by which we seek to protect ourselves from the strain and destabilising uncertainty of engagement. To Nancy, you should not only know where you stand but you should act on it, too: wade into the fray in any way you can.

Virginia, who felt strongly enough about injustice in the world, saw the lure of avoidance. 'Intellectually, there is a strong desire either to be silent; or to change the conversation . . . and so evade the issue and lower the temperature.' Relief is in company where you all comfortably think alike, as Sylvia Townsend Warner observed in Barcelona. 'Agreement', she found, 'was a considerable aid to conversation.' Virginia described exactly the sense of impending social danger familiar to anyone who has been trapped in a train carriage with someone on their way to a far-right rally, or at dinner with some old friend of the family who has a racist/sexist/other opinion to share: 'Nerves erect themselves; fingers automatically tighten upon spoon or cigarette; a glance at the private psychometer shows that the emotional temperature has risen from ten to twenty degrees above normal.' Yet I could not imagine Nancy letting it slide. After all, there is always a risk that your silence will be taken as tacit agreement, or tacit defeat.

The Spanish war was only the latest in a series of moments when Nancy and Virginia's lives did not cross but rather glanced off from one another. Two very different approaches to life, coming, I was starting to think, from quite similar places. Two poles around which my questions were congregating.

Between the two women there was none of the 'great affection' that Leonard felt for Nancy. His sympathy for the wild socialite the Woolfs published may have been part of the problem. More than twenty years after Virginia's death, Leonard would frankly admit to having found Nancy 'enchanting'. There's a story about her sitting in his lap at a party.

In earlier days, this lonely, enthralling, sought-after figure had pricked at Virginia's insecurities. Consider her suffering in 1926 when, dulled by a sleeping draught, she skipped a party held by Raymond Mortimer and then 'envied them; & thought, when Raymond telephoned . . . & said how lovely Nancy had looked, that I had missed the greatest sight of the season'. But Nancy seems to have provoked in Leonard exactly the caring instinct that he trained so firmly on Virginia, and if Virginia felt any wariness it was probably in that too-familiar vulnerability coming close to home. A year before the Woolfs published Nancy's *Parallax*, she described Nancy in her diary, slipping 'into easy desperate sounding chatter' at a party, 'as if she didn't mind saying everything – everything – had no shadows, no secret places – lived like a lizard in the sun, and yet was by nature for the shade'. She protected herself in the best way she knew: by withdrawing. For Virginia, the secret places were everything.

Writing (and reading) is frequently considered a form of escape, even if only a temporary one. It's an odd form of escape to be sure, a retreat fertilised after all by the world being evaded. If the ivory tower Nancy wrote of was a physical and mental sequestering for intellectual work, it stood on the other – opposing – side from engagement with the outside world and its painful developments. Yet Nancy believed that authors had a special productive sensitivity, which was framed by others around this time as a deeply symbiotic relationship with humanity. This was a reason for opposing fascism as a form of self-defence (damage to humanity is damage to the artist), but it was also a belief that the true artist cannot fail to respond to outside agitation, to the great issues of their era.

By the time of the Spanish war, this question of the artist's relationship to the agitated, agitating world around them was under debate. Since they are, as Virginia put it that December, 'in such close touch with human life', does an artist have a place at the centre of the fray or does their ability to contribute to humanity rely on a certain right (and ability) to withdraw? Is it crucial for a healthy society, as her old friend E. M. Forster contended, to allow 'the mind to escape'?

When Nancy returned to France from Madrid, she seized an opportunity to seek a statement on the war from James Joyce and came up against exactly this divergence. She received a strident telling-off. Joyce would provide no such thing, she later told his biographer, 'because it [was] "politics"'. 'Politics' was 'getting into everything'. T. S. Eliot, when she later asked him for a declaration, would tell her that 'at least a few men of letters should remain isolated', claiming that special position for writers – a place above the fray. The author Norman Douglas, one of her closest friends, boasted, 'If Fascists annoy me, I hop it. If Communists annoy me, I hop it,' turning neutrality into merely the good fortune of having options. Compared to the fate of Lorca, or thousands of other Spaniards, deciding to transcend 'politics' starts to look like little more than an assumption of privilege – the ultimate identification with the powerful. (Some people live with their backs against the wall, which gives them little choice but to face the trouble.)

To Nancy, 'Spain [was] not "politics" but life'. She might just as well have argued that *politics* is life, as Martha Gellhorn would many years later: 'Politics is everything,' she wrote. 'If we mean to keep any control over our world and lives, we must be interested in politics.'

In the late 1930s, there were those who saw allowing the mind to escape as simply setting it out to pasture in the pleasant fields of denial, a kind of 'ostrich ignorance' that Julian Bell lambasted when he penned a riposte to Forster. There were, even earlier, critics who would take a swipe at Virginia for such a thing as 'work[ing] on too small a canvas . . . express[ing] too exclusively the "sheltered" point of view', as if the work should be traceable to a contemporary position as much as the writer herself was supposed to be.

For foreign writers who went to Spain, the Civil War threw questions of confrontation and evasion into sharp relief. Nancy's visas came with a time limit, which meant that staying for the duration – full immersion – was never an option. When she got home from Madrid, she told Langston Hughes that Spain was still 'close, both geographically and emotionally'. Yet leaving offered the best opportunity to process what the war might mean. And it was still outside of Spain that the best chances lay for rallying international support for the Republic.

So Much to Be Done

Nan Green

London: October 1936

In October, the Young Communist League planned a massive anti-Franco rally in London's Trafalgar Square, where they hoped to raise funds to send aid to the Spanish Republic. But events overtook them: the leader of the British Union of Fascists, Oswald Mosley, announced an extraordinarily provocative march of his own through the streets of East London for the same day. Under pressure from local party branches, the rally plans were changed. Instead of a protest against Franco, the organisers had seventy-two hours to muster a confrontation with fascism at home.

They kept the same slogans. Chalked messages appeared on walls and pavements: 'Everybody to Aldgate on 4th October 1.00 p.m. THEY SHALL NOT PASS.'

The crowded boroughs of the East End, with their large Jewish population, had become a target of British fascists that year. Jews were described by street-speakers as 'rats and vermin', 'a species of sub-humanity', and their businesses were attacked in fascist wrecking missions. Local MPs had tried to raise the alarm in Parliament but little was done; nor did local communities find much support forthcoming from prominent Jewish organisations. The *Daily Worker* printed directions for the rally; the *Jewish Chronicle* carried warnings not to join the demonstrations. Taking matters into your own hands meant looking for new allies. When tens of thousands of people assembled to obstruct the BUF march, they came from the Stepney Jewish People's Council Against Fascism and Anti-Semitism, from the International Labour Defence League, from the Labour and Communist parties. Among them were men who would later volunteer for the International Brigades. Trade unions had been mobilised, recruiting not just Jewish sweatshop workers but exactly the people Mosley wanted to set up as their enemies: dock and railway workers of Irish heritage.

In the streets where the BUF was expected to march, barricades were thrown up using piles of furniture and paving stones. Four tram drivers agreed to halt their vehicles at strategic locations, while on Cable Street an entire lorry full of bricks was overturned to block the way.

Nan Green was one of the Communists who gathered. She had lived in London for four years by now, and she had seen this solidarity in action before. With George, she ran a second-hand book stall on Caledonian Market, with a noticeably less profitable side business in communist literature. When, having refused pressure from the market authorities to remove the political pamphlets, they were threatened with a BUF meeting on the site opposite – trouble sure to follow – the other stallholders had patrolled in front of their stand, swinging the wares of the second-hand motor parts sellers in a warning fashion. The fascist meeting never took place. But Nan was convinced that 'wherever one looked – France, Spain, even Moseley [*sic*] and his Blackshirts in England, fascism was in the ascendant'. In socialism, in the example of the USSR, she thought they had found the answer.

On 4 October, Nan held clumps of tiny leaflets in her pockets. Her instructions were to release them if Mosley's procession could be prevented: the leaflets told people to gather afterwards at Victoria Park.

'From out of the narrow courts, alleyways and main thoroughfares,' one demonstrator described,

> came the steady tramp of marching feet, growing in intensity as the columns were swelled by reinforcements. A forest of banners arose, borne aloft, with the watchwords *THEY SHALL NOT PASS* emblazoned in a multi-variety of colours . . . Loud speaker vans . . . patrolled the streets booming out the message for *all* to rally to the defence lines at Cable Street and Gardiner's Corner.

Appeals to the authorities to divert the BUF march had fallen on deaf ears. Instead, to maintain order, the entire mounted division of the Metropolitan Police had been drafted in, alongside 6,000 foot

police – vastly outnumbering the BUF supporters assembling opposite the Tower of London.

An open Bentley pulled up. Mosley gave the fascist salute and
stepped out to inspect the ranks of waiting Blackshirts. They were
the most eye-catching feature of his party, a personal militia recogni-
sable by their black uniforms and thuggish reputations.

Incensed protestors surged forward, held back only by the police
cordon. Mosley was told that his march would have to wait until
the barricades could be cleared. That meant sending in the mounted
police.

In the narrow streets, people plunged through the plate-glass
windows of shops or were trampled under the horses' hooves. They
fought back with a barrage of bottles and stones. Each time the police
broke through one line of defence, the anti-fascists simply fell back
behind the next. The protest organisers had foreseen the violence and
arranged medical points along the way. Taxi drivers ferried reinforcements into the skirmish and the wounded out. What became known
as the Battle of Cable Street raged for the next two hours, until the
Police Commissioner finally gave up and rerouted the fascist march,
ordering Mosley to withdraw.

Nan hurled her leaflets into the air and watched them flutter down

around her. She never forgot the sense of triumph as 'the immense crowd' stirred around her at her bidding, forming itself into a victorious procession to the park.

A few months later, the poet Stephen Spender hitched a lift with a convoy of British volunteers as it passed through Barcelona. Spender was on a disillusioning visit to try to rescue an old boyfriend who'd volunteered for the International Brigades and now wanted to come home. But some of the men Spender met impressed him. There was a Communist musician he described, in an article called 'Heroes in Spain', as 'fat, frank, bespectacled and intelligent' (later he revised this to 'firm and stolid'), whose sincerity stood out. George Green, Spender later concluded, was 'one of the few people who came to Spain with undivided hearts'.

I'm not sure that can be true: George had left Nan and their two young children behind to go to Spain. It was a decision they had made together. 'Listen,' she wrote to a relative who criticised him for going: 'George and I are thinking of more than our own children, we are thinking of the children of Europe, in danger of being killed in the coming war if we don't stop the Fascists in Spain.'

When Nan met George on a rambling holiday in 1928 – the year Nancy found Henry Crowder in Venice – he was a cellist in the first-class orchestra on a Cunard liner, the *Aquitania*, and had only two weeks of leave left on land. She saw 'a rather bear-like figure over six feet tall with a broad face and kind, gentle grey eyes behind steel-rimmed spectacles'. In a photo of the two of them on another walking trip, George looks just as she described him. They're both in shorts (Nan's father was horrified) and she is fresh-faced and tomboyish with a grin that speaks of contentment and possibility. By the time George was back on the boat she had agreed to marry him.

Until he arrived, rambling had provided the great joy in Nan's life: a way of expanding out of an existence that otherwise felt narrow and restricted. When George found work in a cinema in Manchester they went together, Nan waiting for him to dash out of the last screening late on a Saturday, walking kit on under his evening attire, to join friends in a run for the train out of the city. They would bed down for the night at a farmhouse before a Sunday of blissful freedom, 'expending our full strength, striding like giants over moor and fell'.

There was plenty she wanted to escape. She was born in 1904, the middle child of five in a family that was 'rising in the world'. Her father, Edward, was general manager of the Raleigh Cycle company, a position he'd worked his way up to from mechanic, and he made sure to send his eldest children to the only private school in the Nottinghamshire village in which they lived. Rising required a strict code of snobbery. Home, Nan remembered many years later, 'was a place where the standards of a good child were impossible, for me at least, to attain. You must be Good, clean, tidy, devout, quiet, *incurious*, well-mannered and obedient'.

None of this prevented a series of misfortunes from sending Nan's aspiring family rapidly back in the wrong direction. Her mother became an invalid during the First World War and was eventually removed to a nursing home, where she died before Nan ever saw her again. Fired at around the same time for refusing to falsify company figures for tax avoidance, her father suffered a collapse that sent him briefly into a nursing home himself.

As so often happens, the family's decline uprooted them and sent them roving. Edward took them to Birmingham, where they moved into rooms above a shop; and then to Manchester in pursuit of work, forcing Nan to give up a scholarship to art school. She took up a series of clerical jobs, each of which she abandoned as her father continued to move around looking for work. During one harrowing period when she was fourteen years old and her father was working in London, she nursed her entire family through the Spanish flu alone. In an epidemic that killed millions, her patients pulled through. Looking back as an adult, she didn't know how she had coped but she did know what the experience had taught her: '*What you have to do, you can do.*'

In George, Nan found someone protective and peaceable; someone free with affection. She would sometimes catch him beaming at her, 'blazing love' in his grey eyes, and be told 'I'm doting on you!' He offered her intellectual companionship, with the additional pleasing discovery that it was rare for them to disagree. There was no aggression or chauvinism in him. He even had advanced opinions about dividing housework. It was going to be union as constant exchange: a life in which everything, including hardship, would be shared. With George she felt '*at home*; there was nothing we could not say to one another'.

After their difficult start in London, things had gradually improved. George played from noon until midnight at the Lyons tea house on Tottenham Court Road (he would also work in other branches) and helped with the children in the mornings. Nan earned a little reviewing trashy novels for the *News Chronicle* and eventually they set up the book stall. At one point she posed as a single, childless woman to get a job in advertising. But, prior to the revolution, there seemed no way out of their financial insecurity. Lyons musicians were hired for a month at a time, so George sometimes found himself without work at short notice and with no recourse to unemployment benefits. They fell behind with the rent, and Nan was visited by a kindly bailiff who carefully informed her that he would look neither in the oven nor under the eiderdown.

Through everything, the Communist Party provided them with a supportive community for the difficult work of activism and the even harder work of keeping heads above water. Nan felt for the comrades who denied themselves the pleasures of family life, rejecting it as a bourgeois indulgence. When free love experiments went wrong, it was Nan and George they turned to: precisely because, George observed, though they too eschewed monogamy, they had built an unfashionably stable relationship on their own terms. 'We were the free ones, really.'

In January 1937, when George and Nan decided he should go to Spain as an ambulance driver for the Republic, friends and family rallied round. Their Jewish landlord cut their rent by a third. Participating in the war was a logical extension of their beliefs, of their transnational analysis of history and destiny. Still, it was no easy or thoughtless thing to leave his wife, a daughter who had just turned six and a son even younger, behind – and without the vital contribution of his earnings. George's departure left Nan to face their own daily battlefront without the partner she had been promised. As much as anything else, it was this delicate balance that they donated to Spain.

George got word of Spender's article and wrote to Nan to ask if she'd seen it. 'I believe the word "fat" is used,' he warned. In Spain, the nationalists were still battling to encircle Madrid, which meant that he was pitched straight into a lengthy and sanguinary confrontation at Jarama, just east of the capital. In March, he sent Nan a statement of faith from a dressing station. If their shared politics had always held world-history importance, it was now loaded with the realest kind of life-and-death implications:

> Here the ambulance-driver waits the next journey: hand tremulous on the wheel, eye refusing to acknowledge fear of the bridge, of the barrage at the bad crossing. . . .
>
> This is the struggle that justifies the try-outs of history. . . . This is our difference, this our strength, this our manifesto, this our song that cannot be silenced by bullets.

The Ironic Detachment

The Mitford Sisters and Esmond Romilly

England: winter 1936–7

The day after the Battle of Cable Street, Oswald Mosley left for Germany where, at the home of Joseph Goebbels and in the presence of Adolf Hitler, he became Jessica Mitford's brother-in-law. Jessica was not one of the wedding guests. She would not be rejoicing over that union. Her sister Diana's relationship with Mosley had set off a chain of events that would fatally expose the limits of the Mitfords' own special brand of ironic detachment. But it was Jessica who, within months, would abscond in a far more dramatic elopement.

Shortly before Christmas, she clipped out a report in the *News Chronicle* about the fate of Esmond Romilly, who had been fighting with the International Brigades. 'Most of the people here', he was reported as saying, 'have now given up the idea that they will ever return to Britain.' But after the battle at Boadilla, he contracted dysentery and was invalided home to England, where he had to inform the families of his fallen comrades of their deaths. He had survived, disillusioned by war and the disorganisation of the Republican side, and yet with resolution undimmed.

Esmond was a second cousin of Jessica's. She had spent years listening to the adults despairing over this disreputable boy who clearly hadn't been thrashed enough, and thinking wistfully about how wonderful he must be. A boarding-school runaway at fifteen, Esmond had brought disgrace on himself long before his enlistment in Spain. With his brother he had founded a magazine for other disaffected youths of privilege, *Out of Bounds: Public Schools' Journal Against Fascism, Militarism and Reaction*, which became cherished contraband in some of the country's most prestigious dorms. The Romilly brothers were a gift to the *Daily Mail*, which delighted in being appalled by them. His own mother had once had him arrested.

When she heard that he had left for Spain, Jessica had experienced a 'now familiar stab of envy'. Where she had dreamed, Esmond had acted. 'I cut pictures of women guerrillas out of the papers,' she would recall in her memoir, 'determined, steady-looking women, wiry, bright-eyed, gaunt-faced, some middle-aged, some almost little girls. How to take my place at their side?'

Polite enquiries at the Communist Party headquarters in London had got her nowhere. Even Esmond's brother, Giles, was unable to help. 'Reading and listening to the agonizing news from the Madrid front,' she remembered, 'the farce of England's "non-intervention" policy, and the barbarous cruelty of Nazi and Fascist forces in Spain, made me feel like a traitor to everything decent in the world. I despised myself for living in the lap of luxury, supported and kept by the very people who were making the "non-intervention" policy possible.'

Then she heard Esmond was back in England. When a relative who had harboured him in the past wrote in January inviting her to stay, Jessica accepted the invitation with a furtive hope.

I like to think Jessica Mitford was travelling on a Cunard liner in the spring of 1936 when she let her first real chance to run away (she'd been waiting since she was twelve) slip through her fingers. The setting, at Spain's Moorish palace, the Alhambra, was perfect, though she conceded that in her 'white linen cruise suit, panama hat, new brown Oxfords' she would have been fairly easy to track down. It was some weeks before the outbreak of war. Her sister Unity had created the diversion: she was wearing her usual swastika badge, which was quickly spotted by the curious Spaniards surrounding the holiday-makers. Jessica could have slipped away as the irate crowd descended on Unity; instead she was hustled back to the cruise ship with her, quarrelling furiously all the way – 'a fist fight and hair-pulling match' – only for them to be sent straight to their cabin in disgrace by their mother.

The conflict between the sisters was less about Jessica's thwarted escape and more about the dramatic schism of their political loyalties. Jessica was eighteen years old then, a debutante who was alienated from her family in principle more than she was in practice. (In photographs she manages the feat of looking as sullen as she does cherubic.) Almost entirely, and patchily, self-educated, she had discovered socialism as an answer to a 'vast puzzle which I had been clumsily trying to solve for years' and become attracted to communism. Most of all she wanted to get away, to have something happen. She followed the exploits of Nancy Cunard in the press as 'a distant star', and 'longed' to become her friend.

The holiday was a belated attempt by Lady Redesdale to entertain her miserable, wayward daughter. Jessica (known as Decca in the family) had a strong suspicion her mother was also on the lookout for an eligible bachelor for her. She wrote home to her eldest sister, Nancy, noting grimly that one of their fellow passengers was suitably entitled. An irreverent riff soon wafted back across the continent:

> There is a Lord on board,
> A Lord on board, poor Decca roared,
> But the Lord on board is a bit of a fraud
> 'Cause the Lord on board has a wife named Maud . . .

It's one of the family ditties with which the Mitford siblings frequently amused themselves, among the more conventional features of a complex lexicon of nicknames and allusions and impenetrable private dialects with which they – and especially the youngest three – enlivened and entrenched their childhood isolation. It also put me in mind of Nancy Cunard's mother and her abrupt insistence, at some point in her fifties, on changing her name from the sludgy 'Maud' to the glittering 'Emerald'. It may be merely a convenient rhyme, but it seemed to me just possible that Nancy Mitford found it appropriate because of the fame and non-aristocratic origins of the extravagant society lady with the American money.

The Mitfords' background was more or less the reverse: they had the pedigree but not the glamour. Their irascible father, Lord Redesdale, was a hereditary peer, and similar to Sir Bache Cunard in the sense that he had no interest in strutting about in town when he could be stomping around his estate in the country. No parties and guest lists of artists and writers and statesmen for his daughters, at least until two of the eldest made breaks for freedom: Nancy into a life as a popular novelist and Diana by marrying perilously young, to the extraordinarily wealthy Bryan Guinness. None of which made much difference for the younger three still trapped in a suffocating, somewhat tyrannised, girlhood. No education either. As Jessica later remembered it, just relentless boredom and each other.

Out in the world, Diana became one of Lady Cunard's favourites. With her feted beauty and a social position secured by wealth, it's tempting to see her as a kind of surrogate daughter for Emerald, triumphant in all the ways Nancy Cunard chose not to be. (Unlike Nancy's mother, Diana had been introduced to Henry Crowder. She later derisively described him as Nancy's 'black friend' – a 'simple soul' who amused her by misidentifying expensive furniture at the home of their hosts.)

Oswald Mosley was one of the up-and-coming young men Emerald liked to accumulate. For a time in the 1920s he had been tipped as a future leader of the Labour Party. In 1930, he resigned from a Labour government in protest over its handling of unemployment, and founded the BUF shortly afterwards, inspired by a visit to Italy. He was a popular orator and his dire warnings of national decay found a ready audience in a nation rattled by poverty, unemployment and a post-war sense of decline. His attacks on mainstream politics, his stirring insistence on regeneration requiring some violently new approach, must have come as a relief to those viewing their moribund country with despair. At least he was lively. In footage of a rally in Manchester he can be seen giving the fascist salute, shrieking something vague about 'a new and revolutionary conception!' He works himself up. 'England lives! And marches on!'

Diana believed in Oswald. Once their affair began, she planned for a life as his shadowy consort while he achieved his destiny of orchestrating the rebirth of the nation. Her enthusiasm caught on in the family. To Jessica's disgust, her parents, persuaded to visit Nazi Germany, 'returned full of praise for what they had seen'. Even Nancy briefly joined the BUF – her biographers suggest out of loyalty to Diana since her true sympathies put her among the kind of leftists Jessica dismissed as 'drawing-room pinks'. Perhaps worst of all, Unity – who, like Jessica, had idolised their exquisite elder sister since childhood – joined the BUF in 1933 when Diana did. She set her sights even higher than Mosley. On pilgrimages to Germany she managed to catch the eye of Hitler himself. 'The first moment I saw him,' she would tell a journalist in 1938, 'I knew there was no one else in the world I would rather meet.'

Unity was by all accounts a strange girl. Striking and ungainly, she seems to have been an uncomfortable combination of gauche debutante and raging fanatic. A self-proclaimed 'Jew hater' who caused consternation at the local village shop by giving the Nazi salute when buying chocolate bars, she proved irresistible material for her novelist sister.

This was where humour, which had once looked a lot like a survival mechanism, began to strain the bonds between siblings instead. In *Wigs on the Green*, the novel Nancy published in 1935 under a hail of sisterly threats and fury, the heroine is a beautiful, wealthy, parochial young fanatic who harangues the locals from a washtub on the village green, and says things like 'Oh! British lion, shake off the nets that bind you' and 'Go away Nanny'. Like much of Nancy's fiction, it's a slight drama, but it's a smart and dastardly satire too, one in which she ridicules the British fascist movement and sends it up as a conduit for the energies and latent passions of bored and undereducated young women.

Mosley, as 'Captain Jack, founder of the Social Unionist Movement and Captain of the Union Jackshirts', is omnipresent but always offstage: an absence demanded by Diana. Unity threatened never to speak to Nancy again if she went ahead with publication. Diana was estranged from her for years. Desperate for publication revenue but leery of being sued by the litigious Oswald, Nancy had attempted a tentative defiance. 'I . . . know your point of view,' she wrote in a mollifying letter to Diana, 'that Fascism is something too serious to be dealt with in a funny book at all. Surely that is a little unreasonable?'

In the 1930s, Nancy Mitford appeared not to feel strongly about politics. It was not part of her pose to feel strongly about anything. But as a woman who had escaped and refashioned her upbringing through humorous fiction, she must have known that mockery is potent because it undermines. She may have poked fun at Diana's future husband, but there's a rebuke in that evasive, reasoning letter. By taking fascism seriously, it was Diana who had betrayed the sisterly code of amused detachment. Less than two years later, Jessica was set to play further havoc with the delicate balance of family bonds and opposing ideologies.

★

Of course Esmond was at Cousin Dorothy's house, 'shorter than I had imagined, very thin, with very bright eyes and amazingly long eyelashes'. In fact, he was waiting for her. Tipped off about Jessica's ambitions, and 'with his usual enthusiasm for fellow runaways', he was already working on a liberation plan.

Esmond had been offered a job as a correspondent for the *News Chronicle* and was planning an imminent return to Spain. Between them, he and Jessica devised a plan for Jessica to go too. A week of preparations followed, with its necessary raft of lies and deception.

In February 1937, they reunited on a boat crossing the Channel to France, then travelled through the country down to Bayonne, where families of Basque refugees were massing in their hotel. While they waited to cross the border, Esmond talked of the Madrid front. Any rebelliousness, Jessica realised, had hardened into something purposeful. 'He had become a committed partisan of the fight against Fascism.'

There were other developments too: a declaration and an engagement. It would be a long wait for the wedding since they were too young to marry without their parents' permission, but it didn't seem to matter. To Jessica, Esmond was 'all that was bright, attractive and powerful'; he had become her 'rescuer, the translator of all my dreams into reality', a person who could solve any of the problems ahead of them. Politics had caught up love on its transforming way.

But even Esmond could not assuage the fact that she had left her father's house for the last time, or that all hell would break loose when her family discovered that she was not on holiday in Dieppe.

Esmond's return to Spain was shaped and overshadowed by the Mitford clan. In mid-February, he had word from the Basque consulate that he and Jessica could board a ship for Bilbao. It turned out to be a 'tiny cargo boat' loaded with 'about a dozen chickens'. The first night, they stayed up late with the crew and captain; eating, drinking and sharing toasts to the engaged couple and the death of fascism. The rest of the three-day voyage was lost, for Jessica, to a spectacular bout of seasickness.

When she got to Bilbao, it was as if she were still in a daze, still reeling from her audacious escape and its unknown consequences; aware, too, that the 'grim, serious town' was existing in an anxious state of suspension. The struggle for Madrid meant that, in the north, the Basque front was quiet. The war was not there yet but it was coming. People crowded the cafés, listening for news over the radio. Hungry children (a common sight even before the wartime shortages) besieged them, begging for a mouthful of the 'grayish bread' or thick, black hot chocolate that made up the menu.

Jessica drifted along with Esmond as he arranged interviews and sought updates from the press bureau, half her mind on whatever might be brewing at home. Because there was not much to report, there was not much of a press presence, and the bureau willingly put them up in a hotel. Esmond apparently, and uncharacteristically, made no attempt to push on any further or to venture beyond official communiqués. They were taken on a long drive to see the front, but not much was happening there either. Jessica was offered the opportunity to fire at the enemy – little figures visible in the distance – but hit a tree. On another trip they visited a jail for political prisoners and prisoners of war and Jessica judged them 'frightfully well treated, in fact . . . much better than they deserve when you think how the fascists treat their prisoners'. They tried to teach themselves Spanish. Theoretically, Jessica was Esmond's secretary, but she couldn't type, so he handled that as well.

Jessica's first intimation of trouble was a summons from the British consulate. The British consul was away, so it was his Basque counterpart who trustingly showed Esmond and Jessica the coded telegram he'd received, signed by the Foreign Secretary, and the three of them decoded it together: FIND JESSICA MITFORD AND PERSUADE HER TO RETURN. Esmond helped compose the reply: HAVE FOUND JESSICA MITFORD. IMPOSSIBLE TO PERSUADE HER TO RETURN.

Then the British consul came back. Jessica and Esmond were told off. Jessica was ordered to return. Again, she refused. But the strength of the forces arrayed against them was beginning to dawn on her. Her parents had turned immediately to the resources people like them had at their disposal: a British destroyer arrived with orders to lure her on board; she was made a ward of court and Esmond threatened with imprisonment if they tried to marry. They held out until the consulate lost patience and issued the first ultimatum likely to have an effect. If they did not leave voluntarily, they were warned, British aid for Basque refugees would be cut off. Unable to judge how sincere this was, Esmond and Jessica left.

And that was it. In a matter of weeks, Jessica's heroic sortie was over. Spain might have played a role in her liberation, but she was now unlikely to return the favour. At home the press was having a field day, shunting the war off the front pages. The papers had spun a straightforward tale of elopement, as if Esmond and Jessica had fled into a war zone because it seemed like a nice place to get married, and so they were robbed even of any recognition of their motives. With little control over the narrative, they had little control over its meaning.

Esmond refused to accept total defeat. They went no further than the south of France, where he settled down to write *Boadilla*, his account of fighting in Spain. Jessica watched him labouring at his recalcitrant typewriter, knowing that the news coming from Madrid depressed him, and wondered what she had cost him. They had evaded their parents, they had found each other, and yet gloom occasionally engulfed them. 'I might have gone back', he was writing of the

International Brigades. 'But I did not go. I got married and lived happily instead.'

Esmond and Jessica were spirited teenagers who knew how to enjoy themselves. Happy was what they were good at. Given what he now knew about it, the front held little appeal for Esmond. Yet there's a shamefacedness in both their accounts. It has something to do, of course, with how historic disasters reduce little human adventures. But that dry summation of Esmond's suggests something more: that their generation did not have the time or the leisure for youthful escapades, for the blissful self-involvement of first love or first escape. Those were indulgences that relied on peace, and peace, he would insist in his book, would not be secure until 'that mixture of profit-seeking, self-interest, cheap emotion and organised brutality which is called fascism has been fought and destroyed forever'.

Much later Jessica became a campaigning journalist, with a particular talent for unearthing exploitation so blatant that it tipped into the absurd (she wrote a surprise bestseller exposing the great scam of American funerals). The Spanish war, which had more than a little madness in it, could have been just the place to cut her teeth as that writer. But that is to ask what the Spanish war could have done for Jessica Mitford, which even she at nineteen would have known was a question posed the wrong way round.

Jessica had been disappointed by Nancy for trying to persuade her home from Spain, afraid of what the adventure would do to her reputation. 'Society', her sister had warned, 'can make things pretty beastly to those who disobey its rules.' In her concern, she put her finger on exactly what distinguished their approaches to life. 'After all', she declared, 'one has to live in this world as it is'. Jessica would spend most of her future career disagreeing.

Later she claimed to have got permission to marry Esmond by letting it be known that she was pregnant, though it seems that Lady Redesdale did most of the persuading on her behalf. However much Jessica and Esmond proclaimed their outcast status, both of their mothers were with them at the British consulate in Bayonne when they were married in 1937. Unity and Diana sent wedding presents. 'If anything happens don't forget there is a spare room here,' Nancy had offered, before adding, with that last-minute inflection they couldn't do without: '(£4.10. bed)'.

★

If you spend much time in the company of Nancy Mitford's characters – in *The Pursuit of Love*, for instance, where she makes good use of her family – you come to feel that she finds everyone in the world faintly ridiculous and probably, in the end, quite harmless. Her favourite characters are able to drift through the vagaries of life if not unharmed then at least unmarked. The outside world can agitate all it likes: certain foundational things remain the same. Father will fume, the house will be unheated, romance will offer the best escape.

Fourteen years after Jessica's flight, though – years in which history intervened even more spectacularly in the sisters' lives – she would refuse permission for *Wigs on the Green* to be republished. 'Too much has happened', she explained, 'for jokes about Nazis to be regarded as funny or as anything but the worst of taste.'

When Nancy Cunard condemned 'the ironic detachment', my hunch was that she really meant a kind of amused belittling or archly disengaged approach – the kind of *Wigs on the Green* air that comes in so handy when you're queasy about earnestness. But there was also something ironic about the idea of the Mitfords' detachment. Jessica, Nancy and Unity were all of them loath to unpick the bonds that connected them. Sometimes it is only when the causal connection between ideas and their outcomes is confronted that a difference of opinions begins to look more like a breach that neither love nor jokes can skirt around.

'Give [Diana] my love,' Jessica once wrote to Unity in Germany, '& hate to Hitler.' In 1937 their paths diverged forever. For most of their lives, Jessica had been the closest observer of Unity's charms as well as her faults; her sparring partner and her companion. That year Unity would graciously offer to be friends with Esmond on the understanding that she would shoot him should the political situation ever demand it, since 'family ties ought to make a difference' even where sides had been chosen. But Esmond, a veteran of burned bridges, expected a complete estrangement from Jessica's family. And, drawn into the realities of the political gulf she and Unity had positioned themselves across, she could no longer disentangle the loved person from the incomprehensible beliefs.

For all their jokes, Jessica believed that she and each of her sisters was 'a terrific hater' – a skill they notably shared with Nancy Cunard. Perhaps when either humour or hatred fail us, the other takes up the slack. Jessica's deepest disappointment in her 'huge, bright adversary' was that ultimately her sister had failed to hate 'intelligently' – as if that were the key, or the absolution, for hating.

In Jessica's eyes, Unity had thrown her lot in with the vilest, 'most deadeningly conformist of all philosophies'. (Unity presumably felt the same about communism.) The hatreds promoted by Nazism corrupted the idea of hating as resistance, the thing that kept them from conformity: 'she had forgotten the whole point of hating, and had once and for all put herself on the side of the hateful'.

Anger, as girls are told, is not an attractive quality. By itself, it's not terribly useful either. Yet what does it say about us if we're not able to muster a little rage in response to injustice, or oppression, or some preventable suffering, or the threat of those things? Nancy Cunard's outrage, her 'longing to fight', may have made people uncomfortable, but it also kept her moving. As a character written by Martha Gellhorn once put it, 'To be angry, you must have hope.'

PART TWO

Arrivals

Martha Gellhorn

Madrid: spring 1937

It's Madrid in the spring of 1937; Martha Gellhorn's first-ever piece of war reporting. The article is destined for *Collier's* – a coup for a young reporter because it is a seriously-taken magazine read by two and a half million people. It is also not a newspaper. There's no need to attempt a precis of developments, of manoeuvring armies or complex alliances. This is just Martha, alone in her hotel room as it gets coated in dust (dust that rises to the windows as sections of the street erupt), listening to the nationalists shell the city. 'You couldn't help breathing strangely, just taking the air into your throat and not being able to inhale it.' In other words, she must be choking, but in prose Martha can contain her panic. The room is a bad place to be: she goes down to the lobby to wait with the apologetic concierge.

In Madrid, she has already learned, there is always waiting. 'You waited for the shelling to start,' she tells us, 'and for it to end, and for it to start again.' From her waiting place she can see others lingering in doorways until they can get back to business. For Madrileños, waiting has become a kind of stoicism, the resilience of a daily life that must persist however badly it is menaced. There are women she will always remember, 'standing in line, as they do all over Madrid, quiet women, dressed usually in black, with market baskets on their arms, waiting to buy food. A shell falls across the square. They turn their heads to look, and move a little closer to the house, but no one leaves her place in line.'

It is all like one long suspenseful pause, punctuated by destruction. A shell lands, 'and there was a fountain of granite cobblestones flying up into the air', another hits 'and a window broke gently and airily, making a lovely tinkling musical sound'. If it all sounds strangely unreal – well, of course it does: this is the bombardment of a European capital, something almost unthinkable in 1937. When it all goes quiet, and out everyone comes and Martha returns to her room, the hotel itself gets struck. A 'whistle-whine-scream-roar and the noise was in your throat and you couldn't feel or hear or think', and the next thing the concierge knows there are very regrettable holes in rooms 218 and 219. The reality is not that you are always waiting for safety, but that you are always waiting to get hit.

Though humanity – usually in the form of its governments – would always disappoint Martha Gellhorn, she liked human beings. The persistence of the women buying oranges in the square, their courage in a choiceless world (starvation or shells?), is exactly the kind of detail that characterised her reporting from Spain. Martha had a certain latitude from writing for a weekly magazine. As she'd have a fictional alter ego tell fellow press people one day, 'I do not write news like you gents. I write history.' By which she meant, she had the time and space to craft long pieces of reportage; to write in a literary style of gifted noticing that sees, in another piece, an injured boy 'twisting his body slowly, as if he wanted to get out of it'; that conveys the strange unreality of so horrendous a thing as war.

Because she is doing the looking for us, just telling us what she sees, she is able to recount scenes of extreme trauma with a cool kind of empathy. In Madrid, what she saw was people: daily lives, ordinary fears and rationalisations.

In Madrid she sees an elderly woman drag a small boy across the square – a crazy dash prompted by a brief pause in the shelling – and she knows why she has done it. She suspects that we all know, on some level, why she would do it. 'You know what she is thinking: she is thinking she must get the child home, you are always safer in your own place, with the things you know. Somehow you do not believe you can get killed when you are sitting in your own parlor, you never think that.' Don't we all indulge in magical thinking to make ourselves feel safe? Isn't that precisely what the Western democracies are doing in 1937, telling themselves that the affairs of a faraway country don't concern them in the least, when all the evidence shows fascism on the march?

> A small piece of twisted steel, hot and very sharp, sprays off from the shell; it takes the little boy in the throat. The old woman stands there, holding the hand of the dead child, looking at him stupidly, not saying anything, and men run out toward her to carry the child. At their left, at the side of the square, is a huge brilliant sign which says: GET OUT OF MADRID.

War suited Martha Gellhorn because extremes suited her. She hurtled between poles: from roughing it in war zones she would submerge herself in total, luxurious retreat; from circulating in the highest echelons of politicians, diplomats and literary celebrities, dressed to the nines and dripping glamour, she was proud of her ability to hack life in the field with 'the boys'; she sought company, then she wanted, desperately, to be alone.

In her travels, which she used to observe history as it was made (meaning, in her lifetime, war), Martha did not flinch from the worst things. It was ordinary things that gave her trouble. Daily life was of interest when seen in extremis, when peril made its persistence heroic. When she dropped out of Bryn Mawr College in 1929, it was returning to the small rules and small minds in her home town of St Louis that frightened her.

The only girl among four children, Martha developed an acute sense for injustice early on. 'Walter and George tried to kill me,' she once informed her parents in a letter pinned up prominently in the house. 'If you don't do something about it, I'm going to leave home.' Later on she credited her parents for raising her no differently from the boys, which wasn't strictly true. 'If it's assumed that men do whatever they want,' she said, 'I just assumed that I did whatever I wanted.'

But when she did leave, her parents were suitably alarmed. Even to them, the safest place for a daughter was at home, being helpful to her mother. Martha borrowed money for a train ticket to New York.

And from New York, she exchanged an article on the North German Lloyd passenger service for a berth to Europe.

When Martha arrived in Paris in 1930, she was twenty-one. 'Scott Fitzgerald, John Dos Passos, Ezra Pound and Nancy Cunard', her biographer would note, 'had all come and gone'. That, it would seem, suited Martha fine. She later contrasted their Paris – that of the 'gifted Americans and British' in the 1920s – with the 'real life' of the Paris she came to know, the city as it was familiar to Simone Weil: 'slums, strikes, protest marches broken up by the mounted Garde Republicaine, frantic underpaid workers and frantic half-starved unemployed'. She scratched a living at various unsatisfying jobs, wrote a novel, became embroiled in an affair with the French journalist Bertrand de Jouvenel; returned to the US; returned to Europe. She visited Geneva, London, saw Germany with Bertrand and went back to America again.

Until then she'd thought trouble was a European condition. She had done bits of journalism before, but in trying to articulate a human portrait of the Depression, which meant working through what she felt about it, Martha began to develop a literary voice that distilled outrage into unforgiving clarity. Because of the special assignment she was set in New England and the Carolinas, this early training taught her to look into parlours when history was happening: to make a point of understanding what something as momentous as war or economic depression meant to the people living it.

In 1936, having returned to explore her idea of a novel about pacifists, Martha left Europe again to spend Christmas with her mother and brother. Her father had died the previous year, wrenching one of the early pillars out of her life, and the three of them fled the family home for the holidays, heading for winter sun. At Florida's southernmost tip, in the sultry island city of Key West, Martha met Ernest Hemingway.

This was a relationship that would cast a long, much-resented shadow over her life and reputation, but in fairness there were many writers of her generation who could say the same. Already the author of *The Sun Also Rises* and *A Farewell to Arms*, Hemingway produced the kind of prose that Martha both dreamed of writing and feared emulating. Big, bearded, heavy-drinking and famous, he was, at thirty-seven, an imposing man.

In the swaggering account he gave friends, Ernest claimed to have caught sight of Martha and her brother in a bar and mistaken them for a honeymooning couple, setting him the challenge of prising the young bride away for himself. The presence in town of his own wife, Pauline, and their two young sons appears not to have been an obstacle. Martha got to know the whole family.

Over the Christmas of 1936, during what Nancy Cunard called Madrid's 'winter of death and dying', Martha and Ernest discussed the escalating war in Spain. She was well informed from her time in Europe. He wanted to go there. Writing to Eleanor Roosevelt, a friend of her mother's who had become something of a mentor, Martha voiced a mix of dread and exhilaration. She believed fascist intervention on the nationalist side would make the war international. And then they could expect a much bigger conflagration.

The letter hints at other developments, too: Hemingway, 'an odd bird' but also 'very lovable and full of fire and a marvelous story teller'. And now she had a doom-laden get-out clause ready to hand: 'If there is a war, then all the things most of us do won't matter any more.'

Back in St Louis, Martha suffered from feeling out of things and wanted 'desperately' to go to Spain. The publication, to excellent reviews, of *The Trouble I've Seen* had done nothing to satisfy her demands of herself, or solve the question of what to do next. The prospect of missing the action, her fear of aimlessness, enabled her to insist with cool perversity, from the safety and comfort of her mother's house, that 'if you're part of a big thing you feel safe; it's only waiting and looking on from the outside that makes one nervous and lost'.

'I have a feeling that one has to work all day and all night and live too,' she confided to Roosevelt, 'and swim and get the sun in one's hair and laugh and love as many people as one can find around and do all this terribly fast, because the time is getting shorter and shorter every day.' Three months later, she was in Madrid.

★

'I had been five days in Spain and had seen many things,' Martha wrote in a typed version of the journal she kept, 'but it was all preparation, it was like learning the grammar of a foreign language. I was waiting all the time for Madrid.'

March 1937 was a good time to arrive. The city's resistance was already passing into legend. A Republican victory at Guadalajara, forty miles to the north-east, had finally broken Franco's fixation on taking the capital. The shelling of the city continued, but Franco's German advisers were now able to persuade him to focus on more vulnerable Republican targets in the north, sending the conflict in the direction of territory Jessica Mitford had just left.

Virginia Cowles, a glamorous and well-connected Vermont native who had distinguished herself in 1935 by securing an interview with Mussolini in the week Italy invaded Ethiopia, arrived shortly after Martha. 'The Republicans had taken great heart at their Guadalajara victory,' she recalled later, 'and now regarded the future with a robust optimism. They talked in terms of large-scale offensives and of the peace they would impose at the end of the war.' As well as fighting spirit, there was still a certain amount of fighting, as the front snaked remarkably close – so close that in places it was part of the city.

It was what Martha was looking for. 'Madrid is not a city and not a battlefield,' she noted down. 'You can hear the firing on the front in University City, just down the end of a street; you can hear the artillery to the west. . . . You live with the war every minute, and yet you walk around the streets as if you were in London or Rome or Vienna, and worry about the same small human things which worry people everywhere, and you laugh and talk with your friends.'

She could reach 'the front as calmly as one would stroll through Central Park', catching a tramway partway then picking across – even Virginia in her high heels – on foot. When he reached Madrid months later, Langston Hughes described trenches that 'curved and zig-zagged through gardens, under fences, and beneath houses', sometimes even passing straight into a house, cutting through its living room or past the stove in the kitchen, before emerging back out into open trench. Visiting the trenches at night, Martha found the enemy was near enough to torment them by playing a song called 'Kitten on the Keys' at top speed, over and over, on a gramophone. Ernest found a blown-open house from which they could watch distant skirmishes on the Casa de Campo as if watching a movie war fought with toys.

Martha would pass along a street of grand houses and realise that all that was standing were the façades; look up at a wrecked building and see a telephone 'hanging by its cord out into the air'. She talked to people, interviewed officials. She visited the grand Hotel Palace, where surgeons now operated by the light of crystal chandeliers and 'Edwardian show cabinets, for displaying jewelry and crocodile hand-bags, held their tools'. The blood on the marble steps was like a warning: inside, the smell and sounds of people in pain nauseated her. There was no morphine and very few trained nurses.

She went shopping with Virginia Cowles. Since the usual clientele of Madrid's luxury boutiques had fled, there were bargains to be had. She passed people commuting to work. The food was drastically bad everywhere – on her first night (as on many other nights) she was served a handful of chickpeas with pungent dried cod – but she was staying in a hotel said to be the only place in the capital with hot water. In other words, life in the city was so much normal and so much nightmare.

In the beginning, Martha's approach was similar to the Valentine Ackland school of thought: one made one's statement by arriving, and the statement was the crucial thing. 'I believed that all one did about a war was go to it, as a gesture of solidarity,' she wrote years later, 'and get killed, or survive if lucky'. She was in Madrid for several weeks before she sent an article to *Collier's*, little expecting them to run it. But they did, and then she wrote more. The *New Yorker* took two pieces of hers; *Collier's* eventually put her on the masthead.

There was by now a vibrant press community strung along Madrid's Gran Vía: between its bars and restaurants, the Hotel Florida on the Plaza del Callao, where Martha took a room, and the crucial landmark of the Telefónica further up. Martha would become a native of these shifting international communities, valuing the camaraderie of people thrown into swift-forming intimacy. 'She liked them very much,' she would write in one of her novels, describing a journalist who bore a marked resemblance to herself, 'and she did not know them at all.'

The Telefónica was one of the first skyscrapers in Europe, both a soaring lookout spot for the city's defenders and a target for its enemies. There, journalists delivered their articles to the Republican press censors and then telephoned them home in their respective languages. Through the shelling and through the night, 'switchboard girls' stayed at their posts, while correspondents could avail themselves of camp beds set up in the corridors. Martha described seeing them 'run from the hotel to the Telefonica, sometimes waiting for a shell to burst and then running before the next shell bursts', all to file a story. On 31 December 1936, Franco's troops had celebrated the New Year by firing twelve shells directly into the city. Ten of them hit the Telefónica. Yet it continued to stand, iconic in its towering resilience, Madrid's mouthpiece to the world.

Journalists were welcome and well treated in a place where good PR was beginning to seem a matter of survival. Despite the Italian ambassador's admission that his country's forces were in Spain (and would stay until Franco had won), the Non-Intervention Committee had so far only implemented measures against foreign enlistments, thereby effectively targeting volunteers for the International Brigades, since the troops sent by Hitler and Mussolini were serving as part of their own national armies. Like the British, the United States pursued a policy of proclaimed neutrality that in practice benefitted the nationalists. The Catholic lobby, firmly on Franco's side, had pressured Congress into blocking arms supplies to the Republic. Yet the embargo did not prevent the president of the Texaco oil company from supplying the nationalists on credit. By the time Martha crossed the border, American passports were being stamped NOT VALID FOR TRAVEL IN SPAIN. (Volunteers snuck in via France, as she had done.) President Roosevelt later regretted disregarding the stream of reports from the US ambassador to Spain urging support for the Republic – a campaign soon paralleled in Martha's letters to the First Lady. But as the British, French, Americans and others stuck to non-intervention, the Republican government hoped to convert them with evidence of the involvement of foreign fascist powers and of nationalist atrocities, and by undoing the early reputational damage to the loyalist alliance. For this, journalists were vital.

Martha kept track of her own acclimatisation. At the end of March she added a note to her diary: 'I am getting so hardened that I forgot this morning's shell which skimmed the house on the corner and went into the fourth floor of an apartment on the Gran Via, killing a 14 year old child and wounding two adults. . . . I was brushing my teeth, and heard it and went on.' At this point in her life, Martha believed that journalism could create change, that injustice went unremedied because not enough people knew about it. Most could not come to Spain and see the shelling of Madrid, the blood in the streets: that was what she could do. Her job, she came to believe, was 'to be eyes for their conscience'.

There is a refrain in Nancy Cunard's poem about Madrid later that year: 'I have seen', she repeats, 'I have seen'. As much as it sounds like a monotone of trauma, the mind skipping insistently over things too terrible to forget, it also articulates a claim to authority. Martha believed that good journalism was 'a form of honorable behavior, involving the reporter and the reader'. Her side of her bargain was bearing witness. (Even collecting her articles in 1959, the corollary was apparently self-evident that 'the point of these articles is that they are true; they tell what I saw'.) She looked where it was uncomfortable to look and reported back. The moral baton passed to her readers.

Whereas some reporters, like Virginia Cowles, based their work around the balanced and comprehensive report, Martha's concept of journalism, and of journalistic truth, rested with this self-assigned role. Again and again she expressed herself in terms of straightforward looking and of conveying what had been seen, an insistence on a simplicity to her work that begins to sound like too much protesting. 'They are shelling the city again,' she noted at the beginning of April. 'This is easy to say or write but not so easy in fact.' Yet the difficult fact of it – the felt experience of the shelling – was not easy to write at all. She laboured over her typewriter, narrating the trouble she'd seen not at the pace of a mad dash to the Telefónica, but in literary accounts that would stand the test of time. She was writing history, as she saw it.

In 1983, the journalist John Pilger interviewed Martha for a television series he called *The Outsiders*. He included Jessica Mitford the same year. It's a pleasure just to watch Martha's gestures. In contrast to the slightly patrician Jessica, she is downright glamorous. She speaks in an authoritative, almost declarative manner. She has recently returned from El Salvador, where she covered, Pilger points out, her seventh war in half a century as a reporter. He asks her about Spain. What affected her there, he says, what guided her later work?

'Well, the bravery, the enormous bravery of the people . . . absolutely unbelievable bravery under appalling conditions.' Bravery and dignity matter to her. As for what stayed with her – 'individual things, I don't know'. She shakes her head slightly, looks up and around as if seeking the answer or a distraction from it. 'Madrid, shells coming into the square in front of the hotel and a queue of women, who were queuing up to get an orange and nobody moving because it was so important just to get an orange to take home to your' – she closes her eyes – 'underfed family.' She has written these scenes.

'I don't know,' she goes on. 'It's very hard to tell you – there were so many – it was a very long time I was there,' she lights a new cigarette, 'and every day there was something that – that,' she looks at him briefly as she flicks at her lighter, speaking with finality, 'moved and impressed me.'

When, in wartime, he asks, should a journalist censor themselves? 'I'd think never.'

When is it impossible to be objective?

This is harder. 'Well,' she begins, 'I – I don't know – I really don't know.' She gets sharper, emphatic – almost angry – when he asks about Dachau, the concentration camp she entered on the day the Second World War ended, in a fulfilment of her 'personal war aim'. (Both of Martha's parents were half Jewish, a fact to which she paid curiously little attention.)

'What was there to be objective about?' she asks. 'It was a total and absolute horror. [. . .] I don't even know what you *mean* exactly by objective. [. . .] I did neither suppress nor invent, I reported it.'

Here some surprise (really it was just disappointment) arose for me that Jessica Mitford had never made it as far as Madrid or fallen in with Martha Gellhorn. They were very different interviewees in 1983 – Jessica enjoying herself, Martha brisk and uncompromising; the two of them drawling in accents with very different origins – but watching the conversations one after the other, just as I was often reading them in close proximity, revealed them as writers who had taken up very similar positions. When Jessica was hailed as a mother of New Journalism, a mode that brought literary techniques of fiction to reporting in the 1960s and '70s, it was a mantle that she inherited from writers like Martha Gellhorn, a style forged in the Spanish war. 'When are you going to get *angry*?' a friend once asked Jessica after reading a draft of one of her exposés. 'Never,' she replied, having learned to lean on humour for her persuasions, 'it is not in my sweet nature to lose my temper, especially in print.'

The less she drew attention to her own presence and point of view, she meant, the more apparent her point became. Presented without editorialising, Jessica's targets damned themselves. Because the point was not that she was not angry. The point was the 'global Moral Messages' she wanted her readers to absorb. Accuracy was 'essential'; objectivity – 'If to be objective means having no point of view, or giving equal weight to all information that comes one's way' – was not.

By the late 1930s there was a cohort of journalists in Europe ready to jettison objectivity as a guiding principle. Martha was partial to words with exactly the kind of monolithic nobility that makes it seem churlish to interrogate them, words like 'good' and 'strong' and 'true'. It's easy to see why 'objectivity', with its emphasis on avoiding the personal response, might be perceived as an affront by someone whose journalistic career was launched in Spain and followed fascism through a world war to the very gates of its final outcome in the camps; why 'truth' (Merriam Webster: 'the state of being the case; sincerity in action, character, and utterance . . .') sat better.

In other words, if you are Martha Gellhorn, then the truth is always there to be seen; it doesn't need to be ferreted out and it isn't achieved by the careful balancing of scales. As her biographer wrote of her: 'Like lying, sitting on the fence was contemptible'; either would have represented a dereliction of her duty as a reporter and as a person. At Dachau, objectivity goes from being a responsibility to something that looks a lot like an abdication from responsibility. (Copied from a cartoon about the climate crisis, a scrap of paper that floated about my desk for months: 'Someone tell the press gallery the fence they are trying to sit on is on fire.')

'If you are seeing something happening,' she said once, 'the idea that you're so brain dead and stony hearted that you have no reaction to it strikes me as absolute nonsense.' You don't see a boy struck from life whilst clinging to his grandmother's hand and feel nothing. The whole truth, to Martha, was the admission of moral positions, human responses.

Yet there's no excess of feeling in Martha Gellhorn's writing. The sheer force of horror in what she describes isn't there because she lets go and floods the page with her first, instinctive reactions, but rather because of the opposite: it's there in the palpable control, as though she is speaking through teeth gritted tight with rage. Her biographer calls it her tone of 'barely contained fury and indignation'. Martha described a process of 'eliminating as much as possible the sound of me screaming'.

Seeing

Gerda Taro

Almería: early 1937

In March 1937, the French magazine *Regards* ran a two-page story on the refugee crisis caused by the fall of Málaga, with photos taken by Gerda Taro and Robert Capa. After capturing the early scenes of elation and fervour in Barcelona for *Vu* magazine – little boys in CNT caps, militiawomen learning to shoot on the beaches – the couple had roved southwards during their first six weeks in Spain, hoping to capture action shots of the fighting, but instead found themselves photographing refugees. When they returned in February, they had a joint commission specifically to document the exodus from Málaga.

Even among the atrocities Franco unleased on his compatriots, Málaga looms large. Far from the Republican centres of Madrid, Barcelona and Valencia, the city was in ill-defended territory at the southern tip of the country, in Andalusia. A third of the militiamen responsible for its defence had no rifles. Perhaps the city's ancientness, the sparkling border of the Costa del Sol or the immovable backing of the mountains had fostered a false sense of security. The nationalist attack apparently came as a surprise.

When it fell on 8 February, thousands of loyalists who remained in the city were shot or imprisoned (in Málaga the executions would go on for years). Tens of thousands of civilians, petrified by the advance of Italian tanks, had poured out of the city and neighbouring villages as Málaga was attacked from the air and the ocean. There was one way out: along the road east, to Almería. Some made the escape by car, others packed their belongings onto donkeys, mules and horses; the rest went on foot. Having overtaken the ruined streets, 'Nationalist tanks and aircraft', one historian would write, 'caught up with the refugees. Letting the women go free, so as to increase the Republic's food difficulties, they shot the men, often in the sight of their families.'

What remained of the families continued along the unremitting coastal road, caught between the ocean to their right and the Sierra Nevada mountains on their left. Instead of escaping the danger, they dragged it with them. Nationalist ships kept pace alongside, shelling the ragged column from the sea. Planes flew overhead, discharging bombs, and Italian units pursued them with machine-gun fire. Mothers pressed their children into the ground to avoid the bombers, flattening themselves against the hard earth. Exhausted men and women lay down at the side of the road to die. The feet of ill-shod children swelled and bled. People lost their minds.

Almería was over a hundred miles away. As the town filled with survivors, the nationalists bombed them there too – apparently aiming for the centre, where people were queuing for food. Taro and Capa had to move through huddles of traumatised people and point their cameras. Gerda's portraits document stunned, inarticulate horror; the silent scream behind Martha Gellhorn's reporting.

It is striking how much the children in this series are holding on to things. Usually they cling to an adult who doesn't seem able to see them, and in the absence of grown-ups they clutch each other, and when alone they hold tightly to blankets. In a group photo Gerda took of adults and children, each of them, even the babies, seems lost in thought, or lost somewhere else. With their preoccupied gazes, the women bring to mind the iconic image of Florence Owens Thompson – the 'Migrant Mother' photographed the previous year by Dorothea Lange – who became symbolic of the Great Depression. Unmoored but waiting, their situation is perfectly related by the suspension of a photograph.

Gerda Taro knew all about displacement. Perhaps, before she came to Spain, she thought she knew everything there was to know about it. When she and Capa met in Paris in September 1934 they were yet to cast away names – André Friedmann and Gerta Pohorylle – that betrayed what they were: hungry, poor, Jewish; immigrants in a country that kept reminding them of their tenuous welcome.

France's early sympathy for German refugees had waned as they kept on coming, becoming more Jewish all the while. This was the Paris Martha Gellhorn first encountered: a city with problems of its own. Immigrants had to somehow prove that they would neither deprive French workers of jobs nor rely on the state to survive, and they had to do so regularly. Many maintained their permission to stay by faking a family income from abroad; most scraped by on freelance work, things like the poorly paid secretarial job that Gerda held for a while, and taking photographs. Gerda and her roommate, a friend from Leipzig, were so poor and underfed that they often spent weekends in bed, conserving their energy beneath blankets.

It was the roommate who brought Gerda and André together. When a scruffy, unshaven guy with a camera asks to take pictures of you in a park, you don't go along without backup, however much you need the money. Accompanying her friend, Gerda found that André had his portfolio to recommend him, and soon her ambition extended to include this dark Hungarian whose talent she believed in. As a teenager André had fallen in with socialists and avant-garde artists in Budapest, and had demonstrated against Admiral Horthy's anti-semitic regime. Arrested, beaten and ordered to leave the country by the secret police, he had then been forced to leave Berlin with the rise of the Nazis just as his photography career was showing promise. He spoke terrible French with a strong accent, was erratic and drank too much: he was barely getting by. Gerda took him in hand, promoted his work, made sure he was presentable and fulfilled assignments. Gerda, he noted admiringly, 'does not put a lock on her mouth if she does not like something'. He had good reason to do as he was told: she was 'even more intelligent than she is pretty'.

For his part, André encouraged Gerda's own burgeoning talent, even shared his camera (when it wasn't in the pawn shop). In a rare photograph of the two of them together, a scrubbed-up André looks at her with undisguised adoration. They were, he said, 'independent comrades' and 'very good friends', which they had decided was crucial if they were to live together. Here was one of those much-trumpeted partnerships of the artistic circles in which they moved – something like what the Greens set up in England. Love and work and ideals on a shared basis. Two young, talented and disadvantaged people: neither of them with the upper hand. Even if André had been looking for a muse-assistant, he wouldn't have found her in Gerda.

Life was still a hard scrabble. 'You can't imagine, Mutti, the way we live,' he reported to his mother, 'hustling all day, and spending the night manufacturing articles. I named Gerda the "Ragged One".' They went backwards and forwards to newspapers, trying to sell their work, and the soles wore through on Gerda's shoes. Ragged Jewish immigrants were not much in demand as photographers, so, at Gerda's instigation, they made themselves into something else: Robert Capa, a cover persona to give the right sheen to André's work; a mirage of glossy success, redolent of America, of privilege and dash, 'like being born again'.

Gerda took the surname Taro, possibly borrowed from a Japanese friend; distinctive in a better, more pronounceable way than Pohorylle. Now she shopped Robert Capa's work around, making up mischievous stories about their glamorous cipher. Capa was recently landed in Europe, and yet, in another sense, he had already arrived. He was someone who could afford a yacht and thus was scarcely in need of commissions. He was so successful that his photographs were worth three times the going rate. They must have enjoyed themselves in that one-room apartment they shared near the Eiffel Tower – where the bed was too small for them to lie on their backs side by side – inventing Capa's carefree life.

The deception doesn't seem to have convinced anyone for long, but the name stuck. Capa was selling more photographs; Gerda had a job in a photo agency. Then they were offered a commission in Barcelona.

Though *Collier's* was lavishly illustrated, Martha's articles from Spain were the first to appear alongside photographs: women and children sheltering in the city subway, ruined buildings. When I opened a file on Spain among her papers, the first thing that revealed itself was a large, dark photo of the view through a hole in the Hotel Florida floor, which appeared alongside her 1938 essay on the bombing. There, visible through the room's broken floorboards, is a miniature figure. On the back, a note reads: 'the man comes with his donkey cart to sell oranges to the housewives'.

By 1937, the photojournalist had become the natural companion to the reporter. Illustrated European magazines like the French *Vu* were setting a standard that became widely imitated (*Vu* was the inspiration behind the hugely influential *Life* magazine; its editor chartered a plane to get his team into Barcelona as quickly as possible after Franco's rebellion). This was the first war in which the story told to the outside world was conveyed as much by images as by text. Smaller, more portable cameras allowed photographers into intimate proximity with the conflict, and some in the Republican press division were quick to appreciate the propaganda power of photos – particularly of the carnage in civilian areas.

'The Spanish government', Virginia Woolf would record with plaintive hyperbole, distributed such images 'with patient pertinacity about twice a week'. Like Martha, she was struck by the broken-open houses of Madrid, the domestic sanctuaries exposed and refashioned from protective interiority (*you are always safer in your own place*) into something merely suggestive of what has been lost. She, too, singled out a parlour from the interrupted scenes of damaged houses: 'there is still a bird-cage hanging in what was presumably the sitting-room'.

Virginia's discomfort is evident in the evasive, half-protesting mentions she made of the photos to her nephew Julian: 'I got a packet of photographs from Spain all of dead children, killed by bombs – a cheerful present.' But it was hoped that the shock would make evasion more difficult. Europe had never before seen the kind of aerial bombardment unleashed on civilians in Republican Spain. (Which is not to say it hadn't happened elsewhere, but when it was the British 'pacifying' Palestinian villages or Italians attacking Ethiopians, it apparently didn't register in the collective imagination in quite the same way.) The Blitz, Dresden, Hiroshima: all that was in the previously unimaginable future. 'Look at their pictures, peoples,' Nancy commanded in 'Madrid 1936'. 'What is the answer to come?'

Gerda and André did not arrive in Spain as impartial observers. Their lives had been shaped by fleeing fascism; now they had the chance to take the initiative: to head towards the monster rather than running from it. The *Vu* plane offered a break from the grind of Paris, from the struggle to pay the rent in a place that accepts you on sufferance; a chance to be welcomed as a comrade instead.

Gerda had sold her first photographs, thereby gaining press accreditation, only six months before the war's outbreak. Her first press pass shows her happy and sure of herself, smiling broadly. Working beside André, she quickly gained confidence and would soon branch out on her own assignments. Determined to distinguish herself, she covered the wreckage in Madrid, trenches in the Jarama valley, and the defeat of Mussolini's troops at Guadalajara. At first, most of their credited images from Spain appeared under the name Robert Capa, their joint creation. (*Vu* only managed a misspelled 'Cappa' among the listed photographers for its Barcelona issue, making no mention at all of any Gerda Taro.) But it was André who was known as Robert Capa – 'Bob' to people, like Martha and Ernest, who came to know him from Spain. The shared guise had and would conceal Gerda's work, helping to ensure that much of it was attributed to him. Gerda doesn't seem to have been someone to willingly accept erasure. The photos from Almería were published with a rare distinction: 'Photos Capa et Taro'.

In a war taking up the young as recruits and casualties, Gerda and Capa still stood out. In the spring of 1937, they were twenty-six and twenty-three. Even their names were new. A Spanish journalist who met them early in the war described them, enchanted, as 'almost children'. He watched them embolden each other under fire with shouts of 'Forward!' They brought good looks and spirit and daring. Hardened soldiers were touched by the sight of them. An International Brigader who met them later that spring on the Segovia front recalled Gerda as 'petite with the charm and beauty of a child'. There were no safe distances with these two. 'This little girl', he concluded, 'was brave'.

Among the German exiles serving in the International Brigades, Gerda was particularly popular, able to chat in their shared language (she also spoke Spanish). Smart and extroverted, with her Marlene

Dietrich eyebrows and high spirits, she must have been a direct challenge to the deprivations of war. But she was also apparently uncompromising in her courage. She once insisted on a dash across dangerous ground in broad daylight simply to visit a Polish battalion that had caught her fancy. It all served her camera, ensuring subjects who trusted – and wanted to please – her.

The same thing happened with a mixed battalion headquartered near the village of Peñarroya. In this increasingly media-savvy war, it's clear that many soldiers learned to pose; that in quiet times they enjoyed the diversion of putting on a show. (This may have been part of what ultimately drove Gerda into greater risks to reach the authentic action.) When Capa showed up with a movie camera, the men recreated an attack for them. In an account left by the German commissar, the morale boost from the attention is obvious. There was also the sight of Gerda, turning up at their headquarters in trousers and a beret over 'beautiful strawberry blonde hair', bearing a small revolver in her belt; his comrades surging towards the sound of her laughter.

★

They build a compelling picture, these sightings of Gerda: a young woman who was equal parts charm and hard-headed courage. A young woman whose person and image were her anti-fascist contribution. There's so much that goes unsaid. Gerda left almost nothing behind in writing – no diaries, no notes, only the odd letter saved by friends – a gap that presents its own question about the limits of that compulsive practice.

Somewhere along the way, Gerda acquired the nickname 'little red fox': possibly deriving from a not-entirely-appreciative designation by a former employer, a woman who ran a photo agency in Paris and didn't much like her; it may even have been a posthumous invention. But it kept recurring for me, that image. Gerda darting along the front. Gerda as an elusive, quick and quick-witted creature, always at the distance of a camera lens.

On another of their joint expeditions, Gerda was in Valencia with Capa to photograph the funeral of General Lukács, a popular

Republican leader who had been killed in recent shelling. Her shots
are unsurprisingly sombre – wounded-looking women holding massive floral arrangements and giving the clenched-fist salute; crowds
of intent and patient mourners – but for once someone else's pictures
seemed more interesting. By coincidence, another photographer had
caught Gerda in the crowd. In one of their pictures they are standing
right behind her: Gerda's neatly cropped hair is in the foreground,
her white neck bared, her camera raised to her eye. It shows her both
in her natural habitat and out of it, taking photos and caught in one.

There was a slight sense of impropriety, looking at these images:
as if I were disturbing someone at work. There should be a glorious
freedom when writing about the past, tracking and commentating
on people who can have no awareness of you whatsoever. But that
would be to misunderstand the way we interact with history (which-
ever direction it is going), the way generations ask something of each
other (*remember this, tell us how*), the way taking a photo is an implicit
acknowledgement of the relationship between the past and the future.
You press down that shutter and the death knell tolls on the moment.

Gerda was never some cute-canny fox caught in the headlights
of someone else's attention. She was doing her own looking. Her
photos are the story of what she wanted to contribute to the Republican 'Causa' and what she wanted from it. Gerda's biographer, Irme
Schaber, has pointed out how much of her film, in between visits to
the front, was given over to subjects for which 'editorial newsrooms
expressed little interest'. Not work to make your name, then (though
she would do plenty of that), but work that could be used in fundraising pamphlets and propaganda bulletins. She wanted to provide
evidence for the Non-Intervention Committee in London, proving
that Italy and Germany were breaking the international agreement.
And all that getting close, right into the ranks and into the action, was
about more than securing the most exciting picture. As Schaber also
notes, Gerda's parents were still in Germany: stripped of their assets,
forced into 'Jewish' housing and trying to secure visas for Palestine.
If this was a war against fascism, Gerda wasn't just documenting it,
she was in it.

The war dragged millions into its mire, but so often Gerda picks

out one individual, one small group to focus on. She worked to the demands of the moment: euphoric snaps of Barcelona, projecting the very self-confidence the Republic was going to need in the summer of 1936; regimented frames in March 1937 showing the new order of a new People's Army. But it's there in that single, kneeling *miliciana* on the beach in Barcelona, as if Gerda had trained her camera on another woman in a role so new it's like the world has gone brilliantly mad and said *see what one person can do.*

Comrades

Martha Gellhorn, Josephine Herbst, Gerda Taro

Madrid: spring 1937

After a few weeks in Madrid, Martha had taken on the airs of an old hand. The crush of company was starting to weigh on her. 'I find everything except the actively involved people very bad, and I have reached the state where human society is again trying for me,' she wrote in the diary. 'I am not a very good person.' She had begun to sort arrivals into camps: the serious and committed (like herself), and the tourists who arrived to see what war was like, perhaps intending to eventually write up a 'definitive' account based on forty-eight hours' experience and a Ministry of Information bulletin. The Spanish Republic had become a cause célèbre, and the spring of 1937 marked the peak of international visitors to the Loyalist zone. Not only reporters and volunteers were arriving, but sympathetic politicians, humanitarians, celebrities. Few stayed for long, but they all had to be housed and fed. At lunch on 3 April Martha complained that there 'was no more room at the table, due to influx of shits now that all is quiet'. The shits in question were a journalist couple called Seldes, a 'nice handsome dumb named Errol Flynn', and Josephine Herbst.

It was true that Josephine had arrived at a relatively quiet moment in the capital, and she herself would later condemn the superficiality of the press presence in Madrid (though there's a layer of hurt and pique in her complaints of finding herself one of many when she was used to being a lonely vanguard). Long, boozy evenings were being spent by journalists on the Gran Vía, in a basement restaurant reserved for those with the right passes. The novelist John Dos Passos described it as a stagey dive where the stock figures of wartime Madrid rubbed shoulders: 'the professional correspondents and the young world saviours and the members of foreign radical delegations. At the small tables in the alcoves there tend to be militiamen and internationals on sprees and a sprinkling of young ladies of the between the sheets brigade.'

Virginia Cowles remembered it slightly differently: a place 'always noisy and crowded and blue with smoke' where she often saw 'women crying and begging to be let in, but no one was allowed to enter without an official pass'.

The Hotel Florida, too, had its seedy side. Carousing went on into the early hours, since there was, after all, little hope of a full night's sleep. 'Quiet' had different connotations in a city with a daily schedule of bombardments from the nationalist trenches.

On 22 April, Josephine was wrenched from sleep at 6 a.m. by 'heavy thuds, shelling beginning, followed rapidly by crashes – house falling slam heavy as wall of water, voices in hall, doors opening, rising voices, more voices as shelling keeps up'. In the corridors, people were pouring towards the back rooms and basement for shelter. International Brigaders on leave, journalists, an extraordinary number of prostitutes weltered down in confusion. Josephine saw a waiter dragging out mattresses. She was shaking. She managed to pull on red socks and a dressing gown, and left her room. Martha, too, came out in her pyjamas: she'd thrown a coat on. Josephine saw her disappear with Virginia, managing 'semi-bravado laughter'. Dos Passos was in his bathrobe, but he had taken the time to shave: a soothing activity. Josephine tried to get a hold of herself, made another attempt at dressing. But this hotel could be the place she died. She hadn't come here to be killed, not at the Hotel Florida 'like a rat in a trap'. The noise was so loud it was almost physical; the shells right there with her. 'Front of hotel seems ripping off. Expect any moment terrible scream, falling rocks and plaster.' Some of them really were landing just outside, 'tearing up pavement, gashing Paramount theater' and spoiling its poster of Charlie Chaplin in *Modern Times*.

When she got out of her room again, Hemingway tried to check on her but she could barely speak. They all clung to courage by ordinary behaviour. They chatted, though Josephine wouldn't remember what was said. Antoine de Saint-Exupéry, future author of *The Little Prince*, who was there to report for *Paris-soir*, brought a courtly touch by bowing to each of the women who staggered past him. Josephine helped get a pot of coffee going. The shelling went on. When it finally subsided, she ventured outside with some of the others and found workmen already repairing the damage in the plaza. Without realising, and even if she did not feel it, she had passed Madrid's test of courage. 'Shall always remember how human you looked and acted', Dos Passos confided later.

But other types of exposure were always possible in the mayhem of the Hotel Florida nights. Ernest and Martha emerging into the chaos from the same bedroom, for instance.

Martha and Ernest in Spain

★

If anything, Josephine had been even less impressed by the sight of Martha Gellhorn than Martha had been to find her on the Gran Vía. If Martha's wariness towards Josephine had anything to do with the fact that Josephine had known Hemingway since the 1920s – legendary days when Martha was still in her teens – Josephine's hostility certainly had something to do with the fact that she knew Hemingway's wife. She regarded Martha, succinctly, as a 'pushing whore'.

In Madrid, Martha and Ernest's affair was soon common knowledge. Like Gerda, Martha had to find a way to pursue her career in a sphere where her partner had greater recognition. They had to negotiate the implications of their gender in wartime, and the implications of their relationships for themselves. Martha was a seasoned traveller and a recognised writer of talent, but in the supposedly masculine arena of war she was less certain of her credentials. On a walk to the Plaza de España the day after Josephine arrived, she listened without really following as Ernest explained the trench and street-barricade system. 'Myself jittery with lack of tobacco,' she noted down, 'and too many people and horribly worried about the writing.'

As an author, Hemingway had staked a claim to war; in Madrid, he staked a claim to Martha. This had irritations and advantages. On her first night at the Hotel Florida he had locked her in her room without telling her, leaving her trapped during an air raid. But his celebrity brought material benefits. None of the difficulties securing transport that Josephine and Langston Hughes would complain of arose for her: the government put two cars at Hemingway's disposal. Martha was too experienced not to appreciate the other ways in which 'belonging' to him could simplify her experience. 'When I was very young, alone and tempting, at the start of my travel career,' she wrote years later, in an unpublished article called 'On Travelling Alone', 'I thought men a blight. Men and boys, the lot. They interfered with my liberty of action.'

The liberties of male life had always attracted her. To a fellow author she had once written of her pity for women, because, she said, they were not free and had no way to make themselves free. Her native society tended to enforce that idea, so that certain attributes of a meaningful life, like freedom and agency, could not be conceived of as anything but male. 'I fairly writhe to think of how fine it would be if I had been a boy,' a young Josephine Herbst agreed. 'That was a huge mistake – I feel sure . . . As it is I'm a girl with the ambitions and aspirations of a boy.'

Gerda – conscious, like Martha, of her own physical attractiveness – felt the effect of her presence among soldiers to be part of her contribution. Hoping to boost morale, she seems to have offered the performance willingly; trying, through her youth and beauty and spirit, to share out her own resilience. (In that reductive, mistrustful way he often had with women, Hemingway reportedly described her as a 'femme fatale'.) Martha also sometimes offered femininity as a tonic; she returned to visit at least one wounded soldier she'd met in the hospitals, bringing camellias and allowing him to suspect that the gesture carried a meaning it didn't.

She, too, saw things in comradely terms. Describing a drive she spent silently fighting off the hands of an Italian commander in the International Brigades – silent so as not to embarrass his driver – she admitted: 'He spoiled it all, of course, in a desperate starved male way: but that can be forgotten as it is understood.' It was an understanding that had to be effortfully maintained. It spoiled, on some level, the idea that you were all comrades, that you would be recognised as comrades first and foremost. Perhaps it spoiled, too, any distinction Martha counted on at the Hotel Florida, where the female population was weighted heavily towards housekeeping staff and sex workers – a desire to distinguish herself that would suggest insecurity as an explanation for the dismissive remarks she made about some Spanish women in her notes.

Occasionally Martha and Gerda's distracting presence was not welcome at the front. Gerda liked to embed herself, wanting to spend enough time with soldiers, she told a colleague, to be able to 'understand them'. But in early May, an Italian commander suffered gallantly in sharing a room for a week with this 'petite, blonde, live wire in her dirty overalls': 'I can't wait for her to leave.'

In a deeply patriarchal country, the new visibility and assertiveness of women was perhaps one of the most revolutionary aspects of the Republican zone. And yet also one of its most precarious. Those *milicianas* Gerda had photographed were soon disarmed and relegated, deemed too upsetting a presence on the battlefield or in the morgue to be allowed, despite the fact that civilian women were dying in the thousands. Sylvia and Valentine had befriended a *miliciana* in Barcelona, a former 'shop-girl' who had proved herself in combat early in the war. Women in the militias were already being 'weeded out', as Sylvia put it, by the time they met. 'So now,' she had noted sardonically, 'though the Fascists have still a good chance of killing Ramona, she is likeliest to be shot in a captured town, or killed as a civilian in an air raid. To the Fascists this will make little difference, a worker dead is a worker dead to them. But it will make a considerable difference to Ramona, so proud in her uniform, wearing her forage cap so jauntily with the tassel dangling above her bright eyes.'

A short story Martha published in 1941 gives a sense of how slippery the position could be – how even in a war, with shells sailing over your head and rifles cracking, you can be imperilled by your gender. In 'A Sense of Direction' she imagines that back-seat encounter going further, luring her protagonist, a female correspondent, into a solitary encounter with an Italian 'Commandante' at the front with the hope of seeing something to write about there.

The correspondent knows, as soon as she arrives and her escorts disappear, laughing, that she has lost control of the situation. The land is beautiful and deserted. She could be anywhere; she could be somewhere safe. 'I was homesick for country like this, lovely gentle and quiet country, and for a quiet unimportant life where you had all the time you wanted to breathe and lie on your back watching the sky, where nothing tragic or harsh happened within your range of vision.'

Whatever she thinks about herself, her reasons for eschewing the quiet life, to the Commandante she is one very specific thing. Perhaps he thinks she has come to Spain to sleep with him, because when she comments on the shelling he asks with condescending encouragement, 'You are interested in the war?' She reminds him that she's a journalist, to which he responds, 'It is a long time since I have had an afternoon on a hillside with a woman.' She tries that polite, unacknowledging struggle, that careful balancing of tone: friendly but not encouraging. The hope is to hold out without giving offence; to not provoke him, to provoke nothing at all. She stays out of reach partly by making conversation. 'Why do you talk so much?' he says.

Later, after a tour of the trenches and dinner with his troops – scenes in which she recognises this man's courage and the mutual adoration between him and his men – she is again in a position of engineered aloneness with him, this time in the dark, this time possibly lost in enemy territory. Knowing the Commandante's poor sense of direction, one of the men had wanted to accompany them back to the car – 'I would walk very far ahead of you, Commandante' – and she had been keen for him to come along. 'Three, I thought, is a nice number at a war where there is an outstanding scarcity of women.'

In one sense Martha accepted this kind of scenario as par for the course: one of the many challenges she chose not to make a fuss about. But she recognised how freighted it was with wider truths about being a woman in a man's world. In the story, though the woman resists the commander, to do so she has to resist a compliant instinct within herself. Self-defence is followed immediately by guilt and then by pleading. 'I did not want to hurt him or spoil any picture he had of himself. Of the two of us he was the one who counted.'

As for a reporter, so for a woman: you are not the story. (Not unless a writer like Martha makes you one.) When Martha talked about her preference for the 'actively involved people', she was surely shunting herself out of significance as much as anyone else. But here her subject's admiration for the volunteers somehow dilutes the standards she holds them to.

In 'A Sense of Direction' the journalist is not impressed by the Commandante – she feels for him. She can see through him precisely because he cannot see her; because instead of comradeship he offers her only familiar male grandstanding. Even in safe surroundings, when they first meet, she chides herself for noticing his shortcomings: 'He did not catch on to jokes very well but he was extremely brave. His men loved him'.

On the way back to Madrid in the car, the journalist realises that the lasting outcome of this encounter will be a joke about how frightened she was in the trenches after dark. Irritating though that is for a woman who likes to parade her toughness, she understands it as an exchange: a consolation necessary to repair the damage done by her resistance. (Or, in another light, a small price to pay for avoiding something worse.) This, she sees, is a way of restoring the balance she upset, so that they end up where they started, where they have to be: brave man and frightened woman. She has discovered one of the shores beyond the revolution's limits.

This ingrained sense of sexual duty made it difficult for women; prodded at demeaning ideas about their contributions that even they sometimes struggled to disentangle. When Marion Merriman, a volunteer whose husband was an International Brigade commander admired by Ernest, was propositioned by soldiers who explained her political duties to her in sexual terms, she gave them short shrift. Yet when she was raped by an officer and decided to keep the secret, his crime became her sacrifice for the cause: 'This is a war, I told myself. Men are dying and maimed. This is my burden.' This was why the forty-five-year-old Josephine Herbst could berate herself for refusing the advances of soldiers: men 'about to die', as she put it, to whom 'she could not give . . . what she had given to so many'. This was why, negotiating a way out of the sexual danger he represents, Martha's character is just as worried about hurting the Commandante as she is about the hurt he may inflict on her.

★

That camaraderie could operate differently across gender lines was a fact well known to Josephine Herbst. She might not have had more familiarity with war than Martha, but she was steeped in American radicalism and she knew that closed doors could be found in the most open male minds. Take the acerbic account she gave in 1931 to the short story writer Katherine Anne Porter, of conversations their friends were having on the most important matters of the day: 'the Scottsboro case, the miners strike and Revolution'. Or rather, the account is not exactly of the conversations themselves, because Josephine was not privy to them:

> a few gents, including Herr Hermann [her husband] and some of our well-known talk-it-overs . . . decided to meet to talk things over, over beer, as you might know. I, being also an ardent talk-it-over longed to partake of this wordy feast, in fact showed a good deal of longing for same, but [received] the usual masculine retort, such as we well know . . . the same gentle stay-in-your-place which may or may not be the home . . . Mister Herrmann departed for thence full of a masculine importance you and I will never know, alas, and came back somewhat boozy but so far as I could see with not one idea the smarter.

When further sessions failed to produce solutions to weighty problems, Josephine ventured to her husband that 'as long as the gents had bourgeois reactions to women they would probably never rise very high in the revolutionary conversations'. Sadly, 'said remarks rolled off like water.'

John and Josephine had originally planned a union that bolted the confines of conventional marriage. 'It will be an even race between us or nothing,' she'd warned him in 1925. They'd met the year before in the Parisian haunts where she got to know Hemingway. Back then, John had all the good looks and easy charm of a favoured son. If anything, he and Ernest were the more compatible of the three: close in age – twenty-three and twenty-four respectively – with shared boyish loves of fishing, sailing and drinking. Josephine had more of the reserve and edge of a person accustomed to struggle. Still, she talked and partied with the best of them. 'I had quite forgotten what young love was,' she told a friend. She was thirty-two but passing as twenty-seven.

Before Paris, Josephine had arrived in New York from Iowa, via the University of California at Berkeley, in 1919: the year the American Communist Party was founded. 'The more I see of the poor – of the underlying population', Josephine told her mother that year, 'the more I believe in revolution and the class war.' But it's not as if she were seeing the poor for the first time when she joined a rally for striking coal- and steelworkers in Madison Square Garden. Her family had long eyed poverty from its quicksand edges. In the city she had her own difficulties: never warm in the winter, never not worrying about how to pay her bills.

Josephine and her youngest sister, Helen, shared a joke that was not a joke about the Herbst family luck, which was something closer to a curse. Their father, William, had retired from selling farm implements on the road to establish a store and stay closer to his wife and four daughters. The business never thrived. It took Josephine two years after high school to save enough money to leave home for university, and even that was a compromise on her real dream to go out of state: she chose the University of Iowa because by staying she could keep her expenses under $200 a year. Before long she was back in Sioux City anyway, because her father's business had failed and her parents needed her.

William found work as a watchman at a warehouse and his two youngest daughters kept alive their hopes of graduating by saving and studying in increments, alternating between coming home and finding jobs away. Both sisters planned to be writers, but most of all, in those early stunted days, they planned to live as much and as boldly as possible. As escape was deferred and deferred again, it became a threadbare ambition, sustained in part by their solidarity, their unwavering belief in the other's superior talent. (There were times when Josephine postponed her own returns to college in order to fund Helen's.) It took Josephine eight years to get her degree; Helen never managed it.

Taking a room in Greenwich Village when she finally made it to New York, working by day for a charity in the Bronx and nights as a bookseller, Josephine stole time for her twin obsessions: literature and revolution. In 1920, two of her stories were published in *The Smart Set*, that magazine of the Jazz Age which had recently launched the career of F. Scott Fitzgerald. She fell in with what her biographer would later describe as 'a shifting population of independent young women . . . artists, actresses and radicals who attracted into their bohemian quarters an equally shifting population of some of the most engaging men in America, including almost the entire mastheads of *The Masses* and *The Liberator*'.

Another stomping ground was the home of 'a Russian-born American socialist who was a semi-official representative of the Bolshevik government'. This, surely, was what she had struck out to New York for: this highly strung, somewhat secretive, intensely feeling scene, where sex mattered more than marriage, workers debated with writers, and revolution had a hand in everything.

And yet this period of triumphant New Woman independence had a brutally short lifespan. Josephine was convinced by her married lover to have an abortion she bitterly regretted. Then Helen wrote asking for help: she had fallen pregnant and wanted a termination. 'Tell me if you know anything,' she begged. But Josephine didn't tell. Possibly because Helen was staying with their parents and Josephine suspected their mother would read the letters, she sent supportive messages and advice gathered from 'friends' instead, never describing the knowledge she'd gained by painful experience. Not that she would necessarily have counselled against abortion if they could have spoken freely: later she said she would have discouraged her sister if only 'it hadn't been successful with me'. Helen found a back-street abortionist herself, developed an infection and died.

Life after that became very hard. 'It seems to me as if my sister's ashes cover the wide world and everything looks grey,' Josephine told a friend. Years later she was still protesting this injustice: that poverty and gender could combine to kill a woman. 'My sister was as lovely a woman as you'll ever see,' she wrote once to John, who never met her. 'She wanted children and life and all she got was death.'

In January 1921, Josephine spent two weeks in a sanatorium recovering from 'nervous exhaustion'; later in the year she was suffering from palpitations so severe that a doctor warned her to expect a life of invalidism. The way she saw it, she had two options: suicide or going to Europe.

By the spring of 1922 she had saved enough money for a ticket on a Cunard liner. More than two years away from home: Germany, Italy, France. On $20 a month she was rich enough to live in Berlin with the abandon she needed: to treat herself to spas and operas, to sleep around, and write. She produced an autobiographical novel distinguished by a visceral description of an abortion. In it, her protagonist waits for the abortionist to begin and realises that she has never read a literary treatment of what she is about to endure. Then she is distracted by the pain.

I thought of this when I learned that – like Josephine – Jessica Mitford and Martha Gellhorn both had abortions long before they were legalised; that Nancy Cunard almost died at twenty-four from an infection that may well have been the result of an illicit termination. Josephine was almost always writing memoir. 'For me the experience of life and the experience of writing are hard to separate,' she explained. What was part of life was rightfully part of literature, there to be dignified and to be resisted. Given the risk of prosecution, Josephine can hardly have expected the novel to be published. She wrote it because she needed to. It was as if, she told a friend, 'at last I'd found a lover who knew all and understood all'.

It seemed telling to me that in the sparsely furnished apartment they took on lower Fifth Avenue after their return from Europe in 1924, three rooms and six floors up, John and Josephine managed to have six chairs about a round table; and that those chairs were the first thing she would list when describing the place decades later. Josephine enjoyed company and she enjoyed making homes to house it. In those days, on the basis of the book they had with them, you could strike up a conversation with a stranger that would carry you through the night, 'overflowing from the speakeasy to the street, from the street to someone's room, to pitch you finally into a dawn exhilarated, oddly at peace', content because this was the life you had promised yourself.

New York was a sharp return to reality. 'If the country was in high-gear prosperity,' Josephine wrote later, 'none of the young people we knew were sharing it.' She got a job investigating working condi-tions for women in laundries and worked as a reader for a publisher of pulp magazines (you needed bootleg gin just to get through the day). When they were desperate for cash, John took to the road as a salesman for a publishing company. That was a punishing way to live. They exchanged loving letters marred by squabbles over money; his exhaustion, her loneliness. Sometimes Josephine mourned the people they could have been if only given a chance, if only life hadn't made itself so difficult. 'I should be wise and gay and wholesome,' she told him, 'and I am only so tired and really ill'.

She published novels in 1928 and 1929; again in 1933 and 1934. On the publication of *Pity Is Not Enough* (1933), the reviewer at the *Herald Tribune* described her as 'one of the few important women novelists'. By the time of its sequel the following year, he was ready to drop the qualifier. She had become 'one of the few major novelists in America today'. Yet in 1927, after six years of imprisonment and international campaigning on their behalf, the Italian anarchists Nicola Sacco and Bartolomeo Vanzetti had been executed in Boston on dubious convictions of murder. Josephine had been following their appeals and had hoped for a last-minute reprieve. Instead, the lights went out at the prison and, for her, on a 1920s in which fiction could be the primary thing.

When that high-gear prosperity collapsed into the Depression, not many people were buying books. John and Josephine got involved in the radical farm movement. They had moved to Pennsylvania, where neighbours were going under, losing their farms and struggling to feed their children. But after John joined the Communist Party and more or less abandoned writing for increasingly secret work as a courier and organiser, Josephine's presence was understood all too often in relation to her husband. And the party's priorities were not always her own. As she had learned to her cost, oppression was never only economic, and yet the left-wing movement of which she was a part expected her to accept that the class struggle was the supreme challenge of their times, that the life of women was too far removed from anything that mattered to be of consequence.

John's entanglements pushed her further into the sidelines. Their marriage had always accommodated his infidelities; in 1932 it had also flexed briefly to allow for Josephine's affair with the painter Marion Greenwood before Josephine called it off for John's sake. But by the time she was reporting in Cuba in 1935, he was embroiled in a relationship with a woman determined to replace her.

This ceding of significance on so many fronts was so intense that Josephine began to experience it as an existential threat. Her rival's triumph became, for her, connected to all that is wrong with a world that rewards selfishness and greed. 'You're like the rich,' she accused John when he ignored her messages from Cuba, 'who say to the poor, what are you complaining about, you have bread to eat don't you, what more do you want.' In scraps and diatribes, writing itself became her retaliation against the blank indifference of that world. A world that – whether as the unfeeling behemoth of capitalism or the withdrawing husband – refuses to hear the cries of the desperate. Flinging out her letters from Havana, obsessing over them in a lonely hotel room, Josephine insisted on her right to signify. Or, as she put it in one of her abject, probably unsent notes to an already departed John: 'This is Josy trying to make her voice heard from hell to heaven.'

In Havana, Josephine had felt her perspective being limited by her personal pain: 'I pity this wretched island but it takes some strong well person to take care of it. Not me.' Yet those itinerant months of 1935 were her most significant as a journalist. Part of the reason she would go to Spain was in hope of 'an antidote to the poison' she had found in Nazi Germany two years before; Spain, she wrote later, would 'put iron into me at a moment when I needed iron'.

Josephine left for Madrid in 1937 without even securing a press commission. Her departure seems to have been one of those decisions that is so abruptly urgent that it is also inexplicable. 'Why do you write a book?' she wrote years later. 'Why do you fall in love? Because. It is the one conclusive answer that comes from the bottom of the well. Later you may dress it up with reasons; some of them may very well apply. But *because* is the soundest answer you can give to an imperative. I didn't even want to go to Spain. I had to. Because.'

Complications

Josephine Herbst

Madrid and its environs, Valencia, Barcelona: spring 1937

When Josephine first dragged her knapsack into the Hotel Florida, covered in dust from explosions in the street, she met with a warm welcome from Ernest Hemingway. But when, later, he reassured her that she had been a good wife to John, she couldn't help pointing out that Hadley (the wife Ernest had left for the wife he would leave for Martha) had been good to him too. Josephine liked and admired Ernest, held fond memories of him from France when he was 'modest, happy', but by now she approached him with a wary competitiveness. On holidays with him and Pauline in Key West, she had always disliked his tendency to goad and dominate the laid-back John. During one visit in 1931, when her marriage was already in troubled waters, he had got at John so unrelentingly that she threatened to take his gun and shoot him. That was apparently the way to handle him. William Pike, a doctor who met them both at the Hotel Florida, later described Josephine as the one person Hemingway never picked on. He even witnessed her intervening to stem the tide of his harangues against other people. Clearly her outward composure, despite the inner travails, rarely wavered. 'H[emingway] respected her for honesty, integrity and calm,' he wrote.

Always sensitive to perceived slights, in Spain Josephine dwelt on the feting of her old contemporary, and the cuckoo of the young, attractive Martha, as if they stood in for a marginalisation that felt more pronounced than ever. For her previous foreign reporting, she had gone where few others had thought or dared to venture – but everyone seemed to have come to Madrid. Arriving without a press assignment had been a serious misstep. It left her without an obvious justification for being there and made the labyrinthine process of securing passes more difficult. Josephine was not entrenched anywhere: she did not have the protections of marriage, she belonged to the radical Left but was not a member of the Communist Party; as her agent would testily remind her, the liberal press she wrote for could not compete in advertising and thus in fees with mass magazines like *Collier's*.

In Cuba she had regretted the endless precarity of her life; the always working for a pittance, the inability to fund security: 'I could . . . be saner if I had not been working so long and continuously for so little'. Why had she done it? What difference had her unpaid articles about struggling farmers made, her reporting on a shoestring? 'I feel as if I would never write again and I think it is all nonsense about it being good for a writer. It is not.'

What grated about Martha was that she appeared too status-conscious, too good at networking: things which smacked of insincerity. Josephine doubted her feelings for Ernest were genuine and found the younger woman pushy, which seems a strange thing for a person of her politics to resent. But it was all of a piece with her impression of Madrid. 'Hate this quality too prevalent here,' she jotted down, 'catering to Somebodies.'

This reverence for celebrity and the idle jostling in Madrid bothered Josephine beyond her own sense of insignificance. She was shamed by her purposelessness, embarrassed by her terror during bombardments, frustrated by her immobility. Without somewhere to write for, she questioned her right to be there, consuming scarce Spanish resources. But she also felt that much of the scene in Madrid was false and insular. It was an impression echoed by Arturo Barea, the open-minded head of Madrid's foreign press office, who later singled out Josephine and a friend of hers from this self-involved mass. 'Apart from some hard-working "veterans" of Madrid,' he recalled, 'such as George Seldes and Josephine Herbst, the foreign writers and journalists revolved in a circle of their own and an atmosphere of their own'.

In contrast to the situation in Franco's zone, the Republican authorities allowed foreign journalists a remarkable freedom of movement. Nor did Barea think the loyalist cause would be served by tight censorship: generally, foreigners were free to report what they wanted as long as they did not divulge military secrets or include inaccuracies. As Nancy Cunard had done, Martha travelled out of the city when she could to small towns and military encampments. This access did not ensure slavish praise for Republican efforts. Martha was outspoken about the lack of efficiency and the limited resources evident everywhere (when she was travelling with Ernest, they often paused so he could show young recruits how to hold and shoot their rifles), but to her these things only highlighted the soldiers' heroism.

Josephine wanted to get out of the city too and see something real, something she knew she was missing in Madrid. One day she came back to the hotel to find Hemingway's collaborators on the pro-Republican documentary film *The Spanish Earth* sitting in a car outside. They were heading out of the city and offered her a lift, so she got in without hesitating. In the hills above Morata de Tajuña, a village south-east of Madrid and close to the front at Jarama, she found what she'd been looking for.

As she would later tell it, Josephine was dropped off at a house where two soldiers were peeling potatoes at a giant kitchen table, so she joined in the peeling and waited for something to happen. Gratifyingly, the men recognised her name from her Cuban reporting. They were wearing the 'cinnamon-colored' uniform of the International Brigades; she knew that the Abraham Lincoln Brigade had suffered massive losses, including hundreds of Americans, in recent fighting in the Tajuña valley. Eventually a man arrived to take her to the general in command nearby. The general gave her permission to visit the front. She was also offered accommodation at a café in the village if she wanted to stay for a few days: a place to embed herself.

To reach the dugout, Josephine and her guide had to cross a dangerous stretch of open ground with a view out over Morata. From there she could see the church and town hall, a man ploughing in the distance, olive orchards and vineyards crowding the hills. She recorded the damaged landscape, marked by skirmishes: the wounded olive trees, the absence of birds, the 'ground itself [with] little plowed-up runnels that burst now and then into star-shaped pockets'. It was a scene she pieced together in snatches. You had to move quickly to get across, and focus on nothing but your objective, not the distant sound of machine-gun fire, not the odd bullet whistling past your body. Up on the hilltop, as she came to know, the earth was often 'streaked with the slime of dead things'.

The men she reached had been at the front for sixty days and were primed for an attack that was anticipated at any moment. Only the background danger of sniping from enemy lines punctuated the waiting. 'Someone gets it every day or so,' Josephine was told later. 'Just a nick here, a nick there.' She was a welcome distraction.

Josephine was sensitive to the fact that foreign visitors – whether soldiers or journalists – could be a mixed blessing for villagers, whose reactions were sometimes more ambivalent than was generally acknowledged. She was aware that the antics at the Hotel Florida wouldn't endear them to everyone. Some Spaniards, she told a scholar years later, 'thought we were pretty ridiculous and just fornicating the time away': an image unflattering in the extreme given the suffering the war was causing within the Spanish population. Yet she put some hostility down to a pride she deeply admired: that the Spanish might 'hate outsiders if they seem to need them'. Particularly conscious of the fact that she was sharing meals with people struggling to get by, she did what she could to fit in around Morata. She sketched portraits for the children and collected twigs for cooking fires with the wife of the local mayor (who was away with the army). She was useful in other ways, too. When Dr Pike encountered resistance to typhoid inoculations in the British and Polish sections, he enlisted Josephine, hoping a woman's presence would shame the objectors into compliance. Instead, she heard them out and talked them round, saving innumerable lives when an epidemic swept through the ranks.

Josephine came into her own. She enjoyed a reciprocal admiration with the volunteers; Pike was not the only veteran to remember her glowingly decades later. Walking along the trenches at Jarama, Josephine pressed every hand that reached out to her, 'and each hand', she noted, 'was different'. She accompanied the doctor to caves carved in ancient times into the mountains above Alcalá de Henares, the city of Cervantes, where local people had retreated from enemy planes, emerging each day to work the fields below. In caverns kept clean as

houses, she and Pike distributed supplies. The women crowded them
with welcome and he remembered Josephine passing 'among them
quietly, compassionately, a few words here, a touch on the shoulder
there'. She was moved by the community's exultation in a new baby,
born in the cave's dark recesses – and by the lingering fear that his
malnourished mother's milk would soon run out. The women were
holding this fort, as they were across the country, and their quotidian
heroism, its riposte to the prevalence of death, struck her unforget-
tably. 'They stood there so full of vigor and spirit, affirming life, that
I wonder where I shall ever see their like again. As one searches for
certain music heard once, so I know that I shall be looking for those
faces, or their like, the rest of my life.'

Interludes at the Hotel Florida began to feel more superficial than ever.
'I was in anguish in Spain, for so many reasons,' she wrote afterwards
to Barea's wife, Ilsa, 'and all that fluff in the Florida was in such contrast to the real thing going on outside.' Her 'Because' for travelling to
the Spanish war may have been partly to test her political mettle, but
it was also a test of the diffuse movement that had long inspired and
frustrated her; perhaps even a test of whether it existed at all. What
she had heard of the Republican struggle had suggested to her the slim
possibility that the revolution – the one kindled in Cuba, on farms in
Pennsylvania, in the hearts of prairie radicals in the Midwest – might
actually be underway: 'there were intimations of possible miracles in
Spain'.

Josephine identified with the people she encountered there, felt and
saw everything intensely, but its significance seems to have been overwhelming. She could not write. Out of her weeks in the country, she
produced only a few minor (and unpolitical) articles, and laboured for
the rest of her life on a memoir that did not appear until the 1960s and
even then only in parts. She described a disembodying turmoil, as if in
Spain she became merely a receptacle for impressions, or a pole around
which they 'came and went . . . sometimes swarming and buzzing'.

She had arrived still processing not only the disruptions in her own
life, but the disorienting experience of the decade so far. Trying to
explain her struggle in Spain years later, she described the 'confusions'

as both social and political. 'The thirties had come in like a hurricane. An entire young generation had been swept up in a violent protest' but had as yet established no satisfactory answers. In 1936, she was already warning against the pressure on 'writers of the left to chant the same song', a process she felt would bankrupt 'the intellectual integrity of the cultural movement'. As a writer, she felt both challenged and threatened; in the midst of a phenomenon she was not yet able to process. 'Politics had engulfed the world,' she explained years later, 'and might devour the writer too, but before he could recognise it as the dragon, he had to attempt to find the way to the lair.'

In May 1937, Gerda was in Valencia, while Capa headed to Bilbao without her to cover the threat to the north now that Franco had turned his attention away from Madrid. Aside from the dangers of travelling alone, in Paris Gerda had been warned against returning to Spain at all for this latest commission. Infighting had broken out on the Republican side – over military tactics and organisation but also over aims and ideology – and the rifts were so violent that her friendships with people linked to the losing party were enough to put her at risk.

It may have been her gregariousness that saved her from trouble. While her friends from home were anti-Stalinists – a dangerous thing to be now in Spain – her affiliations spanned the political divide. At the Alianza, the union of anti-fascist intellectuals where she stayed when she was in Madrid (and where she helped install a basic dark-room in one of the bathrooms), she was described by her host as one of their most popular guests. Perhaps her new employment by Nancy Cunard's former lover, Louis Aragon, for the Communist-run paper *Ce Soir* gave her a sense of security, too, though it wasn't enough to put her friends' minds at rest.

In the Republican alliance, the dark side of Soviet support was becoming apparent. Backed by NKVD agents, Communists were pursuing a policy of infiltration and manipulation, relying on Stalinist tactics to consolidate power and effect purges of opposition. Communism had never before been a significant force in Spanish politics and had never in peacetime rivalled the popularity of anarchism, but in the absence of other international allies the Republican leadership struggled to contain their influence. Early that month, in what became known as the 'Events of May', hostilities erupted on the streets of Barcelona, causing bloodshed among the Communists and their rivals: the anarchists and Trotskyist POUM. The anarchists were persuaded to stand down, and before long Communist aggressors were operating with an apparently free rein. They launched slur campaigns accusing their opponents of conspiring with Franco. The POUM was eventually outlawed and its leader, Andreu Nin, arrested in a wave of persecution. The Communists claimed that Nin was then rescued by Falangists; in fact he was tortured to death by NKVD operatives.

These divisions had much to do with why Josephine could never get a grip on what she thought about the Spanish war, why Morata de Tajuña and the 'collective enterprises' she visited in Catalonia gave her hope while the city power-centres depressed her. She also headed to Valencia that month; following, in a sense, the sources of her disquiet.

Josephine was far from alone in her confusion. The allegations against the POUM were so extreme that many helplessly assumed there must be something in them. When George Orwell – who had fought in a POUM militia and narrowly escaped arrest by Communists in Barcelona that May – sent Nancy a furious letter denouncing the Communist 'reign of terror' there, she uneasily assumed he had become 'a Trotsk[y]ist' and was out to 'damage . . . Spain'. By this point she had not been in Spain herself for months and, though she immediately sought more information about Orwell (whom she didn't know personally), his protest did not cause her to question her support of the Republic.

The merciless ascendancy of the Communists, paralleled by the secretive slaughter then underway in the USSR, caused some terrible collapses of faith in Republican quarters. Comrades in the US toed the party line in condemning the POUM, but, to Josephine, the matter was worryingly – suspiciously – opaque. 'There are many things in Spain that are far from simple', she wrote to the editor of the *New Masses* on her return. 'While I think there were crooks in the leadership of POUM I know honest men followed too. Why are these things not cleared up?'

For Josephine, for whom the role of literature was 'to make clarity out of obscurity, to clear a path in the jungle', the atmosphere of suspicion and distrust – the scrambling of truth – was so antithetical to what she had wanted to find in Spain as to be incapacitating. She identified with the anti-nationalist struggle as something she understood in her marrow as the revolt of the human spirit against the various forces that crush it; was seeking a force that went beyond the factionalism and theorising she knew from home, something purer and further-reaching and less well-defined. The political machinations that went on and the actual military considerations left her cold, and she was distrustful of the Communist emphasis on efficiency, on postponing the social revolution until after the war had been won. For her, she wrote years later, 'the war was a genuine revolutionary affair or it was nothing'.

Martha and Ernest frustrated her with their apparently unquestioning partisanship. By the time of the Events of May, they were already on their way back to the US, the footage for *The Spanish Earth* complete. Even so, Martha privately admitted to finding some Communists 'sinister folk and very very canny'. Ernest was certainly aware of shadowy executions and torture on the Republican side; Martha must have been too. Yet she made no mention of these things in her articles. Her silence suggests how taking sides demanded, for her, accepting allies without question – admitting to no doubts. When, like Martha, you decide truth means simply recounting what you've seen – without suppression and without invention – you summon, or perhaps evade, the question of where you've chosen to look.

For many sympathisers, it was hard not to let the promise of Republican Spain outweigh any reservations. There was, after all, enormous spending on education, huge transfers of land ownership, industrious child-welfare programmes, an anarchist Minister of Justice who could proclaim publicly, 'For the first time, let us admit here in Spain that the common criminal is not an enemy of society. He is more likely to be a victim of society.' The Communists officially shared the goal of reinstating Spanish democracy, so that supporting them did not have to mean supporting the idea of a new Soviet regime. Martha was not a woman to put her faith in ideologies, and the priority of defeating fascism remained always within her sights. If any reminder were needed, there were the 'irregularly broken' teeth and 'nailless pulp' for fingertips of the Gestapo victims in the International Brigades. For her, taking sides without equivocation was what made it bearable. As she had the hero of a story she wrote about Robert Capa explain a decade later, 'In a war you must hate somebody or love somebody, you must have a position or you cannot stand what goes on.'

The need for a united front against fascism seemed paramount; the news emanating from Barcelona unfathomable. Josephine discussed her confusion with a British correspondent who was similarly stumped. When he managed to secure a car to Valencia, still the seat of the government since its evacuation from Madrid, he invited her along to see if they could get to the bottom of things.

One of the last entries in Josephine's diary from Spain describes a stop on the road to Valencia, which she later included, slightly reworked, in her memoir. In it, she gets into conversation with a loyalist officer at a filling station, who remembers her from a visit she'd made to Guadalajara. Then a civilian hears them speaking Spanish and approaches. At first the man listens respectfully but soon he can't contain his curiosity. He peppers the officer with questions about Josephine, then listens some more, friendly and amazed. He can't resist a final intervention: 'But she understands everything!' he exclaims to the soldier. Yes, the soldier responds, a little dismissive, she is very clever, *'Muy inteligente.'* 'Brave,' the man corrects, *'muy valiente.'*

'But I was far from understanding everything,' Josephine remembered. 'About the most important questions, at that moment, I felt sickeningly at sea. As for being *valiente*, who wasn't? If I wrote it down in my journal, it was to put heart in myself, if only to say, Come now, be *muy inteligente*, be *valiente*. Just try.'

In Valencia, where the Communists were consolidating their advantage, she made notes on a mass meeting called to denounce the POUM. Diligently she recorded the accusation, but she got no closer to anything she could comprehend. *'Quotes,'* she wrote at the bottom of a page. 'Don't believe.' Moving on briefly to Barcelona, where barricades were still standing from the street fighting, she found nothing more illuminating.

At this point, unable to clear a path through the jungle, she took advantage of her proximity to France and left for Paris. She was exhausted, had lost twenty pounds, and told herself she would come back once she'd recuperated. She was wrong.

It was no relief to leave. In Toulouse, where her plane landed, Josephine sat in a café and sobbed. It would take years for her to understand what she had been mourning. She did not realise yet that her years of international reporting, of hope and faith, were almost over.

Sometimes it was very simple. On a country road one day, Josephine was pursued by a woman who wanted to show her a photograph of her son, killed at nineteen. Beyond her maternal pride ('why just look at his legs, did anyone ever see such height to a man'), she had a message for Josephine and, through her, the international community. Shaking her fist towards the enemy in the hills, 'Fascista, she says, malo. An old woman from the sidelines yells also, malo, malo. They want me to be very sure that the enemy is very wicked.'

That April on the French border, with news of the destruction of the Basque town Guernica rattling through the radio, Jessica Mitford had heard an 'old Basque woman' cry 'Allemanes! Criminales! Animales! Bestiales!'

And during Nancy Cunard's frustrating early days in Aragon, when she struggled to find a way to the front, she once squandered an entire morning on the road, hoping to hitch a lift somewhere. An old man approached her, shouting about fascism. He stamped hard on the ground, as if to say, 'one must stamp on it like this, like this!' Then he 'shot me a black look and asked if I had understood him. Yes,' she recalled afterwards, 'yes, I had understood, well understood. Yes, it was there, on the side of the road . . . that this old man appeared and gave the finest of all the many fine descriptions there have been, and will be, of Fascism in the world'.

In the force of these encounters, which never dissipated, was their vindication for taking a stand, for choosing a side despite its imperfections. One contribution Josephine was able to make in Madrid was to broadcast to the US over the radio. She spoke with pride of the American volunteers, celebrating what she believed, enviously, was their clarity of purpose. 'They walked out of [their] world, deliberately,' she said, '*knowing why they left.*' What she comprehended about these people, what she was drawn to, was that they were living in a way that had meaning according to their convictions; they were not blindly stumbling through a terrifying world that was not of their making, but moving with purpose towards one that was.

In Spain she encountered people convinced that the story of their sacrifices was as important as the sacrifices themselves. She felt they counted on her to preserve it. In her memoir she would fulfil her duty to the men in the trenches, who had asked her to 'please remember'. Her role became to convey their clarity, even if she was losing most of her own; to ensure that it remained intelligible across whatever divisions it had to travel.

Giving Away Secrets

Martha Gellhorn and Josephine Herbst

New York: spring, summer 1937

When Martha got back to New York in May, she found it difficult to be away from Spain. She found it difficult to speak of the war to people who hadn't been there and so surely couldn't understand how much it mattered. She found it difficult to be separated from what she cared about, and, as battles continued in her absence, to have bad news reach her from a distance. Leaving Spain only confirmed her need to be there. 'I do not know what one could do there,' she admitted to Hemingway in June, 'but surely that is the place to be.' She was learning her first lessons about the loneliness of a war reporter away from war, alienated by a world that doesn't tarry just because you know more than you did before. In only a few weeks, everything had changed for her: 'none of the old things are good, and none of the friends speak the old understandable language'.

But talking about Spain was exactly what she had committed herself to do, having signed up to give a series of lectures about the war. It was work that she found draining and in some way invasive, and she quickly began to question its value. 'I[t] is terribly hard to talk about Spain to those smooth uncomprehending faces,' she complained to Ernest. 'It is like giving away secrets.' How to convey things she believed had to be experienced to be comprehended? How to be worthy of the confidences of suffering and hope with which she had been entrusted? To Eleanor Roosevelt she said she persisted because she didn't know what else to do, because the memory of people who needed help dogged her whether she was useful to them or not. (And her influence was greater than she admitted. It was thanks to Martha's lobbying that she, Ernest and Joris Ivens were invited to the White House to screen *The Spanish Earth* that July.) 'I want to do a book on

Spain fast', she had announced to a friend on her return, 'and I want to go back.'

★

Perhaps the rush was partly to assuage the fact that she could leave at all – another of those inescapable distinctions she recognised, like writing of soldiers as a non-combatant; distinctions that could only be a defining feature of her experience of Spain. It put me in mind of an excursion she described once, one pleasant day when she and Hemingway took a break in a park because the shelling had lapsed. 'We were sick of the war,' she wrote. 'We had no right to be, since we were not the men in the trenches, nor were we the blind American in the hospital at Salices, nor the little Spaniard in the first-aid post near Jarama, who had no arm.'

Doing a book – going back. For all she involved herself, the escape valve of a foreign passport (what she would later call 'the great unfair advantage of choice') made the immediate stakes for Martha very different than they were for Spaniards, or for those members of the International Brigades who were already exiles from fascist countries.

Martha believed it was in the democracies' interests (in her own interests, then) to support the Republic, but her relative freedom suggested awkward questions about investment; ones, I was finding, that seemed to crop up, in different guises, with other marriages between writers and politics too. Going back was something, but without further work Hotel Florida life could be the kind of empty gesture Virginia Woolf dismissed soon afterwards in a different context as affording 'emotional relief' to the privileged trying to reach across classes 'without sacrificing middle-class capital, or sharing working-class experience'.

Virginia knew what it was to be one of those smooth, uncomprehending faces Martha hated. Listening to working-class women discuss problems that affected them ('questions of sanitation and education and wages') – something she had done over years of involvement with the Women's Co-operative Guild – she had found that the problem was the difficulty of escaping her own identity, her lack of personal investment in principles that mattered deeply to them. 'If every reform they demand was granted this very instant it would not touch one hair of my comfortable capitalistic head,' she wrote frankly, acknowledging her privilege. 'Hence my interest is merely altruistic. It is thin spread and moon coloured. There is no life blood or urgency about it.' Comforting though it might be to have the 'correct' emotional response to suffering (to those photos arriving from Madrid), as Josephine had declared with the title for the first volume of her trilogy: pity is not enough. This was surely the message embodied by the volunteers Martha admired in Spain, people for whom solidarity was an active position that couldn't be held from a distance.

Going back, then – even though she was not Spanish and could easily come home again. To deny the distinction would be to claim something that wasn't hers, which raised another question: where was the line between solidarity and shameless presumption, even appropriation?

For me, it was a question that brought Nancy Cunard to mind, overstepping in ways that have undermined so much of her work, emerging at the opposite pole from Virginia Woolf. It was a problem that seems not to have occurred to Nancy, but which should probably have absorbed more of her attention when she was planning the *Negro* anthology: how to offer service to a movement (or minority) whilst avoiding the fallacy that it is yours to hijack – or simply missing the point entirely. Nancy walked the line between solidarity and appropriation, and her wavering goes some way to explaining why her political efforts have been downplayed and often regarded with suspicion.

When people really care, she wrote once, 'the tragedies of suffering humanity become as their own'. It should be the kind of approach that makes for a better world. But this, and the work she did to shed so many of the trappings of her background, gave Nancy the idea that she could 'speak as if I were a Negro myself'. She was the type of white person who, as one scholar has put it, 'went to Harlem . . . with the pioneering idea that they could *volunteer* for blackness'. This was pioneering not least for its implication that 'race is a social construction and not an essential aspect of our being'. The denial of difference – a consoling approach for someone who preferred not to countenance the idea of benefiting from the status quo she condemned – became central to Nancy's version of solidarity.

It's one of the strange conundrums of a woman who so readily saw race and class intersect in the oppression she protested, that she could so disregard the implications of her own identity. She opposed racism because its injustice appalled her, yet by claiming blackness for herself she reneged somewhat on that perfectly sufficient reason – failed to recognise how racism operates, refused to admit to the reality of power and where it resides in this world. It's hard to look now at, say, the solarised photos (taken by Barbara Ker-Seymer) that she posed for in the late 1920s, which had the effect of making her skin look black, and take her seriously at all. The average Harlemite in the 1930s might have found the idea of Nancy speaking for them outrageous enough (if not entirely surprising); the idea of her speaking *as* one of them would surely have seemed not only laughable but grossly insulting. You could take your pick from a hopeless mix of reasons, none of which can be the whole story, to find an explanation for the more extreme aspects of her approach to solidarity: unrequited longing, sheer insensitivity, the impulse of a spoiled woman who liked to shock; some kind of statement about our common humanity and the labels we construct to deny it.

If Nancy seemed, as usual, to have posed problems rather than solving any, others had also grappled more intentionally with similar difficulties well before they reached Spain. As a middle-class intellectual and a Communist, Sylvia Townsend Warner had found there was a certain level of discomfort in protesting a state of affairs which, in class terms at least, was not particularly to her detriment. Early on in her membership of the party, she had written with half-embarrassed gratitude to a working-class comrade, thanking him for his welcome – despite her and Valentine coming 'from such a dubious quarter, middle-class homes and genteel upholstery' (a position of comfort not dissimilar from arriving in Spain as a non-combatant from a country at peace).

Yet she was still attuned to the way that she, like any individual, comprised a knot of identities that could not easily be delineated into oppressor/oppressed, privilege/disadvantage. In a lecture about 'Women as Writers' she gave specific attention to working-class female writers, using the platform to direct attention further down the scale of visibility. It prompted her into a kind of self-deprecation. 'It may well be that the half has not been told us', she warned: 'that unbridled masterpieces, daring innovations, epics, tragedies, works of general impropriety – all the things that so far women have signally failed to produce – have been socially, not sexually, debarred.'

Perhaps Sylvia's humility (she seems to dismiss her own fiction entirely) is a necessary part of solidarity. When I came across the South African poet William Plomer's acknowledgement that the *Negro* anthology's 'influence augmented other influences already at work' in the service of change, it occurred to me that he was describing exactly what an ally should aspire to: amplification of the cause and not the contributor.

Sometimes Nancy was a little clearer about where she stood. Describing a speech given by Langston Hughes in 1937, she wrote that he represented 'a most vital link between his people, who are of colour, and our own white world'. (Langston had more usually found himself in the position of representing and parsing African American culture for white well-wishers, as if the value of his work lay in this service it could provide for them, but he was open to more fruitful possibilities of cooperation, particularly as an aspect of radical politics.) Here Nancy saw them both as in-between people, kindred pilgrims beating a path across an ill-tended bridge. Poets like him, she went on, were 'building a road between, a road called Understanding'. Poets like her, too. Later that summer, sending Langston a copy of the article, Nancy claimed a place for herself on the same path, embracing him 'as a co-traveller on our one road'.

Maybe that's where the book Martha was trying to write came in. Imagination is often offered as a way of building bridges, of thinking a way out of prejudice or into compassion. Some of Nancy's dreamed-up ideas about Africa can make imagination feel like a red herring. Yet there's a moment in Virginia's novel *The Years*, whose completion had pushed her to the edge of breakdown in 1936, that made me think she also had at least some faith in that impulse of communication, that work that literature does.

The novel follows a family, the Pargiters, over several generations, but never really gets purchase on any of them. It is full of half-articulated thoughts and missed connections; of people feeling their way towards common understandings only to be swamped by conventional discourse and its superficial exchanges, by the sheer difficulty, in fact, of speaking openly – and of knowing how to express what it is one wants to say. But they keep trying. Perhaps the only real defence against tyranny *is* to keep trying. Peggy Pargiter, in a moment of opportunity with her brother, manages to convey 'only a little fragment' of what she intended. 'But . . . she felt relieved of some oppression; her heart thumped; the veins on her forehead stood out. She had not said it, but she had tried to say it.'

'I suddenly realise that I am not going to finish my book,' Martha confessed early in July. 'I can't even do it properly because it is really too close to me and I feel it all too hard and can't get away from it and look at it clearly.' Time away from Spain, necessary to write a book, was hard to justify when events there were so important. By August, she and Ernest had sailed back to Europe, travelling separately in an attempt at discretion. (Though her great unfair privileges meant they indulged in parties in Paris, and that she could steal some days alone on the coast, before they made their way back to Spain in September.) But before she left, there was the speaking to get through.

A crowd of thousands – 'young, enthusiastic, eager' – descended on Carnegie Hall that summer for the opening of the Second Congress of American Writers. It was still a Popular Front affair, backed and organised by the American Communist Party, but involving speakers selected by profile rather than strict political affiliation. Proceedings were dominated by the threat of international fascism.

Onstage, Martha sat among more than 350 delegates. Later, she gave a talk on 'The Writer Fighting in Spain', by which she meant not only the soldiers who wrote and the writers who fought, but also the journalists who took risks to cover the war. Her formulation rang with a kind of bravado (not only a habit of Hemingway's) that rebuked all those she was finding difficult to tolerate: anyone, in other words, who wasn't 'actively involved'. A true writer could not be an aloof intellectual. (Nor was it clear that they could be a woman.) 'A writer must also be a man of action now,' she announced. 'He is a man who has known where he belonged.' If not in Spain, a year might be spent with striking steelworkers or addressing 'the problems of racial prejudice'. 'If you should survive such action,' she promised, 'what you have to say about it afterwards is the truth, is necessary and real, and it will last.'

It's a position that is easy to ridicule (that dramatic 'if'), establishing stakes that writers could be forgiven for finding unjustified. Consider Dawn Powell's dry summation of Hemingway's speech: 'writers ought to all go to war and get killed and if they didn't they were a big sissy'. But Martha's was a high-stakes age, and it shows her at the same conclusions as Nancy Cunard and Simone Weil: that a writer must see and experience for herself, must ensure – as far as is possible – that she knows of what she writes.

Josephine had lingered in Europe until the end of June and did not attend the New York congress. 'Platform speaking never gave me much,' she claimed later, 'I need books and quietude.' Nevertheless, she managed her own round of speaking engagements on Spain, and experienced a similar disquiet to Martha's. '[I] have been so terrified at the indifference embedded in people,' she told Katherine Anne Porter in August, 'their inability to respond really, the kind of deadness.'

There was also the growing disenchantment between her and the Communist Party. She kept up a regular correspondence with people she had met in Spain and followed the news closely, but being of practical use was more challenging when the aid bodies were almost all organs of the party. Some of her relative silence in print was probably down to a reduced appetite for her work. *The Nation*, which had agreed to publish several pieces from her, only ever took one; Josephine blamed this partly on the fact that she wrote more positively about anarchist policies than Communist ones. 'There was one thing you couldn't do when you came back from Spain,' she observed much later. 'You couldn't begin to talk in terms of contradictions. Everyone I knew wanted the authoritative answer.'

When she did get back to the US, she headed straight to the writers' retreat at Yaddo before spending most of the rest of the year alone at her house in Erwinna in Bucks County, a place somewhere to the west of New York, in Pennsylvania. Erwinna mattered intensely to Josephine. She had made the enormous sacrifice of marrying (to please her father-in-law) in order to obtain it, and fought ferociously to keep it after her divorce. In a life that always skirted precarity, her possession of that home was some modicum of protection, its walls providing an ill-equipped ballast against an extremely uncertain income. By the end of her life, the cottage had become an apparently inseparable part of her story. Setting out on her research in the 1970s, Josephine's biographer was told over and over about an elderly lady 'poor and isolated [with] no plumbing in her old stone farmhouse'.

When I leafed through Josephine's files in the Beinecke Library at Yale University – a map of Spain, copies of International Brigade newspapers, studio photographs of antecedents – I lingered over several contact sheets of pictures of her in later life. They were taken in the well-tended garden at Erwinna. Josephine smokes, she talks, she raises her arms above her head, sits with legs crossed on the stone steps, listens with chin on fist; in almost an entire sheet of images she is apparently giving a tour of the shrubbery. The animated radical is there in the gestures, and in the background is the side of the house with its white fence.

The photos were taken in 1965, but I had also seen a snapshot of Erwinna from 1928, the year Josephine moved there with John. That photo seemed to have been taken in winter: the small trees in the foreground were bare, and the whole image has a bleak and lonely look. The house stands in an otherwise apparently uninhabited valley, a white stream beckoning at a bottom corner of the photo. It isn't visible, but a shaky cedar bridge once crossed the stream, chained on one side to a tree. It took John's carpentry skills and Josephine's determination to make their new home habitable, and they had no plumbing or electricity. In those days, Erwinna was remote and rural: the couple had a whole fifteen acres to themselves. Eventually friends alighted on houses nearby for seasons away from the city. The proximity to New York was both a blessing and a curse: by 1939, Josephine was complaining about Hollywood people ('the Dorothy Parkers') turning up and buying weekend getaways, spoiling the atmosphere. But Josephine and John had always found their wealthier neighbours useful: a ready source of cash when they were collecting funds for the poorer ones.

A few weeks before travelling to the US, idly googling, I had seen 'The Josephine Herbst House' listed for sale online. It was described as a 'Creekside Retreat' and priced at almost a million dollars. I thought of a scene in one of Josephine's novels, then, where she describes

impoverished Bucks County farming families returning to the old homesteads they had been forced to sell, just to marvel at the renovations by rich weekenders.

In the summer of 1937, Josephine went back to Erwinna, to the house where she would now live alone, and to the novel interrupted by her abrupt departure to Spain. In 1933 she had published the first volume of her monumental Trexler Trilogy, *Pity Is Not Enough*, and followed it swiftly with *The Executioner Waits* the following year. Now she settled down to complete the series with a book she would call *Rope of Gold*. Rather than picking up where she had left off, she began again. She wrote the novel, her biographer records, in 'the greatest [isolation] which she had ever so far experienced'. (She left Erwinna only at the end of the year to visit Washington, where she was among the leaders of a demonstration at the State Department protesting the arms embargo.) She did the opposite of Martha: she stuck with the book. 'If it weren't for my work,' she wrote later, 'and my own real absorption in it, I would have been swamped many times.'

Josephine's ambitions for the Trexler novels were at once intimate and grand: to pay tribute to her mother's people and to write a history of American society. Through this amalgam, she thought she could find a way to understand the age she was living in. At around the time *Pity Is Not Enough* was published, she had explained the trilogy to Katherine Anne Porter as an attempt to answer her own confusion, the same impulse that would later take her to Spain. 'I keep feeling in my own life this constant need for further interpretation of the present', she wrote, describing what she came to see as the chief contribution literature could make. As her plans for the trilogy fell into place, she had suddenly seen 'the whole business in a sort of span'. She knew how the books would unfold, and she saw that the life of her forebears spoke directly to her life in the twentieth century.

Josephine's mother, Mary Frey, came from Pennsylvania, which meant that the move to Erwinna had felt like a kind of homecoming. Mary had kept generations of Frey family documents hanging in sacks from the rafters of her house, and as a child Josephine had listened to them heave and sigh when the wind blew through the attic. Eventually they became the bedrock for *Pity Is Not Enough*, though the trilogy had its deepest roots in the family stories her mother had raised her on.

The trilogy is intensely personal, closely autobiographical. Explaining it, Josephine would later speak of the 'haunting history' of her family's 'natural decay and end', which seemed a sad and strange thing to say when she and two of her sisters were still alive (even if she was partly speaking in class terms). *Pity Is Not Enough* chronicled Mary Frey's penurious background and hard-working youth in post–Civil War America, while *The Executioner Waits* drew up to contemporary life, belonging to the two youngest daughters of Mary's fictional alter ego, Anne Wendel (née Trexler): Vicky ('a fierce creature who knew how to use her tongue') and Rosamond, who dies before the novel's end. When she returned to *Rope of Gold* in 1937, Josephine had outstripped her mother and was processing recent history at pace.

All of the struggle she knew and inherited went into the novels. The Trexler-Wendel family is never secure, and Anne Wendel is forever plotting ways to offer some little help to her spirited younger daughters as they painstakingly put themselves through college. Vicky makes her way to New York and eventually meets Jonathan Chance, her John Herrmann. By the end of the second novel their marriage is already in jeopardy, their early optimism beaten down by the reality of being poor.

Yet these individual lives are only part of the span, a reach that is both temporal and social. For Josephine, the Frey/Trexler inheritance gained significance only through its 'wider implication'. Reading the novels, I was struck by how much they draw into their scope. The breadth of cast and geography was bewildering. There are factory workers, anarchists, Communist Party organisers, ineffective liberals and sanctimonious bourgeoisie; there are movements like the Industrial Workers of the World, which Josephine remembered from her youth; there are strikes and farmers protesting foreclosures. Josephine used her Depression-era reporting as much as her personal history. After concentrating on the US in the first two novels, she began to work in lives in other countries, too: labourers in Cuba, soldiers in Spain. Characters emerge from the gloom of history only to subside back into it: people real and imagined, named and unnamed. The overwhelm of *Rope of Gold* began to seem like an expression of Josephine's state of mind that summer, though it might be more accurate to say that the range of the novel was her response to confusions that reached their peak in Spain. In returning to literature, with its potential to make clarity from obscurity, she was searching out a through line.

Writing, keeping in mind what she called 'a Marxian theory of class', allowed Josephine to bring it all together: wandering souls, isolated farming families, an unhappy female journalist, her wealthier relations and her long-dead ones – all can be seen in relation to one another. In her roving faithlessness (no one family, movement, era or town holds the floor for long) she admits the puniness of the individual and tries to bring into view what they cannot see.

Inspired by a Diego Rivera fresco she saw in Mexico – 'a sort of dual study . . . the big painting above and underneath the precise delineation of almost historical facts' – Josephine attempted a similar method for the Trexler novels. She wanted to show individuals paddling on a tide of history unfathomable to them, with trends and movements rolling on beneath, as imperceptible in their entirety as a great whale passing beside a tiny raft. For her, the past was ever present: creatively nourishing but also always at work in human life. As Vicky finds in *Rope of Gold*, it 'had a way of tolling like some bell'.

Josephine's heroes' chances lie in solidarity. Others know this before them and fear it. 'My God,' one government relief official thinks in *The Executioner Waits*, 'if they ever realized they were in the same boat, if they ever quit tearing at each other's throats, if the little storekeeper ever got it into his head that his friend, his only friend was the poor farmer, not the rich banker, where in hell would the system be then?'

As news emerged of the Moscow show trials and her faith in the Soviet Union faded, Josephine would claim (and this may have been a stretch) never to have been 'absorbed in organizations and only in politics so far as they were giving me some understanding of the world'. Nancy Cunard's belief in the special sensitivity of writers would have resonated with her. For Josephine, it meant being especially attuned to one's era, something she called 'a complete relationship between the writers and the situation'. That could never be anything but personal and political. This was why, as critics have noted, her trilogy maps out her own progression as much as history's: from the pessimism of her youth, to the convert's faith in radical organising, to Vicky's hard lessons – in politics and in love – about trying to build a future when you can't escape the spectral tolling of the past.

If, in 1937, Josephine was not yet writing much about Spain, she was in a sense writing about what Spain meant to her. The decline of her hopes for it was not the only difficulty. Remembering her response to the arts of the 1920s, she once recalled her 'longing for a still, small voice, for a spokesman not for the crash of breakers on the rock but for the currents, down under, that no eye could see'. Perhaps the cymbal clash of war and revolution in Spain – the explosive moment – was simply the wrong material for a writer who sought out the long rolling currents of history, who wanted to hear the whispers as much as the shouts they became.

Towards the end of the trilogy, a labour organiser called Steve Carson has helped occupy the plant where he works in Detroit. All the strife and disappointed hopes of the thousand pages before this seem to have culminated in one promising strike, one awakening of collective power. Carson rises early, his comrades still sleeping around him, and finds the scene beyond the windows quiet and snowy. 'This was what it was like,' he realises. 'Not like you thought, but like this. The excitement of it was churning inside him like watching a big newsreel of the world, like looking at a history of your own life.'

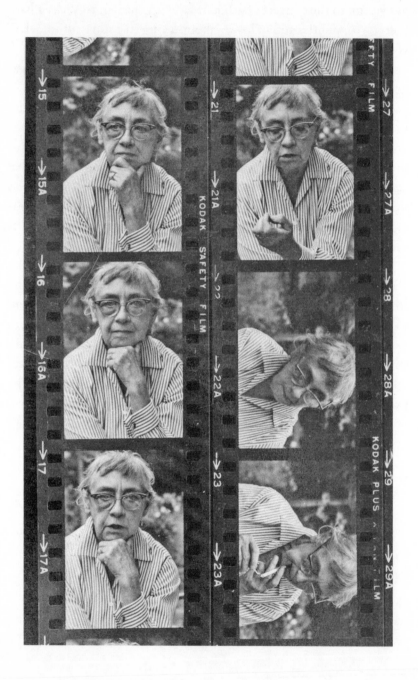

'The threat of war, irresponsibly conjured nearly a fortnight ago, still hovers over North China. Partial mobilization has been ordered in Japan . . . Japan's temper is warlike, and China will not yield beyond a certain point without offering at any rate the show of violence.'

'Sabre-Rattling', *The Times*, 22 July 1937

Merely a Writer

Virginia Woolf and Nan Green

London: spring, summer 1937

When Virginia Woolf's nephew Julian came to visit her – rang at her door on a day she was happy – she stood at the top of her stairs and sought to tease him. 'Who is that?' she boomed dolefully. The familiar, large-limbed figure 'started', she remembered later, '& laughed & I let him in'. Virginia was hoping for Leonard, the person with whom to share her treasure: she'd just come in carrying a copy of the *Evening Standard*, and in it a glowing review of her new novel, *The Years*. But Julian was a pleasant surprise. She hoped he would stay – invited him to – but he was visiting to ask for a telephone number and seemed disinclined to linger. Eventually she left him alone with the *Evening Standard* and went to find what he wanted. When she returned he was browsing a different page and made no mention of her triumph.

Virginia didn't press him to stay, although she wanted to. She wasn't good at making her fondness felt. She'd been a central figure all through his childhood, but there was awkwardness between them sometimes; tactless responses to his literary efforts that couldn't be undone. Now there was the Spanish Civil War. Julian was planning to join the International Brigades. His mother and aunt were trying urgently to stop him, both somehow convinced that if he went to Spain he would not come back.

When Virginia came to write this encounter down, the review of *The Years* sat at its unacknowledged heart; unmentioned by either of them and yet a matter of huge significance. Her labours over the novel had almost cost her her sanity. Publication had been postponed in 1936 – she couldn't face the proofs. Convinced the book was a failure, each piece of acclaim the next year was a stay of execution for her psyche. She had rallied, was revelling in her relief.

But Julian's response is significant too. Did he even notice the review was there? Virginia had left the paper open at the crucial page, but that's not what he was reading when she returned. At first she thought of drawing his attention to it – 'Look how I'm praised' – but then thought better of demanding recognition from a younger writer yet to receive his own. A novelist in her position ought not to need to do that. Besides, Julian may have seen the review and chosen not to comment. To him it might not have seemed important.

Here's a telling detail: in Virginia's recollection, Julian not only overlooks the review, he turns away from it – 'I think to the politics'. It is so symbolic of a debate between them that it is hard not to see a novelist's sense of order and meaning at work. Julian, flipping straight from literature – Virginia's domain – to the pages that matter.

In 1937, Julian was intent on picking his side. 'It's too late for democracy and reason and persuasion and writing to the New Statesman, and Virginia signing letters saying its all a pity,' he had written recently to his brother. 'The only real choices now are to submit or fight.' It wasn't that Virginia was entirely unsympathetic to Julian's position, or unaware that they were separated by history. She, like Nancy and Sylvia, had been a horrified witness to the First World War; he was a son of the 1930s, with poverty, decline and fascism on his mind. 'He says politics have got more & more on his conscience,' she noted in her diary. 'They're on the conscience of all his generation. So he can't be merely a poet, a writer. I see his dilemma.' There's a whiff of self-deprecating irony in that 'merely', that generous understanding, but it wasn't a dilemma Virginia denied. She just didn't see why he had to break his mother's heart and go to Spain. She could not accept war as an answer to anything.

On 22 June 1937, a trail of Spanish refugees passed through Tavistock Square. Bilbao had fallen and, in May, the British government – to the vociferous protest of the BUF – had grudgingly offered sanctuary to several thousand Basque children. Groups of them were still being handed around the country, indifferently welcomed. Perhaps some of the smartly dressed and sombre children Robert Capa had photographed on the Bilbao docks while Gerda was in Valencia were among them. Overheated from doing her shopping in June weather and black clothes, Virginia was on her way home when she saw them:

> Children trudging along; women in London cheap jackets with gay handkerchiefs on their heads, young men, & all carrying cheap cases, & bright blue enamel kettles, very large, & saucepans, filled I suppose with gifts from some Charity – a shuffling trudging procession, flying – impelled by machine guns in Spanish fields to trudge through Tavistock Sqre, along Gordon Square, then where?

It seemed to her that she was the only person on the street struck by their appearance. Perhaps it was their sheer incongruousness – seeming 'like a caravan in a desert' – that brought tears to her eyes while others went on unastonished. The memory she put down in her diary was a miniature flood of detail: colour displaced into London drabness; kettles and saucepans unmoored from homes and exposed in the street to scrutiny; one boy 'chatting' against the absorption of his companions; and people trudging, though they fly. Though Virginia could guess at what they'd come from (she'd seen the pictures), imagination failed her when it came to their destination. And curiously, though it was a little over two weeks since he had left for Spain, when she wrote about seeing them she did not mention Julian.

Two days later she was onstage at the Royal Albert Hall, trapped in the tailwind of the microphone so that the words from all the speeches rattled over her in duplicate. 'The last [meeting] I swear' she promised herself. Then again, she reported to a friend, 'they collected £1500 for the Basque children'.

All that was required of her at the fundraiser was her presence, her name on the flyers. So she sat for hours as speakers solicited donations. Pablo Picasso had let the organisers use a detail from his painting *Guernica* on the posters. The great Paul Robeson, whom the American papers had once baselessly claimed as a lover for Nancy, addressed the crowd. Rallying his audience, Robeson insisted, 'The artist must take sides. He must elect to fight for freedom or for slavery. [. . .] Again I say, the true artist cannot hold himself aloof.'

Yet somehow the evening failed to involve Virginia. She found the meeting 'all very stagey empty and unreal'. This was a problem she encountered frequently. The gesturing of life could not interest or convince her as much as life's murkier undercurrents within the mind. (She also fell prey to a Nancy-ian impulse when she exoticised Robeson's voice as redolent of the 'hot vapours of African forests': recording the sound rather than the content of his address.) 'I think action generally unreal', she told Stephen Spender, thanking him for his praise of *The Years*. 'Its the thing we do in the dark that is more real; the thing we do because peoples eyes are on us seems to me histrionic, small boyish'. Displays of involvement, such as Julian's decision to volunteer in Spain (Vanessa had at least managed to persuade him to go as a driver and not as a soldier), were difficult for her to comprehend, or perhaps she was simply reluctant to acknowledge them. Remarking on her nephew to Spender, she wrote only that she felt he was making 'a mistake'.

The thing we do in the dark. 'How I loathe the publishing of books,' she told a friend in the weeks before *The Years* came out. 'What I mind is being hooked & hauled to the surface when my natural dwelling is in the dark at the depths.' Virginia craved uninvaded space, both mental and temporal, where creativity could thrive uninterrupted and unobserved. When requests for her presence on committees and stages arrived, she reacted with instinctive resistance. She had refused to attend the First International Congress of Writers in Paris in 1935 because the interruption would cause 'a weeks misery' just when she was 'getting ahead' with *The Years*. She tried to swear off all socialising that offended the fertile dark ('I shall only pick up some exacerbating picture: I shall froth myself into sparklets').

In 1937, as everyone seemed to be at war or on stages talking about it, she was trying to concentrate on her next feminist tract, which finally had the name – *Three Guineas* – that it would keep. But there was the inarguable reality of the quiet caravan on Tavistock Square. There was the photographic evidence of what they'd fled. And that summer there was Julian, unseeable in Madrid, whose imperilment threatened to break through the 'magic bubble' of a new book surging.

That summer Nan Green was visited by Wogan Philipps, the good-looking, aristocratic painter husband of the novelist Rosamond

Lehmann. Wogan was one of the people in Spain Virginia Woolf had asked anxiously for news of, seeking potential allies among friends and acquaintances for dissuading Julian: Wogan had volunteered as an ambulance driver at the same time as George. They'd driven in the same convoy through France and worked the same battlefields in the same horrendous conditions.

Wogan had been wounded in the spring and invalided home. But he would have been of no use to Virginia – he still believed in the cause. He told Nan that what the Republican medical units were missing, apart from supplies and enough medics, was administrative personnel who could keep the whole thing running. He was visiting to persuade her of something she had begun to suspect herself: that she too should go to Spain.

Over the previous months, Nan had kept the family afloat. She got an office job which let her out early enough to meet Frances and Martin after school and, with babysitting help from her father-in-law, had been able to keep up with her responsibilities as branch secretary for the Communist Party. It was hard but she managed because she had to, and because she had comrades who helped her. Her pride in George filtered through the family. A local election came around, and a Conservative canvasser made the mistake of knocking on their door only to be dispatched by a six-year-old Frances, who told him: 'My Daddy has gone to Spain to fight the Fascists.' But the more Nan heard about what was happening in Spain, the more she wondered if home might not be where she was needed most.

The Congress

Sylvia Townsend Warner

Barcelona, Valencia, Madrid: summer 1937

The road from Valencia descended around hairpin bends beside precipitous drops, only to rise again balletically, taking travellers from one world to another. An embarrassment of orange groves and oleanders and roses growing where they pleased along the dusty road gave out at last to the plains around Madrid, 'a vast austere tableland' where corn was grown. In July 1937, while Martha was giving speeches in the US, Sylvia Townsend Warner wrote a description of the harvest underway in Spain. 'The reapers', she recorded, 'are too sunburned to look hot. Faces and bared arms are dark, shining with sweat they look like oiled wood. The men wear broad-brimmed straw hats, the women muffle their heads in thick kerchiefs, sometimes they have a white cloth bound over the mouth. This prevents the rasping straw dust from irritating the throat. The dust settles on faces and bared arms, the flies buzz . . .'

This was the first crop that would be harvested for the reapers and not for landlords. And yet, watching them, Sylvia saw men and women bound to long-learnt motions of ages: 'Subdued to this rhythm, working on under the heavy sun, the corn-dust flying, the flies buzzing, the beat of the swollen vein, the ache in the loins . . . to those who reap it can this harvest of 1937 seem so very different from the harvests of other years?'

After a year of war, how much had changed? That summer, finally back in Spain, she and Valentine had a chance to judge. Weeks after American writers gathered in New York, the Second International Congress of Writers for the Defence of Culture assembled two hundred delegates from at least twenty-six countries for sessions in Paris and, pointedly, in Republican Spain.

~

The American and International Writers' Congresses had both been
inaugurated in 1935, products of a mood of internationalism in the
arts. Writers nominated themselves as a new kind of public servant:
professional communicators preparing to take over where diplomats
had failed – literature at its most assertive. Delegates had debated the
role of the writer and of the individual in society, nations and cultures, creativity; as if, in the conscientious talking-through of ideas,
they could hold off the gathering threat, or at least demonstrate its
alternative.

As seemed to be the way, the International Congress had multi-
plied, leading to the establishment of the International Association of
Writers for the Defence of Culture, for which Sylvia would serve on
the executive committee; and, in Spain, the Alianza de Intelectuales
Antifascistas which was now running facilities in Madrid, Valencia,
Barcelona and Alicante. In 1935 it was agreed that the next International Congress would be held in two years' time, in Madrid. Despite the war, the Republican government reaffirmed its intention to
play host, turning the 1937 assembly into an opportunity for writers
to express their solidarity on Spanish soil.

Not all of their governments made it easy for them. When Sylvia
and Valentine applied for visas in England, they found themselves with
passports stamped NOT VALID FOR TRAVEL IN SPAIN instead. Sylvia was
disgusted to be told, with 'patience and firm serenity', that 'culture'
was not a 'valid reason' for travel. *Business*, on the other hand, most
emphatically was. They went to Portbou with forged documents.

The Congress opened in Valencia on 4 July. Sylvia and Valentine
were the only women in the British delegation. They were also a
little late.

After assembling in the drowsy heat of Portbou on 3 July, the delegates had to be transported more than five hundred kilometres along
the mountainous coastal road to Valencia. The British writers were
assigned a Rolls-Royce and a driver who was excited to show what
the car could do, which meant a journey not only arduous but terrifying, and not made any easier by the number of wrecked cars they
passed on the road. At Barcelona, less than halfway to the Congress,

his exhausted passengers accepted an invitation to spend the night at the Hotel Majestic instead of pressing on. When they finally reached their destination late the next day, they were rushed straight to the town hall where, in a chamber hung with the names of Republican martyrs, their session was already underway.

Over the next eight days, they would shuttle from Valencia to Madrid, and from Madrid back to Valencia and Barcelona, for a series of meetings, receptions and tours, before closing in Paris. Many speeches were given, songs sung, commemorations observed, resolutions and tributes made. There was eating, drinking and a certain amount of squabbling. For some of the attendees, doubts hovered about the point of it all.

Delegates could offer the Republic two coups: they could demonstrate to the outside world that the sympathy of prominent writers internationally lay heavily with the Republican side, and they could act as witnesses to the argument that the war was less a civil conflict than an assault on civilians. To Spaniards, and the Spanish writer-delegates, they hoped to offer the morale boost of solidarity.

As writers, they were not generally engaged in work with quantifiable effects; the impact of their presence in Spain was just as incalculable. But from inside an actual war the efficacy of thinking and talking may have showed itself a little differently than it had done in Paris two years before. Soldier-delegates like Josephine's friend Gustav Regler, who had attended the 1935 conference as a writer, put their efforts at a harsh perspective.

As they toured, feasting in hungry towns and receiving tribute, others asked themselves whether their presence was even appropriate. Some of the delegates clearly found themselves walking a narrow line – that tenuous division between types of looking: voyeurism on the one side, a vital act of acknowledgement on the other.

In the British delegation, the poet Stephen Spender, who had admired George Green earlier in the year, felt queasy about taking 'a luxury tour of a war-shattered country'. Strangely, though, he reserved his greatest hostility for Sylvia and Valentine, who appeared in his 1950s memoir under the contemptuous designation of 'a Communist lady writer, and her friend, a lady poet'. Sylvia, he sniped, 'looked like, and behaved like, a vicar's wife presiding over a tea party given on a vicarage lawn as large as the whole of Republican Spain'. He didn't like that she called everyone 'comrade', resented manipulations by which she got her way (that extra, delaying night in Barcelona was all her fault) and satirised Sylvia and Valentine's solicitude towards each other.

A clue about the source of his dislike can be found in an account he wrote shortly after the Congress, describing one of the few stimulating conversations he enjoyed there. With the French novelist André Malraux he had privately discussed politics and poetry. The environment, Malraux contended, shaped a poet's vocabulary. Spender explained this further: 'Set the poet in simple surroundings of the earth, the ox, the woman and the mountain, and the imagery suggested by this environment will recur in his poetry.' Sylvia understood that when a woman detaches herself from the landscape and reveals the ability to speak, it can be upsetting. Surprise becomes hostility. A woman, she noted once, 'must be kept within bounds'.

It's not hard to imagine that Spender was offended not by Valentine and Sylvia's manner with each other, but by their intimacy, or that his descriptions of Sylvia's manipulations were resentful accounts of her authority as a seasoned activist within the British Communist Party (it was Sylvia who had – at short notice – organised the British delegation to the Congress).

But he was also outraged by Sylvia and Valentine's refusal to acknowledge (in his presence) signs of internal Republican violence. Their loyalty certainly seemed to be not so much to the Republican side as to a certain faction within it. In a review written that year of new books about Spain, Valentine had adhered to the Communist Party accusations against the POUM with chilling precision, describing the POUM's 'convincingly Fascist appearance' in Barcelona: something she had not appeared to notice when witnessing an exhilarating POUM procession in 1936. Sylvia's fervour also remained entirely undimmed, despite the reality check of their return.

This was a different Spain from the one they had known nine months before. The palpable uptick of danger when they reached Madrid left

Valentine badly shaken. She watched bombers 'spitting and raging' over the street while 'snub-nosed chaser planes' pursued them in a pandemonium of engine noise. When she went outside afterwards, women were queuing for milk – women who must have been visible to the pilots firing. She was horrified by the damage Madrid had sustained. War was 'INFINITELY worse', she told a friend, than she had ever imagined. Weeks later, she would acknowledge that 'every day makes the [hoped-for] victory a lesser one, except for glory – for the country is bleeding and the people are dying'.

To Sylvia, the landscape seemed forbidding. Mountains preoccupied her: in her writing their outlines fall heavy on the people in their captivity; they rear, like creeping shadow-monsters, at the backs of injured soldiers; they guard her reapers with 'the watchfulness of tyrants'.

Yet she was clearly still under the country's spell, enchanted by the improbable improvisations and sheer magical fortune that seemed to keep life going in the Republican zone. ('Pieces of luggage mystically secured to the backs and bonnets of cars', for instance, that 'by a simple piece of twine remain there, floating serenely above any ordinary laws of gravity, over four hundred kilometres of impassioned road', or the 'elastic-sided streets' that seemed to expand as their car passed impassable trucks.) Reading her admiration for all she encountered, it's hard to tell whether Sylvia's enthusiasm could only be sustained by convincing herself she'd found perfection or if it simply made everything seem perfect. In the general frugality of her life, the main extravagance she allowed herself was in expression. And she held fast to the thrill of ideals, to an overarching right-side-of-history sense that coloured her entire outlook on the Republic. To use one of her own phrases, no 'middle-class idea of compromise' could be allowed to penetrate.

In *New Yorker* mode, she took proprietary pleasure in watching the delegates succumb to Spain's charms. They had all arrived severe and business-like, determined to prove that they weren't there on some glorified holiday, but began, irresistibly, to enjoy themselves. Sylvia was not insensitive to the possible dissonance of 'discussing questions of culture and humanism within earshot of the battle', as she described it, but found the delegates' reception on their travels affirming. What

pleased her most was to be met with cries of '*¡Viva los intelectuales!*' She
felt they were welcomed 'not as curiosities, not even as possible propa-
gandists, but as representatives of something . . . valued and understood'. For once she could exist as an intellectual 'without feeling the
usual embarrassment and defiant shrinking'.

Sylvia was aware of Spender's contempt and had plenty with which
to reciprocate. Perceiving his disillusionment with the Communist
Party, which to her demonstrated only a failure of commitment, she
suggested he be expelled before he beat them to it and left. In her
view, party membership had been detrimental to his work. This per-
turbed her. It mattered, she felt, 'if our methods are such as to damage
imaginative workers'. Unlike many in the party leadership (as Josephine had more astutely understood), Sylvia clearly believed writers
to be politically valuable by the quality of their work as much as for
their public profile.

At home Sylvia felt that the mistrust of the British ruling class
for culture – its dismissal of people like her as 'either genuine cranks
or affected ones' – filtered through society, preventing intellectuals
from taking up productive public roles. Worst of all, she feared people
who saw this ineffectiveness simply assumed 'that we are only a pack
of idlers'. But in Spain, refugees offered them a position of service.
As they had done with Josephine and Martha and Nancy, Valentine
recalled Spanish women 'telling us what we must write when we
returned, what we must say'.

Rather than question her place in Spain, Sylvia drew from their
welcome much-needed reassurance that she was not an interloper. It
mattered to her to demonstrate that literature belonged to everyone.
Pointedly she stated in a report that more than 4,000 soldiers had
reached the status of 'literate' during the single month of May, thanks
to the efforts of the Cultural Militia. If this wasn't self-evidently good,
'the clacking of typewriters' audible in the streets affirmed the need:
it came, she explained, from the public letter-writers' booths, where
people queued patiently to pay strangers to transcribe their messages
to loved ones because they could not write the words themselves.

★

In the novel Sylvia completed the following year, a local schoolhouse gains intense symbolic significance as the site of a last stand in a peasant rebellion. *After the Death of Don Juan* transplants the labourers she observed on progress around Spain to an eighteenth-century Andalusian village. The novel plays with the legend of the libertine Don Juan (as expressed in Mozart's opera *Don Giovanni* and in a play by Molière), keeping the opening premise more or less the same: while attempting to rape the virtuous virgin Doña Ana, Don Juan is interrupted by the lady's father, whom he murders. A statue is erected in the old man's memory and Don Juan, as disrespectful of death as he is of patriarchs, mockingly invites the figure to dine with him. His marble guest duly appears, calling on Don Juan to repent, and when he fails to do so Don Juan is dragged down into hell.

Sylvia's novel picks up jauntily in the aftermath, when a newly married Doña Ana insists that Don Saturno, Don Juan's father, must be informed of his son's demise. Reluctantly, her husband sets out with his new wife and a retinue of their servants for Don Juan's ancestral village of Tenorio Viejo. There, they are taken aback to find not only that Don Saturno is sceptical about the story, but that the entire community seems disinclined to grieve. The death of Don Juan, if it has happened, would be a blessing for everyone.

Describing the novel to Nancy Cunard, Sylvia called it, a little coyly, 'a parable, if you like the word, or an allegory or what you will, of the political chemistry of the Spanish War, with the Don Juan . . . developing as the Fascist of the piece'. She would also categorise the book as 'definitely a political novel – at least perhaps I should say it's a political fable'.

For years, the abject poverty of Tenorio Viejo has persisted because of the endless demands of funding Don Juan's lifestyle. The cost of all the raping and shopping and drinking has been borne by the peasants, and their over-cultivated, increasingly unyielding land. And yet, for the villagers of Tenorio Viejo, Don Juan is merely an emblem of the bondage that prevents their flourishing. Even if the Devil has taken him, one of them remarks, 'we shall not be rid of him . . . We have more on our backs than the son of Don Saturno.'

Literacy is closely bound up with resistance in *After the Death of Don Juan*. Don Saturno's visitors are shocked by his reforming indulgence towards his tenants; appalled to discover that he has allowed them a schoolhouse and that they can all read. ('How could the son of such a father escape damnation?' Doña Ana thinks.) He accepts the risk, that in 'time the arts of reading and writing will force them to realise the wretchedness of their state, and then to resent, and then, perhaps, to amend it'; he anticipates a 'hive of revolutionaries', and gets it.

In this, Sylvia was picking up a message insistently relayed by the Republic. After the Congress, Valentine would write an article about the instruction books distributed to soldiers, which ended with a letter of welcome from the Minister of Public Education. 'A new world opens in front of our eyes and your understandings,' he told them. 'This magnificent world we shall conquer if in one hand we hold the lesson-book and in the other the rifle with which we can guard our right to education'. Despite the horrors Valentine perceived, the compensations observed in Valencia had been thrilling:

> new men walk, new women people the streets,
> and children stoop over schoolbooks, having at last truth before them.

~

Though in a very different novel from *A Rope of Gold*, Sylvia, like Josephine, drew a connection between the past and the promising, imperilled present. To them, the Spanish war was not solely a stand against fascism but a class war: a rising of the oppressed, a collective that spanned not only continents but centuries. In contrast to many observers, Sylvia could admire the rural poor without idealising their condition. At home, she and Valentine kept themselves well informed: Valentine's investigation into declining living standards for rural workers, *Country Conditions*, had been published shortly after they got back from Barcelona in 1936. To Sylvia, the imagined villagers of Tenorio Viejo were noble but their circumstances were not, nor did their nobility derive from some untutored simplicity. They are allowed to strive for better – they verge on the entrepreneurial – and are allowed to resent their position. When Don Juan finally reappears, scuppering hopes for improved lives, the villagers refuse to accept him. Instead, they besiege the castle, triggering a rebellion.

The nobles summon the army and the rebels are slaughtered. As their enemies lay waste to the homes of their future widows, a few survivors gather in the schoolhouse. Defeat seems not to crush them. In this moment of crisis, of self-assertion, uncertainties have been swept away, leaving purpose and unity in their place. A hatred that, untapped, can only corrode impotently from within has been transformed into revolutionary momentum. A villager named Diego exults in the new collectivity, in a new substance to love and hate that Sylvia relished in Barcelona:

> The mistrust, the unsatisfied egoism which had tormented him all his life long had shrivelled and vanished. He felt secure in the love of his fellows, brotherly affection laced them all, living and dead, into a harmony where there was no compulsion, no bending of the individual from its true intonation. Secure in love, secure in hate. His hate was released and ran loose, beautiful in the sunlight, rejoicing like some wild animal loosed from a cage in which it would have grown unmuscular and scabby.

~

Sylvia had seen how a cause that transcends our self-absorption can, paradoxically, restore us to ourselves. She had seen it work for Valentine. Dulled and depressed by what Sylvia described as 'the rather parochial outlook of our Party visitors' in Dorset – but also by an inescapable awareness of her lesser recognition as a writer – Valentine was visibly revived by the Congress. 'Madrid', Sylvia observed, 'replaced her in herself.'

When she gave Valentine a copy of *After the Death of Don Juan*, Sylvia inscribed it with the novel's description of Ramon, a villager who is noted for the 'steadfastness by which he lived according to his creed'. A tribute to Valentine, this was also surely a tribute to their life together. Sylvia's love for Valentine had been revelatory, redirecting her life and redirecting her fiction. *Summer Will Show*, her chronicle of lesbian love set against the 1848 upheavals in Paris, had described a revolution of feeling as much as of politics. With this next novel she was striving for the next political step: a portrait of a collective rather than anything so individualistic as a personal emancipation.

In *After the Death of Don Juan*, Don Saturno's position as hostage to his son's extravagance has always exposed the limitations of his good intentions. If Don Juan is Sylvia's fascist, his father serves as the liberal who lacks a communist's ruthless intensity of purpose and so achieves nothing. This kind of ineffectiveness haunted Sylvia. In a speech she gave about the Spanish war, she warned that the conflict was a lesson for their age. 'On whether we learn that lesson or not,' she told her audience, 'depends whether this crusade will be a step towards victory or merely a period in which some of us make speeches and some of us make good resolutions.'

Sylvia was determined to put her fiction and her energies to work on behalf of others, but she never considered her own literary contribution sufficient. Instead, she took on all the relentless organisational and campaigning work that the Communist Party expected of its childless, unmarried, female members, and she remained ever aware of the voices that went unheard. (To a friend, she admitted the relief of the chores, sometimes: of going from interior struggles to external ones, facing practical setbacks instead of 'introspective disappointments'.)

Her chosen position as a writer of the Left required an uneasy balance between humility and self-belief. She counted herself out of the lives that mattered while weaponising her work because she believed it could make a difference. In finding the 'right' subjects, she had to tune her writing to other voices. But, rather than hesitating before the possibility of speaking for others, she relished her ability to roam. Asked once about the inconsistency of subject matter in her work, she protested by quoting Walt Whitman: 'Within me I contain millions!'

For Sylvia, a novel's success depended, at least in part, on the clarity of its message. There was no question of waiting for the muse to strike, or descending into the subconscious to resurface with your best work: for the right kind of creative combustion a writer must begin with an idea and a purpose. 'When the unequivocal statement matches itself to the predetermined thought and the creative impulse sets fire to them,' she declared, 'the quality we call immediacy results.'

That struck me. In the progression from *Summer Will Show* to *After the Death of Don Juan* it is possible to trace an author's political development, but I had been wondering if it was also a mark of something less organic – of the dictates of Communist literature, say, and whether those could have undermined her faith in her radical instincts. (Though if they did, there's enough comedy in the novel to stand testament to Sylvia's irrepressible sense of humour.) Reading Spender's disparagement, his snide noting of the lady novelist with her special lady poet friend, underlined just how radical was her writing about women who loved each other, women who recognised their responsibilities to the collective but also embraced similar freedoms for themselves. Sylvia knew through her own skin and soul how different kinds of liberty are often bound together. As much as we can speak on behalf of others – can lend our voices – she understood that there is no substitute for allowing people to speak for themselves. To deny a person the ability (or the platform) to do so is the real crime: the travesty of men and women queuing to have their letters written.

There is a photograph of Sylvia addressing the Congress on its opening night in Valencia. It catches her in the midst of speech: eyes half-closed behind round spectacles, mouth open, arms reaching out and down towards the table in front of her. She looks almost beatific. She is wearing a rumpled blouse with a frilly confection around the neck, her hair is pinned up in little coils; it's possible, likely even, that she is still in the outfit she wore on the sweltering drive from Barcelona. She looks tired, and something about her stance makes it seem as though her strength for the speech is coming from elsewhere.

Judging by the angle of the picture, Gerda must have been somewhere below Sylvia, rather close, looking up at her – watching the speech through her lens – waiting for the right moment to press the shutter down. Sylvia could hardly have failed to notice the slight figure taking pictures, part of the audience and not part of it. In the moment, she is facing straight ahead, lost in her message of salutations to the Spanish people, but perhaps at some point they caught each other's eye. Gerda must have been waiting for Sylvia to look her way.

Sylvia gave the speech in French, so Gerda would have had no

trouble following it. But the proceedings of the Congress did not hold
her attention for long. That night, rumours arose of a huge mobilisation outside Madrid and she was immediately diverted by finding a
way to the front.

Reckonings

Gerda Taro, Julian Bell, George Green

Brunete: summer 1937

Julian Bell knew something was up even before Gerda did. On 1 July, less than a month after he'd arrived, he wrote to his mother from Madrid: 'There is a sudden crisis here – at last – and rumours of an attack.' Having come to Spain to observe war, to learn from it, he was chafing to see action up close. The deficiencies of his unit had been getting to him. Even the open secret of the coming offensive seemed amateurish and risky. He was getting, he said, 'very angry over organization' – or rather, the lack of it. Yet it was all valuable experience for the political future he expected to have. Exhausted by the demanding work, surrounded by other ambulance drivers as tired and committed as he, he judged his days in Spain 'a better life than most I've led'.

Generally Republican morale was at this time perilously low. A series of defeats had punctured faith, and Communist infiltration was wrecking unity. Officers either joined the party or risked costing their men weapons, rations, even medical aid. Tactics shifted to align with a sly and aberrant logic intelligible only to those familiar with Soviet realities. Pockets of discontent had erupted within the International Brigades, where the unbending brutality of some commanders meant it was suicide to follow their orders and suicide to resist them. Volunteers, some of whom had expected a six-month tour, were finding themselves trapped.

When Madrid refused to fall, the nationalists had trained their might on the north and taken Bilbao in mid-June. Further losses in the Basque Country would be disastrous and so a diversion was planned at Brunete, a village twenty-five kilometres west of Madrid. The best of everything at the Republic's disposal would be thrown into the attack, in what was intended as a great display of Communist prowess.

Seventy thousand men, including all five International Brigades, were mustered alongside the largest concentration so far of tanks, guns and aircraft.

Troops and equipment were amassed in and around the Escorial, a vast sixteenth-century royal and monastic complex to the west of the city. Hospitals were established and, in one of the palace's imposing courtyards, a motor pool where the ambulances of the Medical Aid service would assemble. George Green was based at a field hospital in an abandoned monastery further down the hill. The hope was to break the stranglehold on Madrid – perhaps even mark the anniversary of the war with a turn in the Republic's favour.

The rumours reached Gerda in Valencia just before the Congress was due to move on to Madrid. As word spread, the press office was besieged with correspondents requesting passes to the capital. Gerda lodged her own appeal with style. Finding the woman who ran the office in Valencia overwhelmed, she left a bunch of flowers on her desk. 'I'm so sorry to worry you when you're so flustered and busy and tired,' she said in a note, 'but I must get to Madrid before the offensive is over.' There may not, officially, have been any such offensive, but Gerda got her pass to Madrid.

The Congress picked up in the capital on 6 July. Early the same morning, a Republican division attacked the nationalists at Villanueva de la Cañada, while another swung on towards Brunete. At the Madrid press office, Arturo Barea was allowed to tell clamouring correspondents nothing. There were no passes to the front.

The next afternoon, soldiers interrupted the Congress with sensational news: the Republicans had taken Brunete. The delegates' response was euphoric. Gerda stayed just long enough to photograph young men with captured nationalist standards on their bayonets, training her camera on their faces rather than the tattered fabric above them. Hardly jubilant, they look up almost anxiously, as if troubled by the responsibility of keeping it all aloft. More than anything, their expressions recall those more familiar images of Madrid, of people gazing into the skies 'not to see sun or stars', as Valentine put it, but in fear of planes.

The message at the Madrid press office stayed the same: no passes to the front. Gerda hailed a car anyway. She knew her way around by now and, more important, the soldiers knew her. This was what she, like Julian, had been waiting for. This was action. Capa had taken their film from the Congress's Valencia opening back to Paris to be developed, so the opportunity, and the risk, was all hers.

Having outstripped their comrades, the 11th Division of the Republican army waits at Brunete. The nationalists call their victory a lie but Gerda is there to provide the evidence: a photograph of Republican soldiers idling in front of a street sign, clear as day. A colleague watches her kneel in the dirt of the road, angling carefully to fit it in the frame: BRUNETE.

Later they pass a group of International Brigaders resting in a field, and stop to eat with them. In parting, they sing 'The Internationale', and he is moved by the sight of Gerda's 'tiny fist reach[ing] for the sky'.

The battle is so close to Madrid that the smoke and glare of its detonations can be seen from the city. Arturo Barea watches the 'dark, flashing cloud' and thinks of the Brunete he knows from childhood, of the 'dun-colored village' of mud walls and desolate fields being blown to pieces by 'clanking tanks and screaming bombs'. This is what the war comes down to for him: resisting the side that wants to keep 'all the Brunetes of my country arid, dry, dusty, and poor as they were'.

While the Congress continues, Gerda can split her time between the front and the delegates, and spends her nights at the Alianza, listening to the radio for the news and singing with friends for their spirits.

Valentine records the nationalist retaliation: 'heavy guns pump[ing] high explosives and incendiary shells into the heart of Madrid – destroying a hospital, wrecking houses, killing and burning women and children'. On the streets, Sylvia has another chance to admire Spanish women under fire, insisting again on their kindness and their fury. Beneath the strain, she will write, every woman she sees bears 'the same expression of indomitable concentrated rage. If you talk to them they are as friendly, as kind, as you please. But the moment they leave off talking this look of whitehot bad temper comes back. It was the most impressive thing I saw in Spain.'

By 10 July, the Congress has returned to Valencia, which means Gerda can focus her attentions on the battle. She is popular with soldiers and friendly with General Walter, the Polish commander of one of the International Divisions, which means she is well informed about where things are happening and able to get there.

The Escorial stands on an elevation, once a vantage point for royal and religious power. If they venture into the gardens in the evenings, the medical staff can watch lights flickering against the sky: anti-aircraft guns and villages on fire.

For all the early celebrations, the reality on the ground is desperate. From the beginning, nationalist resistance has been stronger than expected, and Republican soldiers are fighting against well-defended targets in the full force of the Spanish summer sun. The Escorial has been overwhelmed since the early hours of the first offensive. The morphine runs out. Flies descend. Staff are officially on twelve-hour shifts but in reality their work is endless.

George Green, temporarily without an ambulance, assists as an orderly. 'We work dourly,' he writes to Nan, 'saying hardly a word, cleaning out rooms, scrubbing, wiring, fixing lights in the theatres and in the triage downstairs'. In the theatre he finds himself acting as 'anaesthetist, all-in-wrestler, stage-manager, settler of disputes between sister and surgeon, selector of raw material from the triage, and secretary – and occasionally assistant surgeon in a consultation capacity when everybody else is too tired to use common sense'.

The nationalists have quickly rallied counter-attacks that cost thousands of lives and exhaust the International Brigades. On the Republican side, there is nowhere near enough water or ammunition. The tanks become furnaces. In the hard earth, it's difficult to dig trenches for shelter. By 11 July, the Republic has lost its initial air supremacy and a relentless bombing of its lines begins to do away with its armoured vehicles. When, on the following day, the German Condor Legion unleashes Messerschmitt Bf 109s, the sky is blackened with more than two hundred planes. The hospitals are among their targets.

Gerda is supposed to return to Paris but she decides to stay. She goes as close to the fighting as she can reach, small and quick, keen to seem fearless and to give exhausted soldiers an encouragement to be so. Lugging both her Leica and an Eyemo movie camera Capa left her – it comes with a heavy tripod, which is soon peppered with bullet holes – she goes recklessly far. There are photographs of the wounded being stretchered into ambulances, and if she was close to the ambulances, she was close to danger. The stretcher-bearers are running terrible risks; half of the British medical unit will be dead before this is over.

In trenches abandoned by the nationalists outside Villanueva de la Cañada, ambulance drivers like Julian catch moments of sleep when they can. They shelter there when enemy planes fly over – when they can. They are on an almost constant loop between first-aid stations at the front and the hospitals at the Escorial, and sometimes the planes trail them, firing. In a confusion of military traffic, they drive slowly through terrain with no cover. Often, they drive at night on damaged, unlit roads, keeping their passengers in jolting agony. At one point, George drives for eighteen hours without a break. Dust and smoke and the smell of bodies clog the air, and they are thirsty, always thirsty. George cannot see how he will survive.

A blistering stalemate sets in. Bodies, scattered liberally across the landscape, turn black and putrid in the sun. For a brief time, after his ambulance is blown up, Julian works as a stretcher-bearer, leading a team of thirty that tries to retrieve the dead in moments of relative quiet. It is unbearably hot.

The delegates of the Congress finish up in Valencia and are scheduled to complete proceedings in Paris with the colleagues who couldn't reach Spain. They cross the border in time for Bastille Day, on the 14th; Sylvia and Valentine march for hours through the streets of Paris in the parade. Nancy Cunard attends the Congress's French sessions, listening with particular admiration to Langston Hughes, who has come to France as one of the American delegates.

Given a lull at Brunete, Gerda permits herself a quick break in Paris with André. They spend Bastille Day with friends, then in the evening go up to Montmartre to while away some time in a little square beneath Sacré-Coeur. André, as Capa, has become a famous photographer thanks to his photos from Spain. Now Gerda's pictures from the early victory at Brunete are in *Ce Soir* and *Regards*, her credit beside them. *Regards* boasts of its fast-moving photographer, who scooped them the 'first and only images of the offensive'. She has made her name, and it isn't Robert Capa.

When she leaves again for Madrid, Gerda promises to return to Paris in ten days' time. Capa wants the two of them to go to China and cover the Sino-Japanese War, which is already pushing Spain off the front pages. Loving her fiercely, he believes he is the only one who can protect her from the dangers of war, by which he also means protecting her from herself. The prospect of China is irresistible. If he can secure them a commission, Gerda says she'll go with him.

Sylvia and Valentine get home on 16 July. Two days later, the British Medical Aid unit takes delivery of a new lorry, which means Julian has an ambulance again. Things are still quiet enough that morning for him to suggest driving out to fill some of the shell holes in the road, to make transporting the wounded easier. But that day is 18 July, the anniversary of the rebel uprising, and Franco has chosen it to launch a ferocious counter-attack.

As Republican troops battle desperately to hold off the nationalists, a relentless flow of casualties resumes, swamping the hospitals. George and Nan's comradeship means he spares her nothing. In a letter probably written during this time, he documents a harrowing, unceasing struggle. 'We worked for three days and nights with never more than two hours sleep and you can't imagine the tiredness of it', he says, 'and yet the feeling of being buoyed up by the knowledge that the triage is full of wounded men who depend on us . . . And Nan, we have some *awful* wounds. Some of them die on the operating table.'

He describes the fight in theatre to save the leg of a smashed-up man who lay unaided on a hillside for twelve hours before reaching hospital; and then, the next day, the fight to remove the leg before gangrene kills him, George watching the rot spread before his eyes on the operating table, disposing of the leg as fast as he can before the soldier comes round and sees it. He describes not being able to answer the man when asked, for a second time, if his leg can be saved. He describes the washhouse at the end of the garden, where the dead are left, and trying to comfort a nurse with 'the simple fundamentals that make us know with no blind faith, that if they kill every Communist and burn every book today and destroy the Soviet Union tomorrow that we shall still win, and the bargain made with the unborn sons of the sleepers in the wash-house will be kept, and we shall build a new world'.

All along, George wants Nan there: because the medical units are desperately understaffed and because he needs her. 'I want you in the night and in the day', he pleads, 'to work with and to sleep with and to wake with and to cry on and to comfort and be comforted by and to hold your hand and to lean on me sometimes at night if you feel like it and to love and to cherish. Please write and say you want all these things too, or come and tell me about them.' Nan reads the letters, feels she has a duty to go; torments herself with the thought of her own children and the ways that they need her too.

At the Escorial, an injured ambulance driver arrives so caked in mud that the doctor (a friend of his) doesn't, at first, see who it is. Julian is conscious, but he cannot survive the wound in his chest. He has a little lingering time to attempt a joke, mutter something in French that the doctor can't identify, and then he slips into a coma. In two days' time, Vanessa Bell will never be happy again.

Almost every day Gerda gets up early – the best for light – and heads to the front from the Alianza. On the Gran Vía she has a reputation now for getting close to the action, for raising morale. A respected American correspondent believes the Loyalist command are glad to have her there because the presence of someone who looks so young, so not-of-the-muck-of-war, reassures the men 'that things couldn't be as bad as all that. They usually were. Or worse.'

From 23 July, the nationalists are on the offensive. The following day they break through Republican lines and reach the edges of Brunete. Things begin to collapse. In one division, four hundred men are reportedly shot for fleeing. Throughout the campaign, desperate shortages have been compounded by problems of communication. At one hospital, a nurse counts twenty different nationalities. How are they all supposed to understand one another?

Commanders afraid to admit to failures have misled their own comrades. After crowing over exaggerated victories, the Republican command has pushed on at irreparable cost. Their flagship offensive will shortly end with a final gain of fifty square kilometres. For this they have sacrificed most of their armoured force and a third of the fighter aircraft deployed, and incurred 25,000 casualties. Which is to say, 25,000 soldiers killed or injured on one side alone.

Gerda gets news from Paris: *Life* magazine will send her and Capa to China. Capa is beside himself with excitement; in Madrid, Gerda tells everyone. The next day she calls on Ted Allan, a Canadian who trails her adoringly but has never yet accompanied her to the front. It is the last day before her return to France; she has an official car and a chauffeur. Does he want to come along?

The front is in tumult. Even Gerda's usually friendly contact General Walter orders them to leave immediately. But Gerda simply makes for a different trench and, while enemy planes fire and Allan cowers in the dirt, snaps photo after photo in a frenzy. In Allan's telling, she is almost crazed by adrenalin, convinced she is taking the photos of her life, vital in the midst of death. He isn't able to persuade her to leave until her film runs out.

On this day Franco will declare the battle over. Colonel von Richthofen, commander of Luftwaffe operations in the Condor Legion and a man not usually impressed with nationalist efforts, is satisfied with that day. 'Countless red casualties, which are already decomposing in the heat,' he will write in his diary. 'Everywhere shot-up tanks. A great sight!'

Gerda and Allan take to the road towards Villanueva de la Cañada, at first on foot and then atop a tank. The Republic is in retreat. Bodies line the verges. When they make it to Villanueva, they see a car transporting injured soldiers to the Escorial and leap onto the running boards. Around them, fields are burning. German planes appear again overhead, flying low and strafing the road; the driver fights to keep control of the car, which careens like a frightened animal. A Republican tank bears down out of nowhere, collides with them where Gerda is clinging. When Allan wakes at the side of the road, she is gone. At the hospital, conscious despite devastating injuries, she asks after her cameras.

The next morning, Gerda's hosts from the Alianza appear at the hospital in the Escorial at a run. They have been told that a young photographer has died there in the night, and that if her body is not identified and claimed, she will have to be buried in an unmarked grave, with all the many dead.

★

When Langston Hughes arrived at the Alianza in Valencia not long afterwards, he found it 'draped in mourning'. The 'body of Gerda Taro, young Hungarian photographer, was lying in state there'. In confusing her nationality, Langston was only replicating a common misunderstanding about Gerda – another assumption that twinned her with Capa. But in another sense, there was now no question about who she was. At the Madrid Alianza, militiamen had stood in a guard of honour over their 'little Hungarian heroine' while a stream of mourners filed past her makeshift coffin and Capa called frantically from Paris to find out why she had not arrived. It fell to Louis Aragon, in his role as editor at *Ce Soir*, to break the news. Then *Ce Soir* took over, preparing the stage for an enormous funeral in Paris – a mass rally of mourning – which would claim Gerda as a Communist martyr, despite the fact that she hadn't been a member of the party. A few days later, a long, slow procession passed through the streets to Père Lachaise Cemetery. Gerda's father had come from Yugoslavia, where her family had finally fled into exile, and found his grief paraded past the crowds. Capa was inconsolable.

Gerda was the first female photojournalist to be killed in action. Not an accolade she would have chosen for herself. First female photographer to get so close to combat; one of the pioneering photographers who changed forever how war was reported; an early opponent of fascism – she earned better ones. But, after a brief posthumous period of celebrity as an anti-fascist heroine, there weren't many others on offer. Some of her images from Spain became iconic, but her credit for them proved ephemeral. In the chaos of the first months of the war, it wasn't uncommon for photographers to entrust their rolls of film to any stranger who was headed out of the country and willing to take them. They were lucky if their pictures made it to a darkroom in Paris, to say nothing of getting a credit if they were published. Gerda and Capa often worked side by side, making it difficult to distinguish what they had each produced. In the relentless danger and dislocation of the years that followed, Capa – his fame only burgeoning with the Second World War – was hardly in a position to be the best custodian of her negatives or her reputation. Nor were there any other heirs to speak for her. Within a few years of Gerda's spectacular funeral, her whole family had disappeared, unmemorialised, into the Holocaust; murdered by the phenomenon she'd hoped would be repulsed in Spain.

Until her work began to be rediscovered in the 1990s, especially through the efforts of her biographer, Irme Schaber, Gerda was remembered, if at all, as the tragic, possibly politically fanatical, wife of the famous war photographer Robert Capa. 'Wife' was a misconception arising with Capa himself: probably one of those instinctive nudges that presses the record from the narrow line of fact out into the wider space of things-felt-to-be-true.

That Schaber could find anything at all about Gerda Taro when she began her research she put down to a same-old story: Gerda was 'in a relationship with a man who later became world famous; she was young and beautiful; and she died under tragic circumstances'. All things that are true; all adding up to so much less than the whole picture.

Looking for Salaria Kea, Part I

Salaria Kea was like Gerda, slipping into the record and out of it, her story in the hands of others. When I looked for her, I looked for a woman named Salaria Kea, or Kee, or O'Reilly. Or, as a high school mention of her had it, Sarah Lillie. Even more than Nancy Cunard, whose papers were eventually stomped into the ground by occupying Nazis, Salaria seemed destined to evade narrative consolidation. Certain records survive because they are deemed more worthy of preservation than others. On the uneven field of remembering, organisation, coherence and posthumous care are everything. Writers have at least this advantage over death and marginality. They are always heckling the unanswering face of history, leaving a trail for memory-gatherers. Salaria seems to have known this herself, since she made several attempts to wrest her story from propaganda-makers. But by that point they had laid down a version of such deceptive clarity – such easeful logic – that she had trouble making authenticity out of what was left.

The place I went to look was New York. It was New York where Salaria was living and working when she decided to volunteer in Spain, and it was in the Tamiment Library – a rusty-looking building on Washington Square – that my best chance of piecing her record together resided.

Salaria came from Akron, Ohio, but in 1937, aged twenty-three, she was working as a nurse at Harlem Hospital when she volunteered to join a medical unit headed for Europe. She left New York in March and became the only female African American nurse to volunteer in Spain. The Abraham Lincoln Brigade, made up of American volunteers, was already heavy with significance as the first integrated military unit in US history. Salaria, pictured with her thick nurse's cape flung proudly over her shoulder to show her AMB badge, became an icon of African American solidarity with Spain, and of the broad spectrum of causes associated with the Republican Causa. The communist and African American press alike ran stories about her; she appeared in at least two contemporary movies about the war. Yet the record of her time in Spain remains confused and confusing.

One of the first accounts I read was a propaganda pamphlet published by the 'Negro Committee to Aid Spain and the Medical Bureau and North American Committee to Aid Spanish Democracy' in 1938, which was devoted entirely to Salaria's story and seemed to rely on her personal testimony. This was the tale of one young woman's political awakening. ('Now she was learning to resist, to organize and change conditions. She emerged with a strong new feeling of group identity.') What drew me to the Tamiment, however, was evidence that Salaria had made several attempts to write her own memoirs of Spain independently. There was, for instance, *While Passing Through*: a sketch that was intended as part of a fuller autobiography, from which excerpts were published in the late 1980s. Four typewritten sheets, numbered six through nine, had been found in an archive in London and identified as part of an account that predated both the pamphlet and *While Passing Through*. (By the time I visited that library, those pages had disappeared.) In the files at the Tamiment, I would also find one of her friends reporting in the late 1960s that Salaria was studying with the famous poet Langston Hughes in order to put her memories down on paper. But my trip to New York clarified very little of this. Not only was this book apparently never completed, but the stories that Salaria did voice proved to be remarkably contentious.

Much of the detail of her life was hard to pin down. One article, from 2011, had her die in both 1990 and 1991; her birthday moved around; neither of her names appeared to have a permanent spelling, and the more I read, the more I found the same stories – originating in some form with Salaria's own accounts – repeated, reworked, challenged, overwritten and adulterated.

Her birthplace, which she usually gave as Akron, was in fact in Georgia. She lost both of her parents early on, but accounts of the circumstances vary, even in those given by Salaria herself. It seems quite possible that she simply wasn't sure of the facts: her father died when she was a baby, a loss that precipitated the kind of break-up that dislodges a family from its foundational memories. It is usually written that Salaria's father was murdered by a patient in the under-staffed hospital for the insane where he worked. Salaria sometimes said that he was killed at sea during the First World War. What his death meant was that Salaria and her three older brothers were taken by their mother to Akron, where she also passed out of the record. Sala-ria grew up in much the same way that Langston's biographer would describe him: as a 'passed-around child'. Handed from home to home and frequently separated, Salaria's brothers nevertheless found ways of looking out for her. None of them were able to graduate high school, but they made sure that their clever, sporty sister did.

New York, representing the best she could find in terms of oppor-tunities, was also a kind of dead end. If racism established roadblocks there, there was nowhere else to go. The 1938 pamphlet located Salaria's political development in Harlem Hospital, where she was involved in the desegregation of the staff dining room very early in her career. Falling in with a group of progressive nurses, Salaria attended lectures and discussion groups, which, according to the pamphlet, furthered her understanding of international systems of oppression. In other words, she started to make connections.

According to Salaria, it was the refugee doctors from Europe who showed her America from a new perspective. The Ku Klux Klan wasn't some terrifying aberration. It existed on a continuum with a government that upheld segregation, and with the subjugation of people in colonised lands, and with a movement in faraway countries that made life verging on impossible for Jews in ways both similar and different from – but resonant with – the way life for her people was often verging on impossible. As the 1938 pamphlet had it, 'what was happening in Harlem' had a relationship 'to events in Europe and Africa . . . When Mussolini advanced his Italian troops from Ethiopia into Spain she understood that this was the same fight.'

'It had seemed that in all the things I had wanted to do I had been rejected in my own country,' she told a journalist in 1975, thinking back on all the obstacles thrown up against her efforts to volunteer her skills. 'I didn't know anything about politics. . . . All I knew about was democracy, and anything that wasn't democracy wasn't for me.'

America might call itself a democracy, she said elsewhere, but 'what democracy meant to me was that we would be all equal . . . they were lying. We weren't all equal.'

Salaria Kea knew how much she had to offer. Of all the things she was denied, in interviews it sometimes seems as if it was the repeated, high-handed rejection of her gifts that hurt the most. At the Tamiment, I watched footage of her in old age, seated on a check sofa beside that photograph of herself in nursing uniform. Her face creases into a fierce expression. 'And why shouldn't I go and help the world?' she says.

Like all reading rooms, the one at the Tamiment Library had a hushed, padded quality in which it was possible to get so absorbed in your material that to look up at the windows and see the world still moving sometimes came as a surprise. It was dark, too. From archives, where the lights are usually dimmed to protect delicate material, everyone outside really does seem to be operating in a different realm entirely.

Even here, in the right place for them, I had struggled to find the records I was hoping for. I had not found a full-length memoir by Salaria Kea. I was low on time. There were limits to what I could order from storage each day and, since the catalogue was various and complicated and I wasn't entirely sure what I was looking for, it felt like pure luck whether what arrived was useful or not. It's often like that. You can spend your morning sifting through photocopies of articles you've read before, only to stumble on something brand new and crucial just as the archivists are ushering you out.

For some reason, it had taken me until the last day before the library closed for Christmas to get to a series of recordings of Salaria that had been made in preparation for a documentary released in 1984. The audio files were stored on CD-ROMs, so I needed a different set of contraptions to listen to them. As I waited for all this to arrive, I felt the day's potential returning.

Salaria must have been about seventy when she gave the interview, and she sounded distant and softly spoken at first, but as the tape settled I heard a light, refined voice, perhaps a legacy of her childhood NAACP coaching, that lilted occasionally with a direct 'look, doll' or 'you understand?' I listened to the conversations for hours. Salaria was often animated, frequently funny or emphatic, and quick to deflect foolish questions. When asked if she'd 'accepted' the fact she wasn't allowed to swim in local pools as a child, she retorted in quick affront: 'Sure you accepted it. Are you kidding? Indeed you accept those things . . . I just thought that was the world. I wasn't in heaven. This was the earth.'

But at a certain point I got the feeling that she was beginning to tire. Her answers became less direct and precise, the thread of her stories a little harder to follow. The interviewers, a man and what sounded like a young woman, were inevitably not asking the questions I would have asked, leaving me to ponder what wasn't being said as much as what was. I began to wonder why they hadn't offered Salaria a break. In the dim, comfortable room, with the headphones hot around my ears, my own attention was beginning to wander.

The hundreds of untapped files were always going to be a distraction. It's hard to quantify the value of your work each day when most of the time in an archive you are waiting; waiting for a revelatory, or confirmatory, encounter that might never arrive.

I refocused. Salaria was speaking about her crossing from America to Europe in 1937, on the SS *Normandie* (elsewhere this was given as the SS *Paris*). Somebody had met her at the port, she was saying, a French journalist. Also – whether this was the same person or their companion, I couldn't quite tell – a woman; a woman whose parents owned a shipping line.

I looked up, startled, my pencil hovering above my notebook. The screen in front of me counted steadily through the seconds. Salaria could not recall the name. I waited, willing her to remember. She was boasting a little now: this person had put her up, she said, as her guest, in one of the best hotels in France. To me that sounded like a familiarly extravagant gesture. Surely if someone bore the name of a shipping line, it would be a reasonable misunderstanding to assume that their family still owned it.

Salaria also wanted the name. She asked the interviewer to pause the tape while she went into the other room to check with her husband. He would know who had been waiting for her in France. When the tape crackled back into life, everyone was laughing. Nancy Cunard! Salaria announced. There was Nancy Cunard.

THE QUESTION

WRITERS and POETS of ENGLAND, SCOTLAND, IRELAND and WALES

It is clear to many of us throughout the whole world that now, as certainly never before, we are determined, or compelled, to take sides. The equivocal attitude, the Ivory Tower, the paradoxical, the ironic detachment, will no longer do.

We have seen murder and destruction by Fascism in Italy, in Germany — the organisation there of social injustice and cultural death — and how revived, imperial Rome, abetted by international treachery, has conquered her place in the Abyssinian sun. The dark millions in the colonies are unavenged.

Today, the struggle is in Spain. To-morrow it may be in other countries — our own.

But there are some who, despite the martyrdom of Durango and Guernica, the enduring agony of Madrid, of Bilbao, and Germany's shelling of Almeria, are still in doubt, or who aver that it is possible that Fascism may be what it proclaims it is :

" the saviour of civilisation ".

This is the question we are asking you :
Are you for, or against, the legal Government and the People of Republican Spain ?
Are you for, or against, Franco and Fascism?
For it is impossible any longer to take no side.

Writers and Poets, we wish to print your answers. We wish the world to know what you, writers and poets, who are amongst the most sensitive instruments of a nation, feel.

SIGNED:

Aragon
W.H. Auden
José Bergamin
Jean Richard Bloch
Nancy Cunard
Brian Howard
Heinrich Mann
Ivor Montagu
Pablo Neruda
Ramón Sender
Stephen Spender
Tristan Tzara

To be able to print you all we want a message from you, a statement in not more than 6 lines. We ask you to phrase your answer on Spain, on Fascism, in this concise form, to send it to us as soon as you receive this—in no case later than July 1. — addressed to:

Nancy Cunard, C/o Lloyds,
43, Boulevard des Capucines, Paris

The collection of answers will be published forthwith. A copy will also be sent to all those who reply.

PARIS . JUNE 1937

The Question

Nancy Cunard

France and London: summer 1937

When Nancy heard the news of Julian Bell's death, she wrote to his father, Clive, confident that he could take comfort in 'the gratitude of the Spanish people to all who come to them in their hour of tragedy', and confident that she, 'as one who was in Spain for so many months' (though not since the previous year), could speak to it. Then she did something less in keeping with a condolence letter. She nudged him on unanswered post. 'You know, I sent you this weeks ago. Will you not answer it Clive?'

Given the timing, there's surely only one thing it could be: the challenge she had sent to many of her fellow writers, asking them to weigh in on the Spanish war. Here she is at her most single-minded and perhaps her most presumptuous: Clive Bell was not only bereaved by the war, but a famously committed pacifist.

It's another moment of Nancy and Virginia skirting each other, too. Leonard replying to Nancy's Question and Virginia not. Virginia, grieving, developing strategies to avoid exactly people like Nancy Cunard.

The first thing I ever knew about Nancy was the commanding broadsheet she dispatched in the summer of 1937, containing the challenge that sent me in pursuit of her and Salaria Kea and others like them in the first place. She addressed it to many of the most important writers of Britain and Ireland, sometimes sending multiple copies with the idea that they'd pass them on. It made its way to George Bernard Shaw and Evelyn Waugh; to T. S. Eliot, James Joyce, Samuel

Beckett; to Rebecca West, Rose Macaulay and the Woolfs; to Cecil
Day-Lewis, Stephen Spender, Louis MacNeice and W. H. Auden.
It reached Aldous Huxley and George Orwell; Vita Sackville-West
and Sylvia Pankhurst. It went to Vera Brittain and H. G. Wells; to
Rosamond Lehmann and her brother, John; to Sylvia Townsend
Warner and Valentine.

Nancy printed her missive in black and red and addressed it, broadly
and grandly, to 'the Writers and Poets of England, Scotland, Ireland
and Wales'. Large type announced: THE QUESTION. Along the left-
hand side of the sheet was added, vertically: SPAIN.

The Question (though technically there were two) appeared perfectly straightforward. 'Are you for, or against, the legal Government
and the People of Republican Spain? Are you for, or against, Franco
and Fascism?'

Nancy assured her writers that she would publish the answers
they chose to send, by which she meant: you are asked to state a position publicly. As far as she was concerned, *not* taking a position was
impossible.

The project centred on her fundamental and appealingly simple
belief in the value of taking sides, and on that arresting proposition –
that history will sometimes present moments when convictions have
to be decided upon, when lines are drawn that must be acknowledged.

Nancy assembled twelve additional signatories (all of them male) to
the questionnaire, but later claimed it solely as her own. It was she
who conceived the idea, drafted the questions, arranged for them to be
printed in Paris, and came up with a list of recipients. Names kept on
occurring to her, until she had mailed out over two hundred copies.
The cooperation of the other signatories was in fact of little significance. 'Had every one of them said "No",' she told a scholar in the
sixties, 'I should have made the little work all the same – and how!
You see in those days there did exist ENTHUSIASM for what was
felt to be good and right and true.'

Nancy then left Réanville: 'Now comes the summer of 1937. I am in the Hotel Arvor, in the Rue Laferrière, in Montmartre, in June or July, and I am very much occupied, for a great many answers arrive rapidly to my Questionnaire'. Her enthusiasm, it turned out, is matched by others. The pamphlet eventually consisted of 148 replies, but at least twenty-five were left out for space, which implies that a great proportion of Nancy's dispatches hit home. She gave herself only two weeks to organise and prepare them for publication, then she was on the move again: to London, to find a publisher. As with the *Negro* anthology, she hadn't been diverted by finding one beforehand (probably she would have printed at her own expense if necessary). Nancy wanted to find a mainstream publisher who could ensure a wide audience, but in England she had trouble finding takers. The larger houses passed, so she offered it to the *Left Review*, where it was accepted at once. They printed 3,000 copies of *Authors Take Sides on the Spanish War* and immediately sold out.

Nancy had not limited her outreach to writers she knew or to those she assumed would agree with her, but she was convinced that the results would overwhelmingly favour the Republic, and she was right. Of the 148 printed responses, only sixteen chose neutrality, and just five were against the Spanish government. (The responses left out for space were all pro-Republican.) In Paris, she had sorted the answers herself, categorising them as 'For' the Republic, 'Against' or 'Neutral'? without adhering to any particularly discernible method, just as her basis for approaching respondents had hardly been scientific. It was a very Nancy-ian enterprise: a freewheeling, instinctive canter from conception to fruition. Some of those who ignored her commands and chose to equivocate were overruled and placed in the 'For' pile, when perhaps they intended to be 'Neutral'. On the other hand, there were statements published under 'Neutral' that could convincingly have been designated as 'For'. And at least Nancy did allow for Neutral. The phrasing of her questions had been unashamedly leading. The point of the questionnaire was not to achieve a balance of opinion. The intention was to publish a declaration.

'It is to be hoped that some methodical person has made a collection of the various manifestos and questionnaires issued . . . during the years

1936–7,' Virginia Woolf later remarked, taking a very dim view of the 'inquisition' to which she felt herself subjected in those days. 'Private people of no political training were invited to sign appeals asking their own and foreign governments to change their policy; artists were asked to fill up forms stating the proper relations of the artist to the State, to religion, to morality . . .'

The deluge was in part a symptom of a boisterous left-wing publishing scene in Britain, which had raised a clamour of little magazines, manifestos and statements. The distrust evident in some responses to Nancy's flyer gives a flavour of the partisanship of the times. It was partly a problem of definitions. Some of the hostile responders assumed that Nancy was asking them to choose between fascism and communism, which she wasn't; others assumed she would leave out anything unfavourable to her position (their responses duly appeared in the pamphlet).

Not everyone was convinced that the simple act of declaring themselves could be of much use. Rebecca West, sending hers in, worried that 'six lines is terribly little and it sounds very trite and boring'. E. M. Forster could not share Nancy's conviction 'that manifestos by writers carry any weight whatever'.

Nancy's questionnaire was in a sense asking too much and asking too little. It is all too easy to sit down in some quiet place, compose a few lines, and settle back satisfied in the fulfilment of a civic duty. 'To scribble a name on a sheet of paper is easy,' Virginia pointed out in the book she was writing that summer, but an expression of opinion was not 'positive help'. On the other hand, it's easy to imagine intellectuals baulking at nailing their colours to the mast as publicly – or as simplistically – as Nancy wanted. A war in someone else's country was surely more complicated than she was prepared to allow.

Yet it's not difficult to see why Nancy thought the project important. At the League of Nations she had witnessed the Republic's fellow democracies still refusing to confront Germany or Italy over their 'invasion' of Spain. 'While the powers pass resolutions,' she had reminded her readers, 'international Fascism kills.' With so much relying on changing the narrative outside of the country, harnessing the opinions of articulate public figures – the publishers listed forty of them down the front cover – and having them sound the alarm in their cumulative authority was a sensible, even inspired, contribution. In the dogfight of the pamphlets, Nancy had compiled a hefty contender. It was a signal that what was happening in Spain was a matter of gravity and relevance. You can almost hear the supporting clatter of Nancy's bracelets as she typed them up: This is worth your attention.

Nancy wasn't asking her respondents to merely lament 'how wicked it all is', as George Orwell would accuse her, but, in stating a side, to do something more difficult: to forsake such unimpeachable generalisations in favour of specifics. But in the pamphlet that emerged, the particularity of Spain – its history and traditions; the nature of its political scene – often fell by the wayside. Much as many of the writers saw the Question as perfectly simple – an elected government could be the only legitimate contender – they also took Nancy's cue in using it as an opportunity to voice their suspicion of the fascist powers in Europe. Nancy had set up a symbol that allowed her correspondents to continue their own debates. To read the pamphlet is to see a cohort of writers pondering their place in the world.

Nancy's exhortation to writers was more than just a statement of faith in their influence. She also saw in fascism an implacable enemy of the arts. In her own statement she declared: 'It is . . . unthinkable for any honest intellectual to be pro-Fascist . . . Above all others the writer, the intellectual, must take sides. His place is with the people against Fascism; his duty, to protest against the present degeneration of the democracies.'

Taking up one's place with 'the people' is clearly a position influenced by communism (which, as manifested at the time in the USSR, would prove just as hostile to intellectual freedom). But, as Nancy did, most of her responders regarded fascism – particularly as demonstrated in the regimes of Hitler and Mussolini – as not just hostile to intellectuals and repressive of artistic freedom but antithetical to culture: mere 'barbarism', as Leonard Woolf and others put it. (As it happened, 'barbarism' was also how Franco described socialism.) Upbraiding the Left in the 1950s, Josephine Herbst would assert that 'an anti-intellectual was basically a fascist position'.

In the responses Nancy received, works of the intellect and

imagination were sometimes understood to bestow 'civilisation' as much as depend upon it. It was in this idea that some writers saw the opportunity to actively take sides without departing from their work as artists and thinkers, and that sent me back again to Nancy's statement – to the qualifier she includes when concerning herself specifically with the 'honest' intellectual. Valentine Ackland expected both 'reason and tenacious courage' from artists: attributes required for making a stand. After all, it's the honest application of the intellect – an uncorrupted deployment of reason alongside the imagination – that helps us to make sense of phenomena confronting us. Without some grounding of shared, acknowledged truths, some basic standard of rational honesty, the collective landscape is only an unnavigable mess of caves and trenches. (It should be what stops us, even, from letting taking sides mean blind, unreasoning allegiance.) This would explain why Nancy saw artists and intellectuals endowed with a special responsibility towards truth, why they were the natural enemies of fascist movements that warped and suppressed it. It seemed to me that her recipients would have appreciated this at once: writers, whether identifying as intellectuals or artists, are already dealers in trust. They have to be able to convince, on some level at least, if they want their creations to move and engage.

As Sylvia's response had it, 'Fascism is based upon mistrust of human potentialities'. Art and scholarship by contrast expressed and enabled them. One writer, who had lived in Spain in the 1920s and returned as a journalist in 1936, described artists in his contribution as a kind of vanguard, whose imagination (when matched by 'the worker's hope', of course) could 'make the future real'.

By which he meant, I think, that we create possibilities by imagining them. It's a beguiling and yet somehow banal-because-obvious idea. Through wilful dreaming, artists and scholars have conjured previously inconceivable worlds – worlds in which people could take to the sky or prevent cholera, or overturn seemingly all-powerful empires – and radical new ways of understanding reality; in thinking the unthinkable, they allow others to do the same.

As any censor knows and fears, in the arts there are secret languages which can encode, and thus protect, independence; that can entrench dissent in realms where it is difficult to identify and impossible to root out. 'Printing! And printing what?' Nancy imagined her neighbours in Réanville thinking, long after she had come to understand the depth of their suspicion. 'A press is very dangerous! It means the dissemination of ideas.' Responding to Nancy's questionnaire, Cyril Connolly, the editor of *Horizon* magazine, pointed out that the aggressive aims of fascist states required a populace that was 'rendered both warlike and servile' – the 'stultifying', in other words, 'of the human race'. When a system relies on the prevention of independent thought, the use of the intellect (the dissemination of ideas) becomes a primary form of resistance.

In a poem she wrote that summer, Nancy claimed a long heritage of resistance for writers, shaming her contemporaries into action by invoking chroniclers who came before them, those who 'wrote and painted and said / Their NO [. . .] against lying': 'then the artist became the act'.

This was not Nancy insisting that writers immediately take up arms – or at least not in the literal sense. This was her great claim for the power of the arts and the attendant responsibility of the artist. Each age asks some new and perennial thing of them. For Nancy, it was not just that the artist must act, but that they must rise to the potential of their art. 'Every man to his battle, child,' she says; 'this is yours'.

'At a time in which the world is full of tensions and alarming confusions, in which the most dangerous elements attempt to attack and destroy the civilisation of Europe, Germany and Italy have found themselves in sincere friendship and common political cooperation.'

Adolf Hitler at a reception for Benito Mussolini, Berlin,
27 September 1937

The Ivory Tower

Virginia Woolf

England: summer, autumn 1937

After doing her duty at the Albert Hall fundraiser for Basque children in June, Virginia had found herself 'in full flood' on her next book, *Three Guineas*. Then Julian was killed and the loss was so massive that it overcame her usual release valve of observing and writing. Instead, there was only the consolation of being necessary to her sister, Vanessa, who had collapsed into what she would later describe as an 'unreal state' that lasted for weeks.

For once, Virginia stayed on the surface, her voice the only sound that could recall her sister from chasms of grief. Virginia – who left unchecked could speak and speak herself into a frenzy, whose animated conversation Vanessa had often watched with a wary eye – Virginia went every day and threw her sister a lifeline. And though, for the time being, Vanessa could not raise herself from silence, Virginia's debate with Julian had only just begun.

When Virginia returned to her diary two and a half weeks after the news reached them, her mood was defiant. If Julian's death represented meaninglessness, 'the immense vacancy' and puny apportionment of life, Virginia's response was to prepare her protest. Writing and thinking represented not only life, but the defiance of death. 'I will not yield an inch or a fraction of an inch to nothingness, so long as something remains.' The problem was re-entering the book she had abandoned on the other side of the cataclysm. How to finish *Three Guineas*? In August she prepared to face another casualty: 'now I suppose its stiff & cold'.

Yet, a week and a half later, she was back in full flow. Leonard and Virginia had driven Vanessa down to Sussex, and in between writing and tending to her sister, Virginia now strode out on her customary walks – accompanied by Julian, 'who stalks beside me, in many different shapes'.

Three Guineas had been conceived with *The Years*, split from the same idea. Virginia had hinted as much to Julian in 1936 when she told him, 'Unfortunately, politics gets between me and fiction. I feel I must write something when [*The Years*] is over – something vaguely political; doubtless worthless, certainly useless.' But what she didn't say was how intimately the politics and the fiction were connected, how hard she had in fact tried to combine them.

Throughout 1935, the year she and Leonard visited Germany, Virginia had flitted between the two books, finding that whatever did not feed one could often fertilise the other. She picked up scraps for the essay in her reading, at parties, in correspondence and in chance encounters with friends: outrage frequently prompted 'floods' of material for the book. Privately she began to refer to what became *Three Guineas* as her anti-fascist pamphlet. In her scrapbooks, clippings built up: evidence for the arguments she was preparing to make. Reports from Germany, Italy, Spain and Britain coalesced within them in ways that strengthened her resolve: side by side they affirmed connections, ways of thinking that stretched as broadly as Salaria Kea identified.

Fascism is ominously present in the margins of *The Years*, but Woolf ultimately fought shy of introducing polemic. She feared it would impede both the reader's engagement and her own creative faculties. By the end of 1935 she had faltered. *Three Guineas* took the blame for her troubles with *The Years* ('Now again I pay the penalty of mixing fact & fiction'). As she faced the challenge of finishing the novel, the lightning flash of ideas for the essay became unwelcome intrusions. Just as the new harshness in her nephew discomforted her, so she feared writing propaganda: suspected it was too rigid to allow for the necessary roaming of her mind.

Everything that Virginia took out of *The Years* remained to be said in *Three Guineas*, and she went on steeling herself against the instinct to retreat or dissemble. 'Lord, what a shivering coward I am,' she

Virginia Woolf

told herself in 1935, 'but not as a writer. No. I stick to that by way of compensation.'

Three Guineas would be an unconcealed manifesto – she hoped it would be her final word on politics. It was her most radical text, but would also be among the least acknowledged. Watching her nephew succumb to the lure of war, living through the aftermath, feeling the need to finish the argument against his going which she had lost: all of this fuelled a book that had been feeding on Julian for years.

A few weeks before he left for Spain, Virginia had witnessed a 'long close political argument' between Julian, Stephen Spender and Kingsley Martin (the editor of the *New Statesman*). She was seated at the same table, but from her account of the evening it sounds as though she simply let them speak, spiriting away the ideas her disagreement provoked for resurfacing in her essay later. While the men debated politics and pacifism, Virginia was there and not there, stirred but not convinced. Her mind worked in its own stream, plotting her response: 'I sat there splitting off my own position from theirs, testing what they said, convincing myself of my own integrity and justice. . . . we

discussed hand grenades, bombs, tanks, as if we were military gents
in the war again. And I felt flame up in me 3 Gs.'

Though she would not deride the principles that had sent Julian to
Spain, Virginia felt she could formulate a more productive response
to the challenge the war posed. 'My natural inclination is to fight
intellectually,' she reflected in her first notes on Julian's death; 'if I
were any use, I should write against it: I should evolve some plan for
fighting English tyranny. . . . one must control feeling with reason.'

Reading *Three Guineas*, it seems at first as though Woolf is circling the
issues, setting up various excuses for speaking her mind. The whole
book is framed as a belated response to a man who has solicited her
advice on how 'to prevent war'. Virginia imagines it among a pile of
correspondence on her desk. There's this letter about peace – long
avoided because don't we always hope someone somewhere else has
the answer? – with a request for a signature on a manifesto pledging 'to
protect culture and intellectual liberty' and appeals for donations from
worthy institutions concerned with women's advancement. Somehow
replying to the question of war, or rather peace, requires dealing with
the whole pile. It turns out that Virginia Woolf's thinking on the
appropriate response to fascism spans it all.

Virginia had long seen Julian as her insight into the male life and
mind. His self-confessed obsession with war gave fuel to her position,
set out in *Three Guineas*, that war is an inherently male affair. In her
view, 'to fight has always been the man's habit, not the woman's'. (Or,
as a character in one of Martha Gellhorn's stories puts it, 'they make
wars because that is what men like'.)

'I'm sometimes angry with him,' she admitted after Julian's death.
As witness to Vanessa's suffering, how could she not be? Yet beyond
this instinctive resentment of the waste was a suspicion of the grand
ideals that supposedly sent men to war in the first place – the kind of
concepts that Simone Weil, after her return from Spain, had that year
condemned as 'words with capital letters . . . all swollen with blood
and tears' – words that in actual fact were 'empty'.

Weren't these capitalised terms merely a grand form of coercion,
resting on cynical claims to a collective that existed only when it

suited the powerful? Virginia remembered the rhetoric of the War of 1914–18. Its hypocrisy offended her: the idea of lauding suffragettes for their support of the war effort when their use of violence in their own campaigns had previously been enough to see them imprisoned. The fact that her correspondent's plea is even addressed to her seems nonsensical. Why not ask the people who start the wars how to prevent them? It's an injustice built into inequality, that the emotional, physical and intellectual labour of fighting society's ills should fall on its least empowered members – on the people already most burdened by them (an injustice, it occurred to me as Woolf's outrage permeated, that allyship at least tries to ease). Now she determined to protest male aggression as her solution to the perennial insecurity of peace.

What is truly provocative in *Three Guineas* is Woolf's clarity about whom the state serves, about the fact that stories about national solidarity, about patriotism and shared values, in fact conceal the unequal apportionment of the benefits of belonging. 'But the educated man's sister – what does "patriotism" mean to her?' she insists. 'Has she the same reasons for being proud of England, for loving England, for defending England? Has she been "greatly blessed" in England?' This is a reminder to think honestly of whom we mean when we start blithely speaking in plurals, to always interrogate the manipulation of language by the powerful.

She turns to some of those clippings she has been collecting: quotations from the British newspapers in which people object to women taking jobs. This brings her out into the open:

> We shall find there . . . something which, if it spreads, may poison both sexes equally. There, in those quotations, is the egg of the very same worm that we know under other names in other countries. There we have in embryo the creature, Dictator as we call him when he is Italian or German, who believes that he has the right whether given by God, Nature, sex or race is immaterial, to dictate to other human beings how they shall live; what they shall do.

'I think I was saying discrimination,' Salaria told her interviewer, 'but when I got over there I learned to say fascism.' Salaria Kea, Langston Hughes, Virginia Woolf, Nancy Cunard: all saw in fascism prejudices known by other names. There are risks to this elision of specificity. Reading the various explanations for why Spain mattered, the answer given is often 'fascism' – and 'fascism' becomes a kind of shorthand that does not always differentiate between different types and extents of prejudice. Yet, used in this way, it also denied the benefit of the doubt (offered through various euphemisms) to dangerous ideologies, to the kinds of elitism that afford basic human dignity to only a narrowly defined side: from Spanish nobles opposing land reform to threatening crowds outside Alabama courthouses. It began to look like an early warning system.

Tyranny, to Virginia Woolf, was not a foreign enemy. Feminists had been 'fighting the same enemy that you are fighting and for the same reasons'. This was her challenge to those interested in peace, those who called themselves anti-fascists, to rise to true solidarity: to see the cause of equality as a cause indivisible from the liberty they championed. To all the people insisting on the need to fight fascism in Europe, she would respond that there was tyranny to confront at home. The idea of picking sides was a distraction: a summons to fall unthinkingly into line. How could war be prevented? By shaking our thinking free from the brutalising, masculinist norms that governed societies and nurtured war in the first place.

She lays a picture down before us: ruined houses and bodies in the background; a man in uniform – Führer or Duce or Tyrant or Dictator – in the foreground. This living, recognisably human form complicates things, implicates us, and yet suggests its own solution, one that may actually go further than Nancy Cunard's efforts for Spain:

> It suggests that the public and the private worlds are inseparably connected; that the tyrannies and servilities of the one are the tyrannies and servilities of the other . . . It suggests that we cannot dissociate ourselves from that figure but are ourselves that figure. It suggests that we are not passive spectators doomed to unresisting obedience but by our thoughts and actions can ourselves change that figure. A common interest unites us . . . How essential it is that we should realize that unity the dead bodies, the ruined houses prove. . . . though we look upon that picture from different angles our conclusion is the same as yours – it is evil.

Looking for Salaria Kea, Part 2

One of the things I especially liked about New York was the grid system. In a city that crowded out the sky, I was sometimes surprised by enormous eruptions of space as I reached one of the avenues and grand vistas unfurled into improbable distances. Walking alongside Manhattan from across the East River one bright morning, I noticed as I went that the city was regularly bisected by light; that for all its traffic and monuments, I could suddenly see right through it.

There was no such clarity in my research, where I was instead still deep in the mire of conflicting detail and narrative confusion. Having caught a tantalising glimpse of Nancy Cunard in Salaria Kea's story, I was now struggling to make sense of it. I was equally coming to realise that something about this kernel of an encounter struck at the heart of the questions of identity and solidarity and truth that I was circling.

Nancy's place in Salaria's story was controversial. In interviews she gave in the years after the Spanish war, Salaria became more open about some details of her experiences there and less open about others. In particular, she became more outspoken about a racist slur thrown at her on the crossing to Spain by a senior member of her own team. And in that particular story, somewhere along the way, Nancy had become involved.

In her later life, Salaria recounted the first meal of that journey several times. In its outline, what she described was this: the medical staff – some of whom she knew and some of whom she was yet to meet – assembled for the first time at a long table in the dining room of the ship that was taking them to Europe. No one could take their seats until the head physician, a Dr Pitts from Oklahoma, arrived to join them. But when he reached the table and found Salaria there, he refused to sit down. Never in his life, he explained to an anxious waiter, had he eaten, nor would he eat, with a '[n—] wench'.

Salaria felt acutely aware in that moment that she was the only black person in the room. Everyone was staring – apparently in silence. The waiters couldn't persuade Dr Pitts to take his seat. And then something remarkable happened: someone stood up for Salaria.

The identity of her defender is hazy (though notably it wasn't another member of the team). In a 1980 interview, Salaria said that eventually the captain appeared to break the stand-off. He had a man with him who turned out to be a proprietor of the shipping line, and also that man's daughter. Gallantly, they swept Salaria up into first class, where she remained as the 'roommate' of the woman until the boat reached France. On arrival, Salaria went on a little confusingly, she was met by Nancy Cunard, 'and she said, I will be her roommate'. Nancy (in this account) continued the rescue, putting Salaria up in a hotel at her own expense until eventually Salaria travelled on into Spain to rejoin her team. I came across other versions, in which Nancy was actually on the boat, and it was there she made Salaria her guest – either in her cabin or just for meals. Or sometimes it is only that Salaria ate at the captain's table for the rest of the voyage. Since the different variants crop up in different places, it's hard to say exactly which of the conflicting details originate with Salaria and which accumulated like tumbleweed as the anecdote rolled down history street.

It seemed odd that Nancy had left no record of this encounter herself. It also seemed unlikely that she had been on the ship given her movements that spring, but the largesse and ostentation of providing for Salaria certainly sounded like the kind of statement she would have relished making. Tracing my way through as many versions of the story as I could find, I suspected that Nancy's presence on the crossing was a misunderstanding (or misremembering) that could easily have something to do with her surname. But the alternative – that she met Salaria at the port and whisked her away – was equally strange: why would Salaria have disembarked alone in France, when her team was destined for Portbou, only to rejoin them in Spain a few weeks later?

One thing I did know, or came to know, was that Nancy Cunard and Salaria Kea had definitely met, and that Salaria had made an impression. In 1939, reporting from a Paris at war, Nancy added a plea to the end of one of her ANP articles: would Salaria Kea, whom she had met in Spain, please get in touch. Another tantalising glimpse, and one that implied a later encounter than Salaria's recollection.

Perhaps Nancy had nothing to do with Dr Pitts or Salaria's first taste of Europe. It is just one appealing version of a story that probably panned out differently. Perhaps several facts – their meeting, Nancy's famous identification with anti-racism, Salaria's humiliation at the hands of someone who was meant to be an ally – drew together in a kind of logical magnetism, different memories making sense of themselves as they mulched down with time.

But it fits nicely. It fulfils something for both women: Nancy gets to stand with the persecuted, to be the rescuer she was driven to be – that on some level she clearly needed to be – and an incident that would have been purely ugly becomes something a little different. In its reparative arc, the story has a fairy-tale element; it grants a wish for the world to become better than it is. In Salaria's telling, she is wronged and insulted, but ultimately respect is restored, and she is treated as an extravagantly honoured guest, her true value recognised. She doesn't even have to confront the evil herself. Others leap to her defence, and she rises above and away from a place where Dr Pitts can discriminate against her with impunity. It's a halfway house to the better world in which there is no discrimination in the first place, positioned appropriately on her crossing to Spain. Salaria had learned to speak up for herself, partly because she had learned she couldn't always rely on others to speak up on her behalf, but here that gruelling diversion of energies is done away with. With Dr Pitts left behind in steerage, things are going in the right direction.

The more I delved, the more placing Nancy at the scene began to seem less interesting than what had gone on at that dinner and afterwards. It was sobering to imagine a table full of white volunteers who were willing to risk their lives in Spain but not willing to risk – what? their solidarity with Dr Pitts? – to call out racism. Perhaps this was why the story, when it began to circulate years after the war, proved hard to stomach.

In 1990, a former Abraham Lincoln Brigade member wrote to Frances Patai, who was gathering material for a book about the women in the American medical units, to refute Salaria's account.

Patai was also inclined to dismiss it. Pitts's slurs were, she reassured the irate volunteer, 'all a figment of [Salaria's] imagination'. Her certainty was apparently nothing to do with Salaria but rather her white colleagues and what they represented. 'It's totally absurd', she continued, 'that Pitts (who may have been a not-good person and a sexist) would make such an outlandish rasist [sic] insult. Had he done so the AMB personnel and the Lincoln volunteers on the boat would have been up in arms.'

Patai pledged that the story would not appear in her book (which in the event was never published), nor in a projected book about African American volunteers, because 'none of us want such an untrue lie to dim the glory of the U.S. volunteers'. I don't know whether she was unaware of the comments of Evelyn Hutchins, who had driven an ambulance in Spain and later told in an interview of the 'infamous Dr. Pitt[s], who kept making problems because Salaria was black and he was a doctor from the South', or whether that account had to be sacrificed to the greater glory too.

When Robert Reid-Pharr, an academic of colour, encountered Salaria's description of this incident, what struck him was not its outlandishness but 'just how very mundane it is'. Dr Pitts's alleged insult was many things, but probably not very shocking to a black woman living in 1930s America.

As Reid-Pharr noted, the reputation of the anti-fascist volunteers becomes, in Patai's response, a rather vulnerable thing: a glory that could weather neither questions, nor reservations, nor challenges. In this approach, which transformed Salaria from ally to aggressor, solidarity becomes something else: a question of conformity rather than unity of ideals or a form of mutual support; it requires the elision of dissenting or qualifying voices to survive. Since the medics on the boat were all on the 'right' side, they were granted an amnesty from interrogation. This produces strange contortions of solidarity: Salaria's self-appointed defenders turn out to need more protection than she does. (And even Patai went on wanting to have everything both ways. Whilst branding Salaria a liar, she insisted that this fact did 'not in any way diminish her bravery, courage, nobility in volunteering'.)

Little wonder that there was no mention of this incident in the 1938 pamphlet dedicated to Salaria. However you spun it, it didn't quite chime with the message people wanted to hear. But Salaria was willing to tell the story, and not just towards the end of her life. She told it to Nancy in 1937, when they were together in Spain. What wasn't difficult to imagine was Nancy's delight when she was introduced to this intrepid young woman – most probably, I soon found, by another of Salaria's admirers: Langston Hughes.

Tightropes

Langston Hughes and Nan Green

Valencia, Madrid and its environs: summer, autumn 1937

Langston must have reached Valencia at almost the same moment Gerda Taro's hearse paused there briefly on its way to the French border. Yet despite the sombre note struck at the Alianza, a year into the war, Valencia was bursting with life. Driving from Barcelona with the Cuban poet Nicolás Guillén (another delegate at the Second International Congress), Langston had been caught up outside the city in a dusty traffic of 'burros, trucks and oxcarts' while on either side of the road orange groves stretched into the distance. In different times, tourist guides had recommended entering Valencia in just this way to appreciate the 'endless garden' of the city's environs, a lush landscape watered by the Turia river. In 1937, they passed elderly peasants who straightened stiffly in the fields to offer the Loyalist salute.

Though bombed from the air and shelled from the sea, this elegant Mediterranean port city was still far removed from the fighting around Madrid and elsewhere, and far better supplied. There was good food to eat and wine to drink – even fresh fish and luxuries like melons and oranges and grapes available. 'And there were parks and bathing beaches, music and dancing, anti-aircraft guns making fireworks in the sky every night, and tracer bullets arching like Roman candles in the air as Franco's bombs lighted up the port.'

The blackout (imposed due to the night-time air raids) was not so strictly enforced in Valencia, and the streets and cafés thronged with people. Soldiers visited on leave, filling the beaches with couples, and Langston was back, as a reporter for several African American newspapers, in the city that had last hosted him in 1924, when he was a young sailor making his way home to America.

★

'Langston Hughes,' Nancy Cunard announced when describing his address to the Paris session of the Congress, 'has had an adventurous round-the-world life.' In his own accounting, by 1937 Langston had been 'all around the embattled world': 'I had seen people walking tightropes everywhere – the tightrope of color in Alabama, the tight-rope of transition in the Soviet Union, the tightrope of repression in Japan, the tightrope of the fear of war in France – and of war itself in China and in Spain – and myself everywhere on my tightrope of words.'

This balancing act was the story of his life so far, which he had spent poised between different worlds, seeking an accommodation between the different things they asked of him and his work; a feat that was also a vantage point.

So much of Langston's life involved acts of delicate evasion, wanting to please his various admirers without being subject to their expectations; lines he negotiated with such grace and charm that his defiance was not always immediately felt. In the twenties he had become one of the stars – if not *the* star – of the Harlem Renaissance. Trying always to reach the majority of black people, he maintained close friendships with white patrons who funded his education and helped to launch and maintain his career, as well as with the well-wishers like Nancy who formed tessellations of art and activism. He delivered books into the hands of white pub-lishers. He saw the threat different groups posed to him: ' "O, be respectable, write about nice people, show how good we are," say the Negroes. "Be stereotyped, don't go too far, don't shatter our illusions about you, don't amuse us too seriously. We will pay you," say the whites.'

When, in 1926, he announced his artistic intentions in a brilliant clarion call of self-assertion, he was striking a warning note:

We younger Negro artists who create now intend to express our individual dark-skinned selves without fear or shame. If white people are
pleased, we are glad. If they are not, it doesn't matter. . . . If colored
people are pleased we are glad. If they are not, their displeasure doesn't
matter either. We build our temples for tomorrow, strong as we know
how, and we stand on top of the mountain, free within ourselves.

Who exactly his people were remained a knotty question. Like
Sylvia Townsend Warner, he wasn't convinced that those he most
wanted to reach had much use for him. 'Whereas the better-class
Negro would tell the artist what to do, the people at least let him
alone when he does appear,' he wrote in the same essay. 'And they are
not ashamed of him – if they know he exists at all.' It sounds like the
kind of unrequited need (what in his magisterial biography Arnold
Rampersad calls a 'psychological craving') that could lead to heart-
break: an artist writing for people too preoccupied with the difficult
business of survival to notice what he was offering.

'Beauty and lyricism are really related to another world, to ivory
towers, to your head in the clouds, feet floating off the earth,' Langston
once wrote. He had a bewitching talent for beauty and lyricism. And
his 'roses and moonlight poems' were never the ones that got him
picketed or threatened or deported. But from the tightrope, it was
clear as day that roses and moonlight were no universal language, no
shared bounty of the earth:

> unfortunately, I was born poor – and colored – and almost all the
> prettiest roses I have seen have been in rich white people's yards –
> not in mine. That is why I cannot write exclusively about roses and
> moonlight – for sometimes in the moonlight my brothers see a fiery
> cross and a circle of Klansmen's hoods. Sometimes in the moonlight
> a dark body swings from a lynching tree – but for his funeral there
> are no roses.

The only solution was another of his balancing acts. As the Depression scattered the promising stars of the Harlem Renaissance, he was
drawn increasingly towards socialism, another predominantly white
movement, and his work showed it. With the exception of Richard

Nancy and Langston in Paris, 1938

Wright, he was the writer of colour most associated with the American Communist Party in those years; seeing, like Nancy and Josephine, the class struggle as integral to any progress towards racial equality. The world might be 'divided superficially on the basis of blood and color', he declared in Paris, but was in reality divided 'on the basis of poverty and power'. Travelling through the USSR in 1932, Langston looked as far as its outlawing of racial discrimination and declared himself satisfied.

But with destitution often at his heels, he had also to reconcile radical writing with more mainstream work that could keep him from penury. From his reading tours of the South, he knew that the voice and form of his more militant poetry was not yet the way to reach the readers he most wanted to engage, any more than his celebrated 'literary' style was. The radical Left was treated with extreme suspicion almost anywhere you could go, and Langston had already begun rowing back from too inextricable an association with it.

Nancy Cunard had sent him irresistible letters in the summer of 1936.

'I sort of wish I was in Spain to see all the excitement,' he had admitted. Finally he was there, 'and nothing', he wrote home, 'could be finer'.

The person he was writing to was a prominent figure in the American Left, at that time serving as the National Secretary for the English Section of the International Workers Order (IWO), and she was also headed for Spain. Louise Thompson was a seasoned political organiser and well versed in mobilising artists. She and Langston had been close friends since meeting in Harlem in the 1920s. (She also knew Nancy Cunard, but had little time for what she regarded as Nancy's emotional interventions.) In 1937, the IWO funded her place on a delegation to Spain that was to assess the priorities for relief efforts.

Louise was not only the sole person of colour on the IWO National Executive Committee, she was also its only woman. In an article written the previous year, she had drawn attention to the 'triple exploitation' of African American women 'as workers, as women and as Negroes'. In Spain, she would narrowly miss another African American woman on a funded mission for aid organisations. Thyra Edwards may have been the person who wrote up Salaria's experiences for the 1938 *A Negro Nurse in Republican Spain* pamphlet. Her primary interest in visiting was the well-being of women and children living under wartime conditions. These were activists for whom being on the 'right' side also meant working on more than one front.

Langston dawdled in Valencia. He gave himself a week or so to enjoy the pleasures there, feeling no great desire to rush into the dangers of the capital and its battlefronts. Eventually, he and Guillén hauled themselves onto a military bus for a thirteen-hour drive along the road that so many people had died to keep open.

When Nan Green reached the English hospital at Huete, a village roughly halfway between Valencia and Madrid, she found, to her 'profound astonishment' that her husband was there. Of all the things she had expected in Spain, this gift of fortune was not one of them. After eight months apart, it was 'sheer and unadulterated joy' to find him.

George's accounts of the shortages and disorder at Republican hospitals had half persuaded Nan to volunteer her services. His comrade Wogan Philipps's visit in July had done the rest. As part of his pitch,

Wogan had offered to pay boarding school fees for Martin and Frances if Nan decided to go. 'I walked up and down for a *whole night* of turmoil,' she would remember later, 'trying to decide what was best.' Wogan's offer was 'a wonderful chance for my kids to get out of the poverty we were in'; she even found a school where the headmaster was a supporter of the Spanish Republic, someone she trusted to provide the kind of environment she wanted for them. But scrupulously she acknowledged the prospect as an escape for her too, a relief from the day-to-day strain of sole responsibility for their welfare. At most, she told herself, she'd be away for six months.

She didn't go in the hope of reuniting with George. Letters from the front were censored and though he had sent her 'carefully guarded' news, including an account of Julian Bell's death, she had only the vaguest notion of his whereabouts. She knew that the horrors he'd seen had persuaded him to deepen his commitment by going from ambulance driver to soldier – that he was planning to join the International Brigades – but she didn't know that a petrol burn had sent him to hospital first. While he recovered at Huete, he had been made political commissar with responsibility for hospital morale. So when Nan appeared, he commandeered her services at once, teaching her to play the accordion over a single afternoon so that she could perform that evening in a recital he had organised for patients.

There's a photo of their little band squinting in the bright sun: George, in a roll-neck jumper and spectacles, cradling a cello and almost schoolmasterly, looks encouragingly towards his musicians. This was how he wanted to spend his life, not fighting on a dusty battlefront. 'My idea of a good time is not being shot-at,' he wrote to his mother that year, trying to make himself understood, 'but is connected with growing lettuce and spring onions, and drinking beer in a country pub, and playing quartets with friends and having my children about me to educate me and keep me human.' In the photo, Nan stands glowering against the light at his shoulder, the accordion spread in a protective curve behind him. She stuck as closely to George as she could at Huete, perhaps unable to quite believe in the luck of their reunion, knowing, too, that it couldn't last.

The hospital was housed in a mammoth twelfth-century monastery, a building of thick walls around an inner courtyard and a large, disused chapel with a new mural painted by a passing International Brigader. Nan was now part of Spanish Medical Aid, an organisation that had been brought into being in London shortly after the outbreak of war through the efforts of Isabel Brown, secretary of the Relief Commission for the Victims of Fascism, and doctors associated with the Trades Union Congress and the Socialist Medical Association. They had organised the convoy in which George and Wogan had come to Spain.

At Huete, Nan officially held the position of 'assistant secretary', which in practice meant handling almost everything that wasn't driving ambulances or tending to patients. She helped keep up the spirits of the staff (the nurses were mostly hard-working Brits and New Zealanders), tried to manage supplies, liaised with the surrounding communities. The reality on the ground proved both sobering and affirming. The hospital suffered crippling shortages of almost everything; visiting vehicles were sometimes relieved of their petrol so the nurses could keep the Primus stoves they used to sterilise instruments going. Throughout her time in Spain, Nan encountered atmospheres that had become (sometimes poisonously) suspicious. At Huete, there were tensions between Communist and non-Communist volunteers, and Nan found herself wondering about the possibility of spies and sabotage. (Later, she was forced to resign from another hospital after being denounced by a hostile superior – a German Communist whose unsubstantiated accusations against her got as far as the Soviet files in Moscow.)

But what felt to her like the bigger picture was there in the growing confidence and autonomy of the villages, in recruiting volunteers among local women who came to the doorways of homes that were still hovels and enthused about the newly available marvels of schooling. Their daughters trained at the hospital to assist the nurses and had the kind of certainty that had so struck Josephine in the brigades. 'Like Cromwell's men,' Nan thought, 'they knew what they were fighting for, and loved what they knew.'

Nan wasn't the only volunteer encouraged by developments outside of the hospitals as much as within them. At the nearby Villa

Paz hospital, once a summer villa belonging to the royal family, one of the American nurses described the local tenants as former 'slaves' who now ate with hospital staff from crockery emblazoned with their former landlord's crest. When Spaniards from a nearby community approached one of the hospitals with a suggestion that the land around Villa Paz and another hospital be cultivated for food, some of the walking wounded volunteered to help. A nurse present at the meeting remembered watching a co-operative forming before her eyes: 'I saw democracy aborning among . . . former servants of the royalty . . . Maybe you bickered once in a while, gripe you certainly did, but you were all united towards one goal: man's right to be free! In 1937 I was seeing almost pure idealism.'

The Villa Paz

Langston Hughes and Salaria Kea

East of Madrid and Madrid: summer, autumn 1937

Langston was having trouble getting transport. Without a car, he got places from Madrid only when someone heading in the direction he wanted to go was willing to give him a lift. That was presumably how, in October, he ended up at the hospital at Villa Paz.

Though Villa Paz was now the 'American Hospital No. 1', its lush gardens carried echoes of an older world, one whose hunting hounds still wandered stubbornly through the grounds like ghosts. There was a swimming pool and huge pine trees and a brook that gushed over falls. When American staff first arrived in the spring, they had found an almost magical abundance of 'roses, lilies, violets, grapes, forget-menots, irises, gladiolas, different varieties of ivy, cherry and almond blossoms' blooming.

Inside, the first contingent of staff had pooled their salaries to rewire the buildings and install a generator. Stables and other out-buildings had been converted into a kitchen, dining room and oper-ating theatres. But it was a hurried, fragmentary transformation, and some of the villa's treasures remained. Dr Barsky, the hospital's chief, remembered 'an enormous bed draped in regal brocade, the blanket woven with a rare floral design and the whole middle of it covered with a gigantic royal crest. Three of our nurses used to sleep in that bed together.' Paintings and tapestries still lined the walls in rooms bearing signs announcing requisition by the Republic. There was a library, where many of the staff left traces of themselves in the form of donated books. The estate's villagers helped with labour and supplies, and on Sundays stood in long, patient queues to get medical attention for their sick and malnourished children.

As the main base of the American medical unit, the hospital received serious cases evacuated from other hospitals closer to the front. Visiting its stately white buildings, Langston reported to his readers about the black doctor from Harlem, Arnold Donawa, who was rebuilding faces at Villa Paz. The nationalists, Donawa told Langston, were using bullets usually seen only in big-game hunting, which exploded inside the body, spraying shards of metal. (Undergoing a painful medical procedure almost thirty years after the war, Nancy Cunard would be assailed by the memory of a doctor lancing an arm at the Escorial, looking, he told her, 'for a "dum-dum" bullet'.) That year, *Heart of Spain*, a documentary film about the war, showed accusatory footage of bandaged men whiling away time under the vast white arches of the hospital's courtyard, victims of the same weaponry. A nurse in a dark dress and white collar cuts away a man's dressings. With thin and dextrous fingers, she reveals the stump of his arm. 'Don't turn away,' the narrator commands. 'This is neutrality. This is non-intervention, Italian style.' It was this nurse Langston wrote home about: 'a slender chocolate-coloured girl' called Salaria Kea.

When Langston met her, Salaria had been at the hospital for six months. For weeks after she arrived, letters of welcome had flowed in from African American brigaders who, when they could get leave, trekked over to the hospital to meet her. As the only African American woman volunteering as a nurse in Spain, Salaria had become a celebrity. Postcards were made with her picture on. She was hailed as a figurehead for a far-reaching solidarity. ' "Salaria Salud!" ' Langston jotted down in his notebook: 'All children for miles around know her name.'

Though Villa Paz was the best-equipped of the American hospitals, it suffered from the privations and inconveniences endemic in the Republican zone. Dr Donawa sent Langston away with a long list of urgently needed medical supplies. The hospital frequently lost power, struggled to keep anything sterile, and fought battles against water shortages and the cold. Salaria was rising to these challenges with an inventive flair. When the hospital lost heating, Langston reported, she filled hot water bottles with soup to keep a hypothermic surgery patient warm. When they ran out of water, she boiled eggs in wine to keep her charges fed. Unsurprisingly, the patients liked her. One described her as 'a very charming person', known for 'her patience, her smile and her wit'. The makeshift conditions gave Salaria the opportunity to demonstrate her talents and to see them recognised. Rules and hierarchies lost their significance. Instead of 'the scolding, transfers and threatened dismissal' she might have expected at Harlem Hospital for stepping out of line, here she was praised for 'courage, bravery and ingenuity' in government dispatches. She was even promoted to head surgical nurse, a recognition unlikely to have been afforded her at home.

Describing Villa Paz years later, Salaria insisted (despite the dumdum bullets and the hungry children) that 'Everything was just lovely.' It was a place that enabled her flourishing. The work was hard and important. She was fulfilling a dream of service closely related to her faith. (Her outspoken sense of doing God's work by volunteering – something that possibly increased as she grew older – was another example of how she complicated a standard narrative. Asked gently by an interviewer about the hostility of the Catholic church towards the Republican side, and vice versa, Salaria was having none of it. 'I met plenty of Catholics right there in Spain,' she said. 'I was with them.' For all the Republican antipathy applauded by Nancy and Sylvia, many Spaniards did keep to their ingrained faith even as they aligned themselves with the side that tried to educate, or otherwise compel, them out of it. In her untidy allegiance, Salaria was representative of most people most of the time.)

At Villa Paz, Dr Pitts was no longer the highest-ranking team member, and within the hospital Salaria was largely shielded from his hostility. She liked and respected the other doctors she worked with, particularly Dr Barsky and Dr Pike (who had admired Josephine's handling of Hemingway at the Hotel Florida) – she felt they kept Pitts in line. Her main companions were anyway her 'gang' of other nurses. 'I miss you just like a little babe miss its mother's milk,' Salaria would write them after they parted.

Langston was clearly drawn to their camaraderie. On the night of his visit, some of the nurses were getting ready for bed in their dormitory, 'discussing same day's events', as one of them recounted afterwards, 'when Salaria Kea suddenly screamed. There was Langston sitting in a corner, just watching us. He apologised, told us he was enjoying the talk'.

~

Spain had reawakened Langston's idealism. After the semi-respite of Valencia, the war was more apparent in Madrid, where the blackout and curfew had to be taken seriously. He was told that almost a thousand people were killed by shelling in Madrid during his three-month stay. Anyone driving in the city after 11 p.m. could be stopped by guards and had better hope they knew the password for the night. But after the draining day-to-day troubles of life in Depression-era America, the company of people surviving on a promise was enlivening. In Madrid, where people had almost nothing, 'they expected soon to have everything'.

Later Langston would describe Spain's countryside with an elegiac lyricism he had honed in years of writing about the griefs and resilience of African American life. With his special ability to see the lovely in the quotidian, his exalting of the earthy and the seedy, he looked with a worldly yet unjaded eye on Spain: a sympathetic observer for a country in the midst of war. He understood that grief was not always expressed as plaint, that humour could be its own resistance. Recalled by Langston, almost everything was beautiful. He mistook the sound of snipers for birdsong and made even the late-night soliciting of prostitutes, as soldiers struck matches in dark streets to see the features of the women hailing them, a firefly masque of flaring and subsiding hopes. Visiting Neruda's former home, the Casa de las Flores, he found it bleak and empty, its famous balconies and window boxes smashed. And yet, there were still flowers growing at the windows and intrepid vines reaching from the balconies.

Madrid was weathering the aftermath of Brunete, and the bombing of nearby Republican trenches sent tremors continuously through the streets. Langston had visited the Brunete front and was shocked by the desolation of a ruined town. No one was left, but there were still 'portions of the dead in the streets'.

But he was not there to see the blood in the streets. Langston was interested in the arrival of people of colour to a country he regarded as innocent of racial prejudice. 'Divided Spain,' he called it, 'with men of color on both sides. To write about them I had come'.

First, he had sought out the African Americans in the Abraham Lincoln Brigade. Of almost 3,000 American volunteers who served over the course of the war, about ninety of them were African American. As it was for Salaria, volunteering in Spain was frequently a consolation for not having been able to join Ethiopia's struggle against Mussolini. (Haile Selassie's desire for good relations with the US government meant well-wishers had been prevented from volunteering there.) Many had recognised the threat posed by fascism's aim, as Langston put it, of 'a world for whites alone'; many simply recognised the nationalists. 'Give Franco a hood', Langston observed that year, 'and he would be a member of the Ku Klux Klan'.

Despite not speaking much Spanish, in a radio broadcast to the US, Louise Thompson claimed to share 'a common language' with her hosts because 'they are fighting oppression, and I come from a people whose oppression is centuries old'. Taking up arms – or being recognised as a comrade – could have huge psychological significance for volunteers familiar with the kind of prejudices associated with Franco and his allies. A quarter of International Brigaders were Jewish. Josephine's friend Dr Pike voiced the kind of broad solidarity frequently expressed when he gave the antisemitism he'd experienced in his life as the 'motivating factor' for going to Spain: 'I was identifying with those who had been badly treated, pushed around.'

Though he admired their courage, Langston couldn't help but feel that black volunteers had absconded from an equally pressing battle at home. Yet, to him, their sacrifices also advanced African American history, breaking new ground for the recognition of black attainments. He was proud that black Americans had come to Spain, not as the musicians and dancers who until then were the 'leading ambassadors of the Negro' in Europe but as 'voluntary fighters' – which is where history turned another page.

Langston noted that many Spaniards were 'quite dark themselves', with, he thought, 'distinct traces' of African ancestry from the long occupation that had followed the eighth-century Muslim conquest of the peninsula (a history which added potent layers to the presence of North Africans in the nationalist army). Towards himself he reported nothing but welcome, though there were stories of African

American volunteers running into trouble when they were mistaken
as 'Moors'.

To his shame, Langston's first reaction on encountering a man of
colour from the other side was a bolt of pure, instinctive fear. Visiting a prison hospital with fellow reporters one day, he grew restless in
the close heat and oppressive stench while the others conducted long
interviews in German and Italian (languages he could not speak). As
he passed down an eerily empty corridor in search of water, he was
'almost startled . . . out of my wits' by a tall, dark apparition, a figure
of deeper blackness than he had ever seen. Langston froze to let the
silent man pass.

Franco's dreaded Army of Africa, the colonial force he had transported to Spain with German and Italian help early in the war, was
powered by the Foreign Legion (distinguished by their slogan: 'Long
live Death!') and Moroccan mercenaries. Though their ferocious
reputation no doubt rested in part on racist assumptions of barbar-
ity, Moroccan soldiers were often deployed as shock troops, sent in
to pacify towns that didn't surrender immediately. They were frequently invoked by nationalist generals as a sexual threat against Spanish women. One British soldier told Josephine that, when facing them
in battle, 'You always kept a bullet for yourself'.

In her journalism of the previous year, Nancy had framed the Arab
fighters as victims of their paymasters. 'The Spanish fascist rebels are
using native troops to massacre Spanish workers almost as miserable
and oppressed as the North Africans themselves,' she told her readers in December. 'These are the methods of all imperialist powers.'
While the Foreign Legion had played a key role in crushing rebel-
lious tribes in North Africa, they were now fighting alongside soldiers recruited in those same territories. (As one historian has noted,
the 'savagery visited upon the towns conquered by Spanish colonial
forces was simply a repetition of what they did when they attacked
a Moroccan village'.)

To Nancy, the importation of these troops was yet more evidence
of the vast structures of oppression that set its victims against each
other, robbing them of their natural allies. Suspicious about fascist

recruitment techniques in North Africa, she had visited Tangier and French Morocco after first leaving Spain, reporting that many had been tricked and press-ganged into joining Franco's army. The Republican leadership was also making efforts to recast this contingent of the enemy in its public messaging.

Rebuking himself in the hospital, Langston sought out a nurse to show him into the small ward of captured Moroccan soldiers. There he struggled to communicate with anyone but a thirteen-year-old boy who had been injured at Brunete and spoke some Spanish. The child had come to Spain with his mother, who had been recruited to cook and clean behind the lines. The boy had ended up fighting. His mother had been killed.

As if to undo his initial failing and restore the possibility of fraternal communication, Langston imagined an exchange between two black soldiers on opposing sides in a poem written to highlight the discordance of black soldiers firing at each other. ('The Moors', he wrote in an article for the *Afro-American*, 'are shooting the wrong way.') In it, a black soldier in the Abraham Lincoln Brigade describes the death of a Moorish prisoner in a letter home:

> I said, Boy, what you doin' here,
> Fightin' against the free?

But the prisoner has trouble answering this question, and that is what sets the two men apart. Where one has taken up a cause, can live and die with purpose, the other suffers a pointless death, his life wasted because he spent it in his exploiter's service. Unlike the politicised 'wide-awake Negroes' Langston kept meeting, and Josephine's International Brigaders, he does not know why he came.

Langston wrote several 'Letters from Spain', a series his biographer would later dismiss as 'proletarian doggerel': verses intended as propaganda to engage 'the common people' reading him at home. He met with similarly robust criticism on the final night of a stay with soldiers at the front, when he gave a reading at an abandoned mill and members of the Abraham Lincoln Brigade proved themselves as assertive culturally as they were politically. In revolutionary Spain, where the arts were considered common property – a participatory experience – even the bard of Harlem's work was not above challenge.

The African Americans in the brigade, some of the soldiers pointed out, did not speak as the man in the poem did. 'They said that many of their Negro comrades in arms were well educated; furthermore, I might mistakenly be aiding in perpetuating a stereotype.'

Langston defended himself. He was determined to speak to those more usually excluded from high art, the 'ordinary Negroes' who would never even have heard of the Harlem Renaissance. This was a poem to persuade and engage, to reassure and influence his readers with easy comprehension. To his front-line audience, Langston conceded that 'of course, most of the Negroes in the Brigades spoke grammatically', but others, including 'plenty of whites as well – had had but little formal education and did not speak as if they were college men'. Someone must write for them, and show that 'even the least privileged of Americans, the Southern Negroes, were represented' in the Brigades. He had written a voice to express that politics, like the arts, was not beyond anyone.

This was Langston on his tightrope of words, forever questioning his art and yet defending it from interference; searching for ways to reach the people he wrote for, to glorify them in modes that did not alienate, and still, physically and creatively, survive as an artist. It was delicate work to delineate his celebration of 'low-down' life – the tones, lexicon and patter of black vernacular, the rhythm of the blues and jazz he loved – from the caricatures that stood in for African Americans in mainstream culture; yet Langston had long salvaged representation from a language that had been appropriated and debased elsewhere.

I wondered if he was still pondering this defence of poetry-with-purpose in Madrid when he typed onto a scrap of paper some lines that never appeared in his collected work. In them he makes 'Poetry'

a working creature, a beast of burden due no special reverence. Poetry can be ridden 'down the muddy road', left untended at the gate and fed in no special hurry: its place is in the muck with the rest of us, ready to bear the poet where he wants to go.

In Spain, Langston solidified his understanding of himself as a writer at a remove from the humanity he sought always to reach. He wanted to be there watching history as it was made, observing events but apart from them, too. Writing was his channel to the world but also somehow his buffer. In the Spanish Civil War, he wrote, he was a writer, not a fighter: someone who watched and recorded, and then offered an interpretation based on his own emotional responses.

His view of a writer's service as not only recording reality, but making sense of it, reminded me of Josephine seeking a 'complete relationship' with her situation. For Langston, writers brought their talent to bear but also their 'background and experience' and, crucially, an ability 'to study, simplify and understand': 'To understand being the chief of these.' If ignorance risked enslavement, and fascism stood for death, writers could offer the opposite. 'Words have been used too much to make people doubt and fear,' he would announce later in Paris. 'Words must now be used to make people *believe and do.*'

★

The following year, when she was furloughed home, Salaria would work tirelessly to publicise the efforts of the American volunteers – work that was partly enabled by a sorority of black women. When Louise Thompson got back to the US, she wrote to Langston in Spain mentioning her idea of raising funds for an ambulance as a donation to the Republic's medical service. On her own return, Thyra Edwards stayed with Louise before embarking on an ambitious multi-city speaking tour with Salaria. Paul Robeson started things off with a donation of $250; the ambulance was dispatched late in 1938: a gift, as Thyra put it in an article, 'from the Race people of America to the people of Republican Spain'.

At Villa Paz, the nurses Salaria worked with were mostly working-class, like her, and she identified with the Spanish women she met, long oppressed by a deeply patriarchal society. And there were her fellow African Americans in the armed forces. Yet she was also conscious of how the facets of her identity combined to set her further apart, how the otherness people singled out to celebrate left her a little alone. In a partial memoir she drafted in the third person, Salaria made this the caveat of her position there. 'Many people visited and remarked on the lone Negro girl serving so diligently', she wrote, 'yet so far was she from any women of her kind'.

Salaria would give many lectures about the war. She spoke at elementary schools, at NAACP meetings and churches, to trade union members and to assemblies of nurses. But she, like Langston, also had a specific message for a particular African American audience. In telling and retelling her own story, she knowingly took on the burden of representation imposed upon her in Spain, offering herself as inspiration. She wanted, she explained in 1980, to show that none of the setbacks and insults in her life had broken or diverted her; to show 'how I came to blocks [but] they didn't turn me away'.

Among the people alive to Salaria's charms was a reticent white Irishman named John Patrick O'Reilly, who had joined the Republican forces early in the war. It's possible that he took part in the defence of Madrid, but by the spring of 1937 he was working as an ambulance driver and orderly at Villa Paz. 'Pat' was tall and lean; a man who sang 'The Rose of Tralee' with 'head thrown back, eyes closed, putting his whole sentimental Irish heart on the performance'; a writer, it turned out, of poems about Salaria.

Like her, he had grown up poor. During the Depression, he had drifted between England and Ireland looking for work, spending time in Oxford labouring at a brickyard, where he sometimes listened in to the speakers declaiming on the university common. By 1936, he had a pretty bleak view of the future. 'I thought there was going to be a war,' he said later, 'and if I was going to be killed anyway, it would be better to be fighting for the poor than for the rich.'

Immediately struck by Pat's good looks, Salaria at first thought of him only as a catch for one of her friends. Even without the almost unthinkable challenges of a mixed-race relationship, there was work to focus on. But Pat won her over. Later she put it down to a well-pitched plea made on a swimming break. Was she really going to 'let the reactionaries take away the only thing a poor man deserved', he asked her: 'his right to marry the one he loved and believed loved him?'

And so a wedding took place at Villa Paz, attended by delegations from the hospital and from the local community; a wedding so festive that several of the guests had to be carried to their cars at the end of the night. From an infanta's abandoned trunks, Salaria's friends bedecked her in regal finery of a kind she had never worn before and never would again. A chorus of local girls sang in place of a wedding march, and a Spanish judge with a handlebar moustache officiated, while Villa Paz's head nurse, Fredericka Martin, looked on as 'proud maman witness'. Dr Donawa gave a speech for the staff; a blinded soldier on behalf of the patients. Instead of rings, Salaria and Pat exchanged fountain pens. Earlier the same day, two journalists – Martha Gellhorn and Ernest Hemingway – had visited the hospital and been told all about the union. They couldn't stay for the wedding, a colleague of Salaria's reported, but they 'took the story'.

Langston also missed the wedding, but he sent back a piece on Salaria and her marriage to the press at home. In private he exclaimed over the match to Louise Thompson: 'Real solidarity!'

In the papers, Salaria was again celebrated as a symbol: a living icon of Popular Front ideals. A public notice appeared at Villa Paz addressed to 'Comrade Salaria', and through her 'all of our brothers of colour', wishing the bride and her new husband 'all sorts of happiness'. More than a love story, the marriage, according to its well-wishers, had 'set another milestone of victory in our struggle against racism!'

Stupid Days

Martha Gellhorn, Langston Hughes, Nancy Cunard

Madrid and Valencia: autumn, winter 1937

At night, the sound of lions in the zoo roaring with hunger reached Langston from across the Retiro Park. There was horseflesh for dinner there and horseflesh for dinner at the Alianza where he was staying, unless nothing so substantial could be rustled up. With access to the city so restricted, it was impossible to keep it properly supplied. Journalists prowled the watering holes of the capital, hunting for bar snacks. Langston lost fifteen pounds. He couldn't afford to frequent the places on the Gran Vía patronised by Hemingway et al., but in the comradely atmosphere of the war he nevertheless met, as he pointedly noted later, 'more white American writers than at any other period of my life', among them Hemingway and 'the golden-haired Martha Gellhorn'.

Martha had once visited the same zoo, on that day when the weather was good and nothing much was happening and guiltily she had wanted some uncomplicated excursion to enjoy with Ernest; the day when they 'were sick of the war' and 'wanted to have a good time, something not exciting or important or grave or memorable but just fun'.

Having longed to return to Spain in the spring, Martha was now finding the days in Madrid just as wretched. There was no good news. The nationalists had been mopping up unconquered parts of the north. Two-thirds of the country was now in their hands. At home, word about her affair with Ernest was out and only she understood 'how bad it will be'. Her twenties were counting down. Private travails bedded down with the war and smothered her spirits. 'Stupid day', she wrote on 9 November, just after her birthday. 'Grey, cold, nothing. Stupid day, stupid woman. I am wasting everything and now I am twenty nine.'

She was preoccupied with the fear of life passing with nothing to show for it, and her helplessness in a war zone only aggravated her horror of purposelessness. Her achievements as a journalist failed to satisfy her. The approach of her birthday had agitated her journal: 'time is going away almost before you can see it'. Despite a feast rustled up by Ernest and another American journalist, the day itself was spoiled by worries about the gossip at home. And there were often quarrels, Ernest unleashing indelible barrages of hostility, and Martha thought, 'Oh God, either make it work or make it end now.'

When they had returned to Madrid in September, they had driven out to look over Brunete, taken and lost in their absence, and seen a land 'still tawny with summer'. Pointing her binoculars in one direction, Martha had watched Republican soldiers washing in a stream; in the other, nationalists picking through abandoned buildings. Even there, even then, it was 'beautiful' to her. But the winter months brought punishing cold, streets tacky with mud, and very little action. The shelling went on. While Langston's swing records played to distract guests at the Alianza, at the Hotel Florida, Martha and Ernest countered the boom and crash with a Chopin mazurka that would forever after remind her of Madrid. Throwing the windows open to protect the glass, on one night they counted the shells, giving up after six hundred. 'You had a feeling of disaster, swinging like a compass needle, aimlessly, all over the city.' And she kept writing of those the needle landed on, of the quiet crowd watching bodies being pulled from rubble until a 'woman reached down suddenly for her child and took it in her arms, and held it close to her'.

When Langston decided to leave, Ernest and some of the other correspondents threw him a farewell party at the Hotel Victoria. After three months of staying at the Alianza, Langston had spent longer in Madrid than his editors had agreed to pay for. He found it hard to tear himself away and yet, like Josephine, he worried about sharing the food of a starving city. Nor could he forget that, as an American, he could 'go home anytime I wanted to'.

Nancy had crossed the border the previous month with the painter John Banting. He was an old friend who had done duty on other journeys: watching in protective admiration as she handled New York's tabloid press in 1932. *Authors Take Sides* was due for publication in Britain in November, but Nancy had not stuck around to see it. As the French authorities clamped down on people crossing into Spain, she rallied from a fever that had confined her to bed and negotiated a way past the 'drawn sabres and bayonets and angry French officials' to get the two of them into Spain. They made for Barcelona, which was colder and hungrier than Nancy had last seen it, and then somehow managed to secure a government car for the long drive to Valencia.

There they found Langston, still on his way out of Spain, who struck John as 'a magnificent and a magnetising man'. Nancy and Langston had been in touch since the *Negro* anthology but they may have met in person for the first time that year. Much later, he described Nancy as 'kind and good', 'cosmopolitan and sophisticated and simple all at the same time'. He had sent her one of his 'letters home' from the imagined Abraham Lincoln brigader and contributed to her fundraising pamphlets earlier in the year. In Valencia, Nancy reciprocated with a copy of a poem later entitled 'Yes, It Is Spain', which she dedicated to Langston.

He also helped arrange Nancy's other pleasing encounter in Valencia: her interview with Salaria Kea. 'You have read of her already', Nancy's article for the ANP began. 'Now it is my good luck to have met her here in Valencia, my privilege to have talked to her quite a while. She is very well known in this country.'

Nancy seemed to think that Salaria was passing through the city on her way to a convalescent hospital on the coast (possibly at Benicàssim, which, Nancy noted, had been bombed twice that week), but it's also possible that she was on a honeymoon granted by the hospital authorities. Nancy appears enraptured with Salaria in the piece, keen to be friends. The 'tall, dark, intelligent' woman, 'with a winning smile and a very pleasing voice', was 'one of the nicest personalities I have met in a long time.' She estimated Salaria to be about twenty-five but also, indulging in a characteristic fantasy, imagined her as 'a young woman born, oh how long ago in Africa, before all the white invasions and conquests'. Sitting together in a quiet hotel room, the two women discussed fascism, racism and Salaria's new husband.

If Salaria had mentioned Dr Pitts's insult to the author of the *A Negro Nurse in Republican Spain* pamphlet, the story had not made it into print. Nancy, however, was openly appalled. 'One would think that Americans who volunteer for any kind of anti-Fascist work over here would realize that Jim Crow simply cannot exist in this country,' she noted tartly. 'Yet Miss Kee spoke of having met with one instance of Jim Crow here, on the part of an American.'

Keen to emphasise the internationalist solidarity she put so much faith in, Nancy assured her readers that 'Spaniards would be very angry indeed' about Salaria's experience. Informed by their new comrades about American race relations, they had proved vocal in their outrage. 'In fact,' she insisted, 'hardly a day passes now without some Spaniard telling me how abominable it is.'

Later, Nancy and Salaria had coffee with 'an English friend' (presumably John Banting) in one of Valencia's cafés. Nancy felt close to Salaria ('I think we both feel we became friends that very first meeting'), and on her side at least their parting was a poignant one. She knew that Salaria was due to join a mobile unit at the front during the next attack – 'Salaria says this as calmly as one says "I'm taking the train" ' – and she also knew that Salaria's happiness with her new husband would be no safer once they were out of the country. Speaking of Pat, Salaria had smiled and said, 'I could not go South with him . . .' But just then in Valencia, as two women able to sit together, unmolested, in a public café and talk things over, 'the whole color question, as it exists in America' seemed to them 'an absolute fantasy'.

Langston and Nicolás Guillén were having trouble getting out of Valencia. Food was still more plentiful in that city, but there were already also more refugees and more rumours than when they had left. The nationalist forces were poised to divide the Republican zone by driving through Aragon and Castellón to the sea. It was said that the government was planning to evacuate further north, to Barcelona, but that did not answer the question of how everyone else would escape. With so many people scrambling for an exit, Langston found himself trapped.

The station was crammed with 'unending' queues, and they were told that there were no tickets to Barcelona for a month. Even the local press office could promise them nothing in the way of transport before Christmas. Then Langston remembered Thomas Cook and Son. The British travel agency had a reputation for being 'wonderfully dependable' – something he could not attest to, having been refused service at its New York branch. But the Valencia office remained insouciantly open and, out of options, he tried them anyway. In the panic-stricken city, he was serenely received by a polite clerk who seemed to find nothing absurd about Langston's request for two tickets on the wagon-lit to Barcelona. When would he like to go? 'Tomorrow,' Langston hazarded.

The following night, he and Guillén left Valencia in style. In France, he headed straight for the station buffet – stunned, after the deprivations in Spain, by its abundance. But like Josephine a few months before him, he found his thoughts straying from the meal. He sat and 'wondered what would happen to the Spanish people walking the bloody tightrope of their civil struggle'.

During this trip, as on others, John Banting marvelled at his resourceful and unrelenting guide. Wherever they went, they met insurmountable obstacles she could force aside and people she knew. Nancy could always keep going. In Barcelona, he took what would become his favourite photo of her. A woman who had sat for many portraits, she had a tendency to slip into poses at the appearance of his camera. But this time he judged his moment right, catching her when she was too tired to stiffen to attention; too impatient to do anything but submit to his lens and try to limit the delay. She looks exactly as if she has just turned back in response to her name; her arm is out in a gesture of appeal and resignation. Sunlight bursts over the large white flower in her lapel, revealing deep grooves of exhaustion on her face. 'If I look closely into the shadows-filled eyes', John wrote years later when he sent it to her, 'I can see such wells of kindness and patience and indomitable love and steadfastness. (And you look pretty cute too by the way.)'

After Valencia they went on to Madrid: a ten-hour bus journey with a single stop along the way. To keep going was only to rise to the

example set by the Madrileños. In 'freezing, starving Madrid under
the December shells' more than anywhere else, Nancy said, she found
'that fortitude, that innate faith in its cause of the Spanish people'.
The lowest temperature of the century was recorded that month in
Aragon. At their hotel, they lifted the rugs from the floor onto their
beds at night for warmth.

One morning, they rose at 6.30, 'in the dark calm, after uneasy
sleep in icy beds', for one of those days that you never forget. The
'authorities' (Nancy: 'bless them, those!') wanted journalists to see the
restoration work underway at Spain's national museum, the Prado. At
the Alianza's urging, the government had established a committee to
oversee the preservation of Spain's artistic riches very early on in the
war, and much of what wasn't evacuated to Valencia was stored at the
Prado. (The committee had also initiated educational programmes,
which helped to discourage attacks on art and architecture belonging
to the church and nobility, but nationalist bombing had caused enormous destruction. When Madrid was first imperilled in November
1936, the Prado, the National Library, the Royal Academy of Fine
Arts and other museums had all been struck.)

Insufficiently fortified by tea 'of a kind' for breakfast, Nancy and
John were taken into the museum's hushed vaults to see restorers
already at work by candlelight. In the echoey gloom, El Grecos rescued from churches received patient ministrations and 'frozen, black
mittened hands' tended to 'very lovely Hieronymus Bosch paintings'.
John noticed damaged armour from the seventeenth century; Nancy
was struck 'to my appallment' by the remains of smashed-up plaster
horses that had once borne 'famous knights'.

When Nancy and John emerged into meagre sunshine, snow was
falling in fat flakes. They had spent longer than they'd realised among
the basement treasures, and the day was brightening. They visited
the headquarters of the International Brigades, then Nancy wanted
to show John the city she loved. While the guns blasted in the quite-
close distance, they walked through the Plaza Mayor, and on until they
were stopped by a sentry at the front. They settled down for a cigarette together. Clement Attlee, leader of the opposition in Britain, had
just visited with a group of MPs, and the sentry confided confident

hopes that 'El Commandante Attlee' would defend the Republic's reputation abroad. British inaction so far could only be down to some misunderstanding.

On the way back into town, Nancy remembered Ernest Hemingway. She hadn't seen him since the twenties, but she took Banting off to the Hotel Florida to look him up anyway. They found him in a warm room, holding court.

Thawing in his hospitality (they each received 'a fine, strong drink'), Nancy and John were welcomed with a Hemingwayish mix of bating and bravado. 'He made some remark about the stimulation of fighting which neither of us liked', John recorded, and a joke about the herbs they were smoking (proper cigarettes were almost unobtainable) that he considered in poor taste. He was also offended, as he was no doubt meant to be, by Ernest's announcement that they had arrived too late to be included in 'a play he had just written about the "war tourists"'. This dubious honour had not been escaped by Martha, whose superficial likeness appeared in *The Fifth Column* as the journalist mistress of an American agent living in the Hotel Florida: a woman described as 'lazy and spoiled' (according to her lover) 'and rather stupid' but nevertheless able to write good pieces for a women's magazine.

It had been a tense stay in Madrid. A lull in hostilities around the city had given Ernest time to write the play, but the Republic was expecting another assault and there were rumours of plans for another diversionary attack, this time at Teruel, in Aragon. 'It rained all the time,' Martha wrote for *Collier's* in November. 'It rained and everyone waited for the offensive to begin.' Everyone seemed convinced that the offensive would be a success: they had only to wait for it. They had to wait through the cold, and the rain. 'Waiting is a big part of war and it is hard to do.'

To her dismay, the battle at Teruel began after Martha had left the city. She was headed for New York, where she would distribute Christmas gifts and reassurances to the parents of Abraham Lincoln Brigade volunteers. Ernest covered the offensive without her, entering Teruel with the Republicans in freezing conditions, before heading to Paris, where his wife was waiting for him.

John felt sure that Nancy shared his dislike for Hemingway, but her own recollection was far more affectionate. Later she was disappointed that he had not used his fame to promote more causes, but on that frigid December day the celebrated writer treated her with a tenderness she never forgot. He removed her boots to warm her feet. Recklessly neglectful of self-care, Nancy was startled and touched by the gesture. 'He was enchanting – such a sympathetic moment – from a non-Spaniard – was never my lot till then, nor yet again.'

In one of Nancy's poems about Spain, she mentions 'These agonies, laced with individual sorrows.' I had always read this as a gesture to the countless injured lives that any national disaster comes down to in the end, but now I wondered if she was also talking about her own wounds, about that guilty way in which our individual anxieties and sorrows, insignificant as they are in the grand scheme of things, remain inescapably significant to us – bind themselves, in fact, to external disturbances until it seems as though they are all part of each other, so that political upheavals become personally invasive and, more riskily, that our own feelings about them can take on a semblance of epic significance.

It's often suggested that people gain release from their own problems by becoming involved with more important matters, as if we can simply swamp our troubles into silence by concerning ourselves with other people's. But that also rustles up a neat explanation for why a person who doesn't have to see a war zone would choose to go there: it's easier to search for self-interest than sincerity when judging the motivations of others.

Martha observed in Spain that the 'same small human things which worry people everywhere' were not blown away by the bombs (even her own could not be shaken off), but how, then, to give them their proper place, if they are to be admitted to the record? When it comes to the problems of ourselves and others and the world at large, scale makes itself felt in illogical ways. There's surely no better illustration of this than a diary written in wartime. In the privacy of idle worrying, all things count, and Martha's observations of what was happening in Madrid, her foreboding assessments of the affair with Hemingway, her accounts of shopping and ageing and despair were all committed to paper together.

As well as conveying the sheer intensity of her emotional investment in faraway agonies, Nancy's poem continues in a way that reminded me of Martha's twenty-ninth-birthday upbraidings during that bleak Madrid November:

> This is the house of time withering away
> And time running, and time at a loss,
> Like a foot forever on the stair, and the return
>   of a dying called winter.

Perhaps this is a problem with birthdays: the way they remind us that however much we might lose track of time, it never loses track of us. Maybe twenty-nine is a particularly difficult year. Milestones come into view and put what you've done so far into less forgiving light. 'To be 29 and unmarried,' Virginia Woolf wrote archly in 1911, 'to be a failure – childless – insane too, no writer.' Nearly thirty years later, the swift transience of our little lives had become a reason to live better. 'What a dream life is to be sure,' she wrote, thinking of Lytton Strachey – her great friend and stimulator, whose death in 1932 had ushered in what Leonard would identify as the beginning, for them, of the 'erosion of life by death'. The idea of a literary legacy seemed uncertain comfort: 'that he should be dead, & I reading him', she went on, '& trying to make out that we indented ourselves on the world; whereas I sometimes feel its been an illusion – gone so fast, lived so quickly; & nothing to show for it, save these little books. But that makes me dig my feet in, & squeeze the moment.' It was not exactly that there was still so much to do; there was, crucially, still so much she wanted to think through.

The developments of the 1930s, as more war became more likely, created the intense pressure of a worsening situation. It's telling that when Martha exhorted her fellow writers in 1937 to take themselves out into the world of activism, she sought to reassure them, too, that 'A man who . . . has given a year of his life to steel strikes, or to the unemployed, or to the problems of racial prejudice, *has not lost or wasted time.*' What writer isn't always craving time? 'I wonder why time is always allowed to harry one,' Virginia pondered in 1935, frantically excited to finish *The Years* and get on with a polemic that nagged to be written. She tried to hold her nerve against the running of the hours. 'If I want more time,' she promised herself weeks later, 'I shall take it. I'm not time's fool – no.'

Towards the end of her life, Martha would come to terms with her fear of wasting time. 'I now think it is as necessary as solitude,' she told a friend in 1987; 'that's how the compost heap grows in the mind.' The combination mattered, because time itself was not sufficient. Time comes in different qualities. To be useful, it has to be the kind that is also space in which to roam, a kind of privacy.

When Sylvia Townsend Warner was a single woman living alone in London, she developed methods for evading the various friends and acquaintances who would drop in, confidently expecting her to be available to them – she would put on her hat before answering the door and pretend to be just heading out. Little wonder that her Lolly Willowes does not turn to witchcraft to restore the inheritance mismanaged by her brother, or to bring herself fame or beauty; she does it when her nephew arrives to shatter her peace. Fond though she is of him, Lolly will marshal plagues to reverse his invasion. That iconic room of one's own Virginia pinned her hopes on was fundamentally a protection from intrusion, from the demands of the world outside: the archetype of a writer's seclusion. A room of her own is a space where a writer can shed all the layers required for being, and simply think, simply write.

Over the 1930s, Virginia developed this further into a personal ideal of 'immunity' – a term that surfaces several times in that long-brewed novel, *The Years*. It came to her after Lytton's death, this shorthand for not letting the world get to you. 'Immunity', she outlined to herself, 'is an exalted calm desirable state'. It reminded me a little of Langston on his tightrope, a precarious and necessary pose. To be immune was to shake loose from the claims the world makes by noticing one. It meant, Virginia elaborated in 1932:

to exist apart from rubs, shocks, suffering; to be beyond the range of darts; to have enough to live on without courting flattery, success; not to need to accept invitations; not to mind other people being praised; to feel This – to sit & breathe behind my screen, alone, is enough; to be strong; content . . . to feel no one's thinking of me; to feel I have done certain things & can be quiet now; to be mistress of my hours; to be detached from all sayings about me; & claims on me . . .

'His Royal Highness acknowledges with smiles and the National Socialist salute the greetings of the crowds gathered at his hotel and elsewhere during the day.'

The Times reporting on the visit of the Duke and Duchess of Windsor
(formerly King Edward VIII and Wallis Simpson)
to Nazi Germany in October 1937

Outsiders

Virginia Woolf

Three Guineas

Virginia Woolf takes her place on a bridge. We are welcome to join her – that, in fact, is her intention. Look: on the other side, a procession is passing. Rows upon rows of men streaming by, in wigs and gowns and other finery. Power is filing past us, in other words, and we can see its progress because there in the crowd are 'great-grandfathers, grandfathers, fathers, uncles . . .': legacies of influence. Rarely does power escape the procession; rarely does it slip away to join us, the observers on the bridge. This is what Woolf wanted us to see (how fortunate that they should be passing at just this moment), because this is a procession that must be kept within our sights even if – we can dream – we should ever be honoured enough to join it. Most of all, she wants us to keep an eye on where it is headed, because whether we are in it or not, we will be swept in its direction. We turn our heads, and see that Woolf is giving us a meaningful look. It's a look that says: *never join*. Become a participant in those ranks if you must, but never merely follow that procession. We strain at first to grasp her meaning: we can belong but we must not? Lean forward – in all the pounding clamour of all those steps, the clink of medals, the rustle of gowns and papers, it is hard to hear – 'Think we must . . .' she is saying. 'Let us never cease from thinking – what is this "civilization" in which we find ourselves?'

England: 1938

Three Guineas was published shortly before the first anniversary of Julian's death. 'If I say what I mean in 3 Guineas', Virginia had warned herself, 'I must expect considerable hostility.' It's easy to cast her up in the ivory tower in the late 1930s, missing the point, and there were many who did. Even decades later, her surviving nephew, Quentin, was still exasperated with her for trifling with minor matters like feminism at a time when vital issues were at stake: why, he would demand, 'involve a discussion of women's rights with the far more agonising and immediate question of what we were to do in order to meet the ever-growing menace of Fascism and war'? This second debate between aunt and nephew, in which Virginia had become the ghost and Quentin the survivor who must interpret the other's position, rehearsed the clash at the heart of 1930s culture over the value of the arts and the intellect, and between pacifism and self-defence. Or, as Quentin put it with ill-concealed contempt, 'were we . . . to scuttle like frightened spinsters before the Fascist thugs?' In his construction, reflection was a cowardly (feminine) evasion.

It's not difficult to understand his enduring impatience. His aunt, he felt, had muddied the waters where clarity and action were needed. Virginia was prescient when she imagined *The Years* (which in her mind formed 'one book' with *Three Guineas*) being dismissed as 'the long-drawn twaddle of a prim prudish bourgeois mind'. In the 1930s her reputation entered a long period of decline, which for decades scuppered her hope that real attention would be paid to *Three Guineas*. As one of her biographers puts it, 'With the rise of the dictators . . . she came to appear a batty lady authoress, out of touch with the brutal world of politics. And so was born the myth of the precious aesthete, withdrawn from the real world'.

Virginia was very aware of the soul-searching going on around her, the tussle over the ivory tower. But to her this was a question of class consciousness and elitism. By 1940 she would speak of a 'leaning tower' inhabited by public-school-boy writers who had finally registered that their background set them apart from the majority. And yet, if the ivory tower represents a certain solitary intellectual independence, Virginia defended it for reasons that put her firmly on the same page as Nancy Cunard. Words were valuable, she wrote in an essay published in the weeks before Julian died, for 'their power to tell the truth'. But they were retiring creatures that needed, like Virginia herself, 'privacy' in order to properly develop. 'Our unconsciousness is their privacy; our darkness is their light.' Two years later, she would be fretting over so much contemporary literature that seemed 'surrounded by a circle of invisible censors'. 'If I say this So & So will think me sentimental. If that . . . will think me Bourgeois.' The lack of privacy stripped 'concentration' and 'beauty' from literature: 'As if the mind must be allowed to settle undisturbed over the object in order to secrete the pearl.' As a refuge for thinking, the ivory tower (a realm that totalitarianism would necessarily seek to conquer) was also the final bastion of resistance.

If Nancy wondered why she received only one contribution to *Authors Take Sides* from the Woolf household, the answer was waiting in *Three Guineas*. As she reflected on the slow progress of women's rights in Britain, Virginia issued a warning. Society was changing but women remained on the outside of power. This, then, was a crucial moment to pay attention to that procession of powerful men: as the opportunity approached to join it, would women fall into line or attempt to change its direction?

Virginia believed that women, through their long exclusion, had become possessors of a history and culture all their own. She wanted them to bring this independent inheritance to bear. As she explains to the man who has asked her advice on how to prevent war: 'Though we see the same world, we see it through different eyes. Any help we can give you must be different from that you can give yourselves, and perhaps the value of that help may lie in the fact of that difference.'

In other words, outsiderness had become their power. The 'daughters of educated men', she believed, had something to offer by virtue of their history of exclusion: an independence of thought that would be jeopardised if they relinquished their outsider's perspective. If they lost it, she feared that women would simply contribute to a system that perpetuated war, and learn to exclude others from their advantages as they themselves had once been excluded.

She proposed an 'Outsiders' Society'. 'It would have no office, no committee, no secretary; it would call no meetings; it would hold no conferences.' Members would commit to a policy of not joining in: they would refuse honours, avoid working in military industries like munitions factories or participating in patriotic displays that 'encourage the desire to impose "our" civilization or "our" dominion upon other people'. Financial independence would of course be crucial, so equal salaries and payment for previously unpaid work like the duties of motherhood were going to need attention. Members would rely on their individual consciences and personal instincts. They would interrogate, question and rise above. In doing so, they might find the strength to do the difficult thing. 'This is what needs courage,' North Pargiter thinks to himself in *The Years*: 'to speak the truth.'

Here is another surprising parallel between Nancy Cunard and Virginia Woolf: that they could both, despite their privilege, identify themselves so keenly as outsiders. Nancy made very deliberate efforts to alienate herself from her native class: picking a side had made living with the enemy impossible. Virginia sometimes insisted on a surprising level of disempowerment. In *Three Guineas* she claimed that 'the daughters of educated men' (of which she was certainly one) had less agency than their working-class sisters, who could at least go on strike in a way that people might notice. For her, power was so concentrated within that procession of privilege that most of humanity could operate, if they wished, as outsiders, despite the spectrum of economic advantage they would represent. In 1940 she would align herself with an audience of working men when she told them, 'we are not going to leave writing to be done for us by a small class of well-to-do young men who have only a pinch, a thimbleful of experience to give us'.

But being an outsider was less about exclusion than about positioning oneself at a tangent that became a vantage point – about maintaining integrity. Martha Gellhorn claimed not-belonging as a virtue, despite her ease in aligning herself with the Spanish Republic. Being an outsider was her chosen position, she once wrote. No group she had ever seen had tempted her: 'I am an onlooker.' Josephine Herbst, who insistently chronicled injustices of sex as much as the injustices she was assured were actually important, placed a further expectation on her work. 'I can't think of any really important imaginative writing,' she once declared, 'which isn't basically critical of the social order.'

★

For a long time, a line from one of Nancy's poems hung on a board by my desk:

I'm of a mood tonight, boy, marked DO NOT TOUCH

Some key to understanding her seemed locked in that taut warning, in the rigid *need* of it. The line comes from 'Yes, It Is Spain', which was written around the time she was trying to get *Authors Take Sides* into print. (It's the poem she dedicated to Langston in Valencia.) In it, she envies the dead, 'safe from the shells and cries and wounds'; safe from seeing the worst humanity is capable of. I could imagine her not wanting to be touched – needing, in the face of all that suffering, to maintain a tight defensive shell against the invasions of contact or comfort. Comfort was not a thing that could be tolerated. Comfort was not going to change anything. It could not help the dead.

Do not touch: a warning from a woman who needed to be alone. When questioned by her biographer, a former lover of Nancy's could recall, 'Once she told me she needed a day absolutely alone,' but also: 'Solitude terrified her.' There was something about the writer's – the outsider's – predicament there too. The pendulum swinging between company and solitude, engagement and retreat. Hemingway put it another way when describing Martha: 'M. loves humanity but can't stand people.' I thought of Virginia Woolf, endlessly curious about other lives and endlessly aware that her imagination could only batter 'like a moth at the flame of so many inaccessible lanterns'; always more comfortable with the mass in the abstract than with individuals who emerged from it: perhaps the reason why politics had to be translated into her own tongue, as she put it, before it could be dealt with.

The important thing for Nancy, I suspected, was not only to have access to solitude but to be able to withstand it. Holding to your own course, your own code, in the face of a hostile and uncomprehending society is a lonely business. Fortunately, that echoing mansion of Nancy's childhood had been a schoolroom in loneliness.

She was always an extraordinary outsider to the causes she chose – constitutionally incapable of party discipline, gifted with tenacity but not with diplomacy, determined to learn but not always to listen. Despite all the friends, all the movements artistic and otherwise with which she intersected, it is hard to see exactly where Nancy Cunard belonged. The same went for Martha, Josephine, Langston . . . They did not quite (did not try to) fit in anywhere. Except, perhaps, in the Outsiders' Society.

In January 2018, a man called John Kiszely posted a picture on Twitter of his father, 'a young doctor with the International Brigade', tending to the body of a woman. When comments on the post suggested the patient could be Gerda Taro, Kiszely added of photo of the reverse, on which someone had written 'Mrs Frank Capa . . . Killed at Brunete.'

When I looked at the post in the spring of 2020, it had 173 comments and had been retweeted 1,600 times. Much as the scrawled caption both eclipsed and suggested the woman's identity, the emergence of the photograph threw up more questions than it answered. In the commentary I followed afterwards between various academics, people seemed inclined to accept that the photo could really be of Gerda. Given the immense propaganda show the Popular Front made of her death, it did seem plausible that someone might have photographed her body.

One of the replies to Kiszely's post included another, eerily similar, photograph: Gerda sleeping, captured by Capa in their Parisian room. In this one she is curled on her side on the narrow bed, covers tossed aside, her striped pyjamas rumpled and caught up around one knee. Her arm is clutched defensively to her chest, but her face has the unguardedness of sleep: mouth open, teeth just slightly visible. Both photos have a transgressive intimacy about them, in which we intrude on states that should be private: sleep, death. What do we think we're doing, you realise after a moment, watching her like this?

There is another obvious parallel in the photos Gerda took of air-raid victims in Valencia in the weeks before she herself was killed.

I thought particularly of a woman photographed on a makeshift mortuary slab, arm flung behind her with that reckless abandon in which children sleep; mouth slightly open. These were the kind of pictures British and American papers largely refused to publish, for reasons of public taste; the kind the Republic put on posters and Nancy pasted into her scrapbook about Spain; the kind we're now used to seeing.

In *Three Guineas*, Virginia is preoccupied with photographs: still haunted by those missives from Spain, perhaps more than ever since Julian's death. 'This morning's collection contains the photograph of what might be a man's body, or a woman's,' she writes; 'it is so mutilated that it might, on the other hand, be the body of a pig. But those certainly are dead children . . .'

In *Regarding the Pain of Others*, Susan Sontag took up the thread of Virginia's response to these photographs to navigate the ethical labyrinth of war photography. Is looking at others' suffering at such a remove 'morally wrong'? There is something uncomfortable about the distance: 'the standing back from the aggressiveness of the world which frees us for observation and for elective attention.' 'But,' she continues, 'this is only to describe the function of the mind itself. There's nothing wrong with standing back and thinking.'

At the time I was first considering the uncompromising challenge Nancy had posed with *Authors Take Sides*, I felt drawn to Virginia's idea of immunity (though conversely I was frustrated, too, with always trying to work out what I thought before I could work out how to act), but I suspected it contained some kind of moral failing – some connection to Norman Douglas's blithe and privilege-reliant expectation of being able to 'hop it'. The more I thought about *Three Guineas*, though, about her struggle to hold to the course her principles demanded, the more 'immunity' came into view as a way to create space for rational engagement rather than as an escape. On that continental trip in 1935, having reached Rome via Germany and Austria, she pondered the 'use' of the notes she was keeping, and concluded that only time and distance would show what they might offer: 'Perhaps when the editing of the mind has gone further one can see & select better.'

Immunity was also a way of managing sensitivity – exactly because the world cannot be escaped – and harnessing it to reach some greater clarity. 'It is a fact', Virginia once wrote, 'that the practice of art, far from making the artist out of touch with his kind, rather increases his sensibility.' Josephine Herbst believed that writers were people who combined such 'unusual sensibility' with 'an unusual sensitiveness to language'. It was dangerous, this receptiveness, and needed to be harnessed to some purpose: otherwise it could 'wound if it flies off without a string to it. . . . It will wound anyhow – but what doesn't? The saving grace is the transvaluation in words. Or, of course, deeds also.'

The carefully cultivated immunity of the 1930s, imperfect though it was, was what enabled Virginia to make the political sally of *Three Guineas*. Her outsiderdom was never complete. But seeking immunity was an effort to not be overcome by the dark threats hovering, which is not quite the same thing as an attempt to dodge them. As a writer she was engaged in work that could not really be explained, that was unpredictable in its sources and its outcomes, that required – for someone who had weathered traumatic brushes with insanity – intense plunges into risky mental territory. Thinking was, for Virginia Woolf, a personal struggle as much as it was her contribution to any battle for liberty (intellectual liberty was as sacrosanct to her as physical). It was her fighting her way up towards the light with the bounty of the depths in her teeth.

In March 1938, Unity Mitford was in Vienna to see German troops march through the streets and crowds cheer for the Führer as their country was annexed. 'Hitler', Virginia noted succinctly in her diary, 'has invaded Austria.' The expansionist aggression evident in Ethiopia, in the German and Italian involvement in Spain, was battering on towards inescapability. When fears of war surged, Virginia looked at Quentin, her surviving nephew, and thought, 'They'll take you.' She stood by her pacifism, but had no hopes of the British government's policy of appeasement. In February she had signed a telegram to the prime minister, Neville Chamberlain, protesting the prospect of a 'rapprochement' with Mussolini – unless he withdrew troops from Spain (the Anglo-Italian Agreements were signed anyway in April). Generally, though, it was understood by now that Virginia Woolf was not available for collective action. When Rosamond Lehmann arranged a protest meeting about Spain at the Queen's Hall, Virginia was not asked to attend. Nor was she invited to the 'In Defence of Freedom: Writers Declare against Fascism' event at which Sylvia spoke in June.

Julian had explained to the older generation (in an essay that the Woolfs, to his intense indignation, declined to publish) that being a socialist intellectual meant 'turning away from mysticisms, fantasies, escapes into the inner life'. It's hard not to read that as a direct challenge to Virginia. While he was alive, she had offered the apologetic 'What can I do but write?' Many months later, she would refuse to concede that action had a monopoly on significance. She offered thinking as her fighting. 'For the 100th time I repeat – any idea is more real than any amount of war misery. And what one's made for. And the only contribution one can make – This little pitter patter of ideas is my whiff of shot in the cause of freedom'.

When the German-Austrian *Anschluss* happened, Nancy was back in France but yearning for the kind of immunity possible only in the eye of the storm. She spoke obsessively of Spain. She went to Geneva to cover another session of the League of Nations – non-intervention upheld again – and on her way back through Paris, 'picked up' Narcisa, a Spanish refugee whose husband had disappeared in the massacres at Badajoz, offering her and her son refuge at Le Puits Carré. In France, she read every newspaper she could get her hands on, and the accumulation became an onslaught that stymied thinking. 'One is worn out, suffocated, emptied of thought. All that remains is a furious sense of indignation. How much I would have preferred to be a regular press-correspondent, to have been right in the vortex at that time.'

PART THREE

Retreat

Salaria Kea, Martha Gellhorn, Nan Green

Spain: winter, spring 1938

'As time went on,' Salaria told an interviewer in 1980, 'they began to bomb the villages.' When Martha, and then Nancy, left Spain at the end of 1937, the Republican army was on the cusp of its last victory of the war. It took the nationalist garrison at Teruel in early January, but could not hold it for long. By the beginning of March, Franco had not only forced the Republicans into retreat from Teruel but had launched his own offensive on Aragon. One hundred thousand men, heralded by two hundred tanks and hundreds of German and Italian planes, were marching towards the sea. Reaching it would mean that they had split the Republican zone in two.

The nationalist advance drove before it a petrified civilian population, who swept into already overcrowded cities. The cities were bombed. Refugees rushed back out into the countryside. Medical units were thrown into motion. At the end of January, a nurse who had served at Villa Paz recorded setting up – and leaving – five hospitals in a week. They used any building available. 'For 2 months', on the Teruel front, 'we slept and ate where and what we could.'

Transferred to a mobile unit, Salaria travelled in convoy to devastated areas, sometimes going perilously close to the front lines. The roads were packed with refugees. 'I can see it,' she would say in the 1980 interview, 'but it's hard to describe.' Field hospitals and convoys were strafed and bombed so often that she became 'almost immune to danger'.

Afterwards, she would be haunted by the children. Ingenious children, who had learned what to forage, who ate frogs and could kill birds with slingshots. Children who lived, to her amazement, in caves. She was haunted by villages where she went looking for casualties 'and it would be just children'. She never forgot being dispatched so close to the front that she could watch the men being wounded before they reached her. 'We worked like there was no tomorrow,' Salaria would say in another interview. 'Everything was just wonderful.'

Martha was in Miami with Ernest when they heard that Teruel had been retaken. She had the same impulse as Nancy: she went back to the vortex. 'I want to be there,' she told Eleanor Roosevelt from the ship to Europe, 'somehow sticking with the people who fight against Fascism.' It was the opposite impulse from Virginia Woolf's: for Martha, physical engagement had become the only bearable response. There was now little hope that the Republic could survive the war, and somehow this fact made the gesture all the more vital. And yet it was with a kind of despair that she offered it. To go back was, in a way, to succumb to the disillusionment she felt coming for her in a great tide of fury. 'I have gone angry to the bone,' she insisted. 'I think now maybe the only place at all is in the front lines, where you don't have to think, and can simply (and uselessly) put your body up against what you hate.'

In March, the Italians introduced a new bombing tactic: attacks that came so close together that it was impossible for people on the ground to know whether the sirens were sounding the all-clear or the alarm. Barcelona was subjected to the most sustained aerial bombardment of the war so far. Nearly a thousand people were killed in a single night on the 18th – a performance Mussolini hoped would please the German leadership, who, his foreign minister noted, 'love total and ruthless war'.

Shortages had made the city hungrier and dirtier. At the Hotel Majestic, where Nancy's friend Angel Goded worked as a waiter, Virginia Cowles saw staff scraping food from used plates to take home to their families. When she arrived, Martha found unwashed sheets – there was no soap – assiduously ironed and replaced on the beds. Everything stank. Exhausted and demoralised, the People's Army and International Brigades continued to give way to Franco's advance.

In April, the nationalists reached the sea. Following developments from the US, Josephine found the news from Spain 'so shocking and so horrible' that she felt as if she 'had watched a boy grow up through sickness and with much promise only to be run over by a streetcar'. She blamed treachery for the worsening position and found the USSR's waning support for the Republic unforgiveable. 'Anyone writing today', she told Katherine Anne Porter, 'should either shut out the papers or get chronic hardening of the heart.'

Eventually Salaria was furloughed home. (Pat had to return to England, but they were hoping to get permission for him to join her in the US.) The pamphlet about her printed that year described a bombing raid on her unit in which she was buried in a trench by an explosion. When she was dug out, it said, she was too badly hurt to continue her work. But Salaria herself played down the injury, calling it 'only . . . a strained back' in an interview in New York. The interviewer explained that it had worsened, forcing 'the courageous little nurse' to leave Spain. Other records suggest she was treated for dysentery in France. In the photo taken of her on her return, leaning confidently against the ship's rail, she is swamped by her coat. More than anything, she looks incredibly young.

So much about Salaria's time in Spain is indistinct. Like some heirloom quilt, the story is overworked in some places and survives only in tatters in others. Certain details stand out with morning sharpness, but the context around them – dates and places, transitions, corroborating evidence – has faded out, obliterated by confusion and incomplete records, the scrambling that upheaval does to memory.

With broken communication and inadequate maps, convoys could get lost in Spain, sometimes even drifting into fatal territory. Fronts moved so fast that field hospitals were in danger of being overtaken. (In May, Nan Green was stuck on an unmoving troop train headed for Barcelona for twenty-fours: unbeknownst to her, the land it had to cross had fallen into nationalist hands.) On at least one occasion in the confusion of the nationalist advance, Salaria became detached from her unit. At the time it was recorded only that she hitchhiked towards Barcelona, where she rejoined a hospital. But in interviews she gave late in life, the villain of Dr Pitts crops up again, orchestrating two separate incidents in which the convoy moved on without her. She recounted stumbling, lost, into nationalist territory, where she was captured and imprisoned for several weeks.

The experience was something she described in that 1980 interview and in quite a pulpy rendering in her unfinished memoir, *While Passing Through*. ('Get up you savage!' a capturing German yells at her, to which she replies with movie-star heroics: 'Shoot you coward!') She spoke of being put in jail and forced to watch executions whilst given to understand that her turn was coming. She said she saw other people, too: Spaniards, perhaps the families of the condemned, who screamed and screamed and were made to clean the blood from the walls before they retrieved the bodies. Eventually, in the dead of night, Salaria was rescued (by whom is vague: she mentions a monk in the interview, a member of the British Battalion, a Canadian, and running) and bundled onto a train destined for Barcelona.

Readers had trouble believing this dramatic account. One veteran, encountering the story in an article after Salaria's death, concluded that she had been 'fantasizing'. Long after reading his objection, I found a paper written by an academic who had been told that, towards the end of her life, Salaria was suffering from some kind of dementia; I knew that her husband had certainly tried to fend off inquisitors in the early 1980s by warning that Salaria's memory had been affected by a spell in hospital.

I wasn't the first to try to make sense of it all. Several scholars have worked to sort Salaria's accounts into some verifiable order. Implausible things happen in a war, and inconsistencies, such as the details that waver in Salaria's tellings, are to be expected over the years. Decades of experience and acquired knowledge overlay and replace each other, especially if you're not a person whose written account was sought-after at the time: if you're a person who was expected to leave others to write your story for you. And as Salaria warned her interviewers, it is hard to organise chaos into words.

But it is also our first instinct: narrative offers a way to impose order on things that detonate meaning. We try to arrange the fragments in ways that repair the damage. History sorts war into distinct phenomena – retreats, advances, fronts – but as Esmond Romilly's

Boadilla made clear to me, a 'retreat' or an 'advance' is nothing so easily encapsulated by language. It can mean hours of crazed bloodshed in which no one seems necessarily to know where they are or where they are meant to be, or even who they are shooting at (only that they're being shot at themselves), and the outcome boils down to a different group of men sitting among the bodies of their comrades in a ruined farmhouse at the end, and the end is probably a lull of indefinite length before the madness starts again.

Among all the accomplished descriptions I read, it was in Salaria's confused and confusing recollections that the sheer chaos of war made itself felt. In her interviews, Salaria tried to explain that missing big picture to people who probably couldn't understand what it was like to be at war. She didn't know how or why certain things happened, she said. All she could offer was glimpses of understanding, slivers of direct experience. (Yet how to provide an answer to their questions without resorting to narrative, with its explicatory offerings of cause and effect?) This was war as a phenomenon that not only broke bodies and families apart, but shattered sense and meaning, too. There is that refrain of Josephine's broadcasts: that the volunteers knew why they came. You can almost feel the relief with which Josephine grasps their certainty. 'You couldn't feel sorry for that army,' Martha added in 1938. 'Everybody you saw knew what he was doing and why.' Those are the ways in which war seems mercifully simple: that story of one side against another.

Repeatedly, people told Josephine, Sylvia, Nancy, Valentine exactly what they wanted recorded – which names, which crimes. In the midst of an enormous conflagration, they knew that something so small as a person could easily be wiped out. By working the war and its stakes back into a narrative logic, preserving some second life for it, writers could restore something to people who were losing everything else.

Even though I never found a full manuscript, even if it was perhaps never finished, the most plausible thing of all to me was that Salaria had tried to write her life. *Why shouldn't I go and help the world?* she had said. Why shouldn't she speak for herself? Why did it offend people that she did? Whatever was provable or not in Salaria's stories (and some of the surviving material reads as though she was experimenting with fiction as much as memoir), Salaria, having survived so much, was searching out words to match what she knew.

It was like watching a woman wrestle with the record, trying to salvage her own meaning from what others had made of her story. Sometimes the tussle played out before my very eyes as I read. Salaria in a 1987 article: 'I saw my fate, the fate of the Negro race, was inseparably tied up with their fate'; Salaria spoken for in the 1938 fundraising pamphlet: 'Salaria saw that her fate, the fate of the Negro Race, was inseparably tied up with their fate'. Which way round did this borrowing go? Whatever she was doing, however intentional it was, in her most contentious stories Salaria had inserted herself into narratives of the war in ways that made her hard to ignore and harder to speak over.

Martha and Ernest followed the Republican line in its retreat. Martha went on fiercely admiring her side, and carefully documenting the intervention of foreign fascist powers. They visited old friends in the International Brigades, and she indulged a patriotic pride in the badly depleted Abraham Lincoln Brigade, loving them, in all their courage and certainty, 'immeasurably'. Like Salaria, she watched the battles. She saw Republicans hold on without cover against harassment from German planes 'bombing and diving to machine gun', trying to delay the enemy advance for long enough to allow an orderly retreat. In her notes she recalled the terror of hearing the planes approach: 'that panicked feeling of where-where-where'.

On the bloated roads it was possible to plot the advance of the enemy by the licence plates on fleeing vehicles. She watched burdened women reach out pleading arms, seeking transport to anywhere, anywhere at all. She heard soldiers describe their retreats and had to answer their questions about 'others who are missing or probably dead'.

It was spring. 'It was such beautiful weather that you could not believe anything so bad could happen.' In April she and Ernest dropped by the hospital unit run by Dr Pike – the friend of Josephine Herbst's with whom Salaria sometimes worked – which was also on the move towards the battlefront. They found his staff sitting down to eat out-side, 'very picnic and gay and camping trip'. It was pleasant. Spain still captivated her. She kept thinking it was all 'too beautiful for the Fascists to have it'.

In May, Salaria arrived home in New York making the same kind of triumphalist statements that Martha had given to the press the year before. 'With every advance of the fascists,' she told the *Daily Worker*, 'the people responded even more courageously. Franco will never rule a fascist Spain.' But in reality there were only two things delaying a Francoist victory: the general's desire to 'cleanse' Spain of everything the Republic represented ('I cannot shorten the war by even one day,' he had written the year before; 'first I must have the certainty of being able to found a regime') and the desperate resistance of his opponents.

During the late spring and early summer, the Republican government extended conscription, pulling into its army sixteen-year-old boys and middle-aged fathers, despite not having enough rifles for them. The hardest-fought battle of the Spanish war was on the horizon. In July, the Republican leadership planned an attempt to reunite Catalonia with the rest of the Republican zone by launching an offensive across the Ebro river, and hoped, in doing so, to recapture Europe's attention. Some 80,000 men were assembled on the riverbank. In the dark early hours of 25 July, the first of them slipped across to kill the sentries on the other side; the rest followed in boats and across pontoon bridges. It was a year since the battle at Brunete had ended. George Green was no longer driving an ambulance. This time, he was a soldier in the army and, this time, Nan was close behind him. Late on the 25th, she, too, crossed the river.

Nan had been made an assistant to the Chief Medical Officer of the 35th Division Medical Corps, part of a unit that included Spaniards, Canadians, Americans and fellow British volunteers. While the unit waited, she had handled admin and made tea: doing her best to keep everyone going. 'It was not my aim to give political pep talks: that was the job of the Commissar,' she wrote afterwards. 'My aim was to try and keep people cheerful.' Until the offensive began, one of the best ways she found to rally them was to start a conversation about food: asking a group of North Americans what a hot dog was turned out to have transformative effects. Once it started, those kinds of distractions were no longer needed.

After crossing the river in the wake of the army, they reached their destination at dawn. 'It was a scene of desolation,' she remembered later, 'with still unburied bodies lying by the roadside, shattered dwellings and huge piles of jettisoned material, papers, suitcases, bedding, even rifles, showing the haste with which the enemy had made his get away.' They set up their headquarters and an emergency theatre in a farmhouse, and got to work.

It was Nan's job to collate and organise the casualty lists sent by the four front-line dressing stations in their division, typing them up and classifying them according to the types of injury ('head wounds . . . amputations and so on'), the weapons that had caused them (mortars, shells, bullets . . .) and the hospital the patient was transferred to. Casualties in the Battle of the Ebro were enormous: 'an avalanche of work descended with which we could barely cope'. Each day the lists reached Nan from the doctors at the front, and each day, for a few agonising moments, she scanned them for George's name.

Nan hated the filth. 'How dirty I am,' she grieved to her sister in August. She'd worn the same ill-fitting clothes for five days, removing them only once to wash 'in a pint of dirty water'. But there were unforgettable consolations too. One of the many things the medical unit lacked was blood for transfusions, which offered Nan, a universal donor, opportunities to make perhaps the most tangible contribution possible. She lay down beside dying men and watched her own blood restore them to life.

Then, the 'first onslaught over', she was able to visit George while his unit had a few days' rest. The British Battalion was now 'a raggle-taggle bunch of weary men, scattered over an arid hillside', but George was alive and they got to spend two evenings 'and one whole night' together on a sofa crawling with lice.

Afterwards, George's unit went back to the line. The Republic did not have the resources to hold on to its early gains, and what Nan would describe as the 'long, slow, desperate and heroic retreat of the

Spanish People's Army' had begun, on one occasion moving so unstop-
pably that her own unit was overtaken, leaving them dangerously
exposed. She heard each boom in the distance as a sound that might
have taken her husband. Every day there were air raids. It was easy to
tell whether or not to take shelter, whether the planes approaching
were friend or enemy: if there was anti-aircraft fire in the sky around
them, the planes were Republican. Only the nationalists still had the
equipment to defend themselves against aerial attack.

Martha wanted to stay but she remained a person who could leave.
With the situation in Europe worsening, her editors were tiring of the
long Spanish conflict. The world's attention had shifted to Czechoslovakia, the country Hitler had his sights on next. 'Not interested
Barcelona [article]', *Collier's* cabled when she wanted to report on the
refugees. 'Stale by the time we publish.'

Obedient to the story, Martha had left for Prague by June. It was
a nomadic year for foreign correspondents trekking from crisis to
crisis. Virginia Cowles had spent only a week in Spain on her return
in February. When she admitted to a Spanish friend that she wouldn't
be staying long, he asked, 'You have other things to do?' Then he
answered for her: 'I understand. Soon new things will be happening.
We are only the first.'

'Neither at the White House nor at the State Department is there at this moment any willingness to make public comment on the European situation, whose danger and delicacy are measured by the deep anxiety which is felt in every sector of official life.'

'Americans and the Crisis', Washington correspondent,
The Times, 1 September 1938

The Equivocal Attitude

Virginia Cowles meets the Mitfords

Nuremberg, Germany: summer, autumn 1938

In August and September 1938, the German city of Nuremberg was bedecked with thousands upon thousands of swastika flags, fluttering festively from window ledges. Golden eagles surveilled a carnival atmosphere. The town had undergone its yearly transformation from historic centre to showcase for the Nazi propaganda spectacle, and was packed with visitors from around the world. For the foreign delegates and journalists, there was tension beneath the festivity: Hitler was scheduled to give a speech on the final day of the rally, and they were expecting it to prove the culmination of the Czech crisis.

Virginia Cowles was lucky to have found a room in town. Hotel space had been reserved for those sympathetic to the Nazi regime: delegates and reporters from Italy, Japan, Nationalist Spain. The British, French and Americans had been relegated to (admittedly luxurious) train carriages drawn up outside of town. The Grand Hotel, usually the place to be seen in Nuremberg, where in previous years dignitaries from around the world had assembled, now offered sparser pickings. When Virginia walked into the lobby in 1938, the most notable people she saw there were the Mitfords.

Virginia approached Unity and her parents with a certain detached amusement. Jessica's sister was a striking figure wherever she went, but in Nuremberg officials were paying ostentatious tribute. The Mitfords seemed oblivious to the prevailing anxiety. Lady Redesdale, when not dragged out to watch Nazi displays with Unity, settled herself into the corner of the hotel lobby and got on with her sewing. Her husband 'wandered about', Virginia remembered, 'with a bewildered air as though he were at a rather awkward house-party where (curiously enough) no one could speak any English'.

Virginia knew the Mitfords: she was friendly with the sole brother, Tom. (Needless to say, Jessica – who had now settled in a working-class district of London with Esmond – was not with them.) Far from distancing herself from them in Nuremberg, Virginia spent time pumping them for insider gossip. She sat with Unity at a special tea given for Hitler, where she watched the Führer and the twenty-four-year-old catch each other's eye, exchange a flirtatious Nazi salute. Afterwards she and Unity shared an SS car on the way to dinner. As one of a select few granted a private audience with Hitler that week, Unity was possibly Virginia's best source on the likelihood of war. (She was sceptical: 'The Führer doesn't want his new buildings bombed.')

Virginia had spent much of the summer driving around England with Martha Gellhorn, who was working on a report for *Collier's*. For weeks, Hitler had been threatening to send troops into Czechoslovakia to 'rescue' its German minority. Martha was fresh from Prague and feeling pugnacious. To gage the public mood in Britain they had dropped into pubs and tried to engage the punters in conversation, finding what seemed to them an extraordinary level of complacency. The jaunt around the country had degenerated into the kind of lecture tour Martha swore she hated. Few were spared her mounting outrage. 'The fact that the working-man in England was not stung to fury (as she was) by the treatment of his brothers in Spain or the doom of his brothers in Czechoslovakia', Virginia recalled, 'struck her as shameful.'

It's tempting to imagine what Martha might have said at, or about, Virginia's dinner with the Mitfords. Virginia was by now as alarmed by fascist aggression on the Continent as Martha was, but they had markedly different approaches to their work. Where Martha was all fierce partisanship, Virginia insisted on considering every angle. Where Martha wrote to confront and accuse, Virginia attempted analyses that carried their own warnings. In Spain, she had been almost unique among journalists in reporting from the Nationalist zone as well as the Republican, something that put her under suspicion on both sides. 'I was curious to hear the Nationalist point of view', she wrote afterwards, 'and felt that until I did I would not have a proper perspective.' Everywhere she went she made contact with influential and well-connected people with apparent ease; she seems never to have let personal convictions obstruct her access to information.

If anything, people's rigidity in taking sides unnerved her. Reflecting on her first stay in the Republican zone, she recalled being 'surprised' by how 'impersonal' the fighting seemed. 'Men killed from conviction, not passion; even in Spain, a man shot his brother not because he disliked him, but because he disagreed with him.' Virginia was an astute observer who took an almost phlegmatic approach in her writing. Ideology alone couldn't swing it for her. In her 1941 memoir she would make it clear that she couldn't confirm her own private sympathy for the Republic until she had spent time with the nationalists. Both sides gave her cause for concern and she was sceptical of democracy surviving the war, regardless of the victor. She was also prepared to write articles saying so, something Martha would not have countenanced.

The access Virginia established with people like Unity had served her well before. Read any history book that deals with the infamous destruction of the Basque town of Guernica in 1937 and you are likely to find Virginia Cowles's evidence of nationalist complicity in the bombing cited, because she was there in Nationalist Spain for an officer to tell her directly: 'We bombed it and bombed it and bombed it, and *bueno*, why not?'

The same year, she had got reassurance that her approach was bearing fruit. A *Sunday Times* article she had written detailing the numbers of German and Italian troops fighting for Franco was quoted repeatedly in Parliament. She was told it had been circulated in the Cabinet and, she boasted in a letter home, soon afterwards the British government challenged Italy over breaches in its non-intervention commitment. Her account had been trusted expressly because she had stopped short of taking a side: the Under Secretary of State felt that hers was 'one of the most objective articles they had read on the Spanish situation'. 'So if the trip to Spain proves nothing else,' she continued, 'at least I think I struck a shrewd blow for democracy.'

Virginia did not wait around in Nuremberg to hear Hitler's speech. She had been shaken by the one rally she'd attended and had gathered

Nuremberg Rally, 1938

enough material to finish her article elsewhere. She headed to Paris instead, preparing herself for a trip to Prague when things got worse, and listened to the speech over the radio.

Virginia Woolf was listening too. 'Hitler boasted & boomed', she recorded, 'but shot no solid bolt.' For all those primed for a declaration of war, the speech came as an anticlimax: Hitler allowed more time for negotiations over Czechoslovakia, which only prolonged the uncertainty. The Woolfs listened not only to his shrieks over the airwaves but the return 'howls from the audience': more of that docile hysteria Virginia had noticed three years before. Hearing them now, she found it 'frightening to think of the faces'.

Hunger

Nancy Cunard and Nan Green

Barcelona: late 1938

The next day, Nancy Cunard read Hitler's speech in the papers before sitting down to lunch at the Hotel Majestic. Then the planes came. And while they bombed, Nancy composed a poem that dispensed with uncertainty. There was a war gathering, but she and Spain were already in it.

> Another country arming, another and another behind it –
> Europe's nerve strung like a catapult, the cataclysm roaring and
> swelling . . .
> But in Spain no. Perhaps and Tomorrow – in Spain it is HERE.

'I know it is no longer "news" when a score of people are killed . . . in an air raid over [Barcelona],' Nancy commented with waspish warning in the *Manchester Guardian* that month, 'although it would be – as yet – in London, Manchester or Paris.' While the world's attention was elsewhere, the bloodshed went on.

In the poem, which she called 'To Eat Today', the planes become bearers of Hitler's threats – 'dashes along the great maniac speech' – and in the carnage Nancy, in a heightened state of noticing, zeroes in and in and in on the toll of the raid: a woman carrying food, 'four children outside, with the house, and the pregnant cat'. She marked the deaths of people whose names she and the pilots and her future readers would never know, she marked the death of a cat who could hardly matter to anyone when death was stalking children, she marked even the flicker of life in a street cat's womb. Imagine being there, at a café in a city at war, knowing that people are starving, that their homes have crumbled, knowing that the news gets worse and worse and it isn't going to get better, having to steel your nerves because the planes arrive in their drone and clatter and killing, feeling the thud and eruption in your bones, and putting a pregnant cat into your protest. It's as if, in that infinitesimal detail of promise extinguished, she found a way to write the vast and incalculable scale of the slaughter.

That day in Barcelona, Nancy again put aside perhaps and put aside tomorrow, rejected equivocation or delay. She saw only the violence of fascism – 'You passed; hate traffics on; then the shadows fall' – and that, unless resisted, it would go on and on. Another country arming, another and another behind it.

Nancy said of those days in the city that 'everything could be summed up now by that terrible word "hunger"'. Since the Republic had lost the agricultural regions of Aragon, food staples were largely imported from sympathetic Mexico. People lived on chickpeas, lentils, sometimes a bit of fish. 'A piece as long as your finger and twice as thick', Martha had established before she left, 'is the ration for one person for two weeks.' That year, the death rate among children and the elderly doubled. Martha was convinced that starvation would be what finally broke Republican resolve. She had hoped to convey this humanitarian crisis through an encounter with one family – but that was the article *Collier's* declined to publish.

It was still written, that stale story. Describing a visit to the Hernández clan, Martha annotated their lives with the big picture. The grandson, a ten-year-old boy who spends his days queuing for food, is shy about the bombs. 'I hide,' he tells Martha confidingly. 'I hide so they won't kill me.' But he also tells her how entertaining it is to watch the women quarrel in the queue. 'Sometimes when the shop runs out of food before everyone is served, the women are wild with grief, afraid to go home with nothing,' Martha explains. 'Then there's trouble.'

The baby in the Hernández household is fretful and sick; her mother hurt by knowing that visitors can't take pleasure in the sight of her. 'Lola pulled the cover back over the bundle in her arms and said, coldly and proudly, "She does not have the right food to eat and

therefore she is not well. But she is a fine child." ' Martha has been to
the children's hospital; she knows the malnutrition figures; she understands why Lola's baby looks the way she does. The nightmare in Barcelona is also seeing what the dream has become. In the hospital, she
had tried desperately not to think of 'the swift dark laughing children
in Madrid'. She could not bear to 'imagine how hunger had deformed
them'. Martha agrees with Lola: she has a fine child. But as she speaks,
she is thinking, 'Maybe we can stop looking at the child, when we all
know she's sick with hunger and probably will not live until summer.'

In the pages of the *Guardian*, Nancy made another plea for food donations, and returned to Paris cold and unwell, having left most of her
clothes for the needy in Barcelona. (Perhaps she left something for
Angel Goded, her friend at the Hotel Majestic too. She had given away
as much money, food and cigarettes as she could manage each time
she'd gone to Spain.) She found the atmosphere in France strained.
Negotiations over Czechoslovakia were faltering. Armies were mobilised. In London, gas masks were distributed and some schoolchildren
evacuated to the countryside: preparations for war. Virginia Woolf
had been dreaming about Julian. 'I implored him not to go to Spain.
He promised. Then I saw his wounds.'

Days after Hitler's speech in Nuremberg, the Spanish prime minister announced the disbanding of the International Brigades to the
League of Nations. By now the brigades were desperately depleted.
They had played a valuable role in some of the war's key battles,
but they had only ever represented a minority within the Spanish
army the Republic had mustered over the years. It was hoped that
the withdrawal of foreign soldiers who had come voluntarily to fight
for the Republic would increase the pressure on the fascist powers to
withdraw the troops they'd sent from their national armies, but it had
little impact while attention remained on the Czech crisis.

Late in September, the British and French negotiated a settlement in
Munich that gave Hitler the Czech territories he wanted. '[The British
prime minister] has given Europe to the dictators,' Martha fumed. In
London, Jessica Mitford watched as the Munich Agreement ushered in
a period of 'drab limbo' that crushed even the spirits of the rebel she

A war orphan eating soup in Madrid (Gerda Taro)

had fallen for. In Esmond's despondent reaction, she wrote later, she saw 'the despair of a generation that has lost control of its own destiny'.

In Spain, the withdrawal of the British Battalion was fixed for 22 September. There had already been a reprieve of a kind for Nan in August, when George was wounded in the head and taken to a hospital. The injury itself healed quickly but he was kept on the ward out of concern over the sores on his legs (a complaint most of them were suffering from, she noted). She had the comfort of knowing that, for the time being at least, he was in no more danger than she was. But once the withdrawal was decided, George appeared at the unit's HQ with a note confirming he'd discharged himself from hospital. He wasn't prepared to miss his battalion's last action in Spain.

Nan had an hour or so with him, time to plan their reunion with Frances and Martin. Her unit would be staying on after the withdrawal to train replacements, so it seemed likely that George would get home before her. He promised to wait. As with so much else, they wanted the reunion of their family to be something they did together. George's father had told them that Frances and Martin were 'fascinated by the idea of a bearded Daddy', so he promised not to shave either. Then he rejoined his unit, and Nan went back to checking the casualty lists for his name.

On 22 September, George's name was not on the lists: Nan had reached the last day of dread. She did not know that, at the front, the enemy was launching an unexpectedly fierce attack or that the British Battalion would be asked to stay in the line for one extra day to help repulse it.

The following night, two soldiers woke her with the news that George was missing. Later she would remember sinking back down without a word, pulling the blanket around her 'suddenly icy-cold' shoulders. A new thought had started up in her head like a needle sticking on a record. *He might be alive, he might be dead. He might be alive, he might be dead.* The next day, her comrades worked together to ensure that she was never alone for a moment. She wanted to be alone. She wanted to find a way to come to terms with this new thought. On it went, over and over. He-might-be-alive-he-might-be-dead. Her children might see a bearded Daddy, they might never see a bearded Daddy.

She went on working, and before long their replacements were trained and Nan was heading back across the river, withdrawing like the remnants of the British Battalion before her. As they passed through the villages she caught sight of people on the streets: not soldiers or medics, but women. She wanted to join them. She wanted to call out to them, 'There you are, my sisters, my dear ones, weep with me!'

In October, what was left of the International Brigades assembled in Barcelona for a farewell parade. Seven thousand survivors, leaving behind more than 17,000 dead or missing comrades. The president and prime minister of the Republic were there to pay their respects. Republican planes flew overhead, on the alert for the enemy. Crowds lined the streets; women flung flowers. Robert Capa, dressed in a suit to mark the occasion, darted alongside the column snapping pictures. In the crowds and in the depleted ranks on display, people wept. 'Leaving Spain, for most of the European volunteers', Martha observed, 'was to go into exile.'

La Pasionaria, that rousing voice of Madrid's defence, honoured the 'gallant comrades of the International Brigades, who helped save the city with your fighting enthusiasm, your heroism and your spirit of sacrifice'. To those now stateless she could offer only a home in an imagined future where the war was over: 'Come back!' she told them. But, through the mothers in the crowd, she also promised them history. One day, she commanded, Spanish women would tell their children stories of the foreigners who came to Spain: 'Recount for them how, coming over seas and mountains, crossing frontiers bristling with bayonets . . . these men reached our country as crusaders for freedom'.

Nan went home via Barcelona. She had been phoning hospitals, 'spending hours shouting down crackling, buzzing, intermittently silent lines'. She knew as well as anyone that in the carnage of a retreat the wounded weren't always properly identified. She thought George could have been shunted northwards, an anonymous body, unclaimed and injured. Somewhere someone might have word of him. Finally, one hospital in the Barcelona area admitted the presence of a George Grey. He was a Frenchman and not badly hurt. Nan fixed on the possibility that he could be hers.

A little over eighty years later, I listened to an interview that Nan gave in 1976. She had been thirty-two when she went to Spain; in her seventies when the interview was recorded. The self-contained woman others remembered from her war service was still very much in evidence. She was well spoken, brisk; ready with impressions and explanations. She had a firm grasp of the dates (and a habit of enunciating each of the years in full, so that 1938 was a drawn-out and intentioned 'nineteen hundred and thirty eight'), but of her own experience she gave, like Salaria, only dislocated anecdotes. She was sometimes wistful, especially when she described Spanish villagers learning, as she saw it, to live socialism. 'Oh, a lot of lovely things happened,' she said. It was all romantic to her still.

When asked about the state of Barcelona in 1938, she offered that the optimism of 1936 and 1937 was gone. 'People were beginning to starve.' But then she admits that she can't really remember. Barcelona in 1938 was vague to her, blurred by her search for George. She was going from hospital to hospital, hoping he was alive, the broken record still on its sustaining rotation.

The hospital she'd spoken to had no George Green when she arrived – it didn't even have a George Grey. None of the hospitals had him. It wouldn't be until March 1939, months after she got home to England, that she had official notification of George's death: a letter giving the date as 23 September 1938, the same day she'd been told he was missing.

There is something specially involving about a voice, particularly when there is no video in the recording to distract attention. Just the direct and disembodied sound of it: one person's consciousness straight to yours. The pauses, the faltering, all have something to say. Emotion lingers, waiting for its opportunity. It's a lot like eavesdropping, like listening at the door of the dead.

Nan may have wanted the unknown women she saw in Spain to weep with her, but really it was she who had chosen to weep with them. She had taken up a place in a war they had no way of avoiding. From the distance of decades, that choice might have seemed like a tragedy, an avoidable, life-shattering tragedy. It did seem that way. But in 1976, Nan's enduring conviction also made it sound like a privilege.

'That was the last day the brigade was fighting on,' Nan says. 'He was killed almost in the last hour of the last day.' She had sped up, reaching George, stumbling as she did so. In the mass of things-that-could-be-said, she had to feel for the ones she wanted. 'I've never felt able to be sorry for him,' she tried. And then she went on:

Because he – he was doing – he was doing the right thing, he was doing his thing and it was the right thing. We all feel that. We had this privilege of being [. . .] straight down the high road of history, in the right cause. And [. . .] he was doing that and he was sure that we would win . . . I think that [. . .] he died flying as it were, you know, like a bird dies.

'My good friends, for the second time in our history, a British Prime Minister has returned from Germany bringing peace with honour. I believe it is peace for our time. We thank you from the bottom of our hearts. Go home and get a nice quiet sleep.'

Neville Chamberlain announcing the Munich Agreement outside No. 10 Downing Street

'But it was relief without hope . . .'

Jessica Mitford, *Hons and Rebels*

The Stricken Field

Martha Gellhorn

Cuba: 1939

In Spain in the winter of 1938, around the time she turned thirty, Martha Gellhorn ran up against the insufficiency of her efforts. She was in a hospital in Barcelona, visiting the wounded, starving children. Decades later, in an afterword to the novel she wrote about the war, she remembered realising she could no longer stand the sight of those wards. 'My work was useless, none of my articles had saved anyone.'

'You can make history darling: I am modest,' she told a friend once. 'All I want to do is see it happen.' But what good does watching do? Martha decided 'to get out. Leave Europe, leave history.' She went back to the US and then, in 1939, in Cuba, she set up home with Ernest Hemingway.

After years on the move, Martha was ready to stop and sort through the accretion of response that was pooled somewhere within her. The obvious thing was to write a novel set in the Spanish war (which is exactly what Ernest settled down to do), but she still couldn't disentangle herself sufficiently to see it. 'Spain was too close,' she wrote later. It meant something to her that she was never able to translate into fiction. Instead, she discovered she 'could control and use the emotions of Spain in writing about Czechoslovakia'.

A Stricken Field is the result of Martha's early, hard, lessons about journalism, about the limits of what she could do. It is a desperately bleak book, a book fit for the times it came from. The novel Martha wrote about Spain is set in Czechoslovakia in the days after the Munich Agreement. Germany has taken possession of the Sudetenland, there is an enormous movement of people, and the Czech government has decreed that those who have fled the Sudetenland must return. For a group of exiles from Nazi Germany who have found refuge in Prague, the approach of the Germans means falling within the reach of the Gestapo again. Like those Martha knew in the International Brigades, they are people running out of places to go.

As a protest against treachery and indifference, the novel is all about Spain. Witnessing the United States, France and Britain abandon (as she saw it) first the Republic and then democratic Czechoslovakia to their fascist enemies demolished any faith she still had in justice and in governments. It also broke the bargain she had with Spain: that for all she derived from the cause, she could believe that, through her writing, she was giving something back.

Because of the war, Martha had got to live the rarest kind of life – a life in which her beliefs and the labours of her days coalesced into a perfect wholeness. The grand but furtive hopes Martha expressed for herself as a writer in the journal she kept in Spain were both intensely private and central to her sense of what would make her life worthwhile. Work was personal; it was also the service she could offer. The work and the conviction fed and fuelled each other, and she got to be part of something more important than her fumbling self. 'I think we got something out of history that is more than anyone has a decent right to hope for,' she affirmed to a poet who had volunteered in Spain. 'We got that perfect fusion . . . of body and soul; of living one's life and believing with one's whole heart in the life around one.'

Martha had always valued fiction more highly than her reporting and, perhaps relatedly, it was now where she felt least comfortable. (Living with the man writing *For Whom the Bell Tolls* can't have helped.) She worried that she didn't have 'the magic' to write a great novel, by which she betrayed the secret ambitions she still retained for her fiction: 'without magic who will weep and who will protest?'

★

In an early scene in *A Stricken Field*, Mary Douglas, the journalist protagonist, watches the 'Special Commissioner for Refugees of the Society of Nations' dispense with representatives of displaced people in a hotel lobby. She watches in a state of battling with her own fury. She wants desperately not to care. Her work has demoralised and exhausted her, and surely a job shouldn't take this much out of you. 'No one pays me to get the horrors over this place; I'm supposed to be a journalist. I'm through work for today. I've worked enough.'

The idea is to walk out of the hotel. It's the end of the day, time to get some dinner, drink some, take her mind off things. The things she's seen will take some drinking. Another representative approaches the commissioner – a woman. Like the others, she is struggling. 'Mary could see what trouble she had with the words and how from time to time, despairingly, she stopped talking and looked around the room as if for help.' In the struggle to be understood, it's crucial to have language at your command. But Mary is a writer, she knows how language can fail us. She appreciates better than most the odds the woman is facing: not just against the uncomprehending commissioner, but against the enormity of the predicament she's trying to express. This, in a way, is Mary's struggle, too. At the end of this trip, she'll have to put this crisis into words, so that maybe, from the safety of their breakfast tables, her readers will begin to understand. Except, of course, it is not Mary's struggle, not in any way at all. She has the magic talisman of an American passport in her pocket. She has a right, as a stranger to this country and its problems, to remain at the distance of a hotel lobby.

When Martha was in Prague in 1938 she compiled a formal report on the refugee crisis. She knew the facts and figures: *A Stricken Field* was her attempt to show what they meant. The novel is her in full, grief-stricken confrontation mode. In it, she won't, or can't, flinch from the horror, and she is determined to have her readers recognise themselves in her characters, to strip them of the refuge their sense of safety offers. She wants us to understand that our world can go mad if we let our attention lapse. There is the rumpled Sudeten German, an ordinary man, battling his disbelief that life could change so much that he would be 'hunted down simply because, all his life, over a pipe and a glass of beer, he had mused placidly on politics, without wishing to change anyone else, but enjoying his own thoughts and guarding them'. There is Rita, a German political exile whom Mary knows, who has lost her brother to the Nazis, whose three years in a German prison is an experience that Mary 'would never understand or share' and who will soon have to disband the surrogate family of refugees she has assembled in Prague as part of her job with a Communist organisation. Mary visits and sees them – children practically – poring over an old atlas, telling themselves that there is a country somewhere that will take them.

And there is Peter, Rita's lover, the person who has allowed her to snatch happiness from the unlikeliest world. Outrage makes Martha audacious in *A Stricken Field*. Few writers would attempt a scene like the one in which Rita listens, hidden, while Gestapo agents torture Peter to death.

The moment in the hotel arrives about halfway through the novel, and marks an unexpected rally of energy, a brief surge of hope. There Mary is, watching, trying to talk herself out of confronting the commissioner. It won't achieve anything, she thinks; she'll just embarrass herself and the other hard-bitten correspondents around her. Then she crosses the lobby anyway. For a moment, she simply refuses to accept the fact of her powerlessness. It's also the point at which she delineates conclusively between writing and doing something.

In 1938, Martha took her report on the refugee crisis to the League of Nations High Commissioner for Refugees. As she told it, she 'saw him and pounded the table as always and shouted and pleaded and explained and described'. The novel follows what actually happened closely: Mary Douglas confronts the commissioner, who turns out to be a human as pained and disillusioned as she, and he finds himself tempted by her energetic resistance to inevitability. Her idea is to delay the expulsion order and buy the refugees some more time to escape the country. She manages to orchestrate a meeting between him and the Czech prime minister, and ropes in an influential French general to help him make the case. In all the cajoling rush, it seems as though behind-the-scenes diplomacy and sheer daring might make something happen where journalism has failed. But in the end, it comes to nothing. Mary is left with 'nothing to do, except leave, safely in a plane'.

★

Writing was the one place Martha Gellhorn belonged: 'the only thing', she realised in Spain, 'which does not bore or dismay me, or fill me with doubt. It is the only thing I know absolutely and irrevocably to be good in itself, no matter what the result.' But *A Stricken Field* didn't solve anything for her. There wasn't even any of that consoling satisfaction you should get out of having at least finished a book: 'I had the feeling I had dropped my work, the hard months of my life, into a well, and there they were, muffled and lost.'

Inside any writer lives a callous magpie who is always at work, pilfering material from what originates often enough as motiveless observation. The magpie's thieving goes on indiscriminately: its watchfulness is part of what makes a writer an outsider, or what makes outsiders suited to writing. Whatever purpose Martha assigned to her writing, it was still born of a process in which she reworked other people's tragedies into material. With the gift of having experienced those awful years first-hand so palpable, it's not hard to see why the exchange was troubling her. 'We do not ask you to come and stare at us as if we were animals,' a helpless refugee rages at Mary Douglas. Unless some tangible benefit to her subjects resulted, the moral angle was hard to discern.

By 1940, after the book was published, Martha was 'suffering . . . both in a sense of personal futility and a lack of confidence in my work'. At that point, Europe was officially at war; before long the German army would march into Paris. Martha got married, entrenched herself in her own version of domesticity, flourished under the Cuban sun, practised her writing, swam in the pool in her own backyard. She had found them a limestone bungalow, the Finca Vigía, on a hill outside Havana, and had it painted pink. From the house you could glimpse the sea. It had a tennis court, a long, large living room and a library, a terrace trailing bright bougainvillea and grounds purple-blue with jacaranda. She experimented with 'relaps[ing] into total cosmic indifference'. 'Ah, balls,' she told a fellow journalist. 'I don't want to think about it.'

★

When I decided to reread *A Stricken Field*, I was staying alone for a short time in a white house that overlooked a valley. On bright days, sunshine would pour over the fields, and I could crunch my way out over frost-crusted grass into a province of fir trees and shaggy horned sheep and earthy smells, in air that was mentholated in its wintry sharpness. Most mornings, though, I woke in darkness, and all that was visible of the valley was a mass of white cloud, as if a ghostly sea had swept in overnight. On those days, the fields would appear and recede through a wash of mist all morning, and I wouldn't know, from one moment to another, if when I looked up from my notes the valley would be there or not. I was unsettled – many people were just then – and I had an uneasy sense of disasters unfolding just beyond my vision.

When I'd got back from visiting Boston to page through Martha's papers, there were twelve weeks of normality left and I had no idea. In all the pessimism that had swamped me as I began to follow Nancy and the others, a global pandemic did not feature: people talked of political and perhaps international conflict, the decline of democracy, the death of the planet itself. Those are disasters that are often discernible in the distance (though I soon learned that scientists had been warning of something like COVID-19 for years); that is why it's possible to avert them. In Europe in the late 1930s, the clock was running down on ordinary life. And any new sensitivity to time passing prompts the question: have I done enough?

Much as they were prescient in seeing fascism threatening international peace – and appalled that it had already taken the peace in Ethiopia – those who went to Spain did not go there merely in an attempt to save their own countries, to save themselves. There is usually a disaster happening somewhere for someone. Martha Gellhorn did not wait for the disaster to reach her before she took it seriously. She did not accept the shelter her privilege offered her as an excuse for doing nothing.

This was the mistake of appeasement, Virginia Cowles would decide: the failure to think as citizens of the world, the attempt to buy peace with denial. 'Appalled by the prospect of more bloodshed, we locked the doors and bolted the windows, each one trusting that although his neighbour might be robbed and plundered, he himself would be spared. We failed to understand that our neighbour's misfortune was our misfortune; that we are all part of the whole'.

Of the 1930s, those years of motion and activism, Josephine Herbst once wrote: 'People cared. It was a decade when people believed in the possibility of their own powers.' Tracing her efforts in those years as I departed my twenties, I was more aware than ever of the ways in which we can be encouraged to shirk responsibility as much and for as long as possible – usually in ways that serve the status quo rather than our own interests. Accepting the idea that our behaviour counts is as alarming as it is empowering. But without that belief in the possibility of change, that outlandish presumption that we can somehow affect how history unfolds, we perish.

In the early days of the lockdown, people spoke of heroes a lot, and it was talk that carried sinister undertones for the people they were praising. It is convenient to think that only certain outstanding individuals make a difference in the world. It lets the rest of us off the hook. Because some people are heroes, we can peaceably expect them to take the kinds of risks we might not countenance for ourselves. The people in this book were imperfect in their commitment, incomplete in their selflessness, sometimes misguided in their affiliations, incoherent or inconsistent in their efforts. They had the power of a certain freedom, the privilege of choices. Spain was not exactly 'their' fight. They chose to overlook those things (those ready-formed excuses) and pick a side anyway. They chose solidarity, and then had to work out for themselves what that meant.

In Caroline Moorehead's biography of Martha, she mentions a night in 1942 – when America had finally joined the war and Martha's marriage was going badly – in which Martha couldn't sleep. Instead, she wrote down: 'If you have no part in the world, no matter how diseased the world is, you are dead. It is not enough to earn your living, do no actual harm to anyone, tell no lies . . . It is not enough.' No wonder she couldn't sleep, if those were the unanswerable questions on her mind. What is ever enough? Doing something, doing anything at all, doesn't quell the question.

Isolation can be unbearable. And yet most of us survive every day by a kind of distancing. We do not treat other people's problems as our own; we can't afford to. How does a writer reconcile those competing instincts of engagement and retreat? Martha's response to the trouble she'd seen was to write, but in order to write, write something she felt was valuable, she had to be able to extricate herself from the roar of the experience, otherwise what fuelled the work could also overcome it. To write was part of the survival mechanism. Creating *A Stricken Field*, she hoped, might be a way to escape what she was writing of: 'to lose oneself in a specific problem of construction, imagination and sentences'. And yet it could only ever be a temporary respite.

Forty-five years after *A Stricken Field* was published, she was clearer about the purpose of her fiction, or rather, she had come to terms with the limits of what she could hope from it: 'Novels can't "accomplish" anything. Novels don't decide the course of history or change it but they can show what history is like for people who have no choice except to live through it or die from it. I remembered for them.'

The grandest expectations she had of her writing had flared and died in Spain. But what little she could do was still something. Or, at least, it was not nothing. In January 1939, when Barcelona fell to the nationalists, Eleanor Roosevelt urged Martha to 'stop thinking for a while'. 'I <u>hate</u> what happens in these times, but ignoring it won't change it,' Martha wrote back:

> And someday if I go on trying to know and understand, I may at last
> get it all in some sort of shape or order, be able really to see how it all
> works together and why, and then maybe I could write something
> that would make just a few other people think too . . . the only way
> I can pay back for what fate and society have handed me is to try, in
> minor totally useless ways, to make an angry sound against injustice.

The Exodus

Nancy Cunard

France: early 1939

While others moved on, Nancy Cunard was trying to get back into Spain. The editor of the *Manchester Guardian* agreed to take her articles if she paid her own expenses, so, with his accreditation, she headed south through France. She got as far as Perpignan, a French city close to the border, and then, on 26 January 1939, she came to an abrupt halt. It was the day that Barcelona fell.

Nancy sensed a disaster gathering. Barcelona's port had been 'bombed without cease', she wrote in the dispatch she rushed to her editor, W. P. Crozier: for those fearing the nationalist arrival there was no escape possible by sea. People were fleeing, under bombardment, along the roads towards France, and French troops were being sent to the frontier to fortify it. A proposal had been made to allow for a protected neutral zone just over the Pyrenees, but no response had yet been received from Franco. Nancy spoke with a handful of women who had already made it into France; they were, she reported, in 'a frightful condition'. 'Daily the number is going to mount,' she warned, 'miserable, dispossessed, and weary peasant women and children will be coming here and to all the frontier stations along the French-Spanish Republican Pyrenees. Some of the passes are under snow.' The French were prepared to admit only 2,000 people a day; the remainder would have nowhere to go.

The next day she travelled to Le Perthus, a quiet village on the Pyrenean border. From there she walked the four miles down the mountain to the Spanish frontier post at La Junquera. It was here, in 'mud, rain, dark and cold', that she found her fears confirmed. A quarter of a million refugees had congregated in the area and now they were waiting, while others arrived behind them.

As a mass of civilians filled the roads heading north, nationalist planes bombed and strafed them. Trains stalled, cars were abandoned; 'in sheer desperation' thousands gave up on the roads entirely and began a trek into icy mountains. Those parents bundled up their children and their belongings as best they could and dragged them on sleds through the snow. They built tiny fires to warm the children's feet. Babies succumbed to pneumonia before their mothers' eyes.

If they finally reached the border, French soldiers stopped them there. But the arrivals continued. Spaniards pressed on ahead of Franco's army, claiming their place with the Republic even as its leaders began to pass into exile. The frontier posts dammed up with people; people who were hungry, bereaved, in desperate need of medical aid. 'I understand they spent the nights standing,' a Quaker relief worker wrote home from Perpignan, 'as one stands in the tube in rush-hours.' It poured with rain.

On 28 January, the French began to open the border to women, children and the elderly, but the crisis continued to escalate by the hour. That morning, Nancy hitched a lift from Perpignan on a provisions lorry headed for Spain. It couldn't pass any further than Le Perthus. The entire distance of the road to Gerona (a Spanish city roughly forty miles away), she reported, was 'filled, blocked, dammed with humanity that is fleeing the advance of the Franco armies. . . . It is all a welter of wretched faces, despairing and patient'.

At Le Perthus, she watched the people coming: 'In the cold wind of this narrow mountain village, with its single main street, have trudged and waited and stood day-long these broken thousands of refugees. I cannot tell how many I have seen pass, not counting those who at this hour are yet waiting all along that hilly road – maybe a mere 4,000 to 5,000. One loses all sense of numbers.'

She knew that this 'ghastly and tragic scene', this 'terrible indictment of Franco and of Fascism', was a tiny fraction of what was to come. Le Perthus was only one of three main frontier towns that were witnessing the exodus: the others were Bourg-Madame and Cerbère (a place Sylvia had described in a sombre wartime poem). 'The tide may rise to as high as 200,000 . . .' Nancy wrote. 'It may be greater yet.'

Behind them was a retreating army; Republican soldiers still desperately trying to hold the enemy at bay. Pablo Neruda heard later that men who had printed his *España en el corazón* at the front were among those heading north, carrying his poetry in their packs.

All kinds of people had been reduced to just one. Nancy saw 'the tradesman, the peasant, the visibly once well-to-do, and . . . those who have been refugees already in some other part of the country, who have lost everything in Asturias, Bilbao, Malaga, Madrid, Barcelona.' Within a few days the president of the Republic himself would cross into France on foot.

People would tell Nancy of the crowd in a railway tunnel near Portbou – the town that had so recently been Sylvia and Valentine and Langston's gateway to Spain – where crammed trains stood immovably for two days as Italian planes pelted down machine-gun fire outside. She asked a schoolmaster why there were so many wounded soldiers on the road and was told that the hospitals, hearing what happened when the nationalists arrived, were advising anyone who could walk to get out. A doctor described seeing a group of lost children high in the mountains, two of them disappearing into a snowdrift before his eyes. It all went into her notes: 'Items of the day'.

Running on aspirin and tea laced with rum, Nancy left Perpignan each morning to reach the frontier by car or train, before joining the thousands on foot in Spain. 'Scenes of horror along the way,' she remembered years afterwards. 'Questioning, noting, talking to hundreds of people in Spanish, memorising things to describe.' She got back in the dark to write up her articles in an unheated and poorly lit hotel room, before finally finding herself something to eat with other journalists late in the evening. The only breaks in the routine were interminable waits at the prefecture, negotiating with hostile officials to get the permits she needed to continue.

Five days after Barcelona fell, Nancy reported: 'There are some 300,000 starving Spanish refugees massing along the frontier of France: as yet only tens of thousands have crossed. It is a major disaster, and the climax has not yet been reached.' She was right. Altogether, an estimated half a million people would cross.

To Nancy, the horrendous spectacle of the exodus symbolised the entire tragedy of the war and of the Spanish Republic, which now seemed certain to be defeated. She had seen suffering accumulate through each of her journeys to Spain during the war: in the refugee crisis it seemed to be reaching a terrible culmination – one she would call, in her poetry, a 'triumph of hell'.

Private charities were making valiant but inadequate efforts to distribute food and shelter to those arriving in France. In anguished telegrams, Nancy begged Crozier to establish a fund for donations from readers. At first he refused. 'Every week', he told her, 'we print letters about the refugees from one country or another – China, Spain, Czechoslovakia, Germany'. She worried he could not appreciate the scale of the crisis. SITUATION CATASTROPHIC, she cabled. And again: UP TO FIVE HUNDRED THOUSAND STARVING SPANIARDS . . . THIS IS A FRANTIC S.O.S. FOR MONEY FOR FOOD HELP STOP.

The fund was opened, and hundreds of pounds arrived within days. Nancy wrote adverts to support it which ran in the *News Chronicle* and the *Daily Chronicle*. 'We are printing at present everything that you are sending,' Crozier assured her in early February. Word was getting through to Britain. On the day Nancy was warning of a 'major disaster', Virginia Woolf tramped through London in a 'bitter cold wind', thinking 'of the refugees from Barcelona walking 40 miles'. That year she sold the manuscript of *Three Guineas*, donating the proceeds to European refugees.

Franco's forces advanced further towards the border. He had rejected the suggestion of a neutral zone and, on 5 February, the French government finally admitted the retreating Republican troops, immediately interning them. A week later, Franco would publish a 'Law of Responsibilities', under which, as one historian has put it, 'supporters of the Republic were effectively guilty of a crime, that of military rebellion, which in Franco's topsy-turvy moral world meant opposing his military coup'. Those in the Republican zone had good reason to flee. The law both signalled towards and prepared the ground for the repression of all who had in any way remained loyal to the Republic.

Nancy watched the People's Army cross. On 6 February she spent the day watching. 'They have come by in thousands and thousands,' she wrote for the *Guardian*. 'Spanish soldiers give up their arms in an orderly fashion. . . . But all this is only the beginning . . . On the mountains each side they come, so that the whole land-scape seems to be moving. Soldiers on horseback, wounded men, women, children, a whole population . . .'

Three days later she saw nationalist troops reach Le Perthus and hoist their flag; watched as, in marked contrast to the imprisoned Republicans, they were permitted to wander about in France still armed. After so much witnessing, this was finally too much. 'I do not want to see Le Perthus tomorrow,' she put down in her report, 'or any day, ever again.'

In her early articles, Nancy had praised the efforts of the French. She wrote of trucks, vans and buses running back and forth to refugee camps, getting people away from the border, and of the French military, *Garde Mobile*, police and specially deployed Senegalese troops doing 'their best' to keep the mass of humanity surging through the frontier posts 'in some kind of formation'. But families were being separated. The Spanish peseta had become worthless, and Spaniards were relinquishing their life's savings for a pittance in francs; cherished belongings were being surrendered at the border. She observed the lack of welcome: 'some of the French population [will] curse them and others say: "Humanity itself commands us to do all we can for such misery." ' If it was an overheard conviction, it also voiced the belief that kept Nancy moving.

Then she got to the camps. When applied to the holding places Spaniards were disappearing into, 'camp' becomes a euphemism. Later, when France was in turn occupied, some of these structures proved useful to the Nazis. By the time Martha Gellhorn reached one in 1945, she had perfected a tone of icy condemnation. 'There are no vital statistics for the Spaniards in France for no one was concerned with their living or dying,' she wrote. 'All we do know is that there were ten concentration camps in France from 1939 on. . . . By the tens of thousands, these Spaniards died of neglect in the concentration camps. And the German Todt organisations took over 7,000 able-bodied Spaniards to work as slaves.'

That February of 1939, thousands were forced into wired-off expanses of sand on the beaches of southern France. '[We thought] we would be received as heroes for having resisted fascism for nearly three years,' one exile would remember. 'We realised that it was in vain.' At first there was barely any food or drinking water, and there was no shelter. Nor was there medical care or sanitation. Inmates were left to perform their own amputations on injured soldiers. There was no clean clothing, let alone bandages. Disease and infection spread as quickly as the vermin; more than 14,000 Spaniards are believed to have died 'from malnutrition, dysentery and bronchial illnesses' in the first six months.

'Some of the camps to which the Spanish refugees are going are not fit to receive human beings,' Nancy protested. She warned that people traffickers were arriving from Marseilles, eyeing up the 'many pretty girls in the Spanish migration', and hinted at one of the reasons for this hostile environment: those agreeing to return to Francoist Spain, she noted, 'have every facility given them to leave'. In private, she described 'nightmare camps', a 'hell' of 'roaring mistral and flying sand'. Appealing for more donations in the *Manchester Guardian*, she insisted: 'When one has seen, as I have, the internment camps and the huge clearing camp at Le Boulou, there is nothing one would not do to help.'

Again she fought for a way to make the situation perceptible. She wrote of 'atrocious' conditions and hardened journalists 'aghast' at what they were finding there. 'All this will no doubt horrify and astound you,' she observed to Crozier. 'I swear to the truth of it.' Yet in Manchester, as she feared, her reports were proving inconceivable. The staff began to question them, only to have them verified by other sources.

Nancy went backwards and forwards to the camps, sometimes walking twenty miles each way to do so. Her articles became more outspoken. She began to make appeals on behalf of interned intellectuals, to whom she gave particular attention partly because so many of them had been non-combatants, and partly because she saw the possibility of a certain kind of survival resting with them: 'the preservation of the culture that is Spain'.

As criticism mounted, the French authorities began to restrict press access. In March, Robert Capa fell back on his old, unfamous, name to sneak a permit to visit the camps. 'We are [all] walking around like dogs after the rain', he told his mother, 'and trying to save our friends.' Nancy launched her own rescue missions. A note reached her from Angel Goded, the waiter (and former hotel manager) she had befriended in Barcelona. He was trapped in a camp at Argelès-sur-Mer. With well-placed faith he wrote, 'I am counting on you to get me out of here, and I know you will.' She not only got him released, she got four other men out too, one of them the writer César Arconada.

She managed to get them as far as Paris, where the entire group, including Nancy, was arrested. Though she had authorisation to take them to Normandy, Nancy was accused of smuggling the Spaniards into the capital. The men were to be returned to the camp. Nancy protested, argued for two days, got them out again. This time she took no chances. The six of them travelled the rest of the way to Réanville in a taxi.

After living with her for two months, Nancy's five guests eventually emigrated safely to South America and Russia, but she was afraid of what would happen to others, especially if war came to France. She asked Crozier to furnish her with letters of accreditation for Mexico, Central and South America, and the West Indies, intending to investigate possibilities for further settlements herself, and eventually headed for Chile.

Almost a third of Spanish territory was still in Republican hands after the nationalists marched through Catalonia. Nevertheless, the French and British governments chose to recognise Franco's government at the end of February. 'And Julian killed for this,' Virginia recorded in disgust.

In March, as Nancy was battling to get her friends out of concentration camps, Franco's forces entered Madrid. Nan Green was having lunch with a colleague in London, waiting for her food with clenched fists. 'Unloose your hands,' her companion told her. Letting them go released a wave of grief. Years later she still remembered the moment. 'I thought till then that I'd cried all my tears.'

The war ended on 1 April. 'These are days that strain the heart,' Sylvia put down that month. For Martha it was simpler still: 'Spain has really broken my heart.'

Twenty years later, after her last visit – the one that landed her in a sanatorium in London – Nancy wished she had died 'under fire' in Spain before the future found her. She tormented herself with the thought that life had been lonely, possibly pointless. What had she done with it? 'Oh,' she admitted to a friend, 'for 1 month I wrote the truth about the exodus into France from Spain in 1939.'

One final scene. *On the mountains each side they come, so that the whole landscape seems to be moving. Soldiers on horseback, wounded men, women, children, a whole population . . .* A woman is doing the best work of her life. She is walking. From the frontier at Le Perthus, or Cerbère, or Bourg-Madame under snow, she walks back into Spain, against the tide.

Epilogue

Britain and France declared war on Germany five months after the Spanish Republic was lost, in response to the Nazi invasion of Poland. Almost two years later, calling on her native America to join the war, Virginia Cowles looked back on the 'ragged soldiers fighting in the mountains near Madrid' and saw them in a procession with all the scenes she had witnessed since: 'the weeping women in the streets of Prague; the tragic refugees streaming across the Polish frontiers; the Finnish patrols slipping through the ice-bound forests of the Arctic; the terrified flow of humanity choking the roads from Paris to Tours'. After reporting during this new war, she settled in Britain, raising a family with the journalist and politician Aidan Crawley, and turned to writing history and biography. (She also composed a comic play about war reporting with Martha Gellhorn. They thought it would make them rich. It didn't.)

When the SS *Sinaia* (a ship chartered via Wogan Philipps's shipping connections) departed from Sète, in France, in May 1939, it took six hundred Spanish families to new lives in South America. On board, Nan Green had responsibility for feeding two hundred babies: the most useful way she could earn her place on the crossing as an observer for the British National Joint Committee for Spanish Relief, which had been working to remove people from French camps and organise their evacuation to other countries. Back in London, she shared a flat with a refugee from Spain who had once been her commanding officer, another comrade from Spain and his Spanish wife. Through positions at a series of committees, she helped to resettle other Spaniards who made it to Britain. Eventually, she became Secretary of the International Brigade Association, and for years she worked tirelessly on behalf of Franco's opponents outside Spain and inside it. In 1986, Martin, who had once been so captivated by the idea of a bearded

George, took Nan's ashes to Spain – to scatter them, he wrote, 'on the soil which had been enriched by my father's body'.

During the Second World War, Sylvia Townsend Warner thought of Spain with guilt and nostalgia and grief. On a summer's night in 1940 she listened to German planes fly over English skies. On the radio, wounded French soldiers sent messages to their families. The next day she busied herself sorting through accumulated things, masses of it the remnants of her Spanish efforts. She had worked 'vainly', she admitted, but she wished she had worked 'a hundred times harder'. That was a war in which there had been a place for her, a contribution she could make. 'This war has not issued a single call for the help of intellectuals,' she complained in her diary. 'It is just – your money and/or your life.'

When it seemed Britain would be invaded, she and Valentine attended local classes in rifle shooting and hand-grenade throwing (Sylvia learning, Valentine teaching). In Dorset they opened their home to evacuees but did not particularly enjoy the company. (They had earlier sponsored the arrival of Ludwig Renn, a German writer and Republican volunteer who had been through the camp at Argelès, and who stayed with them until his emigration to America in 1939.) A better marriage of minds arrived when they bumped into Nancy Cunard by chance in Dorchester, transforming what had been a corresponding acquaintance over Spanish matters into a close friendship that lasted until the end of Nancy's life.

After Valentine died of cancer at their home in 1969, Sylvia stayed on, incredulous and irritated that the loss had not killed her too. Despite and because of this disappointment, she continued to publish short stories and poetry until her death in 1978, when she was eighty-four. Valentine's love was 'everywhere', she had written after her bereavement. 'It follows me as I go about the house, meets me in the garden, sends swans into my dreams.' They are buried together in East Chaldon.

A piece of advice Sylvia offered in 1938 to a friend who was thinking of going to Spain took up prime position in my notes as I finished this book. Equality, democracy and peace seemed no less embattled in Europe and the US than they had when I started. There was war again in Europe. There were fresh and devastating assaults on women's rights in America. Racism, sexism and climate change had prompted new eruptions of protest, calling progress further into question, while the government in my own country was seeking new means for restricting the right to stage peaceful demonstrations. My pursuit of Sylvia, Valentine and the others had proved a timely instruction in the importance (and limitations) of paying attention. For, as Sylvia wisely advised her friend: 'when the house is on fire it is best to be awake'.

The Nazis famously had a list of almost 3,000 British citizens they would arrest the moment they invaded. Sylvia's name was on it. She and Valentine were on other lists, too. Still members of the Communist Party (though, according to her biographer, Sylvia was no longer 'a paid-up member' and Valentine would resign in the 1950s), they remained under MI5 surveillance during the war. Even after the USSR was invaded by Germany in 1941 and joined the Allies, suspicion remained. In the US, which entered the war at the end of that year, the authorities took to calling those who had opposed Franco and his allies in Spain 'premature anti-fascists', as if it was only reasonable to oppose a thing once your country had declared war on it.

Sacked from her job in a propaganda office in 1943 and interrogated by the FBI, Josephine Herbst clung to her truth as if her life depended on it. As the investigators read aloud from her record, questioning her about it, she saw herself locked in a tussle over her own story. 'Moments like this can relegate you to a dungeon, with nothing to contemplate except your own abyss,' she wrote afterwards. In those moments, you save yourself by holding to the meanings you have. Given the opportunity, her enemies would wrest her history from her, and that would be an end to the trying to understand.

> I had no intention . . . of apologizing or stuttering away my birthright or ceding to strangers the ground rights to my own experience, my own mistakes. Or even to my own ignorance. To do so would close the debate. What I understood very well was that the dry rattle of all these *It is Reported*s might be calculated to reduce some of my best

yesterdays to outworn slogans; telephone numbers of people who were
no longer there, or were dead; and foxed files.

They could take *It is Reported that in Madrid, in 1937, you broadcast in
behalf of the Spanish Loyalists*, turn it inside out, and find me involved
in a conspiracy, where I saw only evidence of my own well-grounded
reasons of the heart.

When she died in 1969, an old friend said that 'Josie, who could
easily get mad and also make you see the fun of getting mad, got mad
always in behalf of other people'. True in its essence, if not entirely
true of this woman whose enlivening conversation and tantalising
memories more than made up for the lashings she could deal out to
young late-life friends like Saul Bellow, John Cheever and various
neighbours. She died two weeks after giving her doctor a message for
them: 'Tell them that I do not repent, that I love life unto eternity,
love and life.'

The designation of 'premature anti-fascist', with its leftist associations, ruined many lives in America. Veterans of the International
Brigades frequently found themselves blacklisted from jobs and relegated to menial roles during service in the Second World War (worse
would follow with the new taking-sides of the Cold War). There was
no work for Salaria in 1939. 'All thumbs are down if you only mention
Loyalist Spain,' she told a friend. But she needed a job for more than the
living – she needed it to get Pat into the country. 'I shall be the happ[i]est
woman in the world when he gets here.' It took until 1940, and then
he was drafted into the army. They both served, though Salaria could
not join until 1944, when the recruitment of African American women
began. After the war, they lived in New York, where Salaria helped
coordinate the desegregation of a number of hospitals. The couple later
retired to Salaria's home town of Akron, Ohio.

The interviewer who visited them in 1980 had the harrowing
impression that Salaria and her husband were living in fear. 'Recently
they feel this rise in the Ku Klux Klan that's now beginning to make
itself felt in Akron.' They took care to enter and leave the super-
market separately, to not be seen together. They'd received threats.

The interviewer added his own observations to the end of his recording, notes that tell of Salaria and Pat in old age: Salaria, 'probably underweight' but still showing all the signs of having been 'an absolute beauty'; Pat a big, quiet man; the two of them somehow obviously compatible. Both of them courageous, both of them 'splendid'.

Jessica Mitford was doubly suspicious in her adopted home: watched by the FBI both for her husband's service in the International Brigades and for her family's links to fascism. She and Esmond had emigrated from London to America in 1939, battered by the death of their baby daughter, Julia, in a measles epidemic, and by the disillusionment of the Munich Agreement.

In 1941, Jessica came close to returning to Britain, wanting to stay as near as possible to Esmond after he chose to enlist with the Royal Canadian Air Force and was posted to England. She agonised for a while about whether to leave behind in safety their new baby, a daughter she had given the Spanish name Constancia, but eventually decided to bring her. LEAVING FRIDAY SO TERRIFICALLY EXCITED DARLING, she cabled Esmond. That day, news returned of his plane missing on active service. Though she did not believe it for many months, Esmond had been killed at the age of twenty-three.

Jessica joined the Communist Party in 1943, soon after marrying the lawyer Robert Treuhaft (with whom she had two more children), and spent most of the next fifteen years working for the Civil Rights Congress from her home in Oakland, California. The couple left the party at the end of the fifties. Jessica's triumphant career as a writer began shortly afterwards: a midlife transition after FBI interventions forced her out of a job. I watched her light up in that *Outsiders* interview with John Pilger when she told him about her dossier in the FBI files. 'It was 350 pages . . .'

Unity's despair at the conflict between Germany and Britain prompted a suicide attempt in 1939 that left her dependent on the care of their mother until her early death in 1948. Oswald and Diana were arrested and imprisoned in Britain in 1940. Jessica, Nancy Mitford and Nancy Cunard were among those who warned against their release. When the SS *Sinaia* had taken Spaniards (and Nan Green) to South

America, Nancy Mitford had been there at the port to see them off. Her husband had been working for the British Joint Committee and she had joined him for a while in Perpignan. This was the moment she confronted her mother's politics. It was clear that the 'first result' of fascism taking over a country, she told her, was 'always a horde of unhappy refugees': 'Personally I would join hands with the devil himself to stop any further extension of the disease.'

In 1940, Virginia Woolf (another person on the Nazis' blacklist) lay awake at night and listened to a dog fight in the sky above her. There was a young man up there, a British pilot, battling with his life to preserve hers. Both of them trapped. Some bold soul had invited her to write another article about women and peace. Very well, she would. Lying in bed, she had been thinking; she has never ceased from thinking. She takes up the thread of *Three Guineas* and continues: 'there is another way of fighting for freedom without arms; we can fight with the mind.' 'Mental fight means thinking against the current, not with it.'

It is not true that Virginia Woolf has never ceased from thinking: everything stops as she waits for a bomb to drop. But when the barrenness of terror passes, life starts up again in her mind, defying death by engaging in the opposite: 'by trying to create'.

After publishing *Three Guineas*, Virginia completed two further books: a biography of her friend Roger Fry and the novel *Between the Acts*, which was published posthumously in 1941. She took her own life in March 1941.

The fall of Paris to the Germans in 1940 felt personal for Langston Hughes. For him it had been, he once said, a place where 'you can be whatever you want to be. Totally yourself.' I was glad to know he'd made it back, years later. But it was Harlem that was home. He died there in 1967, and fittingly his ashes are interred there beneath the floor of the Schomburg Center for Research in Black Culture.

Martha Gellhorn did some of the best reporting of her life in the Second World War, a period during which her five-year marriage to

Ernest Hemingway disintegrated. In 2019, I read in the news that a blue plaque had just been added to the building in London that was her home for the last twenty-eight years of her life, commemorating her as 'a pioneering war correspondent whose passionate but lucid reporting style became highly influential in the practice of journalism'. Since she had died in 1998, I was surprised it had taken them so long.

In 1975 – five years after she moved into that flat – Martha returned to Madrid. She came back on the day Franco died ('there was nobody I wanted dead more than Franco') and checked into the Hotel Palace, where she had stepped over blood in 1937 to reach the injured soldiers being treated there. 'The clientele was very young then,' she wrote, but this time she sits in a room she remembers with such fury and grief, and her company is old men getting misty-eyed over the funeral playing on the television. Sickened by 'this Spain where the only "heroes" are Franco's Falange and the war monuments only commemorate Franco's dead', she goes looking for the Retiro Park, where she and Ernest had that pleasant excursion snatched out of wartime, and finds in her taxi driver an instant comrade. You can talk safely in a taxi – no one is listening. For the rest of the trip she hails taxis, looking for the grey-haired drivers, and finds Republican veterans with whom she has 'good old-soldiers' chat[s]'.

In 1940, when France was invaded, thousands of Spaniards still languishing in French custody joined the Resistance and played a part in that country's eventual liberation. Thousands of others were sent to Mauthausen concentration camp, where the majority perished. Some Spanish volunteers believed an Allied victory would restore their own Republic, but Franco remained in power for another thirty years, eventually tolerated by the Western democracies as a Cold War ally against communism. His ruthlessness persisted, as the historian Paul Preston writes, 'in the labour camps, the five hundred thousand prisoners, and the 150,000 executions on which his dictatorship was built'. Democracy did not return to Spain until 1977.

For decades, much of the history of the Spanish Civil War was researched and written by people outside of Spain. This was not least because, in the words of the historian Helen Graham, 'an attempt to obliterate the memory of the defeated' was 'integral to the totalitarian aspirations of victorious Francoism'. It was a state of affairs so far from what Nancy Cunard expected, from what she believed should be the case. 'No, it is the poets, the writers, the artists of Spain itself', she wrote from Madrid in 1936, 'who will immortalize forever this terrible and magnificent Odyssey. I have seen them, I know them.'

Nancy understood that any writer has two lives. She and Sylvia both worked over the post-war years to translate and place Spanish writing, helping to keep it in circulation. Efforts for the Spanish Republic in exile were what brought Nancy into friendship with Nan Green, too.

Nancy was in South America when the war broke out. Hers was another name on the Nazi arrest list. Instead of staying where it was safer, she slowly made her way back to Europe. She took refuge in London and found work with the Free French, suffering the grim shock of daily office work and tormented by the total silence from her home in occupied France.

In 1946 she made the first in a long series of returns to Spain: writing reports for *Ce Soir* on Franco's dictatorship and still hoping the democracies might unseat him. 'Spain is as complex as the heart,' she wrote – and, for her, as endlessly tormenting. As the new Spanish reality began to sink in, she swore to be 'WITH the Spanish workers for ever and AGAINST their enemies who are and always have been mine'. This was a promise she kept. For years she went on travelling into Spain, often making clandestine trips over the Pyrenees, smuggling people, money and – some said – arms to help sustain the pockets of resistance across the border.

Over time, onlookers became less willing to excuse the furious outbursts, the sexual roaming, the inconvenient demands of Nancy Cunard. Alcohol took its toll with a kind of compound interest. What was exciting about her gradually became absurd. When she died in a Parisian hospital in 1965 (she had been found in the street, unconscious), it was an end that lent itself to the drawing of steep trajectories. Yet John Banting, one of her greatest friends, did not trust the motives of those who wielded pity as a weapon. One way of 'throwing into disrepute her outlook on life and that of all others who hold a similar outlook', he warned, was to 'say that of course she was "ineffably charming" but [that she also] had a "fatal fondness for lost causes" and a "compulsive inclination towards self-destruction." ' After all, as Spain demonstrated, a cause isn't lost by itself but through lack of support, and the concept of self-destruction is a convenient one for those engaged in, or ignoring, the destruction of others. One way of dismissing, unanswered, all those uncompromising questions Nancy posed through her life and during it would be to dismiss as a tragicomic case the woman herself.

Of all the notes I have on Nancy, I bear in mind Maroula Joannou's reminder that her 'call for legislation to end racial discrimination . . . was greeted with incomprehension and hostility whenever she tried to broach it in white circles as she frequently did'. That was a law that came into being in the UK only after her death.

When France was liberated, Nancy went back to Réanville to face the ruin of her home. It was a sight she would describe repeatedly in print. Her former neighbours had pillaged at will. Then German soldiers had taken over. It seemed everything about Le Puits Carré had offended them. The house was wrecked, not through misuse or the ravages of war but through intended desecration. The doors were gone, the windows smashed. That deep well, where she cooled wine the summer Langston visited, and they had sat out long into the night, talking, then listening as her Spanish guests played the flamenco music of their own lost home: that was clogged with refuse, excrement, even a dead sheep; worse, her books flung down there, too.

For days she picks painfully through her house and garden, scavenging for scraps of her past. There is a drawing by Wyndham Lewis crumpled under a tree; paintings (degenerate art) full of bullet holes, torn apart; the portrait Eugene MacCown painted of her in Paris in 1923 looking like someone has thrust a bayonet through it. Someone has stoned her African sculptures; taken a hammer to a box of type. Daubed *Achtung, Waffen!* on an outbuilding. All her papers, the voluminous correspondence, most of the records from the *Negro* anthology and *Authors Take Sides*: it is all gone. The roof is missing where the Hours Press used to run.

Only the old Mathieu hand press still stands, monolithic among the ruins, having, by its size, 'defied' the wreckers. Nancy contemplates the damaged tin box of type. 'This, passingly, seemed a symbolic exclamation: "Damnation take all print!" And how well illustrated here was that famous cry: "Death to the intellect!" which was shouted in Germany and then in Spain.' Fascism has been visited on her home. But how symbolic, too, that her press had proved too lasting to destroy.

Or put it this way. Some months after the Nazis occupied Paris, someone vandalised Gerda Taro's gravestone in Père Lachaise, chiselling away the tribute that connected her to Spain. By then, Capa had managed to escape Europe via a passage to New York (his exit visa was signed by the Chilean consul, Pablo Neruda). He was killed in 1954 when he stepped on a mine in Vietnam, photographing for *Life* magazine.

In 1939, he had left his studio – and its negatives – in the care of his darkroom manager, Imre Weiss. As the Nazis gained on Paris, Weiss joined the thousands fleeing. He bicycled as far as Bordeaux with the studio's legacy in his backpack. Then, in a last-ditch attempt to save the negatives, he persuaded a Chilean he met on the street to take them, hoping he would entrust them to the Chilean consulate for safe-keeping. Weiss got out of France but was interned in French Morocco. (Capa and his brother helped to secure his release in 1941, and he made it to Mexico.) The negatives disappeared into the catastrophe.

Except. In December 2007, three cardboard boxes packed with rolls of film arrived at the International Center of Photography in New York. They contained 4,500 negatives from the Spanish Civil War: pictures taken by Robert Capa, Gerda Taro and their friend David Seymour ('Chim'). The discovery was, as Gerda's biographer put it, 'a sensation in the history of photography'. The odyssey of those boxes is still not entirely clear. Somehow, they had ended up among the belongings of a Mexican diplomat – a fate that meant they became known as the 'Mexican Suitcase'. He may not even have known what he had in his possession when he eventually packed up to return home. They might have survived precisely by being lost. Decades later, they were inherited by someone whose nephew began to make enquiries about them; enquiries that eventually reached the notice of Cornell Capa, André's brother, who had been searching for the missing film for years. Analysis of the negatives enabled the attribution of hundreds of new photos to Gerda, a huge advance in understanding the extent and significance of her work.

The ICP holds other recoveries, too: stashes of photos by Gerda and André serendipitously turned up by researchers over years and countries. I think of them – little rolls of film; notebooks measuring only 8 x 10 inches and filled with tiny contact images; twenty-seven vintage prints stuffed into an attic – like leaves blown away in a storm and caught up in secret places. Too tidy, too pretty an image for the destruction that invasion and internment and genocide does, for the way they waste and pervert human potential, obliterate both people and what they've created. When millions have died before their time, recovered photographs are hardly something to rejoice over. It is too tempting, too sentimental, to exult in those recoveries as if they are more meaningful than the fact that Gerda Taro did not get to live beyond the age of twenty-six. But I admit to a thrill from the story of the Mexican Suitcase. I admit to imagining those negatives and contact sheets and vintage prints as tiny pockets of resistance – statements of the unquenchable human drive to create and to record – that will flare up as often as they are extinguished, and will keep on being found.

Selected Bibliography

First and foremost

Ackland, Valentine, *For Sylvia: An Honest Account* (Chatto & Windus, 1985)

Bell, Vanessa, *Selected Letters of Vanessa Bell*, ed. Regina Marler (Pantheon, 1993)

Cowles, Virginia, *Looking for Trouble* (1941; Faber & Faber, 2010)

Crowder, Henry, with Hugo Speck, *As Wonderful As All That?: Henry Crowder's Memoir of His Affair with Nancy Cunard, 1928–1935* (Wild Trees Press, 1987)

Cunard, Nancy, *Grand Man: Memories of Norman Douglas* (Secker & Warburg, 1954)

——, *GM: Memories of George Moore* (Rupert Hart-Davis, 1956)

——, *These Were the Hours: Memoirs of My Hours Press, Réanville and Paris, 1928–1931* (Southern Illinois University Press, 1969)

——, *Selected Poems*, ed. Sandeep Parmar (Carcanet Press, 2016)

—— (ed.), *Negro: Anthology* (Wishart & Co, 1934)

—— (signatory/ed.), *Authors Take Sides on the Spanish War* (Left Review, 1937)

——, Langston Hughes and Louise Thompson, *Poetry, Politics, and Friendship in the Spanish Civil War: Langston Hughes, Nancy Cunard and Louise Thompson*, ed. Anne Donlon (Lost & Found: CUNY Poetics Document Initiative, 2012)

Gellhorn, Martha, *The Trouble I've Seen* (1936; Eland, 2012)

——, *A Stricken Field* (1940; Virago, 1986)

——, *The Heart of Another* (1941; Home & Van Thal, 1946)

——, *Two by Two* (Simon & Schuster, 1958)

——, *The Honeyed Peace* (1954; Penguin Books, 1958)

——, *The View from the Ground* (1959; Atlantic Monthly Press, 1988)

——, *The Face of War* (1959; Atlantic Monthly Press, 1988)

——, *Travels with Myself and Another* (1978; Eland, 1983)

——, *The Selected Letters of Martha Gellhorn*, ed. Caroline Moorehead (Henry Holt & Company, 2006)

—— and Virginia Cowles, *Love Goes to Press* (1946; University of Nebraska Press, 1995)

Green, Nan, *A Chronicle of Small Beer: The Memoirs of Nan Green*, ed. R. J. Ellis (Trent Editions, 2004)

Herbst, Josephine, *Pity Is Not Enough* (1933; University of Illinois Press, 1998)

——, *The Executioner Waits* (1934; Warner Books, 1985)

——, *Behind the Swastika* (Anti-Nazi Federation, 1936)

——, *Rope of Gold* (1939; Warner Books, 1986)

——, 'The Starched Blue Sky of Spain', *The Noble Savage*, no. 1 (1960)

——, *The Starched Blue Sky of Spain and Other Memoirs* (HarperCollins, 1991)

Hughes, Langston, *The Big Sea: An Autobiography* (1940; Hill and Wang, 1963)

——, *I Wonder as I Wander* (1956; Hill and Wang, 1993)

——, *The Collected Poems of Langston Hughes*, ed. Arnold Rampersad and David Roessel (Vintage, 1995)

——, *The Political Plays of Langston Hughes*, ed. Susan Duffy (Southern Illinois University Press, 2000)

——, *The Collected Works of Langston Hughes, Volume 9: Essays on Art, Race, Politics, and World Affairs*, ed. Christopher C. De Santis (University of Missouri Press, 2002)

Judd, Peter Haring, Sylvia Townsend Warner, Valentine Ackland and Elizabeth Wade White, *The Akeing Heart: Letters between Sylvia Townsend Warner, Valentine Ackland and Elizabeth Wade White* (Handheld Press, 2018)

Mitford, Jessica, *Hons and Rebels* (1960; Indigo, 1996)

——, *A Fine Old Conflict* (Vintage, 1978)

——, *Poison Penmanship* (Farrar, Straus & Giroux, 1979)

——, *Faces of Philip: A Memoir of Philip Toynbee* (Knopf, 1984)

——, *Decca: The Letters of Jessica Mitford*, ed. Peter Y. Sussman (Phoenix, 2007)

Mitford, Nancy, *Wigs on the Green* (1935; Penguin, 2010)

——, *The Pursuit of Love* (1945; Penguin, 2010)

——, *Love in a Cold Climate* (1949; Penguin, 1987)

——, *Love from Nancy: The Letters of Nancy Mitford*, ed. Charlotte Mosley (Houghton Mifflin, 1993)

Mosley, Charlotte (ed.), *The Mitfords: Letters between Six Sisters* (Fourth Estate, 2007)

Neruda, Pablo, *Memoirs* (Penguin, 1978)

Romilly, Esmond, *Boadilla* (1937; The Clapton Press, 2018)

Warner, Sylvia Townsend, *Summer Will Show* (Chatto & Windus, 1936)

——, *After the Death of Don Juan* (1938; Virago, 1989)

——, *A Garland of Straw* (Chatto & Windus, 1943)

——, *The Diaries of Sylvia Townsend Warner*, ed. Claire Harman (Chatto & Windus, 1994)

——, 'Sylvia Townsend Warner's Spanish Civil War Love Poems, with an Introduction by Mercedes Aguirre', *Journal of the Sylvia Townsend Warner Society*, vol. 19, no. 1–2 (2020), pp. 64–9

Weil, Simone, *The Iliad or The Poem of Force*, trans. Mary McCarthy (Pendle Hill, 1956)

Woolf, Leonard, *Downhill All the Way* (Hogarth Press, 1975)

Woolf, Virginia, 'Introductory Letter', *Life as We Have Known It*, ed. Margaret Llewelyn Davies (Hogarth, 1931; Virago, 1977)

——, *A Letter to a Young Poet* (Hogarth Press, 1932)

——, *The Years* (Hogarth Press, 1937)

——, *Three Guineas* (Hogarth Press, 1938; 1943)

——, *The Letters of Virginia Woolf, Volume 2: 1912–1922*, ed. Nigel Nicolson (Harcourt Brace Jovanovich, 1976)

——, *The Letters of Virginia Woolf, Volume 6: Leave the Letters Till We're Dead*, ed. Nigel Nicolson (Harcourt Brace Jovanovich, 1980)

——, *The Diary of Virginia Woolf, Volume 3: 1925–1930*, ed. Anne Olivier Bell (Penguin, 1980)

——, *The Diary of Virginia Woolf, Volume 4: 1931–1935*, ed. Anne Olivier Bell (Penguin, 1982)

——, *The Diary of Virginia Woolf, Volume 5: 1936–1941*, ed. Anne Olivier Bell (Penguin, 1985)

——, *Moments of Being*, ed. Jeanne Schulkind (Harcourt Brace Jovanovich, 1985)

——, *The Essays of Virginia Woolf, Volume 6: 1933–1941*, ed. Stuart N. Clarke (Hogarth Press, 2011)

The Nancy Cunard Collection, Harry Ransom Humanities Research Center Library, University of Texas at Austin

The John Banting Collection, Tate Gallery Archive

The *Guardian* Archives, John Rylands University Library, University of Manchester

The Walter Strachan Collection, the Charles Burkhart Collection, the Kay Boyle Papers and the Herman Schrijver Collection of Nancy

Cunard, Morris Library, Southern Illinois University Library, Special Collections

Josephine Herbst Papers and Elinor Langer Collection of Josephine Herbst, Beinecke Rare Book and Manuscript Library, Yale University

Sylvia Townsend Warner and Valentine Ackland Collection, Dorset History Centre

Fredericka Martin Papers, Tamiment Library and Robert F. Wagner Labor Archives, New York University

ALBA Collection, Tamiment Library and Robert F. Wagner Labor Archives, New York University

John Gerassi Papers, Tamiment Library and Robert F. Wagner Labor Archives, New York University

Julia Newman *Into the Fire* Research Files, Tamiment Library and Robert F. Wagner Labor Archives, New York University

Martha Gellhorn Papers, Howard Gotlieb Archival Research Center, Boston University

Victoria Ocampo Papers, Houghton Library, Harvard University

Hugh Douglas Ford Collection, McFarlin Library, University of Tulsa

Marx Memorial Library

Biographies and criticism

Bell, Quentin, *Virginia Woolf: A Biography* (Pimlico, 1996)

Berry, Faith, *Langston Hughes: Before and Beyond Harlem* (Lawrence Hill & Company, 1983)

Bevilacqua, Winifred Farrant, *Josephine Herbst* (Twayne Publishers, 1985)

Cañete Quesada, Carmen, 'Salaria Kea and the Spanish Civil War', in Rosalía Cornejo-Parriego (ed.), *Black USA and Spain: Shared Memories in the 20th Century* (Routledge, 2019)

Cassara, Catherine, 'Eyewitness to Missing Moments: The Foreign Reporting of Josephine Herbst', doctoral thesis, Michigan State University, 1988

Chisholm, Anne, *Nancy Cunard* (Sidgwick & Jackson, 1979)

Donlon, Anne, 'Things and Lost Things: Nancy Cunard's Spanish Civil War Scrapbook,' *Massachusetts Review*, vol. 55, no. 2 (Summer 2014), pp. 192–205

Ehrhardt, Julia C., *Writers of Conviction: The Personal Politics of Zona Gale, Dorothy Canfield Fisher, Rose Wilder Lane, and Josephine Herbst* (University of Missouri Press, 2004)

Fielding, Daphne, *Those Remarkable Cunards: Emerald and Nancy* (Atheneum, 1968)

Ford, Hugh (ed.), *Nancy Cunard: Brave Poet, Indomitable Rebel, 1896–1965* (Chilton Book Company, 1968)

Gilyard, Keith, *Louise Thompson Patterson: A Life of Struggle for Justice* (Duke University Press, 2017)

Gordon, Lois, *Nancy Cunard: Heiress, Muse, Political Idealist* (Columbia University Press, 2007)

Gordon, Lyndall, *Virginia Woolf: A Writer's Life* (revised edition, Virago, 2006)

Harman, Claire, *Sylvia Townsend Warner: A Biography* (Minerva, 1991)

Hastings, Selina, *Nancy Mitford: A Biography* (Hamish Hamilton, 1985)

Joannou, Maroula, 'Nancy Cunard's English Journey', *Feminist Review*, vol. 78, no. 1 (2004)

Langer, Elinor, *Josephine Herbst: The Story She Could Never Tell* (Little, Brown & Company, 1983; 1984)

Lebrun, Bernard, and Michel Lefebvre, *Robert Capa: The Paris Years 1933–54* (Abrams, 2012)

Lee, Hermione, *Virginia Woolf* (Chatto & Windus, 1996)

Light, Alison, *Mrs Woolf and the Servants* (Bloomsbury, 2008)

Lovell, Mary S., *The Mitford Girls: The Biography of an Extraordinary Family* (Abacus, 2002)

McLellan, David, *Simone Weil: Utopian Pessimist* (Palgrave Macmillan, 1989)

McLoughlin, Kate, *Martha Gellhorn: The War Writer in the Field and in the Text* (Manchester University Press, 2007)

Moorehead, Caroline, *Martha Gellhorn: A Life* (Chatto & Windus, 2003)

Mulford, Wendy, *This Narrow Place: Sylvia Townsend Warner and Valentine Ackland: Life, Letters and Politics, 1930–1951* (Pandora Press, 1988)

Preston, Paul, *Doves of War: Four Women of Spain* (HarperCollins, 2003)

Radin, Grace, *Virginia Woolf's The Years: The Evolution of a Novel* (University of Tennessee Press, 1982)

Rampersad, Arnold, *The Life of Langston Hughes, Volume 1: 1902–1941; I, Too, Sing America* (Oxford University Press, 1986)

Robins Sharpe, Emily, 'Salaria Kea's Spanish memoirs', *Volunteer*, vol. 4 (December 2011)

Rogoyska, Jane, *Gerda Taro: Inventing Robert Capa* (Jonathan Cape, 2013)

Schaber, Irme, *Gerda Taro: With Robert Capa as a Photojournalist in the Spanish Civil War*, trans. Friedrich Ragette (Axel Menges, 2019)

——, Richard Whelan and Kristen Lubben (eds.), *Gerda Taro* (ICP/Steidl, 2009)

Stansky, Peter, and William Abrahams, *Journey to the Frontier: Two Roads to the Spanish Civil War* (W. W. Norton, 1966)

Swaab, Peter, 'Sylvia Townsend Warner and the Possibilities of Freedom: The Sylvia Townsend Warner Society Lecture 2019', *Journal of the Sylvia Townsend Warner Society*, vol. 20, no. 1 (2020), pp. 63–88

Whelan, Richard, 'Gerda Taro: Heroic Witness', *Aperture*, no. 172 (Fall 2003), pp. 52–65

Wiedemann, Barbara, *Josephine Herbst's Short Fiction: A Window to Her Life and Times* (Susquehanna University Press, 1998)

The Spanish Civil War and related history

Aguirre Alastuey, Maria Mercedes, 'The Spanish Civil War in the Works of Nancy Cunard, Martha Gellhorn, and Sylvia Townsend Warner', doctoral thesis, UCL, 2015

Alexander, Sally, and Jim Fryth (eds.), *Women's Voices from the Spanish Civil War* (Lawrence & Wishart, 1991)

Annan, Noel, *Our Age: English Intellectuals Between the World Wars* (Weidenfeld & Nicolson, 1990)

Barea, Arturo, *The Forging of a Rebel* (Granta, 2001)

Baxell, Richard, *Unlikely Warriors: The British in the Spanish Civil War and the Struggle Against Fascism* (Aurum, 2012)

Beevor, Antony, *The Battle for Spain: The Spanish Civil War 1936–1939* (Phoenix, 2006)

Bessie, Alvah, and Albert Prago (eds.), *Our Fight: Writings by Veterans of the Abraham Lincoln Brigade, Spain, 1936–1939* (Monthly Review Press, 1987)

Birn, Anne-Emanuelle, and Theodore M. Brown (eds.), *Comrades in Health: U.S. Health Internationalists, Abroad and at Home* (Rutgers University Press, 2013)

Blain, Keisha N., and Tiffany M. Gill (eds.), *To Turn the Whole World Over: Black Women and Internationalism* (University of Illinois Press, 2019)

Bogacka-Rode, Magdalena, 'Straight Record and the Paper Trail: From Depression Reporters to Foreign Correspondents', doctoral thesis, CUNY, 2014

Bradshaw, David, 'British Writers and Anti-Fascism in the 1930s: PART TWO: Under the Hawk's Wings', *Woolf Studies Annual*, vol. 4 (1998), pp. 41–66

Buchanan, Tom, ' "Beyond Cable Street": New Approaches to the Historiography of Antifascism in Britain in the 1930s', in *Rethinking Antifascism: History, Memory and Politics, 1922 to the Present* (Berghahn Books, 2016)

Calver, Katherine Elizabeth, 'Authors Take Sides on the Spanish War: a dossier', doctoral thesis, Boston University, 2016

Carroll, Peter N., *The Odyssey of the Abraham Lincoln Brigade: Americans in the Spanish Civil War* (Stanford University Press, 1994)

Cowan, Andrew, 'The Guerrilla War against Franco', *European History Quarterly*, vol. 20, no. 2 (1990), pp. 227–53

Cunningham, Valentine, *British Writers of the Thirties* (Oxford University Press, 1988)

—— (ed.), *Spanish Front: Writers on the Civil War* (Oxford University Press, 1986)

Deacon, David, *British News Media and the Spanish Civil War: Tomorrow May Be Too Late* (Edinburgh University Press, 2008)

Donlon, Anne, 'Archives of Transnational Modernism: Lost Networks of Art and Activism', doctoral thesis, CUNY, 2014

Dowson, Jane (ed.), *Women's Poetry of the 1930s: A Critical Anthology* (Routledge, 1996)

Ellis, Steve, *British Writers and the Approach of World War II* (Cambridge University Press, 2014)

Gardiner, Juliet, *The Thirties: An Intimate History* (HarperPress, 2010)

Graham, Helen, *The Spanish Civil War: A Very Short Introduction* (Oxford University Press, 2005)

——, *The Spanish Republic at War, 1936–1939* (Cambridge University Press, 2002)

Griffiths, Richard, *Fellow Travellers of the Right: British Enthusiasts for Nazi Germany 1933–39* (Oxford University Press, 1983)

Hernon, Ian, *Riot! Civil Insurrection from Peterloo to the Present Day* (Pluto Press, 2006)

Hochschild, Adam, *Spain in Our Hearts: Americans in the Spanish Civil War, 1936–1939* (Houghton Mifflin Harcourt, 2016)

Holmes, Rose, 'Make the Situation Real to Us Without Stressing the Horrors: Children, Photography and Humanitarianism in the Spanish Civil War', in Johannes Paulmann (ed.), *Humanitarianism and Media: 1900 to the Present* (Berghahn, 2018)

Huggins, Nathan Irvin (ed.), *Voices from the Harlem Renaissance* (Oxford University Press, 1976; reprint 1995)

Joannou, Maroula (ed.), *Women Writers of the 1930s: Gender, Politics and History* (Edinburgh University Press, 1999)

Julia Newman (dir.), *Into the Fire: American Women in the Spanish Civil War* (First Run Features, 2002) [film]

Kaplan, Carla, *Miss Anne in Harlem: The White Women of the Black Renaissance* (HarperCollins, 2013)

Kelley, Robin D. G., *Race Rebels: Culture, Politics, and the Black Working Class* (The Free Press, 1996)

Marco, Jorge, 'Rethinking the Post-War Period in Spain: Violence and Irregular Civil War, 1939–1952', *Journal of Contemporary History*, vol. 55, no. 3 (2020), pp. 492–513

Marcus, Jane, *Art and Anger: Reading Like a Woman* (Ohio State University Press, 1988)

——, *Hearts of Darkness: White Women Write Race* (Rutgers University Press, 2004)

Montefiore, Janet, *Men and Women Writers of the 1930s: The Dangerous Flood of History* (Routledge, 1996)

Moynagh, Maureen Anne, *Political Tourism and Its Texts* (University of Toronto Press, 2008)

Nelson, Cary, 'The Aura of the Cause: Photographs from the Spanish Civil War', *Antioch Review*, vol. 55, no. 3 (Summer 1997), pp. 305–26

Piette, Adam, *The Literary Cold War, 1945 to Vietnam* (Edinburgh University Press, 2009)

Preston, Paul, *We Saw Spain Die: Foreign Correspondents in the Spanish Civil War* (Constable, 2008)

——, *The Last Days of the Spanish Republic* (William Collins, 2016)

——, *The Spanish Civil War* (revised and updated edition, William Collins, 2016)

Regler, Gustav, *The Owl of Minerva: The Autobiography of Gustav Regler* (R. Hart Davis, 1959)

Reid-Pharr, Robert F., *Archives of Flesh: African America, Spain, and Post-Humanist Critique* (NYU Press, 2016)

Robins Sharpe, Emily, *Mosaic Fictions: Writing Identity in the Spanish Civil War* (University of Toronto Press, 2020)

Rosenberg, David, *Rebel Footprints: A Guide to Uncovering London's Radical History* (Pluto Press, 2015)

Rosenstone, Robert A., *Crusade of the Left: The Lincoln Battalion in the Spanish Civil War* (Pegasus, 1969)

Sender Barayón, Ramón, *A Death in Zamora* (University of New Mexico Press, 1989)

Shapiro, Martin F., 'Medical Aid Provided by American, Canadian and British Nationals to the Spanish Republic During the Civil War, 1936–1939', *International Journal of Health Services* (July 1983), pp. 443–58

Smethurst, James Edward, *The New Red Negro: The Literary Left and African American Poetry* (Oxford University Press, 1999)

Sontag, Susan, *Regarding the Pain of Others* (Hamish Hamilton, 2003)

Spender, Stephen, *World Within World* (Hamish Hamilton, 1951)

Stein, Louis, *Beyond Death and Exile: The Spanish Republicans in France, 1939–1955* (Harvard University Press, 1979)

Stott, William, *Documentary Expression and Thirties America* (University of Chicago Press, 1973; 1986)

Swados, Harvey (ed.), *The American Writer and the Great Depression* (Bobbs-Merrill Company, 1966)

Thomas, Hugh, *The Spanish Civil War* (1961; Eyre & Spottiswoode, 1964)

Veatch, Richard, 'The League of Nations and the Spanish Civil War, 1936–9', *European History Quarterly*, vol. 20, no. 2 (1990)

Weintraub, Stanley, *The Last Great Cause: The Intellectuals and the Spanish Civil War* (Weybright and Talley, 1968)

Notes

Abbreviations

ACOSB: *A Chronicle of Small Beer*
ASF: *A Stricken Field*
BPIR: *Brave Poet, Indomitable Rebel*
Dorset: Dorset History Centre
EH: Ernest Hemingway
FOW: *The Face of War*
GT: Gerda Taro
H&R: *Hons and Rebels*
HGC: Howard Gotlieb Archival Research Center
HRC: Harry Ransom Center
IWAIW: *I Wonder as I Wander*
JB: Julian Bell
JH: Josephine Herbst
JM: Jessica Mitford
LH: Langston Hughes
MG: Martha Gellhorn
ML: Morris Library
MUL: Manchester University Library
NC: Nancy Cunard
NG: Nan Green
SBS: *The Starched Blue Sky of Spain*
SK: Salaria Kea
STW: Sylvia Townsend Warner
VA: Valentine Ackland
VC: Virginia Cowles
VW: Virginia Woolf

While researching this book, I benefitted from the work of many scholars who went before me. For most of my subjects, there were critical and biographical studies available, including some excellent biographies. I want especially to acknowledge, and express gratitude for, Elinor Langer's biography of Josephine Herbst, Caroline Moorehead's of Martha Gellhorn, Arnold Rampersad's of Langston Hughes, Anne Chisholm and Lois Gordon's two biographies of Nancy Cunard, Claire Harman and Wendy Mulford's books about Sylvia Townsend Warner, and Irme Schaber's work on Gerda Taro. For the history of the Spanish Civil War, I have relied on the work of several distinguished historians of Spain but especially the work of Paul Preston and Hugh Thomas. Preston's *Doves of War*, which is dedicated in part to Nan Green, was also invaluable in confirming some of the context for Nan's own memoir.

I have followed the historian Helen Graham's example in capitalising 'Republican' to refer to those who supported the Spanish Republic during the Civil War, to distinguish them from those with ideologically republican affiliations.

Throughout, square ellipses have been used to indicate cuts in quotations of poetry or speech, in order to distinguish them from pauses or ellipses in the original. Otherwise, cuts are indicated in textual quotations with unbracketed ellipses.

No Perhaps, No Tomorrow

1 *in the most real*: JH to Mary and Neal Daniels, 17 February 1966, Box 5, JH Papers, Beinecke.

2 *Prematurely anti-Fascist*: STW to William Maxwell, 5 May 1967, *The Element of Lavishness: Letters of Sylvia Townsend Warner and William Maxwell 1938–1978* (Counterpoint, 2001), p. 174.

2 *Thinking is*: VW, *Diaries*, vol. 5, 15 May 1940, p. 285.

3 *not mad*: BPIR, p. 325.

3 *there is nothing*: Arthur F. Kinney, *Dorothy Parker* (Twayne, 1978).

3 *grave mistake*: Dominic Tierney, 'Franklin D. Roosevelt and Covert Aid to the Loyalists in the Spanish Civil War, 1936–39', *Journal of Contemporary History*, vol. 39, no. 3 (July 2004), pp. 299–313.

4 *It is clear*: NC, 'The Question', *Authors Take Sides on the Spanish War.*

5 *citadel of capitalism*: Annan, p. 178.

6 *gender-based violence*: Kate Gilmore, June 2019, quoted in Jacqueline Rose, *On Violence and On Violence Against Women* (Faber & Faber, 2021), p. 2.

6 Vox gains: Jason Xidias, 'Vox: The Revival of the Far Right in Spain', CARR Research Insight (Centre for Analysis of the Radical Right, 2020).

8 *resist authority*: *Concise Oxford English Dictionary* (11th edition).

8 *who would eventually rule*: Franco's rule lasted thirty-six years, in addition to his years controlling the Nationalist zone during the war.

9 *Delve a little further*: Beyond Nancy Cunard, Josephine Herbst, Martha Gellhorn, Langston Hughes, Jessica Mitford, Sylvia Townsend Warner, Valentine Ackland; also, for example: Simone Weil, Gustav Regler, Nicolás Guillén, Muriel Rukeyser, Dorothy Parker, John Cornford, Arthur Koestler, Anna Seghers, André Malraux, Mulk Raj Anand, Antoine de Saint-Exupéry, Tristan Tzara, and many more.

9 *We knew*: Quoted in Moorehead, p. 134.

11 *We [writers]*: MG in Henry Hart, *The Writer in a Changing World* (League of American Writers, 1937), p. 67.

12 *Grim as*: JH to Mary and Neal Daniels, 17 February 1966, Beinecke.

12 *I was probably*: JH, *SBS*, p. 135.

Preludes

Unless otherwise noted, quotations by JH are taken from her articles in the *New Masses* and *New York Post* in 1934 and 1935 and from *SBS*; VW's quotations are taken from Volume 4 of her *Diaries*; NG's quotes are from *ACOSB*; NC's are taken from *Grand Man* and those by her friends are from *BPIR*; where MG has been quoted it is from *FOW* and her article 'Ohne Mich: Why I Shall Never Return to Germany', published in *Granta* in December 1992.

13 *ready to make*: JH, quoted in Langer, pp. 177–8.

17 *Everything very quiet*: JH to Katherine Anne Porter, July 1935, quoted in Langer, p. 210.

18 *if the Nazis*: Schaber (2019), p. 24.

19 *When you* and *going to parties*: Quoted in Rogoyska, p. 24.

20 *savage silliness*: Leonard Woolf, *Downhill All the Way*, p. 192.

20 *Can there be*: Quoted in Lyndall Gordon, p. 324.

21 *not simply traditional*: Harman, p. 62.

22 *priests in*: STW, quoted in Harman, p. 140.

23 *have a notice*: Quoted in Mulford, p. 83.

23 *Their chief occupation*: Quoted in Frances Bingham, *Valentine Ackland: A Transgressive Life* (Handheld Press, 2021).

23 *the slough of Art . . . However bewitched*: Quoted in Mulford, pp. 75 and 66. The friend and fellow writer was Arnold Rattenbury.

24 *The choice for all*: Quoted in Mulford, p. 82.

25 *50,000 members*: Gardiner, p. 437.

26 *twenty-two-year-old*: Sources differ on Salaria's date of birth, but the most likely is June 1913.

26 *more trouble*: *Cleveland Magazine* interview with SK and Pat O'Reilly, 1975.

28 *quite impossible*: NC, quoted in Chisholm, p. 47.

29 *permanent state*: NC, *Grand Man*, p. 71.

29 *had to find her*: Quoted in Lois Gordon, p. 139.

29 *a perfumed imitation*: Aldous Huxley, *Point Counterpoint* (Chatto & Windus, 1928).

29 *the most photographed*: Wartime newspaper article, quoted in Lois Gordon, p. 64.

30 *in lush, smiling*: NC, *Grand Man*, p. 78.

30 *She writes poetry*: Quoted in Lois Gordon, p. 120.

30 *were worth while*: NC to Walter Lowenfels, 3 October 1959, 1/1/MSS 085, ML.

30 *Her focus was*: NC was never a Communist or much interested in political theory; she also expressed great hopes of the Communist project.

32 Literacy figures: Beevor, p. 121. Life expectancy: https://ourworldin data.org/life-expectancy.

33 *so grim*: MG to Hopkins, quoted in Moorehead, pp. 94–5.

35 *their own clauses*: NC, *Grand Man*, p. 106.

35 *Events in France*: NC to LH, 20 August [1936], *Poetry, Politics, and Friendship in the Spanish Civil War*.

Part One

Beginnings

STW's *New Yorker* article is 'A Castle in Spain' from the 2 January 1937 issue; her *Left Review* article, 'Barcelona', was published in December 1936. I have also quoted from her article 'Catalonia in Civil War', published in the *New Masses*, 24 November 1936. Unless otherwise noted, the poems by Sylvia quoted in this chapter come from her 1936 booklet for Valentine, which is held among their papers in Dorset. These poems were published in the *Journal of the Sylvia Townsend Warner Society* in April 2020. I have quoted from the first, second, third and fourth poems in the booklet, as well as from 'Portbou'.

39 Population figures: Beevor, p. 459 fn.

39 *There was*: Thomas, p. 182.

39 *so engrossing*: NC, *Grand Man*, p. 107.

40 *a blur of smoke*: Dorothy Giles, *The Road Through Spain* (The Penn Publishing Company, 1929), p. 38.

40 For Barcelona's history, I have drawn on Chris Ealham, *Class, Culture and Conflict in Barcelona, 1898–1937* (Routledge, 2004).

40 *self-governing*: Self-government was suspended after the 1934 uprisings, but restored by the new government after the February elections.

40 *huge, self-absorbed*: Thomas, p. 6.

41 *The government does not*: Quoted in Beevor, p. 89.

41 *the discipline*: NC to LH, 20 August, *Poetry, Politics, and Friendship*.

42 *The people are lovely*: Ibid.

42 *We are going to inherit*: Quoted in Thomas, p. 289.

43 *We are perpetually half-packed*: STW to Elizabeth Wade White, 29 August 1936, D/TWA/A80 Dorset.

43 *a gesture*: VA, quoted in Mulford, p. 88.

44 *the supreme farce*: Pandit Nehru, quoted in Preston, *Spanish Civil War*, p. 159.

44 *never surprised*: NC to LH, 20 August, *Poetry, Politics, and Friendship*.

44 *respectables . . . propaganda*: STW in a 1975 interview, quoted in Mulford, p. 124.

44 *find out*: NC to Victoria Ocampo, 5 October, Victoria Ocampo Papers, Box 7:224, Houghton Library, Harvard (translation from the French by Sara Willis).

45 *At the border*: IWAIW, p. 321.

45 *the anarchist F.A.I. . . . the early days*: STW to Elizabeth Wade White, 14 November 1936, D/TWA/A80, Dorset.

46 *If one wants*: Ibid.

47 *You cannot imagine*: Ibid.

48 *Here all the churches*: NC to LH, 20 August, *Poetry, Politics, and Friendship*.

48 *People like Asunción*: STW, quoted in Harman, p. 154.

48 *If I go to Spain*: VA to STW, 20 August 1936, D/TWA/A05, Dorset.

48 *Righteous indignation*: STW, quoted in Harman, p. 100.

49 *The forsaken*: STW, *Diaries*, p. 70.

49 *It was like a battle*: STW, *Summer Will Show*, p. 102.

49 *I've never seen people*: STW, quoted in Mulford, p. 124.

51 *I remember very vividly*: VA, *For Sylvia*, p. 67; p. 100.

52 *unprecedented . . . combination of*: Mercedes Aguirre in her introduction to the publication of the poems in the *Journal of the Sylvia Townsend Warner Society* (2020).

53 *the only one*: 'Journey to Barcelona', the fifth in the booklet, was the only poem of this collection published during STW's lifetime.

54 *Female militia members*: There were probably only ever about a thousand women militia members at the front, but many more were armed and in place in rear areas. Historians have identified as 'a notable phenomenon of the war . . . the spontaneous growth of a women's movement' (Thomas, p. 120). Women received the same legal rights as men in Spain only with the Republican Constitution of December 1931.

55 *I can only make*: Undated letter from Felicia Browne to Elizabeth Watson, TGA 201023/2/8, Tate Gallery Archive.

55 *When I realised*: Weil, quoted in McClellan, p. 120.

55 *a certain lightness*: Ibid., p. 98.

56 *a period rich*: McLellan, p. 123.

56 *her will to overcome*: Harold Acton in *BPIR*.

56 *War is a malignant*: FOW, p. 2.

56 *atrocities on both sides*: Beevor: 'we are probably faced with a total figure for killings and executions by the nationalists during the war and

afterwards of around 200,000 people. This figure is not so very far from the threat made by General Gonzalo Queipo de Llano to republicans when he promised "on my word of honour as a gentleman that for every person that you kill, we will kill at least ten" ' (p. 105).

57 *of the ghastliness*: NC, 'Blacks in Spanish Revolution Fighting on Side of Royalists', *Pittsburgh Courier*, 22 August 1936, p. 7.

57 *free, cultured*: VA, Review of 'Behind the Spanish Barricades', 'Spain in Revolt' & 'Spain Today', mss, R (SCL)/3/17, Dorset.

The Battle for Madrid

Where Esmond Romilly is quoted in this chapter, quotations come from *Boadilla*. The account of the nationalist advance on Madrid, and their numerical strength at this time, comes from several sources, but particularly Anthony Beevor's *The Battle for Spain*. NC's notes from this period are quoted in Lois Gordon.

59 *It had been a day*: NC to Walter Lowenfels, 1959.

59 *days and days . . . a marvellous*: NC to LH, 6 December [1936].

59 *continue, work*: NC to Victoria Ocampo, 5 October, Victoria Ocampo Papers, Box 7:224, Houghton Library, Harvard.

60 *snow in the new*: NC, 'Madrid 1936', *Selected Poems*.

60 *hard . . . little by little*: NC to LH, 6 December.

60 *Nationalist generals*: Approximately 40 per cent of the Spanish Assault Guard and 60 per cent of the Civil Guard defected to the rebels, bringing the nationalist forces to an estimated 130,000 officers and men. The Republic had roughly 90,000 soldiers but more than a third of these came from the people's militias rather than being trained soldiers. Beevor, p. 88.

60 *Every day*: Barea, p. 580.

62 *constant*: NC to LH, 6 December.

62 *Population just looked*: NC, quoted in Chisholm, p. 313.

62 *defend Madrid*: quoted in Thomas, p. 320.

63 *It's estimated*: Beevor puts the figure of International Brigades volunteers between 32,000 and 35,000 plus 5,000 in the CNT and POUM. Helen Graham has 'some 35,000'.

63 *For your freedom*: Graham, *Spanish Civil War*, p. 44.

64 *gave courage*: Herbert Matthews, quoted in Preston, *We Saw Spain Die*, p. 45.

65 *By the end*: According to Hugh Thomas, three of the British volunteers survived but one was wounded out. Eight had been killed in previous actions..

65 *hellish*: NC to LH, 6 December.

65 *It is ghastly*: NC interview, *Pittsburgh Courier*, 12 December 1936, p. 5.

The Paradoxical

Neruda's descriptions of Nancy and Le Puits Carré are taken from his *Memoirs*. Unless otherwise noted, Nancy's accounts of her affair with Henry Crowder are from *Grand Man*.

67 *his body dumped*: As of July 2021, the location of Lorca's body has never been identified.

69 *a people*: NC, *Negro* foreword.

70 *a tall, imposing*: NC, TWTH, p. 148.

70 *Opinion reserved!*: NC to Anthony Thorne, quoted in *BPIR*, p. 295.

70 *introduced an entire . . . made*: NC to Anthony Thorne and NC to Charles Burkhart, quoted in *BPIR*, pp. 295 and 329.

71 *full of the London . . . plus never drawing*: Brian Howard, quoted in Chisholm, pp. 164–5.

71 *the colour question*: Quoted in Chisolm, p. 220.

71 *enemies, enemies*: Quoted in Lois Gordon, p. 200.

71 *The trip was a nightmare*: Shortly after they separated for good in 1935, Henry signed a contract with a white journalist to write an exposé of his relationship with Nancy. If this later account of their time together is anything to go by, Nancy's behaviour had become very wearying very quickly. Perhaps the colour difference between them, to which Nancy paid so much attention, blinded her to other significant divergences. Henry was a man of conventional views. They argued hotly over his disgust for lesbians; he despaired of Nancy's lack of class discernment and found her promiscuity particularly hard to stomach. There was also the tendency towards confrontation, the never drawing a line. Fear of

legal action by Lady Cunard made Henry's version unpublishable at the time. Had she seen it, Henry's repudiation of their affair would surely have devastated Nancy. In his telling, soured by the recent bad break-up, the love that redirected her life was an unnatural, squalid thing; doomed from the start by a freight of history and external prejudice two people could never hope to overcome.

73 *indignation, the fury*: NC to Hugh Ford, 1964, quoted in Chisholm, p. 191.

73 *Auntie Nancy's Cabin*: Quoted in Kaplan, p. 282.

73 *No chance is ever missed*: NC, *Negro*, p. 197.

74 *Just another white woman*: Quoted in Chisholm, p. 202.

75 *one of the first*: Marcus, *Hearts of Darkness*, p. 128.

75 *the finest anthology*: Quoted in Gordon, p. 173.

75 *A facsimile edition*: An abridged edition of the *Negro* anthology released in 1970 (after Nancy's death) arguably did more harm than good by disproportionately retaining texts by well-known white contributors and adding material about Nancy herself. Feminist scholarship, for example by Jane Marcus, brought renewed attention to Nancy's work (Sandeep Parmar's selected edition of her poetry was published in 2016) and a complete facsimile edition of the *Negro* anthology appeared in 2018, published by Nouvelles Éditions Place.

75 *major, unique*: Sarah Frioux-Salgas and Mamadou Diouf, quoted in Anna Girling, 'More than a Muse: Reassessing the Legacy of Nancy Cunard', *Times Literary Supplement*, 11 January 2019.

75 *Everything!*: LH, *The Big Sea*, pp. 252–3.

76 *from the heart*: NC to LH, March 5, *Poetry, Politics, and Friendship*, p. 18.

76 *the revaluation*: Locke, *The New Negro* (Albert and Charles Boni, 1925), p. 15.

77 *Look at harshness*: LH, 'Call to Creation'.

77 *Come and see*: 'I Explain Some Things', quoted by Mark Eisner in the *Paris Review*, https://www.theparisreview.org/blog/2018/03/26/pablo-nerudas-poetry-of-resistance/.

77 *time-instinct*: VA, quoted in Harman, p. 136.

Facing Facts

79 *we never stop*: VW to JB, 11 March 1936, *Letters*, vol. 6, p. 21.

79 *the most flaming*: VW to JB, 14 Nov 1936, *Letters*, vol. 6, p. 83.

80 *Figures suddenly emerged*: VW, *Diaries*, vol. 5, 24 November 1936, p. 36.

80 *Agreement*: STW, 'A Castle in Spain'.

81 *Nerves erect themselves*: VW, *Three Guineas*, p. 233.

81 *great affection*: Leonard Woolf, *BPIR*, pp. 58–9.

81 *envied them*: VW, *Diaries*, vol. 3, 3 March 1926, p. 64.

81 *into easy desperate*: Quoted in Lois Gordon, p. 45.

82 *in such close touch*: VW, 'Why Art To-Day Follows Politics', *Essays*, vol. 6, p. 75.

82 *the mind to escape*: Quoted in Steven Shapin, 'The Ivory Tower: The History of a Figure of Speech and its Cultural Uses', *British Journal for the History of Science*, vol. 45, no. 1 (March 2021), p. 12.

82 *because it [was] 'politics'*: NC to Richard Ellmann, 1 October 1956, quoted in Calver, p. 309.

82 *Politics is everything*: MG, 'White into Black', *Granta*, 1983.

83 *ostrich ignorance*: JB, quoted in Stansky and Abrahams, p. 303.

83 *work[ing] on too small*: Quoted in Lee, p. 625.

83 *close, both*: NC to LH, 6 December, *Poetry, Politics, and Friendship*.

So Much to Be Done

Unless otherwise noted, quotations in this chapter are taken from *ACOSB*.

84 *rats and vermin*: Quoted in Rosenberg, *Rebel Footprints*.

85 *From out of the narrow*: William J. Fishman, 'A People's Journée: The Battle of Cable St.', in Frederick Krantz (ed.), *History from Below: Studies in Popular Protest and Popular Ideology in Honour of George Rudé* (Concordia University Press, 1985), p. 388.

87 *fat, frank*: Both of Spender's descriptions are quoted in Preston, *Doves of War*, p. 140.

87 *George and I are*: NG, quoted in ibid., p. 137.

90 *Here the ambulance-driver*: Quoted in ibid., p. 143.

The Ironic Detachment

Unless otherwise noted, quotations by Jessica Mitford are taken from *H&R*, and those by Esmond Romilly are from *Boadilla*.

93 *a distant star*: JM, 'A Ship Without a Sail', *New York* magazine, 14 May 1979.

94 *black friend*: Diana Mitford, quoted in Chisholm, p. 157.

95 *The first moment*: VC, *Looking for Trouble*, p. 158.

95 *I . . . know your point of view*: Nancy Mitford to Diana, 18 June 1935, *Love from Nancy*, p. 68.

97 *frightfully well treated*: JM to Lady Redesdale, 5 March 1937, *Decca*, p. 24.

100 *If anything happens*: Nancy Mitford to JM, *The Mitfords*, p. 83.

100 *Too much has happened*: Nancy Mitford to Evelyn Waugh, quoted by Charlotte Mosley in her introduction to *Wigs on the Green*, p. ix. Nancy and Diana eventually patched up their relationship, but by then, Nancy had come to take her sister's politics seriously. During the Second World War, she was among those who supported Diana's imprisonment.

100 *Give [Diana] my love*: JM to Unity, [1935], *The Mitfords*, p. 67.

101 *family ties*: Unity Mitford to JM, 11 April 1937, *The Mitfords*, p. 90.

101 *To be angry*: 'Till Death Do Us Part', *The Novellas of Martha Gellhorn* (Picador, 1994), p. 337.

Part Two

Arrivals

MG's articles from Spain for *Collier's*, including 'Only the Shells Whine', quoted in this chapter are collected (under different titles) in *FOW*. The typed journal she kept in Spain (also quoted in this chapter) is held in Box 1, Folder 7 of her papers at the Howard Gotlieb Archival Research Center in Boston. I also quote from undated notes held in the same collection.

106 *I do not write news*: MG, *ASF*, p. 9.

106 *twisting his body*: MG, 'Madrid to Morata', *New Yorker*, 24 July 1937.

107 *If you don't*: Quoted in Moorehead, p. 17.

107 *If it's assumed*: *Witness History: Martha Gellhorn*, BBC World Service, 2015.

108 *Scott Fitzgerald*: Moorehead, p. 37.

108 *gifted Americans . . . slums, strikes*: MG, quoted in McLoughlin, p. 21.

109 *winter of death*: NC, 'December 1936, Madrid', *Selected Poems*.

109 *an odd bird . . . If there is a war*: MG to Eleanor Roosevelt, 8 January 1937, *Letters*, p. 46.

109 *if you're part*: MG to Eleanor Roosevelt, 13 January 1937, *Letters*, p. 46.

109 *I have a feeling*: MG to Eleanor Roosevelt, 8 January 1937, *Letters*, p. 45.

110 *I had been five*: 'En route to Madrid', Box 1, Folder 7, MG Collection, HGC.

110 *The Republicans had taken*: VC, *Looking for Trouble*, p. 30.

110 *Madrid is not*: MG, undated notes from Spain, Box 1, Folder 7, MG Collection, HGC.

110 *the front as calmly*: MG, 28 March, Notes from Spain, Box 1, Folder 7, MG Collection, HGC.

110 *curved and zig-zagged*: LH, 'Madrid's Flowers Hoist Blooms to Meet Raining Fascist Bombs', *Afro-American*, 27 November 1937.

111 *hanging by its cord*: MG, undated notes from Spain, Box 1, Folder 7, MG Collection, HGC.

111 *Edwardian show cabinets*: MG, 'When Franco Died', *The View from the Ground*, p. 311.

111 *I believed that all one*: FOW, p. 15.

111 *She liked them*: ASF, p. 8.

112 *run from the hotel*: MG 1937 speech, reproduced in Hart, *The Writer in a Changing World*, p. 66.

113 *I am getting*: MG, 31 March, Notes from Spain, Box 1, Folder 7, MG Collection, HGC.

113 *to be eyes*: MG introduction to the 1959 edition of *FOW*, p. 1.

113 *a form of honorable*: Ibid., p. 3.

113 *the point of these articles*: Ibid., p. 6.

113 *They are shelling*: MG, 6 April, Notes from Spain, Box 1, Folder 7, MG Collection, HGC.

115 *When are you going*: JM, *Poison Penmanship*, p. 24.

115 *global Moral*: JM, quoted in Sussman, p. xv.

115 *If to be objective*: Ibid., p. 345.

116 *Like lying*: Moorehead, p. 6.

116 *Someone tell the press gallery*: This was a First Dog on the Moon strip.

116 *If you are seeing*: MG, *Witness History*.

116 *barely contained fury*: Moorehead, p. 91.

116 *eliminating*: MG, quoted in Moorehead, p. 499.

Seeing

André Friedman/Robert Capa's quotes in this chapter are taken from his letters to his mother, which are quoted by Jane Rogoyska in her *Gerda Taro*.

117 *Nationalist tanks*: Thomas, p. 373.

121 *The Spanish government*: VW, *Three Guineas* (Hogarth ed.), p. 20.

121 *there is still a bird-cage*: Ibid., p. 21.

121 *I got a packet*: VW to JB, 14 November 1936, *Letters*, vol. 6, p. 85.

122 *a misspelled 'Cappa'*: The misspelled *Vu* credit is pointed out by Lebrun and Lefebvre, p. 89.

122 *petite with the charm*: Quoted in Rogoyska, p. 161.

123 *beautiful strawberry blonde*: Quoted in Schaber et al. (2009), p. 26.

124 *another photographer*: The pictures of Gerda at the funeral were taken by Emilio Rosenstein, a Polish Jewish doctor volunteering in Spain. See María José Turrión, *El País*, https://english.elpais.com/elpais/2018/02/12 /inenglish/1518429171_470029.html.

124 *editorial newsrooms*: Schaber et al. (2009), p. 23.

Comrades

In this chapter I have again quoted from MG's notes, dated and undated, from Spain, held in Box 1 of her collection at the Howard Gotlieb Center. 'On Travelling Alone' is also held there, in Box 20. 'A Sense of Direction' was collected in MG's *The Heart of Another*. JH's description of the night of 22 April is taken from a diary held in Box 62, Folder 3, among her papers at the Beinecke Rare Book and Manuscript Library at Yale University. Any of JH's letters quoted in this chapter and not otherwise attributed are reproduced in Langer.

126 *the professional correspondents*: John Dos Passos, *Journeys Between Wars* (Harcourt, Brace, 1938).

127 *always noisy*: VC, *Looking for Trouble*.

128 *Shall always remember*: John Dos Passos to JH, 1939, Box 5, JH Papers, Beinecke.

129 *pushing whore*: JH, Spanish journal, Box 62, Folder 3, JH Papers, Beinecke.

129 *Myself jittery*: MG, 4 April, Notes from Spain, Box 1, Folder 7, MG Collection, HGC.

129 *When I was very young*: MG, 'On Travelling Alone', Box 20, Folder 3, MG Collection, HGC.

129 *they were not free*: Quoted in Moorehead, p. 234.

130 *I fairly writhe*: Quoted in Langer, p. 37.

130 *He spoiled it*: MG, 24 April, Notes from Spain, Box 1, Folder 7, MG Collection, HGC.

130 *understand them*: GT, quoted in Schaber et al. (2009), p. 25.

130 *petite, blonde*: Quoted in Schaber (2019), p. 96.

131 *weeded out*: 'I Saw Spain', STW, *The Fight*, February 1937, p. 6.

133 *This is a war*: Marion Merriman in *Women's Voices from the Spanish Civil War*, p. 169.

133 *about to die*: JH, quoted in Langer, p. 215.

135 *a shifting population*: Langer, pp. 53–4.

135 *a Russian-born*: Ibid., p. 58.

136 *My sister was*: JH to John Hermann from Berlin, August [1935?], Box 15, JH Papers, Beinecke.

136 *has never read a literary treatment*: This is observed by Julia Ehrhardt in *Writers of Conviction*.

137 *the result of an illicit termination*: Lois Gordon finds it more likely that Nancy's near-fatal infection was caused by an abortion than Anne Chisholm does.

137 *For me the experience of life*: JH, from a draft of a fellowship application, quoted in Ehrhardt, p. 140.

137 *If the country was in*: SBS, p. 56.

138 *I should be wise*: JH to John Hermann, [undated], Box 15, JH Papers, Beinecke.

138 *one of the few*: Reviews quoted in Langer, pp. 144 and 161.

139 *You're like the rich . . . This is Josy . . . I pity*: JH to John Hermann, [undated], Box 15, JH Papers, Beinecke.

139 *an antidote*: SBS, p. 135.

139 *put iron into me*: JH to Ilsa Barea, Box 2, JH Papers, Beinecke.

139 *Why do you write*: SBS, p. 132.

Complications

Unless otherwise attributed, JH's quotes in this chapter, including her description of EH, are taken from *SBS*.

140 *H[emingway] respected her*: 'A kind of dignity accompanied her, he told me.' William Pike to Elinor Langer, 25 February 1980, Box 4, Elinor Langer Collection of JH, Beinecke.

140 *without an obvious justification*: It also probably informed later suspicions that she had gone as a Soviet spy. In his book *The Breaking Point*, Stephen Koch claims that Josephine went as some kind of NKVD agent, a hypothesis deemed highly unlikely by the historian Paul Preston. If she was a spy, it seems odd that she had such trouble establishing herself in Spain. She was, however, a little better connected than she later suggested – after all, she had at least secured a pass to enter Spain and was able to speak with certain officials there, possibly through existing connections with German communists, one of whom gave her information about the execution of a Spanish friend of John Dos Passos that remains shadowy.

141 *I feel as if*: JH to John Hermann, [undated], Box 15, JH Papers, Beinecke.

141 *Hate this quality*: JH Spanish journal, Box 62, Folder 3, JH Papers, Beinecke.

141 *Apart from some*: Barea, p. 655.

143 *thought we were . . . hate outsiders*: JH to Hugh Ford, 10 November 1962, Tulsa.

144 *among them quietly*: William Pike to Elinor Langer, 25 February 1980, Beinecke.

144 *They stood there*: JH notes for radio broadcast, Box 62, Folder 5, JH Papers, Beinecke.

144 *I was in anguish*: JH to Ilsa Barea, 26 August 1963, Box 2, JH Papers, Beinecke.

145 *writers of the left*: 'Josephine Herbst Protests', *New Masses*, vol. XVIII, no. 11 (10 March 1936), p. 20.

145 *Politics had engulfed*: JH to Burroughs, 22 October 1959, Box 3, JH Papers, Beinecke.

146 *a Trotsk[y]ist*: NC, quoted in Andy Croft, *Comrade Heart: A Life of Randall Swingler* (Manchester University Press, 2003), p. 68.

146 *There are many things*: JH to Granville Hicks, September 1937, quoted in Langer, p. 227.

147 *to make clarity*: JH to Mr Hall, February 1968, Box 2, JH Papers, Beinecke.

147 *the war was a genuine*: JH to Hugh Ford, 10 November 1962, Hugh Douglas Ford Collection, University of Tulsa.

147 *sinister folk*: MG, quoted in Moorehead, p. 151.

147 *For the first time*: Quoted in Thomas, p. 368.

148 *irregularly broken*: MG, 'The Third Winter', *FOW*, p. 41.

148 *In a war*: MG, 'Till Death Do Us Part', *Two by Two*.

148 Quotes: Quoted in Langer, p. 223.

149 *Fascista, she says*: JH draft for a radio broadcast, Box 62, Folder 5, JH Papers, Beinecke.

149 *old Basque woman*: H&R, p. 219.

149 *one must stamp*: NC, undated notes, Nancy Cunard Collection, HRC.

Giving Away Secrets

151 *I do not know . . . none of the old things . . . I[t] is terribly hard*: MG to EH, 17 June 1937, Box 24, Folder 7, MG Collection, HGC.

151 *I want to do a book*: MG to John Gunther, 10 May, quoted in Moorehead, p. 154.

152 *We were sick*: MG, 'Zoo in Madrid', *Harper's Bazaar*, 1937.

152 *the great unfair*: MG, *View from the Ground*, p. 74.

152 *without sacrificing*: Footnotes to *Three Guineas*.

153 *If every reform*: VW in *Life as We Have Known It* (1977 Virago edition).

153 *the tragedies of suffering*: NC, quoted in Kaplan, p. 310.

153 *speak as if*: NC, quoted in Kaplan, p. 297. Indeed the watchful US State Department described her in 1932 as having 'gone Negro'.

153 *race is a social construction*: Kaplan, p. xxvi.

154 *from such a dubious*: STW, quoted in Harman, p. 141.

155 *influence augmented*: Quoted in Carole Sweeney, *From Fetish to Subject: Race, Modernism, and Primitivism, 1919–1935* (Greenwood, 2004), p. 73.

155 *building a road*: Quoted in Anne Donlon, 'Archives of Transnational Modernism: Lost Networks of Art and Activism', p. 102.

156 *I suddenly realise*: MG, *Selected Letters*, pp. 55–6.

156 *young, enthusiastic*: Notes by an attendee, quoted in Franklin Folsom, 'The League of American Writers As I Found It', *CEA Critic*, vol. 56, no. 2 (Winter 1992), pp. 8–19. Folsom points out that the League 'saved sixty antifascist European writers from the Nazis through the complex work of the League's Exiles Writers Committee'.

157 *writers ought*: Quoted in Moorehead, p. 156.

157 *Platform speaking*: SBS, p. 124.

157 *[I] have been so terrified*: JH to Katherine Anne Porter, quoted in Langer, p. 228.

157 *There was one thing*: SBS, p. 131.

158 *poor and isolated*: Langer, p. 8.

160 *If it weren't*: JH to Ruth Herschberger, [undated], Box 15, JH Papers, Beinecke.

160 *I keep . . . the whole business*: JH to Katherine Anne Porter, 27 February 1933, Box 21, JH Papers, Beinecke.

162 *a sort of dual*: Ibid.

162 *absorbed in organizations*: JH to Katherine Anne Porter, 1938, quoted in Langer, p. 232.

162 *a complete relationship*: JH to E. H. Russell, 4 May 1956, Box 22, JH Papers, Beinecke.

162 *as critics have noted*: Winifred Bevilacqua, for example.

163 *longing for a still*: SBS, p. 84.

Merely a Writer

166 *Who is that?*: VW, quoted in Quentin Bell, p. 257.

167 *Look how*: Ibid., p. 258.

167 *It's too late*: Julian Bell, quoted in Lee, p. 667.

167 *He says politics*: VW, *Diaries*, vol. 4, 17 July 1935, p. 332.

168 *Children trudging*: VW, *Diaries*, vol. 5, 23 June 1937, p. 97.

168 *The last*: VW to Janet Case, *Letters*, vol. 6, p. 139.

168 *The artist must*: Royal Albert Hall, 'Spain and Culture, in Aid of Basque Refugee Children', 24 June 1937, https://memories.royalalberthall

.com/content/spain-and-culture-aid-basque-refugee-children-under-auspices-national-joint-committee-0.

168 *all very stagey*: VW, *Diaries*, vol. 5, 25 June 1937, p. 98.

169 *I think action*: VW, *Letters*, vol. 6, 30 April 1937, pp. 122–3.

169 *How I loathe*: VW to Ethel Smyth, 1 March 1937, *Letters*, vol. 6, p. 111.

169 *I shall only*: VW, *Diaries*, vol. 4, 22 October 1935, pp. 347–8.

169 *magic bubble*: VW, *Diaries*, vol. 5, 11 July 1937, p. 101.

The Congress

Quotations in this chapter from STW's published articles are taken from the *New Statesman and Nation*, 31 July 1937, 'What the Soldier Said', *New Frontier* (held in Dorset – and published in *Time & Tide*, 14 August 1937, quoted in Cunningham, *Spanish Front*). Stephen Spender's comments were published in his 1951 memoir, *World Within World*. Valentine's poem, 'Valencia, July 1937', was published in the *New Masses*.

174 *Set the poet*: Spender in *New Writing*, ed. John Lehmann (Autumn 1937).

174 *convincingly Fascist*: VA, Review of 'Behind the Spanish Barricades', 'Spain in Revolt' & 'Spain Today', mss, R (SCL)/3/17, Dorset.

175 *spitting and raging*: VA, 'Congress in Spain', unfinished mss, D/TWA/A56, Dorset.

175 *INFINITELY worse*: VA, quoted in Harman, p. 165.

175 *every day makes*: VA to Elizabeth Wade White, *Akeing Heart*, p. 103.

175 *like creeping shadow-monsters*: See 'Benicasim' (1938). Mercedes Aguirre, in her PhD thesis 'The Spanish Civil War in the Works of Nancy Cunard, Martha Gellhorn, and Sylvia Townsend Warner', makes the point that 'the threatening presence of the mountains is a common motif in Warner's writing about Spain' and connects these two pieces of writing.

175 *Pieces of luggage . . . elastic-sided*: STW, draft for piece on Spain, D/TWA/A24, Dorset; *Akeing Heart*, p. 83.

175 *middle-class idea*: STW to Elizabeth Wade White, *Akeing Heart*, p. 94.

176 *telling us*: VA, *Daily Worker*, VA 1937 Diary, D/TWA/A72, Dorset.

177 *a parable . . . definitely a political*: STW, quoted in Mulford, p. 123.

178 *A new world*: Quoted in *Akeing Heart*, p. 106.

178 *new men*: VA, 'Valencia, July 1937', *New Masses*, 30 November 1937.

179 *the rather parochial*: STW, quoted in Aguirre, p. 122 fn.

179 *Sylvia inscribed it*: This observation is Wendy Mulford's in *This Narrow Place*.

180 *On whether we learn*: STW, quoted in Harman, p. 172.

180 *introspective disappointments*: STW to Elizabeth Wade White, *Akeing Heart*, p. 73.

180 *When the unequivocal*: STW, 'Women as Writers' (1959).

Reckonings

Julian Bell's letters quoted in this chapter are reproduced in Stansky and Abrahams. The statistics of the Battle of Brunete are cited in Beevor, who also quotes von Richthofen. George Green's letters to Nan are quoted in Preston, *Doves of War*.

184 *I'm so sorry*: Quoted in Rogoyska, p. 186.

185 *tiny fist*: Ibid., p. 203.

185 *heavy guns*: VA, 'Harvest in Spain', mss, 18 July 1937, R(SCL)/3/12, Dorset.

185 *the same expression*: STW, quoted in Harman, p. 162. JH also loved the 'magnificently wrathful' matriarchs she saw in Spain.

186 *villages on fire*: Irene Goldin in Alexander and Fryth, pp. 146–7.

187 *half of the*: Stansky and Abrahams, p. 409.

189 *that things couldn't be*: Jay Allen, quoted in Rogoyska, p. 203.

191 *draped in mourning*: IWAIW, p. 328.

191 *Capa called frantically*: Capa's fears had already been inflamed by a small newspaper notice about the death of 'Miss Taro'.

192 *in a relationship*: Schaber (2019), p. 6.

Looking for Salaria Kea, Part 1

Unless otherwise noted, all quotations are taken from recordings of interviews with Salaria held in the Julia Newman *Into the Fire* Research Files and John Gerassi Papers at the Tamiment Library and Robert F. Wagner Labor Archives.

194 *a woman named*: Salaria has been described (by Anne Donlon) as someone 'whose name is perennially misspelled'. I've gone with the spelling she gives in an interview I listened to at the Tamiment ('K-E-A'), which is in the collection of Julia Newman's research materials for *Into the Fire*.

194 *she made several attempts*: Anne Donlon suggests that the 'Negro Nurse' propaganda memoir published in 1938 was written by Thyra Edwards. Dating the later memoirs Salaria wrote herself – extracts of which have occasionally been published – has proved difficult, though Emily Robins Sharpe notes that the fullest version of *While Passing Through* is dated 1973. WPT was written by Salaria, but seems to draw very directly from previously published writing about her.

195 *Four typewritten sheets*: These are mentioned in Carmen Cañete Quesada, 'Salaria Kea and the Spanish Civil War'.

196 *passed-around child*: Rampersad, p. 3.

196 *It had seemed*: SK, *Cleveland Magazine* interview, 1975.

197 *what democracy meant . . . And why*: SK interview, Julia Newman Research Files, ALBA 226, Series 1, Box 2, Tamiment.

The Question

Unless otherwise attributed, the quotations in this chapter are taken from *Authors Take Sides on the Spanish War*. VW's quotes are taken from *Three Guineas*.

201 *the gratitude*: NC to Clive Bell, 24 July 1937, CHA/1/156, King's College, Cambridge.

202 *Had every one*: NC to Hugh Ford, 1961, quoted in Chisholm, p. 240.

202 *Now comes the summer*: NC to Richard Ellmann, quoted in Calver, p. 308.

204 *The deluge*: Curiously, in *Three Guineas*, Woolf suggests that the proliferation of such manifestos could be down to the decline of aristocratic salons held by women like Lady Cunard. Without these private spaces, 'the intelligentsia, the ignorantsia, the aristocracy, the bureaucracy, the bourgeoisie, etc., are driven . . . to do their talking in public' – raising the idea of Nancy fulfilling, with her questionnaire, the kind of role at which her despised mother so excelled.

204 *While the powers*: NC, 'Tells of League's "Behind the Scenes" Attitude On Ethiopia', *Pittsburgh Courier*, 19 June 1937, p. 24.

204 *harnessing the opinions*: The following year, Donald Ogden Stewart took up the idea and canvassed American authors in *Writers Take Sides: Letters About the War in Spain from 418 American Authors*. John Steinbeck and William Faulkner were among those who put their opposition to Franco on record.

205 *how wicked*: Eric Blair to Stephen Spender, 2 April 1938.

205 *an anti-intellectual*: JH to Mr Branch, 4 February 1957, Beinecke.

207 *Printing!*: NC, *These Were the Hours*, p. 199.

207 *Every man*: NC, 'Yes, It Is Spain'.

The Ivory Tower

Unless otherwise noted, quotations come from Volumes 4 and 5 of VW's *Diaries*.

209 *unreal state*: Vanessa Bell to Vita Sackville West, 2 April 1941, VB, *Letters*, p. 475.

210 *Unfortunately, politics*: Quoted in Lee, p. 694.

212 *to fight has*: VW, *Three Guineas*, p. 13.

212 *they make wars*: MG, 'Week-end at Grimsby'.

212 *I'm sometimes angry*: VW, quoted in Lee, p. 697.

212 *words with capital letters*: Simone Weil, 'The Power of Words', 1937.

213 *I think I was saying*: SK interview, Julia Newman Research Files, ALBA 226, Series 1, Box 2 Tamiment.

Looking for Salaria Kea, Part 2

215 *Salaria became more open*: Shortly after asking a friend fretfully in 1974 if they thought she 'might be on Nixon's enemy list' (SK to FM, 9 January 1974, Fredericka Martin Papers, Tamiment), for instance, she played down the communist beliefs of her colleagues in the American Medical Bureau (and possibly her own). There is evidence that Salaria may have joined the Communist Party before departing for Spain, but in later

years she claimed not to have noticed so much as a trace of communism in Spain, and denied that she knew anything about communism.

216 *I came across*: A photo in the Frances Patai Papers at the Tamiment Library shows the medical team waving onboard a ship. The caption on the back puts this as their arrival in 'Espana' in April 1937 – Salaria is visible in the second row, which implies she did arrive with them.

217 *In 1990*: This version had a member of the Cunard family on the ship, which gave rise to one of his objections: the idea 'that a "Mrs Cunard" had invited her to dine for the rest of the voyage in the first-class dining room'. There was 'a major discrepancy', he said: ' "Mrs. Cunard" of the Cunard Line family – a British steamship company would not have been travelling on the S.S. Paris – A French line which was *our* ship' (Reid-Pharr). This 'discrepancy', if relating to Nancy, was no such thing. As she told Langston Hughes in Paris, she did not sail on Cunard ships because 'the line segregated Negroes' (Hughes, p. 318).

218 *all a figment*: Quoted in Reid Pharr, p. 66.

218 *I don't know whether*: I came across Evelyn Hutchins's comments in Dr Carmen Cañete Quesada's article 'Salaria Kea and the Spanish Civil War'. Emily Robins Sharpe points out in *Mosaic Fictions* that fellow volunteers on the same ship were among those who later challenged Salaria's account, though she could find no evidence that Pitts himself ever denied or confirmed the encounter.

218 *just how*: Reid-Pharr, p. 64.

Tightropes

Unless otherwise noted, LH's accounts of his time in Spain come from *IWAIW*. NG's accounts in this chapter are drawn from *ACOSB*.

221 *has had an adventurous*: NC, 'Three Negro Poets', in *Critical Essays on Langston Hughes*, ed. Edward J. Mullen (G. K. Hall & Co., 1986), pp. 93–6.

221 *'O, be respectable'*: 'The Negro Artist and the Racial Mountain'.

222 *We younger*: Ibid.

222 *unfortunately, I was born poor*: LH, 'My Adventures as a Social Poet', *Phylon*, vol. 8, no. 3 (1947), p. 212.

223 *divided superficially*: LH, quoted in Rampersad, p. 345.

224 *I sort of wish*: LH to Richard Wright, quoted in Donlon, 'Archives of Transnational Modernism', p. 98.

224 *and nothing*: LH to Louise Thompson, 26 July [1937], *Poetry, Politics, and Friendship*.

225 *My idea of a good*: George Green, 21 August 1938, Marx Memorial Library, SC/VOL/GGR/1.

227 *I saw democracy*: Lini De Vries in Alexander and Fryth, p. 144.

The Villa Paz

228 *roses, lilies*: Rose Freed in Alexander and Fryth, p. 130.

228 *an enormous bed*: Quoted in Hochschild, p. 136.

228 *There was a library*: Including a Columbia University Press publication about American public opinion inscribed with the name of one Sarah L. Kee that was still there seventy years later: https://pdlhistoria.word press.com/hospitals-and-medical-support-for-the-spanish-republic/.

229 *for a 'dum-dum'*: NC to NG, quoted in *BPIR*.

229 *'Salaria Salud!'*: Quoted in Donlon, 'Archives of Transnational Modernism', p. 103.

229 *a very charming person*: LH, 'N.Y. Nurse Weds Irish Fighter in Spain's War' *Afro-American*, 11 December 1937.

230 *the scolding*: Quoted in Robins Sharpe, *Mosaic Fictions*, p. 95.

230 *Everything was just . . . I met plenty*: SK interview with John Gerassi, 1980, John Gerassi Oral History Collection, ALBA.AUDIO.018-152,153, Tamiment.

230 *I miss you*: SK to Fredericka Martin, 7 January 193[?], Fredericka Martin Papers, Tamiment.

230 *discussing same*: Ray Harris in Alexander and Fryth, p. 135.

232 *a world for whites*: Quoted in Carroll, p. 78.

232 *Give Franco*: LH, 'Soldiers from Many Lands,' *Afro-American*, 18 December 1937.

232 *a common language*: Quoted in Gilyard.

232 *Taking up arms*: The black press, through reporters like Langston, Nancy and Thyra Edwards, kept their home communities supplied with news

of volunteers of colour, and those same communities raised substantial donations for the Republican cause. A young James Baldwin even achieved his first publication at twelve with a piece inspired by the news from Spain (Kelley, *Race Rebels*).

232 *A quarter*: Graham, *Spanish Civil War*, p. 44.

232 *motivating factor*: Quoted in Birn and Brown, chapter by Walter J. Lear: 'American Medical Support for Spanish Democracy, 1936–1938'.

232 *advanced African American history*: Oliver Law, recently killed at Brunete, had been the first black man to command a mixed American company.

233 *You always kept*: SBS, p. 145.

233 *The Spanish fascist*: NC, 'Blacks in Spanish Revolution Fighting on Side of Royalists', *Pittsburgh Courier*, 22 August 1936, p. 7.

233 *savagery visited*: Preston, *Spanish Civil War*, p. 206.

234 *proletarian doggerel*: Rampersad, p. 351.

236 *down the muddy road*: This poem is quoted in Donlon, 'Archives of Transnational Modernism'.

236 *background and experience*: LH, 'Writers, Words and the World', 25 July 1938, *Collected Essays*, vol. 9, p. 198.

236 *from the Race*: Quoted in *Poetry, Politics, and Friendship*, p. 39.

237 *Many people visited*: SK, *While Passing Through*, quoted in Robins Sharpe, *Mosaic Fictions*, p. 95.

237 *how I came*: Gerassi interview, ALBA.AUDIO.018-152,153, Tamiment.

237 *head thrown back*: Fredericka Martin to SK, 1972, Fredericka Martin Papers, Tamiment.

237 *I thought there was*: *Cleveland Magazine* interview, 1975.

238 *let the reactionaries*: Quoted in Sharpe, *Volunteer*.

238 *proud maman*: Fredericka Martin, 19 January 1972, Fredericka Martin Papers, Tamiment.

238 *took the story*: If either of them wrote the story up, I never came across it.

238 *Comrade Salaria*: Quoted in Donlon, 'Archives of Transnationalism', p. 104.

Stupid Days

LH quotations in this chapter are taken from *IWAIW*. John Banting's account of his stay in Spain is reproduced in *BPIR*. NC's interview with SK

was published as 'Salaria Kee Plays Hero Role in Spanish [*sic*] War', ANP,
8 Jan 1938. Quotations from VW in this chapter are taken from Volumes 4
and 5 of her published *Diaries*.

239 *Stupid day*: MG, 9 November, Notes from Spain, MG Collection, HGC.

240 *time is going*: MG, 28 October, Notes from Spain, MG Collection, HGC.

240 *Oh God*: MG journal quoted in Moorehead, p. 136. 'Quarrels' may not
be the word for them. Martha describes one such argument, in which
EH attacked her 'without opposition'.

240 *still tawny*: Quoted in Moorehead, p. 161.

240 *You had a feeling*: MG, 'City at War', *Collier's*, April 1938.

241 *drawn sabres*: NC, *Grand Man*, p. 110.

241 *kind and good*: LH in *BPIR*.

242 *One would think*: Nancy doesn't share further details of this incident,
and it's possible she is referring to some kind of opposition to Salaria's mixed-race marriage, but she also pointedly refers to the lack of
Jim Crow in the café where they eat together. There is some evidence
that Salaria had previously been involved in a relationship with Oliver
Law, a black commander killed during the Brunete offensive; perhaps
even married him in a ceremony that would have been considered legal
under the Republican laws at the time. This may explain some of the
reticence – and hesitation – hinted at among Americans when it came
to Salaria and Pat's wedding: a concern about the marriage following
on so swiftly from Law's death. Of course there may very well also have
been discomfort about the mixed-race marriage – or the expectation of
disapproval from audiences at home – despite the welcome with which
it was greeted elsewhere.

243 *If I look closely*: Copied onto the back of the photo by NC. Reproduced
in Chisholm.

244 *that fortitude*: NC, *Grand Man*, pp. 165–6.

244 *The lowest temperature*: Preston, *The Spanish Civil War*, p. 280.

244 *Nancy and John were taken*: Nancy mentions that she and John were sent
to the Prado with a 'responsible' interpreter – she noted how unneces-
sary this translator was, given her fluent Spanish, but apparently did not
further ponder the fact of their receiving an escort.

245 *a fine, strong*: Quoted in Chisholm, p. 244.

245 *lazy and spoiled*: Quoted in Moorehead, p. 168.

245 *Waiting is a big*: MG, 'City at War'.

246 *He was enchanting*: NC, quoted in Chisholm, p. 244.

246 *same small human things*: MG, undated notes on Spain, Box 1, Folder 7, MG Collection, HGC.

247 *This is the house*: NC, 'Pamiatnik – Memorial of Bittersweet', 1937.

247 *To be 29*: VW, quoted in Lee, p. 307.

247 *erosion of life*: Leonard Woolf, *Downhill All the Way*, p. 250.

247 *has not lost or wasted time*: My italics.

248 *I now think*: MG to Victoria Glendinning, published in the *New Yorker*, 22 June 1998.

248 *immunity*: VW's biographer, Hermione Lee, dates its arrival to 1932 and links 'immunity' to 'anonymity', 'also a favourite word from now on', and to the genesis of *The Years* (Lee, p. 625).

Outsiders

Unless otherwise attributed, quotes are taken from the Hogarth edition of *Three Guineas* and from Volume 5 of VW's published *Diaries*. NG's quoted accounts of the Battle of the Ebro period are from *ACOSB*.

252 *involve a discussion*: Bell, p. 205.

252 *were we . . . to scuttle like*: Bell, p. 186.

252 *one book*: Quoted in Radin, p. xviii.

252 *With the rise*: Lyndall Gordon, p. 366. As the reaction to *Three Guineas* showed, there was little tolerance for variety in response to the challenge from fascism by the late 1930s (and among the younger generation of writers, almost none for pacifism). We only have to cast our minds back to Stephen Spender's antipathy towards Sylvia and Valentine for an example of the ways in which the 1930s literary Left marginalised women. Often it did so ostensibly on the grounds of class (marshy ground for someone like the public-school-educated Spender) but throughout the movement there was a privileging of the male perspective over the female.

252 *Our unconsciousness*: VW, 'Craftsmanship', *Essays*, vol. 6.

253 *they would refuse honours*: Woolf practised what she preached. Here she is turning down an honorary degree in 1935: 'The veil of the temple . . .

was to be raised, & as an exception she was to be allowed to enter in. But what about my civilisation? For 2,000 years we have done things without being paid for doing them. You can't bribe me now' (*Diaries*, vol. 4, p. 298).

254 *This is what needs courage*: VW, *The Years*, p. 289.

254 *we are not going*: VW, 'The Leaning Tower', *Essays*, vol. 6.

254 *I am an onlooker*: MG, quoted in Moorehead, p. 7.

254 *I can't think*: JH, quoted in Wiedemann, p. 72.

255 *I'm of a mood*: NC, 'Yes, It Is Spain'. The copy I found in the Beinecke, dedicated to Langston, is a draft of this poem entitled 'Ballad of the Two Wars'.

255 *Once she told me*: Raymond Michelet, quoted in Chisholm, p. 173.

255 *M. loves humanity*: EH, quoted by MG in *Travels with Myself and Another*, p. 56.

255 *like a moth*: VW, 'Street Haunting', 1927.

257 *morally wrong* and *the standing back*: Sontag, p. 106.

257 *Perhaps when*: VW, *Diaries*, vol. 4, p. 314.

258 *It is a fact*: Quoted in Marcus, *Art and Anger*, p. 107.

258 *unusual sensibility*: JH to Mary and Neal Daniels, 17 February 1966, Beinecke.

259 *Anglo-Italian Agreements*: The agreements effectively recognised Mussolini's seizure of Ethiopia, but sought a reduction of Italian troops in Spain.

259 *turning away from mysticisms*: Quoted in Stansky and Abrahams, pp. 280–1.

259 *What can I do*: VW to Julian Bell, quoted in Lee, p. 694.

259 *One is worn out*: NC, *Grand Man*, p. 111.

Part Three

Retreat

263 *As time went on*: John Gerassi interview, ALBA.AUDIO.018-152,153, Tamiment.

263 *left Spain*: It's a little unclear when exactly Nancy and John Banting left Spain, but it would have been either late December 1937 or January 1938.

263 *For 2 months*: Gwen Jensky, Fredericka Martin Papers, Box 9, Tamiment.

263 *almost immune*: 'I Would Return to Spain if I Could, Nurse Says', 21 May 1938, *New York Amsterdam News*.

263 *and it would be*: Gerassi interview, ALBA.AUDIO.018-152,153, Tamiment.

264 *We worked like*: SK interview, Julia Newman Research Files, ALBA 226, Series 1, Box 2, Tamiment.

264 *I have gone*: MG to Eleanor Roosevelt, March 1938, *Letters*, p. 58.

264 *Nearly a thousand*: Statistics from Preston, *Spanish Civil War*, p. 284; Ciano quoted in Beevor, p. 333.

264 *so shocking*: JH to Katherine Anne Porter, quoted in Langer, p. 232.

265 *Anyone writing today*: Ibid.

265 *the courageous little nurse*: *Daily Worker*, 18 May 1938.

265 *drifting into fatal territory*: The nurse Una Wilson, for example, described being lost on the road for three days and almost being caught by fascists at Teruel.

266 *Get up*: SK, *While Passing Through*, quoted in Reid-Pharr.

266 *fantasizing*: Quoted in Cañete Quesada.

266 *memory had been affected*: Letter to Fredericka Martin, October 1983, Fredericka Martin Papers, Folder 30, Tamiment.

267 *You couldn't feel*: FOW, p. 41.

268 *I saw my fate* and *Salaria saw*: 'While Passing Through', *Health and Medicine* (Spring 1987); Negro Nurse pamphlet.

268 *immeasurably*: MG to Eleanor Roosevelt, 24 or 25 April 1938, *Letters*, pp. 59–61.

268 *that panicked*: MG, 10 April, Notes from Spain, Box 1, Folder 7, MG Collection, HGC.

268 *She watched burdened women*: MG to Eleanor Roosevelt, 24 or 25 April 1938.

268 *others who are missing*: MG, April 21, Notes from Spain, HGC.

268 *It was such beautiful*: MG, April 15, Notes from Spain, HGC.

269 *very picnic*: MG, April 21, Notes from Spain, HGC.

269 *too beautiful*: MG to Eleanor Roosevelt, 24 or 25 April 1938, *Letters*, pp. 59–61.

269 *With every advance*: *Daily Worker*, 18 May 1938.

269 *I cannot shorten*: Quoted in Preston, *Spanish Civil War*, p. 275.

270 *How dirty*: Quoted in Preston, *Doves of War*, p. 169.

271 *Not interested*: Quoted in Moorehead, p. 174.
271 *You have other*: VC, *Looking for Trouble*, p. 117.

The Equivocal Attitude

Unless separately credited, all of Virginia Cowles's quotations are taken from *Looking for Trouble*.

275 *she seems never to have*: Cowles's lack of fervour stripped ideology from some of the most sacred images of the Republic. Josephine Herbst was moved for the rest of her life by the sight of illiterate soldiers learning to read and write in the trenches, learning, as Langston Hughes put it, 'to escape from the darkness of ignorance'; it was an image that cropped up repeatedly as an example of the Republic's ideals and accomplishments. To Cowles, however, there was a self-evident and practical explanation. Given the lack of officers in the Popular Army, promotions had to be made from within the ranks. 'Since few of the peasants could read or write, an accomplishment essential for officers,' she explained later, 'schools were opened at many headquarters and education became a feverish part of military life.'
275 *So if the trip*: Quoted in Bogacka-Rode, p. 122.
276 *Hitler boasted*: VW *Diaries*, vol. 5, 13 September 1938, p. 169.

Hunger

The article of MG's that *Collier's* declined, quoted here, was eventually published in *FOW* as 'The Third Winter'. NG's quotations come from *ACOSB*, unless otherwise attributed.

277 *I know it is no longer*: NC, letter to *Manchester Guardian*, 16 September 1938.
278 *everything could be*: NC, *Grand Man*, p. 155.
279 *I implored him*: VW, *Diaries*, vol. 5, 17 September 1938, p. 172.
279 *has given Europe*: Quoted in Moorehead, p. 180.
279 *drab limbo*: H&R, p. 153.
281 *fascinated by*: Green, p. 96.

281 *Seven thousand*: These statistics for the International Brigades are given in Beevor, p. 366.

283 *That was the last day*: NG interview with Bill Williams, 1976, IWM Oral History Collection, 815.

The Stricken Field

Unless otherwise noted, all quotations are taken from *ASF* or MG's Afterword to the 1985 edition published by Virago.

286 *You can make*: MG to Allen Grover, [undated].

287 *I think we got*: MG to Edwin Rolfe, [undated], quoted in Moorehead, p. 184.

287 *the magic*: Quoted in Moorehead, p. 190.

290 *the only thing*: Ibid., p. 123.

290 *total cosmic*: Ibid., p. 218.

292 *Appalled by*: VC, *Looking for Trouble*.

292 *People cared*: JH to Mr Hall, February 1968, Box 2, JH Papers, Beinecke.

293 *If you have no part*: Quoted in Moorehead, p. 222.

293 *I hate what happens*: MG to Eleanor Roosevelt, January 1939, *Letters*, pp. 72–3.

The Exodus

Unless otherwise noted, all quotations in this chapter are taken from NC's letters and articles published in the *Manchester Guardian* or her letters to its editor, W. P. Crozier, which can be found (in person and online) at the John Rylands Research Institute and Library at the University of Manchester (https://luna.manchester.ac.uk/luna/servlet/Manchester~12~12).

294 *La Junquera*: Throughout this chapter, I have used the place name spellings NC used at the time, rather than the Catalan spellings.

294 *mud, rain, dark*: NC, 'Notes on the EXODUS FROM CATALONIA, Jan–Feb 1939, made on the spot, recopied in Toulouse', HRC.

295 *in sheer desperation*: Stein, p. 25.

295 *I understand*: Edith Pye, in Alexander and Fryth.

295 *The tide may rise*: At this point, Nancy judged that 80 per cent of refugees arriving were women and children, the rest elderly men, the disabled and the wounded.

296 *Items of the day*: NC, 'Notes on the EXODUS FROM CATALONIA'.

296 *Scenes of horror*: NC, *Grand Man*, p. 158.

297 *triumph of hell*: NC, 'Sequences from a Long Epic on Spain'.

297 *Every week*: W. P. Crozier to NC, quoted in Lois Gordon, p. 248.

297 SITUATION CATASTROPHIC: NC to W. P. Crozier, telegram, GDN/B/C290a/19, MUL.

297 UP TO FIVE HUNDRED: NC to W. P. Crozier, quoted in Lois Gordon, p. 248.

297 *We are printing*: W. P. Crozier to NC, 7 February 1939, GDN/B/C290A/28, MUL.

297 *bitter cold wind*: VW, *Diaries*, vol. 5, 31 January 1939, p. 203.

297 *supporters of the Republic*: Preston, *Spanish Civil War*, p. 297. Soldiers who entered France before this had been handed over to the Francoists.

298 *She observed*: Nancy also made the point in her notes that 'The authorities were not, as was often said, taken by surprise; there can be no question about that': as early as 26 January, she recorded, the Perpignan Prefecture had given the figure of up to 200,000 expected.

298 *There are no vital*: MG, 3 March 1945, *Collier's*.

299 *we would be received*: Lluís Martí Bielsa testimony, Museu Memorial de l'Exili (MUME).

299 *from malnutrition*: Preston, *Doves of War,* p. 180.

299 *nightmare camps*: NC to W. P. Crozier, 30 March, GDN/B/C290A/58, MUL.

299 *All this will*: NC, undated note, GDN/B/C290a/23, MUL.

300 *I am counting*: Quoted in Gordon, p. 259.

300 *And Julian killed*: VW, *Diaries*, vol. 5, p. 206.

300 *Unloose your hands*: ACOSB, p. 102.

301 *These are days*: Quoted in Mulford, p. 103.

301 *Spain has really*: Quoted in Moorehead, p. 191.

301 *for 1 month*: NC to Janet Flanner, 19 July 1960, Solano/Flanner Papers, Library of Congress.

Epilogue

302 *ragged soldiers . . . the weeping women*: VC, *Looking for Trouble*, p. 459.

303 *on the soil*: Martin Green, introduction to *ACOSB*, p. xiv.

303 *vainly . . . This war has not*: STW, *Diaries*, p. 106.

303 *It follows me*: STW, quoted in Harman, p. 300.

304 *when the house*: STW to Elizabeth Wade White, October 1938, *Akeing Heart*, p. 172.

304 *Moments like this . . . I had no intention*: SBS, p. 107.

305 *Josie, who could*: Alfred Kazin eulogy, Hugh Ford Papers, Tulsa.

305 *premature anti-fascist*: One egregious example is that of Dr Barsky, the colleague Salaria had so admired in Spain, who was jailed for several months in 1950 for refusing to hand over the files of the Joint Anti-Fascist Refugee Committee (which included the names of donors and recipients of aid) to the House Un-American Activities Committee.

305 *All thumbs*: SK to Fredericka Martin, [undated], Fredericka Martin Papers, Folder 29, Tamiment.

305 *I shall be the*: SK to Fredericka Martin, 7 January, Fredericka Martin Papers, Folder 29, Tamiment.

305 *helped coordinate*: For Salaria's role in desegregating New York hospitals, see Robins Sharpe.

305 *Recently they feel*: Gerassi transcript, John Gerassi Papers, Box 5, Folder 8, Tamiment.

306 LEAVING FRIDAY: Quoted in Sussman, p. 92.

307 *first result*: 25 May 1939, *Love Nancy*, pp. 113–4.

307 *there is another . . . by trying to create*: VW, *Essays*, vol. 6, p. 244.

307 *you can be whatever*: LH, quoted in Hilton Als, 'The Elusive Langston Hughes', *New Yorker*, 16 February 2015.

308 *a pioneering war correspondent*: English Heritage, 'Gellhorn, Martha (1908–1998)', https://www.english-heritage.org.uk/visit/blue-plaques /martha-gellhorn/.

308 *there was nobody*: 'When Franco Died', published in 1976, reproduced in MG, *The View from the Ground*.

308 *Mauthausen concentration camp*: Stein (p. 108) asserts that, of 12,000 Spaniards who ended up in Mauthausen camp, only 2,000 survived. Beevor puts the figures lower.

308 *in the labour camps*: Preston, *Spanish Civil War*, p. 298.

309 *an attempt to*: Graham, *Spanish Civil War*, preface.

309 *No, it is the poets*: NC to Victoria Ocampo, 5 October, Victoria Ocampo Papers, Box 7:224, Houghton Library, Harvard.

309 *She and Sylvia both*: Nancy also put Sylvia in touch with several exiles with whom she corresponded in the 1940s, including at least one Republican for whom Sylvia acted as a conduit for messages to and from his family in Spain; she also sent the family packages of supplies from England.

309 *Spain is as complex*: NC to Walter Strachan, 26 Sept [1946], Morris Library.

309 *WITH the Spanish*: Quoted in Gordon, p. 306.

310 *throwing into disrepute*: John Banting, *BPIR*, p. 179.

310 *call for legislation*: Maroula Joannou, 'Nancy Cunard's English Journey', p. 160.

311 *This, passingly*: NC, *These Were the Hours*, p. 206.

311 *his exit visa:* Lebrun and Lefevre, p. 190.

311 *a sensation*: Schaber (2019), p. 7.

312 *The ICP holds*: See, for example, http://users.clas.ufl.edu/burt/Mexican%20Suitcase/The%20Mexican%20Suitcase_%20The%20Story.pdf.

Acknowledgements

I am grateful to the staff at the following libraries and archives for their help and support, often during the challenges of lockdowns: the Tate Archive, the John Rylands University Library at the University of Manchester, the Morris Library at Southern Illinois University, the Beinecke Rare Book and Manuscript Library at Yale University, the Dorset History Centre, the Tamiment Library and Robert F. Wagner Labor Archives at New York University, the Howard Gotlieb Archival Research Center at Boston University, the Houghton Library at Harvard University, King's College Archives at the University of Cambridge, the McFarlin Library at the University of Tulsa, the Marx Memorial Library, the Manuscript Division at the Library of Congress, Senate House Library at the University of London and the New York Public Library. Thank you, too, to Stephon Lawrence and Kendra Sullivan at Lost & Found: the CUNY Poetics Document Initiative.

A special thank-you to Casy Calver, for sharing notes on Nancy Cunard with a total stranger made desperate by archive closures – an act of scholarly fellowship of which I feel sure Nancy would have approved. For kind and helpful responses to my questions, I am also deeply grateful to Paul Preston and Angela Jackson. Thank you, too, to David Wurtzel for scholarly solidarity and for sharing an article about Martha Gellhorn.

I am grateful to all at the Robert B. Silvers Foundation for their support of this book through a 2020 Silvers Grant for Work in Progress. Huge thanks also to all at Gladstone's Library, especially Louisa Yates, Rhian Waller and the staff at Food for Thought, for four idyllic weeks in 2022 as a writer in residence.

For their kind hosting and enjoyable company, thank you to Will, Lizzie, Isaac, Eddie and Arthur Paget in Boston and to Firat Adriansen and Adriana Vink in New York.

I am fortunate in my editors. Thank you to Bea Hemming at Cape and Maris Dyer at Knopf for their care and attention. Sander van Vlerken at Athenaeum was a valued early reader. I'm grateful, too, to everyone at Cape and Knopf who worked on this book, especially Clara Irvine and Leah Boulton at Cape, and to Gemma Wain, who copyedited it.

Tracy Bohan has long had my gratitude and admiration, as do many of her colleagues at the Wylie Agency. Thank you to Sarah Chalfant, Charles Buchan and Jennifer Bernstein. In New York, I was fortunate in both Katie Cacouris and Hannah Townsend as my champions.

A general haze of gratitude extends also to friends and family: you know who you are. I find there is a great deal of overlap between trusted early readers and most necessary-to-well-being people. I'm grateful to Pete Tibbits for (among other things) his interest in this book and his comments on it. I'm grateful for Sara Willis, my first and most forgiving reader. I could barely get by without the editorial eye and friendship of Ella Griffiths. I'm grateful every day for Julian Walton. And this book is dedicated to Cat Watling, in helpless awe and with loving gratitude.

List of Illustrations

Page 200: *Nancy's questionnaire.* Harry Ransom Center, the University of
   Texas at Austin. By permission of the Literary Estate of Nancy Cunard.

Page 211: *Virginia Woolf.* MS Thr 564 (Box 2: 76), Houghton Library, Harvard University.

Page 223: *Nancy and Langston in Paris, 1938.* Langston Hughes Papers. James
   Weldon Johnson Collection in the Yale Collection of American Literature, Beinecke Rare Book and Manuscript Library.

Page 227: *Nan and George Green at Huete.* Marx Memorial Library and
   Workers' School, London.

Page 276: *Nuremberg Rally, 1938.* Picture Alliance / DPA / Bridgeman
   Images.

Page 280: *War orphan eating soup, Madrid.* Gerda Taro [War orphan eating
   soup, Madrid], 1936. The Robert Capa and Cornell Capa Archive, gift
   of Cornell and Edith Capa, 2010 (TAG1936.2.7.51).

Index

Page numbers in *italics* indicate images